LIVING UPC

LIVING UPON THE WAY

SELECTED SERMONS OF
E. STANLEY JONES ON SELF SURRENDER

REVISED EDITION

Anne Mathews-Younes

LIVING UPON THE WAY:
SELECTED SERMONS OF E. STANLEY JONES ON SELF SURRENDER
By Anne Mathews-Younes

Copyright © 2018 by The E. Stanley Jones Foundation

Previously published by Lucknow Publishing House, 2008

Revised edition published with permission by
The E. Stanley Jones Foundation
Email: anne@estanleyjonesfoundation.com
Website: www.estanleyjonesfoundation.com

Cover and Interior Design: Shivraj K. Mahendra

ISBN-13: 978-1724745736
ISBN-10: 1724745735

MADE IN USA

DEDICATION

Nainan, Saramma, and Selena Thomas
With gratitude for your support
and many shared blessings.

CONTENTS

Preface to the 2018 edition 8

Acknowledgment 9

Preface to the 2008 edition 10

Introduction 12

I. The Career of E. Stanley Jones in Retrospect 17

II. Preacher and Preaching:

Theology, Evangelism, Testimony 45

III. The Necessity of Conversion 57

IV. Presentation of the Sermons 69

1. My Life's Convictions 72

2. We Live in a Moral Universe 95

3. God is Behind the Moral Universe and is Love 117

4. Jesus is Incarnate God 141

5. The Center of the Incarnation is the Cross 167

6. The Way to Live is by Grace and Receptivity 189

7. The Christian Way is the Nature of Reality 229

8. The Gift of the Holy Spirit is the Birthright
    of all Christians 251

9. The Kingdom of God is God's Total Answer to
    Man's Total Need 299

10. The Way to Meet Unmerited Suffering is to Use It ... 321

11. Love is the Strongest Force in the Universe
    and Will Win 341

12. Jesus is Lord! 365

13. Jesus is the One Perfect Gift We Have to
    Give to the World 395

V. Conclusion 419

Appendix 1 425
Appendix 2 433
Sources Cited 437

About the Author 445
About the E. Stanley Jones Foundation 447
Other Publications 449

PREFACE
TO THE 2018 EDITION

NEVER did I dream that when this book was first published in 2008 that it would launch me on an effort to ensure that all 28 of my grandfather's books would be back into circulation by 2025. That year marks the 100th anniversary of uninterrupted time in which the United Methodist Publishing House (Abingdon Press) has had at least one of Jones' books in print. To my knowledge Jones is the only author that Abingdon Press has had in print continuously for 100 years. That is something to celebrate and this little book launched that effort which the E. Stanley Jones Foundation has now assumed!

For that reason we thought that it would be good to reprint these 15 outstanding sermons by Jones which so beautifully illustrate his convictions, life-transforming and life affirming message which rings true with enduring relevance.

This book could not have been reprinted without the assistance of the Rev. Shivraj Mahendra, whose publishing and editing skills were essential to this project. I don't know how Shivraj finds the time to move these E. Stanley Jones reprinting projects forward with his good humor and publishing expertise. I am deeply grateful to him and his ever-prescient advice and guidance. Gifted people surround me and I am blessed because of them. I trust that in turn this book will bless you.

ANNE MATHEWS-YOUNES, ED.D., D.MIN.
President, The E. Stanley Jones Foundation
August 2018

ACKNOWLEDGEMENTS
(2008)

To my loving parents who contributed
to my enduring connection to E. Stanley Jones;

To Bob, Nick and Nora who delighted
in my enthusiasm for this project;

To Brenda who provided invaluable support
and spoke deep words of encouragement;

To Nancy,
whose keen eye kept me from error;

To the Christian Ashram family;
and

To E. Stanley Jones,
who helped set me upon **The Way.**

PREFACE
TO THE 2008 EDITION

IT is a matter of deep pride that I was asked by my daughter to write this preface to her book on the study of some of her grandfather's sermons. This study was undertaken as a part of her work for a Master's degree in theological studies at Wesley Theological Seminary in Washington, D.C. This was not merely a part of her personal desire to understand Jones' work more fully, but also to demonstrate its importance for her own religious development and the significance of his message to Christian thinking and to Christians throughout the world.

Though written more than half a century ago, Dr. Jones' sermons still ring true with enduring relevance today. Anne's commentary on her grandfather's message reveals the power, wisdom and insight of his pragmatic and reasoned understanding of Christianity. In a larger sense, this book is a labor of love and a testimony to Anne's deep admiration and respect for her grandfather, for the sermons contained in this volume were never written down. A consummate orator, Dr. Jones would hold forth and deliver these sermons extemporaneously. Fortunately, over the years, many of his sermons had been tape-recorded by Christian Ashram-goers. Anne's first task was to track down and transcribe these scratchy recordings. Yet, that laborious process of transcription truly immersed Anne in her grandfather's unique understanding of Christ's message to the world. I first heard Dr. Jones in 1937 at a capacity crowd at New York's Madison Square Garden. I was immediately transfixed by his approach to the gospel, in a way that I had never heard before. That night, Dr. Jones shared with the audience his very personal and real understanding of Jesus, and for the first time, I understood Christ's message not only as religious doctrine, but also as infinitely sensible and wise.

The following year, I was sent to India by the Methodist Board of Missions to begin my missionary endeavor on that Asian subcontinent. Jones' first book, *The Christ of the Indian Road*, had already taken the Christian world by storm and had an especially strong impact on Christians in India. Soon after my arrival in India, I learned that Dr. Jones was to hold meetings in the nearby city of Poona. I traveled to Poona to hear him, and I had the opportunity to meet the great man personally. Incidentally, that was also where I first met (and would eventually marry) his daughter, and Anne's future mother, Eunice. Shortly thereafter, I was invited to a month-long retreat at Dr. Jones' Sat Tal Christian Ashram in the lower Himalayas where I began to fully appreciate the depth of his Christian wisdom.

My long friendship with Dr. Jones truly changed my life, and it my sincere hope that Anne's book will introduce a new generation of Christians of her grandfather's life-transforming and life-affirming message.

This book is the result of Anne's extensive travels with her grandfather in India as well as in the United States. She had long been intrigued by the way he sought to relate his sermons to the development of his Christian theology. She discovered that the two were closely connected, and her desire to examine this relationship provided the driving motivation for this book.

I believe that her grandfather would heartily rejoice in the way in which she deals with his message. It has always been the aim of his speaking and writing to relate Christ's message to Christian faith and life. I believe that he would be most gratified to see that his granddaughter has so clearly acknowledged this in this book.

JAMES K. MATHEWS

Bishop, United Methodist Church
2008

INTRODUCTION

E. Stanley Jones (1884-1973) was described by a distinguished Bishop as the "greatest missionary since Saint Paul."[1] This missionary/evangelist spent seventy years in the ministry of the Methodist Church and of Jesus Christ. He was an Evangelist, apostle, missionary, author of twenty-nine books, statesman, Bishop-elect (who resigned before ordination), founder of Christian Ashrams, ecumenical leader, and spokesman for peace, racial brotherhood, and social justice, and constant witness for Jesus Christ. Jones was a confidant of President Franklin D. Roosevelt. He was nominated twice for the Nobel Peace Prize, and his ministry in India brought him into close contact with that country's leaders including Jawaharlal Nehru, Rabindranath Tagore, and Mahatma Gandhi (www.christianashram.org).

His approach to evangelism would not be to attack the non-Christian faiths, but to present Christ as the universal Son of Man without the trappings of Western culture. This new

---

1   United Christian Ashram web site www.christianashram.org

approach to evangelism was directed at the high castes and educated of India who responded to his message. According to Graham "Jones was one of the most widely known and universally admired Christian missionaries and evangelists of the twentieth century." In 1938, *Time Magazine* called him "the world's greatest missionary evangelist." Even after a severe stroke at the age of 88 robbed him of his speech, Jones managed to dictate into a tape recorder his last book, *The Divine Yes*. He died in India on January 25, 1973.

As a well known, engaging, and powerful evangelist, in his life time, Jones preached tens of thousands of sermons and lectures.[2] He typically traveled fifty weeks a year, often speaking two to six times a day. He was recognized as an evangelist who did not require you to leave your intellect at the door. According to Graham, Jones had a life changing impact on the millions of people throughout the world who heard him speak or read his books (21). While the books of E. Stanley Jones remain widely available, a broad selection of his sermons have yet to be compiled, transcribed, and/or published.[3]

This book provides the reader with the complete annotated text of fifteen of Jones' sermons — sermons that are representative of his career and that illustrate his twelve life convictions.[4] These sermons illustrate how Jones uses the

---

2   For example, in a 1936 sermon at Madison Square Garden, 20,000 were in attendance, with 8,000 making personal decisions to follow Jesus (Graham, 248). Mathews writes about this Madison Square Garden experience, "E. Stanley Jones was 52 at the time and at his height of his powers as a speaker. I had never heard anything like him. It was an overwhelming experience to hear anyone who could plead the cause of Christ so eloquently and effectively" (9).

3   There is one sermon included in his posthumously published book, *The Divine Yes*. In addition, *The Encyclopedia of Preaching* (1971) includes three of his sermons, from 1933, 1937, and 1955.

4   1. We live in a moral universe. 2. God is behind this moral universe and is Love. 3. Jesus is incarnate God. 4. The center of the incarnation is

ubiquitous theme of *Self Surrender and Conversion* in all his preaching.[5] These two "events" are the underpinning of his belief that the Christian **Way** is the **Way** to live. Conversion sets us upon the **Way**.[6]

Conversion for E. Stanley Jones was the core element in Christian life, and he frequently preached on this verse from the Gospel of John, "No one can see the kingdom of God without being born from above (anew)" (John 3:3), as well as on the words of Paul, "So if anyone is in Christ, he is a new creation: everything old has passed away; see, everything has become new" (2 Cor. 5:17). Jones had a way of embedding the topic of conversion – in fact the necessity of conversion – in virtually all of his writings, sermons and conversations.

Jones viewed conversion as "the law of life." Jones writes that "the demand for conversion is not merely written in the texts of Scripture – it is written into the texture of our beings and in the texture of our relationships. Life just can't live unless it is converted to a higher level" (Jones, *Conversion*, 33). It is self

---

the Cross. 5. The Way to live is by grace and receptivity. 6. The Way of Christ is written into me and into the nature of reality, and The Christian Way is the natural way of life. 7. The gift of the Holy Spirit is the birthright of all Christians. 8. The Kingdom of God is God's total answer to man's total need. 9. The Way to meet unmerited suffering and injustice is to use it. 10. Love is the strongest force in the universe and will win. 11. Jesus is Lord! 12. Jesus is the one perfect gift that we have to give the world.

5   Self surrender is the surrender or yielding up of oneself, one's will, affections, etc. to another person, an influence, or a cause. Conversion is spiritual change from sinfulness to righteousness, a change of attitude, emotion, or viewpoint from one of indifference, disbelief, or antagonism to one of acceptance, faith, or enthusiastic support, especially such a change in a person's religion. (www.dictionary.com)

6   While this concept of "the Way" is a part of many of the sermons included in this book, see in particular "My Life's Convictions," page 72 and "The Word Became Flesh," page 365, for further commentary on Jones' view of the Way. Jones believed that the Ten Commandments were not only written in the Bible, they were written into life.

surrender and conversion that address the human condition of anomie and contribute to the healing of the human psyche.[7] Surrender and conversion, according to Jones, lead directly to health and wholeness.

Jones' view of conversion goes beyond merely changing the individual and focuses on changing the social order as well. Institutions as well as persons, according to Jones, require conversion. The personal gospel is, of necessity, complimented by the social gospel. For Jones, the possibilities of self surrender and conversion introduce us to the Kingdom of God, which for Jones meant nothing less than building the mind of Christ into human society, i.e., converting the world — *now*. "Jones believed that the only kind of a world worth having was a world patterned after the mind and spirit of Jesus and responsive to Jesus' message of the Kingdom of God. He would spend his entire life trying to transform the world from as it is to how it ought to be" (Graham, *The Totalitarian Kingdom of God*, 165).

To date, the sermons of E. Stanley Jones have not been available in any systematic format for public review and/or use. It is timely that these sermons be made accessible to a wider audience for his topics remain relevant and his observations from nearly fifty years ago were often prescient. These homilies offer the unique opportunity to read as Dr. Jones addresses a range of human needs, which at their core — point to the human need for self surrender, conversion, and the opportunity to follow Christ upon the **Way**. Ultimately, I hope that these initial materials may serve as the first step in a process

---

7 Jones explains in his autobiography, *A Song of Ascents*, the necessity of self surrender. In the Ashram movement, "We try to put our finger on the central problem of life – the problem of self centeredness. To do so we insist on self surrender. A woman said, 'I've found you out. You have only one remedy – self surrender.' I laughed and said, 'I am glad that you found me out, for I had found myself out. I cannot go down any road with anybody on any problem without running into the necessity of self surrender '" (230).

to publish the sermons of E. Stanley Jones under the auspices of the The E. Stanley Jones Foundation.[8] For the purposes of this book, each sermon is introduced by brief commentary. The sermons are then presented in their entirety with annotations as needed to explain some of his references, sources, and illustrations to an audience who is reading them some forty to fifty years after he delivered them.

This book begins with a review of E. Stanley Jones' career as a missionary evangelist in Chapter I, followed by Jones the "Preacher" in Chapter II, and then a summary of E. Stanley Jones' thinking on the "necessity" of self surrender and conversion in Chapter III. The fifteen sermons are presented in Chapter IV, and are sequenced in the order that Jones' "convictions" were stated in the first sermon presented which is entitled, "My Life's Convictions." The book offers a conclusion in Chapter V.

---

8   Information on the Foundation is available at the following website: www.estanleyjonesfoundation.com

I

████ ████

THE CAREER OF E. STANLEY JONES IN RETROSPECT

THE EARLY YEARS

E. Stanley Jones was born in Clarksville, Maryland on January 3, 1884.[1] He grew up in a family of four children. He was close to his mother, Sarah Evans Jones, but was reportedly somewhat more distant from his father, Albin Davis Jones who worked as a toll collector along U.S. Highway #40, the "National Road."[2] He was greatly influenced and supported by his first grade teacher, Miss Nellie Logan, and they maintained an active and

---

1   A very fine biography of Jones was written by Stephen A. Graham. It is entitled, *Ordinary Man, Extraordinary Mission: The Life and Work of E. Stanley Jones* (Nashville, TN: Abingdon Press, 2005).

2   Additional information about the apparent alcoholism of his father is in the Commentary for the sermon entitled "The Christian Faith and the Body."

intimate correspondence for years until her death.[3] It was Miss Logan who was at his side at the altar of the Methodist church in Baltimore when in February 1901, at seventeen, he accepted Jesus Christ as his personal savior and Lord.[4]

After his conversion, Jones worked at a law library in Baltimore and then as an insurance agent "writing and collecting industrial insurance in a poor section of Baltimore" (Jones, *A Song of Ascents,* 44). These two positions enabled him to support his family and save sufficient funds to attend college. He was licensed as a local preacher shortly before he left Baltimore, Maryland to enroll in Asbury College, in Wilmore, Kentucky in the fall of 1903.[5]

According to his autobiography, Jones was looking for a college where his spiritual life would be cultivated and where there would be nothing to hinder, but all to assist in his growth in faith (Jones, *A Song of Ascents,* 67). Jones did well at Asbury, was elected student body president, and was judged to be both an enthusiastic and able student. In the course of his time in

---

3   "Miss Nellie maintained close times to the Jones family throughout her life giving Jones spiritual, emotional, and financial support. In addition to her long correspondence with Stanley, she gave regular financial support from her own income to the mission work of E. Stanley Jones and his wife Mabel. She also wrote to Mabel and to their daughter Eunice and sent birthday and Christmas gifts to all of them" (Graham 33).

4   Additional information about E. Stanley Jones' conversion is in the sermon entitled, "The Marks of a Christian Church."

5   According to Graham, Asbury College was founded by the Rev. John Wesley Hughes, and its origins were in the Holiness movement. "In accordance with the doctrine of Christian perfection, which was first preached by John Wesley in the Great Awakening of the eighteenth century, the Holiness Movement emphasized both salvation and sanctification. Today sanctification is often referred to as the experience of being filled with the Holy Spirit. Sanctification is just as much a work of God as conversion and is both instantaneous and continuous" (24).

college, Jones received the "second blessing" of being filled with the Holy Spirit. (Jones, *A Song of Ascents*, 68).[6]

TO INDIA

In *A Song of Ascents*, Jones recalls the experience of leaving the United States for India.

> No one from the mission board came to see me off...I was given no orientation, no briefing on what to do as a missionary, no manual of instruction on how to travel. I was given a Hindustani grammar, forty pounds in British gold, and a ticket to Bombay via Britain, a handshake and sent off (75).

Jones began his work in India as an ordained minister in the North India Conference of the Methodist Church.[7] He was appointed to the English Methodist Episcopal Church in Lucknow, India, most often called the Lal Bagh Church. According to Graham and others, Jones was an eager student of Indian culture, and he would write about his early days in India, "My greatest asset was my colossal ignorance; I had no inhibition. All I knew was evangelism – people needed to be converted, to be changed" (Jones, *A Song of Ascents*, 80). Graham writes that in 1910 Jones would be released from the Lal Bagh church to do Conference evangelistic work among the Indians and the Europeans. (59).

Jones's first evangelistic work was among the low castes and outcasts of India as was the practice of virtually all Christian missionaries in India. However, he soon began his outreach to the intelligentsia. He enjoyed "energetic discussion/debate with the educated Hindus and Muslims but would readily

---

6   See the two sermons on the Holy Spirit in Chapter 4 for details on Jones' experience of this "second blessing" of the Holy Spirit.

7 "At that time there were 170 Methodist missionaries serving in India. Between 1896 and 1919, the number of full Methodist church members in India tripled to 74,000" (Graham 47).

admit that `in the final analysis, Christianity is NOT an intellectual proposition that can establish its own superiority over other religions by clever argument. Christianity is true because it reveals the truth of God's love for man in the person of Jesus Christ" (Graham, 62).

MABEL LOSSING JONES

Jones married Mabel Lossing (1878-1978) in 1910. Their one child, Eunice, was born in 1914.

Mabel Lossing was commissioned with the Women's Foreign Mission Society of the Methodist Episcopal Church and was sent to India to be a teacher in 1905. (Graham, 73) Mabel was a pioneer of progressive education and developed the instructional model having women teach boys, which was unheard of at the time. Her school in Sitapur proved to be enormously successful, and this innovation contributed to a paradigm shift in the manner of elementary school education in India (Graham, 76).[8] "Mabel Lossing Jones stayed in India as a missionary until 1946 when she returned to the United States where she continued to do fund raising through writing and speaking to support her school virtually until her death at the age of 100" (Graham, 104). Her school in Sitapur, India is still thriving, and its support is supplemented by an endowment that she established during her lifetime with resources, in large part, saved from her extremely modest missionary salary. E. Stanley Jones once made this comment about his wife's public speaking skills:

> Mrs. Jones is not known very widely as a speaker and yet she is a very remarkable speaker. In Dubuque where she spoke a great deal, I was told at the close of an address, 'You

---

8   Mabel Lossing Jones corresponded for 25 years with Mahatma Gandhi on a number of educational subjects. Her daughter and son in law remained close friends of Gandhi's family for years.

are good but your wife is better.' And it was not said as a joke (Graham, 74).

Like her husband, Mabel Jones was an outspoken critic of discrimination. Graham remarks that "Mabel was especially sensitive to the status of women in Indian society and taught sexual equality in her school. Her boys' school, staffed entirely by women teachers was itself a direct challenge to the strict and complete separation of men and women in Indian education" (88). While Dr. Jones evangelized among the intellectuals of India, Mabel Jones educated hundreds of boys, many of whom would grow up to provide leadership in the Indian society (Graham, 90). Mabel Jones would write, "The longer I stay in India the more I am convinced that any work done by a Christian in the spirit of Christ is Christian work just as much as preaching. Lives often speak louder than words" (Graham, 91).

A NEED FOR HEALING

After several years in India, E. Stanley Jones began to experience a series of what were described as mental breakdowns. Jones writes, "My body did not throw off disease as before and I began to have nervous collapses. As a consequence, at the end of eight and one half years, I was ordered to go to America on furlough. So at the end of my first term as a missionary I ended up with a call and a collapse" (*A Song of Ascents*, 86). He continues,

> I knew I was called to put Christ into the minds and souls and purposes of the intellectual and political leaders of this new awakening India. But when I looked at my resources – intellectual, spiritual, physical — there were question marks bordering on dismay. That I should respond to this call was clear. How I was to do it was far from clear (*A Song of Ascents*, 87).

It would appear that Jones' repeated "breakdowns" were the result of job related stress (he served as a District Superintendent, the agent of the Methodist Publishing House in Lucknow and continued traveling as an evangelist), depression, and the lingering physical effects of tetanus, as well as the difficulties of living in India with the intense heat and disease. At about this same time, Jones became ill with appendicitis. He would later acknowledge that he was experiencing inner conflicts and was living and preaching beyond his experience. (Graham 108) These two factors contributed massively to his profound spiritual unrest. He left India on furlough in 1916, but upon his return to India in 1917, the physical complaints continued, and Jones felt that he was finally unable to carry on. In fact, after 8 years in India (and the furlough — for rest and renewal - in the United States) Jones was mentally, spiritually, and physically exhausted. He believed that he was done for. He writes,

> I knew the game was up — I would have to leave the mission field and my work to try to regain my shattered health. As I knelt in prayer in the Lal Bagh church, I gave up my shattered health to Christ and surrendered everything to God that I was healed. I rose from my knees a well man (*A Song of Ascents,* 89).[9]

Jones now had the spiritual resources to continue his evangelistic work. He was convinced that these same resources would be available to all who are truly converted. Jones describes this profound experience of healing as follows:

> Without that total rescuing from weakness to strength, from confusion to certainty, from inner conflict to unity, from myself to his Self, I doubt whether I would have had the

---

9   We will see in the course of this book the significance of this full and complete surrender for it was only when E. Stanley Jones was completely helpless and turned everything over to Christ, that he received the guidance of the Holy Spirit that was to direct the rest of his life (A Song of Ascents, 90).

nerve to undertake this work to which I had been called. It was too demanding, too baffling, and too overwhelmingly difficult to match it with bare human resources. As I look back, I now see that it was good that I should start with so little, for I could take so much (*A Song of Ascents*, 90).

Once he surrendered his all to Christ, Jones had the full resources of Jesus available to him. He would often tell his audiences that that he became strongest just where he was weakest, i.e., in nervous energy. The transformation was finally complete.

A NEW BEGINNING

According to Graham, Jones, with no advanced degree and without a real seminary education, now worked diligently (with the support of the Holy Spirit) to prepare himself for this new task of preaching Christ to the educated of India. Typically he would spend three months each year preparing a series of lectures, which he would then use throughout the year. He turned many of these lectures into his books. Jones read widely from the religious literature of Hinduism and Islam and became knowledgeable about current events in India and in the West as well as the current psychological, religious and philosophical literature relevant to his focus (Graham, 112).[10] He would take notes on virtually any conversation or reading that he believed helped him present the message of Christ to his educated audiences. Throughout his life, he was a searcher for illustrations and verification of his core message that self surrender and conversion are necessary for all.

---

10 Jones' daughter, Eunice Jones Mathews, recalls that, when she first heard him speak publicly before a large non-Christian professional audience, she shuddered as the audience began to question her father only to discover that not only did he "hold his own," he did a splendid job of responding to the most difficult of questions. She was startled by his competence and deeply proud! (personal communication)

Graham writes:

> It was as a result of this intentional involvement with the
> educated of India that Jones moved farther and farther away
> from his narrow and somewhat parochial constraints of his
> Wesleyan Holiness background and training. He was
> beginning to discern that God was not limited by human
> concepts of exactly how and to whom the gospel should be
> presented (147).[11]

While Jones was not inundated by converts among the
educated classes of India, he found that many practiced
Christian principles in their lives and work but did not seek
baptism or join a church. Some more conventional and
conservative missionaries asked if these followers of Christian
principles were really Christian (Graham 148). Jones recognized
– much to the dismay of some of his fellow missionaries –
that the Holy Spirit could work through other channels: "The
Holy Spirit is working far beyond the borders of the Christian
church. If the church can bring Christ to India, well and good;
if not, then if He comes through other channels, we say, Amen!"
(Graham, 148) Gandhi, according to Jones, would be a
representative of this "irregular or other channel" of
Christianity.[12]

Jones would write in *Christ of the Indian Road*,

> Gandhi's movement left a new spiritual deposit in the mind
> of India. The cross has become intelligible and vital. Up to a
> few years ago one was preaching against a stone wall in

---

11 Prabhakar writes that Jones took advantage of the intellectual
revolution occurring in India among the educated and used it as a vehicle
to present Jesus Christ to the educated of India. (8)

12 "Gandhi's non violent non cooperation was not the cross, but he grasped
the principle lying in the cross and dared to apply it on a national scale,
betting his life on the validity of that principle, and won!" (Jones, *A Song
of Ascents*, 140).

preaching the cross in India. The doctrine of Karma has little or no room for the cross in it. But with this teaching of Gandhi that they can joyously take on themselves suffering for the sake of national ends, there has come into the atmosphere a new sensitivity to the cross. (78)

Jones first met Mahatma Gandhi in 1919 and apparently in that first conversation, Jones asked Gandhi this question, "What must Christians do to make Christianity naturalized in India?" Gandhi replied insightfully, "All Christians must live more like Jesus Christ. You should practice your religion without adulterating it or toning it down. You should emphasize the love side of Christianity more, for love is central to Christianity and you must study more sympathetically the non-Christian religions to find the good in them and to have a more sympathetic approach" (Jones, *A Song of Ascents* 132). While Gandhi never converted to Christianity, Jones did find him to have "Christianized" concepts, and Gandhi's comments clearly went to the heart of what would be necessary to have Christianity "naturalized" in India.

India, under Gandhi's leadership, was on the march toward freedom and Jones was involved. Graham helps us understand Jones' response to the rising Indian nationalism of the 1920s:

Jones was well aware that Western culture and tradition, which shaped and directed his presentation of the Christian gospel and which he took for granted, were, in fact, an obstacle to the dissemination of Christianity in India. He knew that if he was going to reach India for Christ he would have to separate the gospel message from its association with Western imperialism. He would have to preach a more truly universal Christ (150).

This idea of the universal Christ would be the foundation for Jones' first book, *Christ of the Indian Road*, (1925) which was his effort to create a more culturally inclusive vision of Christianity (Graham 186) in which he preached a "disentangled Christ" differentiated from Western civilization and un spiritual Europeanism" (Graham 149).[13] Jones believed that India could have Christ without Western civilization (Jones, *Christ of the Indian Road*, 17). He made the case that Indian philosophical structures were as valid as Greco-Roman philosophy for framing an articulation of the Gospel. Jones writes, "As we look back to Christianity we largely see it through the binoculars of Greek metaphysical and Roman law" (*Christ of the Indian Road*, 166). He would assert that this Western perspective would limit the capacity for Christianity to be "naturalized" in India. Instead, we should look to India to develop the capacity to "universalize" Christianity. He writes in *Christ of the Indian Road*:

> The religious genius of India is the richest in the world. As that genius pours itself into Christian molds it will enrich the collective expression of Christianity. But in order to do that the Indian must remain Indian. He must stand in the stream of India's culture and life and let the force of that stream go through his soul so that the expression of his Christianity will be essentially Eastern and not Western (203).

Graham clearly understood the power of Jones' first book and its implications for Christian missions. He writes:

---

13 In Jones', autobiography, *A Song of Ascents,* he relished this particular illustration of the impact on India of the disentangled Christ. He writes, "A Hindu principal of a college was chairman of one of my meetings and in his closing remarks he said, Jesus has stood four times before the door of India and has knocked. The first time he appeared he stood in the company of a trader. He knocked. We looked out and saw him and liked him, but we didn't like his company, so we shut the door. Later he appeared, with a diplomat on one side and a soldier on the other, and knocked, we looked out and said, we like you, but we don't like your company. Again we shut the door. The third time was when he appeared as the uplifter of the outcasts. We like him better in this role, but we weren't sure of what was behind. Was this the religious side of imperialism? Again we shut the door. And now he appears before our doors as the disentangled Christ. To this disentangled Christ we say, "Come in. Our doors are open to you" (110).

Christ of the Indian Road was a frontal assault on the cultural prejudices of most European and American Christian missionaries in the late 19ᵗʰ and early 20ᵗʰ centuries. Jones was one of the first Western Christians to realize that in Asia, Africa, and Latin America the Christian gospel was often betrayed by being enmeshed with the economic and political self aggrandizement of Western nations. In so doing, Jones declared his moral and intellectual independence from Western political and religious imperialism (159).

Jones was a careful student of both Indian culture and was sensitive to the impact of his presence as a missionary. According to Graham, Jones was well aware of what was going on in India, both spiritually and politically. Jones internalized and used his "awareness" and called for "all Western Christians in India, beginning with himself, to be more sensitive to the spirit of Jesus Christ in their adopted country. Jones perhaps surprised many of his Western Christian colleagues as he recognized the presence of the Holy Spirit in the most unfamiliar places and in the most unexpected ways as he continued to discover the Christian truth in Hindu theology" (Graham 167).

Jones concluded that the best way to live in India as a Christian missionary would be to have his message focus on the person of Christ.

> I saw that I could take my stand at Christ and before that non Christian world refuse to know anything save Jesus Christ and him crucified. I saw that the gospel lies in the person of Jesus, that he himself is the Good News, which my one task was to live and to present him *(Christ of the Indian Road,* 12).

In presenting Jesus to a non-Christian audience, Jones would insist on a personal relationship with Jesus, that is, he would insist on self surrender and conversion.

A Focus on Self Surrender and Conversion

Very early in his career, Jones would emphasize the necessity of self surrender and conversion. In 1924, before the publication of *Christ of the Indian Road*, Jones would preach, "It is possible to cross the seas and leave your home and your friends and give up your salary and everything else and yet not give up the final thing — the *surrender of one's self.* And some of us have realized what that means and in that extreme moment we have said, "Lord, that last thing, take it. I want nothing but that, and I choose nothing but the knowledge of God" (Graham, 168).

It would be in the Christian Ashram movement that Jones would develop and articulate his belief that **self surrender** is the first step in following Jesus.

THE CHRISTIAN ASHRAM MOVEMENT[14]

As Jones worked to indigenize Christianity in India, he established the Christian Ashram movement, modeled on his experiences in Gandhi and Tagore's ashrams.[15] Jones believed that the Christian faith as a universal faith benefits from using indigenous forms to express its message. According to Jones, many group movements have arisen in modern times as a result of the desire to put back into the Christian Church the Koinonia, the Fellowship, mentioned in the Acts of the Apostles, which was born out of the coming of the Holy Spirit (*A Song of Ascents*, 232). Jones tells the readers of his autobiography, *A Song of*

---

14 The majority of the sermons contained in this book were presented at Christian Ashram meetings in the United States. For that reason and because so many of them reference component parts of the Ashram experience, a brief overview on the intent and the workings of the Christian Ashram experience is included. Some of this information is from the United Christian Ashram web site www.christianashram.org.

15 See Appendix 1 for an overview of the component parts of a Christian Ashram.

Ascents, just how the Christian Ashram movement was conceived:

> I knew that I was to be a missionary and an evangelist but I saw that many evangelists after a few years of fruitfulness end up quoting themselves and using phrases of sermons that may have been effective, but are now merely slick, like a coin from constant usage. The danger is that lacking a close-knit fellowship to discipline them, they (evangelists) become dogmatic, cocksure, and wordy – they are telling others what to do, but no one tells them what to do (214).

Jones decided that, to counter this tendency, he needed a group fellowship, and he believed that, without it, he would have been a "lone wolf" (Jones, *A Song of Ascents*, 233). He therefore created the Christian Ashram and lived in that fellowship, "testing out his ideas with the group and passing on what passed muster" (*A Song of Ascents*, 233). The Ashram became Jones' spiritual home. He would write, "It is an unbreakable fellowship that does not depend on meeting together as a group, but it depends on meeting together in Jesus (*A Song of Ascents*, 234). Graham noted that, "Jones' ashrams not only provided a disciplined fellowship, which gave him a sense of belonging and a source of accountability, they also tested his sensitivity to the Inner Voice and his obedience to Gods direction as well as the integrity of his message" (350).

The present International Christian Ashram movement grew out of a tiny beginning in Sat Tal, India.[16] Jones would describe the Ashram at Sat Tal as a kind of forest school for meditation, prayer and thought that was designed to "produce a type of Christianity more in touch with the soul of India" (Graham 192). The word Ashram is from the Sanskrit: *a*=from and *shram*=hard work, a retreat from hard work into a forest school under a Guru or Teacher. "The Ashram would be an exemplary communitarian structure which allowed the values

---

16 Sat Tal means "seven lakes." This Christian Ashram in North India is still operating.

of the Kingdom of God to be lived" (Bundy 7). There were, of course, adaptations to the Indian Ashram that would reflect the Christian message. For example, the Indian Ashram has a Guru, or Head, around whom the Ashram revolves and from whom it takes on its characteristics. The Christian Ashram has a Guru, but it is not a human guru, rather Jesus Christ is the Guru.

Jones intended that the Ashram would be a group fellowship focused on Jesus, and that it would operate as a miniature Kingdom of God. All are welcome at an Ashram as there are no distinctions regarding race, ethnicity, age, gender, denominations, or professions. One United Christian Ashram document states that an Ashram "is an attempt under guidance of the Spirit to be the Kingdom in some real way and experience God's redemptive invasion of our often broken selves" (See Appendix 1). Jones spoke of our "broken selves" by saying:

> The biggest barriers that we have — are within us. They are fears, resentments, guilt, impurities, inferiorities, jealousies, and emptiness. These are the things that separate us from each other and from ourselves and from God (A Song of Ascents, 224).

The first meeting at an Ashram is termed the "Open Heart" – a term often mentioned in E. Stanley Jones' sermons. Participants are asked, "Why have you come? What do you want? What do you need? We begin with ourselves for we believe that we are all in need and that God is going to work on us all" (Jones, A Song of Ascents, 224). The last day at an Ashram is the meeting of the "Overflowing Heart," where many participants discover that the Ashram fellowship has become redemptive. Problems and anxieties are said to be "dissolved" in the context of the group redemptive experience. The personal transformations are remarkable. Jones delights in telling this story in his autobiography:

> We try to put our finger on the central problem of life - the problem of self centeredness. To do so we insist on self

surrender. A woman said, 'I've found you out. You have only one remedy – self surrender.' I laughed and said, 'I am glad that you found me out, for I had found myself out. I cannot go down any road with anybody on any problem without running into the necessity of self surrender (*A Song of Ascents*, 230).

A twenty four-hour Prayer Vigil runs throughout the Christian Ashram in hour long shifts. Jones writes, "Some people wonder how they can pray for an hour. But they do. Prayer groups are also established in each Ashram where they pray for the needs brought to the group and then share with the others how they have found release and victory" (*A Song of Ascents*, 228). Jones would write in his autobiography that the "Prayer Vigil raises the spiritual temperature of the Ashram" (228).

One night during the Christian Ashram, the leaders preach on "Healing and Christianity" and close the sermon with a healing service.[17] Jones comments:

We do not make physical healing the emphasis in the Christian Ashram. Rather, self surrender and conversion are emphasized which often results in remediation and freedom from physical disease. We are not absolutists in regard to healing...Some disease must await the final cure in the resurrection when we get our immortal bodies. So God will heal us now or give us power to use the infirmity — not bear it but use it — until the final cure when we get the immortal body (*A Song of Ascents*, 228).

Jones emphasizes that the Christian Ashram is deeply Christ-centric and deeply Church-centric: "It is not the intent of the Ashram to take people away from their churches and absorb their loyalty and love apart from the churches. We are trying to make the Christian Ashram a movement that inspires new life into persons who become refreshed and renewed and

17 See sermon entitled, "The Christian Faith and the Body," p. 229.

therefore better pastors and better church members" (Jones, *A Song of Ascents*, 226).

Graham summarizes the impact of the Christian Ashram as follows:

> For Jones, the Christian ashrams were the consummate expression of the kingdom of God. They embodied all the distinctive features of his thinking, preaching, writing, and action. His ashrams were evangelical in the broadest sense, proclaiming the good news of God's saving and redeeming power though Jesus Christ not only to individuals but also to society as a whole (354).

THE EMERGENCE OF A WORLD-WIDE EMISSARY FOR CHRIST, JUSTICE, AND PEACE

During the tumultuous years when India was seeking independence from Britain, Jones would speak out repeatedly for India's right of self government. As noted earlier Jones was supportive of the rising Indian nationalism of the 1920s. Jones' outspokenness resulted in his being denied a visa to return to India during World War II. It was in that interim that Jones developed the Ashram movement in the United States.[18] Once he was able to return to India in 1946, he became "deeply involved in negotiations with the political leaders of the Congress Party and of the Muslim league, including both Nehru and Jinnah where he focused on two issues, the deadlock between the Hindus and the Muslims concerning Pakistan and the status of Christian missionaries in independent India" (Graham, 321). He would insist and was largely successful in ensuring (for a time) that Christian missionaries would be free to share their faith in India. While he was involved with matters concerning the creation of Pakistan, Jones, like Gandhi, would

---

18 The first Christian Ashram was held in the United States in 1940. The sermon entitled "Faith and Science," tells the interesting story of Jones' "on time" arrival to this meeting. p. 95.

be greatly saddened that reconciliation between Hindus and Muslims was so problematic. Jones was a great believer in reconciliation and fellowship among the various religious groups.

During his time in India, Jones established what he termed the Round Table Conference as a way of having fellowship with non-Christians. These dialogues, initiated in the 1930s, would typically include about 30-40 invitees, generally two-thirds non-Christian and the rest Christian. In introducing the meetings, Jones would say:

> Here we are a group of people more or less religious. We have been using religion as a working way to live. We have had various approaches to religion – the dogmatic, the controversial, the traditional and the nationalistic. Let us take an approach more akin to the method of science. We have all been experimenting with religion as an hypothesis to solve the problems of life. What have we verified? What has become real to you? Will you share with us your verification? Tell us what you have found through your faith. What does it do for you in your everyday life? I suggest that no one argue, no one talk abstractly, no one discuss the other person's faith pro or con and no one preach at the rest of us; but you simply tell us what you have found in your experience (*A Song of Ascents,* 239).

Jones was intensely interested to learn about the *religious experiences* of his colleagues at these Round Table Conferences. He discovered that it was at the point of *experience* that Christianity differentiated itself from Hinduism and Islam. The necessity of self surrender and conversion was unique to Christianity. In retrospect, Jones would comment that he was a "bit surprised at the daring of these Roundtable sessions, for Christians and non-Christians alike were `putting all their cards on the table'... This was a showdown" (*A Song of Ascents,* 239). However, according to Jones, "In every situation, the trump card was Jesus. Jesus made the difference" (*A Song of Ascents,* 239). Overall, according to Graham, these Round Table conferences provided Jones with immense opportunities to learn from his Hindu and Muslim friends as he came to appreciate their insights (183).

Not only would Jones support India's right for freedom from British rule, encourage reconciliation among the religious groups in India, and strive to learn from his Hindu and Muslim friends, he was also an outspoken and early critic of segregation in the United States.[19] Graham comments that Jones viewed racism as "spiritual treason against God." He writes as follows:

I would be remiss if I did not reemphasize here what an enormous debt the American civil rights movement owes to E. Stanley Jones. Almost entirely unknown today is that fact that Martin Luther King, Jr., learned about Gandhi's theory and practice of nonviolent civil disobedience from Jones. While Jones felt that his book on Gandhi was a failure, King said to him, "It was your book on Gandhi that gave me my first inkling of non violent cooperation." However, Jones' work on behalf of freedom for African Americans began earlier. In 1944 Jones wrote: "Unless effective measures were taken to end racial discrimination in the United States, then Negroes, probably joined by whites, may have to resort to non cooperation, by picking out certain injustices, and then, through volunteers trained in nonviolent methods, refusing to obey these specific injustices and taking the consequences of that civil disobedience." The origin of Jones' thinking in this regard was his emphasis on the kingdom of God, a kingdom without prejudice and available to all. Racism was a form of spiritual treason against God and he was well aware of the negative impact that America's racism would have across the world (374).

Martin Ross Johnson comments that it was surprising that Jones should have come out as a social prophet in the way that he did. Given his profoundly evangelistic and devotional

---

19 Jones' observations about the necessity for racial justice are addressed in the Sermon entitled, "Who Do You Say That I Am?"p. 141.

orientation, it is both extraordinary and extremely significant. And his concern for social justice was both theoretical and actual — throughout his life he involved himself in social justice activities. (280).

Jones' deep concern for social justice also thrust him into the role of peace negotiator. Jones' autobiography and Graham's biography of Jones tell this story of Jones' efforts to prevent the Japanese attack on Pearl Harbor:[20]

> Just prior to the U.S. involvement in the war, Jones became an unofficial negotiator among diplomats in Washington, D.C. representing Japan, China and the United States and would meet with President Roosevelt on December 3, 1941 in an 11th hour off the record session that came very close to postponing if not preventing the Japanese attack on Pearl Harbor. The Japanese diplomat Terasaki would later write that the Emperor told him that if he had received the cablegram from Roosevelt a day sooner he would have stopped the attack on Pearl Harbor. (Graham, 277).

In the late 1940s Jones increased his evangelistic work in Japan and Scandinavia, and when he was in his mid-seventies, he expanded into doing evangelistic work in Africa. Jones would say about his work as an elder statesman, "As the years come and go I feel less and less that I'm doing things...I'm just letting God do things through me" (Graham, 356).

Well into his 80's E. Stanley Jones continued his world-wide evangelistic work. He would be nominated for the Nobel Peace Prize in 1962 and would receive the Gandhi Peace Award in 1963.

---

20 Chapter 6 in *The Totalitarian Kingdom of God* by Stephen Graham has considerable detail about Jones' efforts as an unofficial ambassador of peace.

THE LAST YEAR

In December 1971, at the age of 88, while leading a Christian Ashram in Oklahoma City, Jones suffered a "brain stem" stroke which profoundly impaired him physically but not mentally or emotionally.[21] After months in rehabilitation hospitals in the Boston area, he returned to India where he learned how to walk again and wrote his final book, *The Divine Yes*.[22] In this last book, Jones writes movingly of how he picked up the pieces of what appeared to be the "wreckage of his life" and gave them back to God. He maintains that God helped him make "a living whole" from that wreckage. He would joyously proclaim that not only has he had the opportunity to preach on how to use defeat and calamity, but now he could "illustrate" it (*The Divine Yes*, 117). He saw his stroke as an opportunity, not a catastrophe. Six months after his stroke, Jones flew from India

---

21 Jones' friend, the Rev. William Berg, visited him in the hospital following his stroke and wrote Jones this letter following his visit: "You have moved me often closer to God and to His task for me. But the greatest moment and the most moving message came this afternoon in your hospital room. I can almost imagine the angels leaning over the parapet of heaven to catch your words. 'For sixty five years he's been sharing Good News. But what will he have to say now? 'Then God created your greatest hour of witness, your most ringing testimony for Christ. Never was your message more clear, 'Nothing has changed. I'm the same person. I belong to the unshakable Kingdom and to the unchanging Person. He may heal me, he may not, but I believe in the divine yes. I see an open door. Perhaps it is to write a book from here. This is not the end, but the beginning. Jesus is Lord!" (Ashram Commemoration Book 16)

22 Eunice Mathews tells the story of how Jones' last book was created:

After my father's stroke in 1970, he was very handicapped by not being able to see anything small such as print. He was determined to put into manuscript form the fruits of his faith. Since he couldn't see, he spoke into a cassette tape recorder. His voice was almost unintelligible. However a friend painstakingly transcribed the material, but the frequent hospital interruptions made continuity of thought very difficult. He returned to India in 1971. The use of Indian stenographers with an imperfect command of English made the manuscript even more disordered and jumbled. Much deciphering was needed.

to Jerusalem to speak at the First Christian Ashram World Congress. The Rev. William Berg, a member of the Ashram leadership group, wrote this commentary about Jones' closing sermon:

> In his closing message, his valedictory to his world family which was a most moving and memorable address, Brother Stanley, with brilliant clarity and Holy Spirit power, reviewed the foundation of the Ashram movement and its basic principles. Speaking from his wheelchair and bound by many physical infirmities, he was the living symbol of liberation and deliverance. Heaven came down and overwhelmed us. On that mountain top, we caught a glimpse of the Promised Land. (Ashram Commemoration Book, 12 and Graham 380)

Jones remained engaged in public affairs, or as he would put it, affairs of the Kingdom of God, almost until the day of his death.[23] For example, just two weeks before he died, he signed a letter directed to then President Nixon deploring the bombing in Vietnam. (Graham, 383)

After my father's death, the manuscript was brought back to me. It seemed impossible that it could ever be published. We struggled with it for months and nearly gave up. What my father had wanted to say was scattered throughout the manuscript, but with no form or order. It seemed a hopeless task, and we put it aside. Then, almost a year later, my husband had an idea: cut up the manuscript paragraph by paragraph and see where the ideas would fall. We did that. We found that most of the material fell into twelve questions which demanded an affirmative answer of "yes," the *"Divine Yes."* The manuscript had miraculously fallen into place — or were we led - into an orderly progression of thought? It was incredible that the paragraphs fit into the twelve categories. They formed a diary - a diary of affliction, if you will and it ended up with the resurrection note. It was indeed spiritually his last will and testament (Logan 201).

23 A few days before his death, Jones dictated this last entry into his diary, "Dear God: Put thy hand upon us as we go forth knowing that the Divine Yes is at last sounded and is the Yes that affirms all the promises of God. They come to their fruition in him. The world is going to find it out - and what a turning and what an opportunity and what an open door it will be. In Jesus' name we ask it. Amen" (Jones, *The Divine Yes,* 15)

In summary, E. Stanley Jones – the missionary/evangelist spent seventy years traveling throughout the world in the ministry of the Methodist Church and of Jesus Christ.[24] While Jones was strongly ecumenical, he was a convinced Methodist all of his life.[25] Jones worked to revolutionize the whole theory and practice of missions to third world nations by disentangling Christianity from Western political and cultural imperialism. He established hundreds of Christian Ashrams throughout the world, many of which still meet today.[26] E. Stanley Jones was a crusader for Christian unity, non stop witness for Christ, and a spokesman for peace, racial brotherhood, and social justice, and constant witness for Jesus Christ. He would readily admit that his quite ordinary life became extraordinary only because he fully surrendered his life to Jesus Christ! (Graham, 21).

---

24 While he visited nearly every country in the world, these are the countries where he spent the most time: India, Sri Lanka, Malaysia, Thailand, Singapore, Palestine, Egypt, China, Burma, Japan, Korea, The Philippines, Australia, Finland, the Netherlands, Holland, Sweden, South Africa, Fiji, Mexico, Cuba, Argentina, Brazil, Canada, and the United States.

25 Bishop Mathews tells this story about his father-in-law's enthusiasm for Methodism, "Jones would tell this story about a man who was in a hotel. At breakfast the waitress put before him a luscious dish of strawberries. The man said, "Take these away and bring me prunes." As E. Stanley Jones concluded his story he said, "As long as there are people like that in the world, there will be people who do not appreciate Methodism" (Logan 187).

26 The 2008 Ashram schedule for North American includes more than fifty Ashrams of various sizes. One of the largest is in Nova Scotia which averages nearly 1000 participants for a week each summer.

E. Stanley Jones at Asbury College,
Circa 1904

E. Stanley Jones in India in the early years

E Stanley Jones & his daughter Eunice circa 1922

Mabel Lossing Jones

*Jones and Mabel,
Lucknow Parsonage*

Jones with Mabel and Eunice en route to India 1938

Jones preaching from the Slave Block in Fredericksburg, Virginia in 1959

This is a copy of E. Stanley Jones' book Mahatma Gandhi: An Interpretation as seen in the Martin Luther King Jr. Library. The book contains a handwritten note by King that says, "This is it! This is the way to achieve freedom for the Negro in America."

Mabel, Stanley and Eunice

II

PREACHER AND PREACHING: THEOLOGY, EVANGELISM, TESTIMONY

JONES would readily admit that his life's work was to preach the good news of Jesus Christ and present the necessity for self surrender. It was said that in his life time, he preached more than 60,000 sermons. During his time in India, he preached in every city in India with a population of over 50,000. (Logan, 190) He pursued his life's work as an evangelist – the result of his own self surrender — and he would spend his life in testimony to the benefits of the gifts of conversion. Jones was guided in his efforts by the Holy Spirit, which he termed his "inner voice." This section will discuss E. Stanley Jones the preacher and will set a context for the reading of his sermons.

Jones would not have described himself as a theologian, nor an author nor a preacher. He was most content with being called an evangelist, the bearer of *good news*.[1] His message was deeply Christ-centered; it did not emphasize doctrine, but experience — the experience of a personal, life-changing relationship with Jesus. Mathews writes, that "when Jones was accused of repeating addresses, he would cite John Wesley, who said one that that somewhere between the fortieth and fiftieth time he preached a sermon, he got it about the way he intended" (Logan 199). E. Stanley Jones intended that his sermons focus on Jesus. Fant and Pinson understood Jones' intent, "His sermons focus in solitary fascination upon the form of Jesus Christ; they do not argue doctrine…they narrate the acts of God in the life of Jesus and all of his sermons come out at the same place…with the necessity for conversion" (316). Scholars have questioned Jones' absence of theological training, but no one has questioned his profound interest in the nature of God's love in Christ.[2] Bundy calls Jones a "folk theologian with virtually no serious theological or missiological education," but Jones made no effort to pretend that he was anything other than an evangelist (2). Jones would write in *The Unshakable Kingdom and the Unchanging Person*, "I'm not a theologian. I am the bearer of Good News" (9). He knew well his academic limitations,[3] but in spite of - or perhaps because of — them, he focused on presenting his readers and audiences the person of Jesus Christ, the possibility and promise of

---

1   Jones would often state that he wrote all of his books out of the necessity to meet some need. "The need produced a certain pressure and the pressure produced the book, perhaps after long thought" (Jones, *The Divine Yes* 112).

2   Reinhold Niebuhr once said that Jones' book *Christ's Alternative to Communism* (1935) was the "most perfect swan song of liberal politics." In the same breath he would acknowledge however that Jones was one of the genuine saints of the missionary movement. (Graham, *The Totalitarian Kingdom of God*, 16)

3   Duke University and Syracuse University would both grant him honorary doctorates.

conversion, and the reality of the Kingdom of God.[4] Very early in his career, a friend told him, "You are not a theologian; you are a divining rod. You tell us where there is water beneath. Remember your function" (Mathews 18).

As an evangelist, Jones was very optimistic about humanity's potential and believed that the implications of the Kingdom of God on all domains of existence were profoundly positive — and realizable. Jones was quite serious about the matter of bringing the kingdom of God to earth — now! According to Graham, "Once he understood and embraced the implications of the Kingdom of God, he believed that he had a divine entrustment to reintroduce the Kingdom to Christianity" (242). In his goal to redeem the totality of human and social structures, Jones felt free to explore, appropriate any good, any truth anywhere, and he included a wide range of these materials in his sermons and books. (Bundy, 13) While Jones' critics felt that he liberally interpreted scripture to meet his pre-conceived ideas, Jones would respond that, while he was interested in the Jesus of scripture, he was engaged in finding Jesus in our contemporary world: "Christ is living today, and I find him in places and movements I had never dreamed of and by the quiet sense of his presence he is forcing modification everywhere" (Fant and Pinson, 316).

---

4   However, it is of interest that Jones was apparently sufficiently concerned by the limitations of his education that he wrote the Methodist Board of Missions the following:

I feel desperately the need of further study. Sherwood Eddy wants me to spend a year with him in Columbia University next year with a small group who will be given special attention by the leading men there. At the same time, I want to get back to India (Graham 172).

According to Graham, Jones did not spend a year at Columbia University, but he did participate in the American Seminar, which brought together American religious and social leaders to study on site the social, economic, and political problems of Britain and Europe. Jones visited Professor Harnack, (referenced in "The Marks of a Christian Church") who was at that time the greatest living theologian. Jones also had meetings at the League of Nations in Switzerland (173).

Jones understood well the conflictual responses toward evangelism. He easily recognized how the *methods* of evangelism would need to change in light of the current cultural climate. For example, in 1938 he wrote:

> The need for Christian evangelism has not changed, but the method of approach had to be changed because the intellectual climate had changed. American culture had become more suspicious of the motives of evangelism. We are being subjected to exploitation all the time. We hear radio music, and we are not quite sure that we can enjoy it, for we know that our feelings of sympathy are being aroused so we will be in a mood to listen to the merits of Palmolive soap or something else. It puts us on the mental defensive. We bring that defensiveness into the religious meeting. We listen with an undertone of suspicion regarding the real purpose of it all. Is it to glorify the individual, to catch a man for this group, to feed megalomania or to get money out of us? (Graham, 248)

Jones would conclude, according to Graham, that evangelism in the future must be "sincerely and simply real" (249). Jones' message is even more relevant today as we are increasingly saturated with commercialism, and many are even more suspicious of the motives of evangelists.

We will see in this selection of Jones' sermons, largely recorded in the 1950s and early 1960s, that he is very clear about his intentions and motives. He does not try to entice his audience to respond to *him,* but asks them to surrender to *Jesus.* He does not berate or condemn his listeners for their sins, but offers them the freedom of self surrender and the love of God. His sermons are testimonies designed to offer the gift of Jesus Christ. He uses frequent illustrations to make his message transparently clear — "You must be born again" — and his stories add reality, applicability, and interest. The illustrations make his sermons memorable. The reader will find scores of them in the sermons that follow in Chapter IV.

Some have commented on Jones' sermons from a homiletical perspective.[5] Mathews writes that Jones did not have the "homiletical eye," what George Buttrick once called a "fearful member," but he was an acute observer of the human scene, of literature and life, alert for anything which would shed light on man's experience of the Gospel. Mathews continues:

> Jones was a superb preacher. At his best many regarded him as the most effective interpreter of the Gospel in contemporary terms that they ever heard. They marvel when they contrast his preaching with what all too often passes for evangelism in our day. For him there was no contradiction between being the Old Testament prophet and the New Testament evangelist. The two belong together (Mathews, 13).

Fant and Pinson, in their *Encyclopedia of Preaching*, state that, "Jones' sermons are not really technically superior ... nevertheless, every message reveals the depth of his perception, the breadth of his travels, and the genius of his descriptive powers" (314). They continue, "His sermons have not received the attention that his books have. Yet there can be no doubt that his sermons make a profound impact upon those who hear him" (315). In fact as noted above E. Stanley Jones' sermons are testimonies.[6] "They flow naturally from experience to

---

5   Homiletics is the art of preaching; the branch of practical theology that treats homilies or sermons. (www.dictionary.com).

6   Jones tells the story of his first "disastrous" sermon in his book, *Along the Indian Road:* "The little church was filled with my relatives and friends, all anxious that the young man should do well. I had prepared for three weeks, for I was to be God's lawyer and argue His case well. I started on a rather high key and after a half dozen sentences used a word that I had never used before, "indifferentism." A college girl smiled and put down her head. Her smiling so upset me that when I came back to the thread of my discourse, it was gone. My mind was an absolute blank. I stood there clutching for something to say. Finally I blurted out: 'I am very sorry, but I have forgotten my sermon,' and I started for my seat in shame and

experience; they are rich with personal illustration; they are not overly involved with organization or exposition" (Fant and Pinson, 315).[7]

It has often been remarked that Jones' preaching style was always succinct and crisp. He knew how to "turn a phrase."[8] He would often repeat words for dramatic effect, juxtapose contrasting ideas with symmetrical phrasing (antithesis), and reverse the word order of a phrase previously employed (antimetabole). He also used assonance, alliteration and paradox to emphasize his message. It is clear that E. Stanley Jones knew the Bible thoroughly whose authors used similar powerful rhetorical devices. Some illustrations of Jones's unique phrasing are as follows:

♦ **Repeating words for dramatic effect:**

I'd see the word *love*, and I would read into it my highest experience of love, but my highest experience of love is not love; it is my highest experience of love." (*"The Word Became Flesh"* Sermon)

Use of word up and up and up – (*"New Birth"* Sermon)

♦ **Repetition**

Repetitious phrases and words like: love, life, live. (*"New Birth"* Sermon)

---

confusion. As I was about to sit down, the Inner Voice said: 'Haven't I done anything for you? If so, couldn't you tell that? ' I responded to that suggestion and said, 'Friends, I see I can't preach, but you know what Christ has done for my life, how he changed me, and though I cannot preach I shall be His witness the rest of my days. ' As God's lawyer, I was a dead failure; as God's witness I was a success (20).

7 Prabhakar comments, that Jones spoke for 45 years at the Maramon Convention for an audience of nearly 50,000 each year. (16)

8 For example; "If you take the gift, you belong to the giver forever.""We don't break God's laws. We break ourselves on them." "Charity without justice is an insult to God" (Logan 195).

♦ **Juxtaposing contrasting ideas with symmetrical phrasing (antithesis)**

When his [Paul's] eyesight went bad, his insight went better! (*"Christian Faith & the Body"* Sermon)

We don't begin with God and we don't begin with man. We begin with the God-Man and from Him we work out to God and from Him we work down to man. Christianity has its doctrines but it is not a doctrine. It has its rites and ceremonies but is not a rite or ceremony. It has its institutions but is not an institution. It has its creeds but is not a creed. At the center is a person.

Christianity is Christ. Christians are people who believe in God and man and life *through Christ*. There is our starting point to work out to God and to work down to man. In His life we see life. If you begin with God you will probably lose God. (*"New Birth"* Sermon)

♦ **Reversing the word order of a phrase previously employed (antimetabole)**

I don't believe in Jesus because of the Virgin Birth. I believe in the Virgin Birth because of Jesus. (*"The New Birth"* Sermon)

♦ **Emphatic synonymous repetition**

Something new had come into society — that was a man – a man for whom Christ died. He was no longer a man. He was a man for whom Christ died. Classes had been wiped out. Here was a new class — a man for whom Christ died. That placed humanity into an entirely different category of being, and it lifted Christianity to a whole new level. (*"Marks of a Christian Church"* Sermon)

♦ **Alliteration**

"Not a verbal word, but a vital word."

I look up through nature and I come to the conclusion that God is law. I am grateful that God is law and that He does not work by whim, notion and fancy but by law and order. Grateful but not satisfied. I want to know not that God is law but whether God is love. Nature can't quite frame the words God is Love. ("*New Birth*" Sermon)

"What Jesus commands he commends."

"In this world, the choice is conversion or chaos."

♦ **Paradox**

My strength is made perfect in my weakness. ("*Christian Faith and the Body*" Sermon)

"Every road that leads away from Jesus Christ has a precipice at the end of it. Every road that leads away from Him means you are sorrowful; you go away sorrowful. All coming to Jesus has a feeling of homecoming. When you come, you feel that you are out of your estrangement, your alienation.

He's like me and unlike me…. ("*New Birth Sermon*" Sermon)

It was easy to listen to Jones preach and his rhetorical skills added to his capacity to engage his listeners. He also often permitted his audience to ask him questions at the close of his public lectures. He seemed to thrive on the cross examination:

> I allow them to ask questions at the close of my lecture. As I usually have from twenty to two hundred lawyers in my meetings each night, to expose myself to their keen minded cross examination is to invite disaster. But when I began this work, these verses were given to me and have become my charter of assurance: "Ye shall be brought before governors and kings for my sake, for a testimony against them and the gentiles…Take no thought how or what ye shall speak: for it shall be given you in that same hour what ye shall speak. For it is not ye that speak, but the Spirit of your Father which speaketh in you (Matthew 10:19-21, *A Song of Ascents*, 112)

Jones was ultimately quite content with his evangelistic approach and God-given message. Jones knew what it was to preach as an evangelist not as a scholarly academic. His early failure when he tried to be God's attorney was sufficient to have "testimony" be his manner of preaching, writing, and living. Yet Graham is curious to understand the popularity of E. Stanley Jones. He writes:

> The reason, according to an editorial published in the *Christian Advocate,* was *not* because of his speaking ability. "His vocal equipment is susceptible to vast improvement. Indeed, it is hard, physically speaking, to listen to him." So it was not the sales of his books, not his preaching abilities. "Rather," the editorial continues, "the conclusion is inevitable that the secret of his success lies in the impression of "reality" which he gives. Mohammedans, Hindus, Christians, Agnostics, who come within range of his Spirit-filled personality, feel that somehow here is a human being who lives in conscious *harmony with God.* If there is anything real in religion, he has it" (172).

This harmony with God is illustrated by what Jones describes as his "Inner Voice" — that direct guidance from God. In college, he established the daily habit of spending two hours each day in devotions, meditation, and prayer. Jones' sermons and books are full of illustrations of how the inner voice guided him. He describes this Inner Voice as follows:

> God guides through the inner voice. That is not the only way that God guides us as he guides us through the scriptures, the luminous word, the life and teachings of Jesus and the inner voice. God speaks directly to us through the framing of words themselves within the mind without being audible. How can we distinguish between the voice of the subconscious and the voice of God? The voice of the subconscious argues with you and tries to convince you. The voice of God doesn't argue; it speaks, and the words are self verifying. You feel it is real and it is (*Christ at the Roundtable,* 128).

In his autobiography, *A Song of Ascents,* Jones continues,

I have a personal listening post. As one gets older I usually awaken earlier. I decided to put a listening post in that blank early morning space. Instead of tossing restlessly trying to get back to sleep, I fill it with a quiet listening: I ask God, 'have you anything to say to me – I'm listening.' Often he lays it on the line: 'You had better change this and that.' And I reply, 'Wait until morning and I'll do it.' But once when I asked if he had anything to say, he replied; 'No, I love you. Go to sleep.' But as I look back on it, I find that the greatest decisions of my life and the most productive have come out of that listening post (190).

Jones was once asked how he was able, in his incessant travels, to keep the sense of God's direction in his speaking. He replied that always before speaking, he made time, not to think about what he was going to say, but to make sure that his mind was open to God, so that God could direct him. The reader will note that Jones begins virtually all his sermons with a silent prayer.[9]

While Jones was not a formal theologian, he did hold core theological convictions. He once asked himself, "You have been a Christian for 50 years; you walked with Christ for 50 years and you have faced life together. What have you learned? What has life taught you in these 50 years? What are the convictions

---

9   Jones' daughter Eunice Jones Mathews and son-in-law, Bishop Mathews were "remembering" E. Stanley Jones at a 1992 Symposium on "Theology and Evangelism in the Wesleyan Heritage" and made these comments about Jones' silent prayer before beginning any lecture or sermon; Bishop Mathews: "By the way, your dad had a special way of beginning an address."Mrs. Mathews: "Yes, he always bowed his head in silence and then after a few moments, he would say, "Amen."Bishop Mathews: "The last time I saw him, about six weeks before his death, I finally asked him a question I had wanted to ask him for a long time: 'What prayer did you use when you did that?' He shocked me by saying that it was not a prayer at all." Mrs. Mathews: "That's right. He repeated this verse: 'You have not chosen me, but I have chosen you and ordained you to go and bear fruit.'" (Logan, 184).

which you hold, or deeper, which hold you?" ("My Life's Convictions" Sermon) He wrote down his convictions and found that there were twelve:

♦ We live in a moral universe.

♦ God is behind this moral universe and is Love.

♦ Jesus is incarnate God.

♦ The center of the incarnation is the Cross.

♦ The *Way* to live is by grace and receptivity.

♦ The Way of Christ is written into me and into the nature of reality, and The Christian Way is the natural way of life.

♦ The gift of the Holy Spirit is the birthright of all Christians.

♦ The Kingdom of God is God's total answer to man's total need.

♦ The Way to meet unmerited suffering and injustice is to use it.

♦ Love is the strongest force in the universe and will win.

♦ Jesus is Lord!

♦ Jesus is the one perfect gift that we have to give the world.

For Jones, the way to discover and experience the reality of these convictions was through self surrender and conversion. His sermons will make this point transparently clear. That was his message and that was the reason that he preached for seventy plus years!

A Portrait of E. Stanley Jones by Shivraj Mahendra

*(Acrylic on canvas [16"x20"]. This portrait was presented
by the artist to The E. Stanley Jones School of World Mission
and Evangelism at Asbury Theological Seminary,
Wilmore, Kentucky on May 17, 2017)*

III

THE NECESSITY OF CONVERSION

**"Except a man be born again,
he cannot see the kingdom of God." (John 3:3)**

WHAT did Jesus mean by this verse? It is important to know what he intended, for according to Jones, Jesus divided all mankind according to whether they had been born again or not. The matter of conversion is as integral to Jones' theology and to his life as it was, according to the scriptures, to Jesus. There was scarcely a book, a sermon, or a conversation with Jones that did not dwell on this subject. He believed that the human need for conversion was everywhere. Conversion is for those inside and outside the church, for the impoverished and the wealthy, for the young and the old, for intellectuals and the uneducated, as well as for the moral and the immoral.

There was no escaping the need of conversion for all. (Jones, *Conversion*, 12)[1]

Jones illustrates his single-minded focus on conversion by sharing an introduction he received from Srinivasa Shastri:[2] Shastri says, "We always know where Stanley Jones is coming out. If he begins at the binomial theorem he will come out at the place of conversion" (Jones, *Conversion* 6). For Jones the matter was simple—modern man was empty; modern man needed conversion.

What then is conversion according to Jones? "Conversion is the penitent, receptive response to the saving divine initiative in Christ, resulting in a change, gradual or sudden, by which one passes from the kingdom of self to the Kingdom of God and becomes a part of a living fellowship, the church" (*Conversion*, 55).

Did the conversion of E. Stanley Jones accord with this definition?

THE CONVERSION OF E. STANLEY JONES

E. Stanley Jones readily admitted that prior to his "conversion" everything in his life was very ordinary:

> My religious experiences and expression began at age five when at church I tried to call attention to myself – all dressed up in a fine new suit – by passing around a

---

1   It was said that the famous preacher, George Whitefield, preached 300 times on the text, 'Except a man be born again he cannot see the Kingdom of God.' When he was asked why he preached so often on this text, he responded, 'Because you must be born again.' While Whitefield preached on the text 300 times, according to Jones, "Life itself is preaching on it daily, from doctors' offices, psychiatrists' couches, conference rooms, factories, our homes, and if we truly know ourselves...from our hearts" (33).

2   A highly respected Hindu who was involved in India's liberation from England who also served as Agent General of India.

collection plate to the adults chatting after service. In retrospect, I realized that I had 'unwittingly run into the central problem in religion, the problem of the self-assertive self[3] (*A Song of Ascents*, 26).

Jones' autobiography tells in considerable detail his conversion story. It is provided here in its entirety for its considerable insights about the significance of this profoundly life-changing experience:

At about the age of 15, I was in the gallery of the Memorial Church, with a group of boys...The speaker was an Englishman, a man of God and at the close of his address he pointed his finger to where we were seated and said, "Young men, Jesus said, 'He that is not with me is against me.'" It went straight to my heart. I knew I wasn't with him, but I didn't want to be against him. It shook me so I took my place among the seekers. I felt undone and wept – wept because I was guilty and estranged. I fumbled for the latchstring of the Kingdom of God, missed it, for they didn't tell me the steps to find it. I wanted the Kingdom of God, wanted reconciliation with my heavenly Father, but took church membership as a substitute. I felt religious for a few weeks and then it all faded out and I was back again exactly where I was before, the springs of my character and my habit formation unchanged. I had been horizontally converted, but not vertically.

As I look back, I am not sorry that I went through that half conversion which was a whole failure. For the fact that I got out of that failure into the real thing may be used to encourage those who have settled down to a compromised stalemate with no note of victory.

The real thing came two years later. An evangelist, Robert J. Bateman, came to Memorial Church. Through his

---

3 We would more likely use the term "egocentric self" in current parlance.

rough exterior I saw there was reality within. I said to myself, "I want what he has." This time I was deadly serious. I wanted the real thing or nothing. For three days I sought. During those days I went to the altar twice but no spark of assurance kindled my darkened heart. The third night came; before going to the meeting I knelt beside my bed and prayed the sincerest prayer I had prayed so far in my life. "Jesus, save me tonight." And he did! A ray of light pierced my darkness. Hope sprang up in my heart. I found myself saying, "He's going to do it." I now believe that he had done it, but I had been taught that you found him at an altar of prayer. So I felt I must get to the church to an altar of prayer. I found myself running the mile to the church. I went into the church and took the front seat. But I was all eagerness for the evangelist to stop speaking, so I could get to that altar of prayer. When he did stop, I was the first one there. I had scarcely bent my knees when Heaven broke into my spirit. I had him — Jesus — and he had me. We had each other. I belonged. My estrangement and my sense of orphanage were gone. I was reconciled. As I rose from my knees, I felt that I wanted to put my arms around the world and share this with everybody. This was a seed moment. The whole of my future was packed into it (*A Song of Ascents*, 26 ff).

Jones understood that church membership does not either imply that conversion has occurred nor automatically convey membership in the Kingdom of God. His horizontal conversion left him limited with no upward potential. However, when he was "vertically" converted, Jones writes that he had "stumbled across the *treasure* of conversion."[4] However, he never forgot the inadequacy of his half or horizontal conversion and would draw on this first experience to provide encouragement and guidance to others on the *steps* to take in seeking real conversion.

---

4   See Sermon on "Self Surrender" for details on this treasure.

His second conversion at the age of seventeen changed the course of Jones' life and from that time on, Jesus was his unequivocal focus. Jones made self surrender and conversion the central issue in the life of a follower of Jesus. What makes a person truly Christian is conversion.

Yet Jones' life was not yet fully integrated, and it would take more than a "vertical conversion" to impact his sub-conscious mind. In his autobiography, Jones describes the experience of having the sub-conscious mind transformed as well:

> After a year of unalloyed joy I found something alien began to come up from the cellar of my life. I felt there was something down there not in alignment with this new life I had found. I was becoming a house divided against itself. I had an unconverted subconscious. In conversion, a new life is introduced into the conscious minds as we consciously accept Christ. The subconscious mind is stunned and subdued by this new dominant loyalty to Christ. Sometimes it lies low for long period, subdued but not surrendered (*A Song of Ascents*, 51).

It was that experience of the negative power of the sub-conscious mind, which in fact surprised Jones, that brought him again to his knees to ask for prayer and support:

> I shall always be grateful to a little group in the church where I was converted. For a year I was on fire – radiant, I know. But then I tripped and sprawled. I said to myself, "What is the use of going to the church meeting tonight; I have nothing to say..." Nothing had been happening to me, I had nothing to say but I went anyway. The rest of them were telling what Christ had done for them, and I sat there with tears streaming down my cheeks, broken-hearted. After everybody had spoken the leader said, "Stanley tell us what is the matter." I said, "I can't, but pray for me." They got on their knees as one man and took me into their arms and took me back to the bosom of God.

When we got up from our knees, I was reconciled with God – with myself and with the group. I shall always be grateful to that little group – they could have broken me for I was a very bruised reed. They could have said, "Yes, I told you so. It's too good to be true." They never uttered that word of criticism, only love. They were a place of redemption, and that is what the Christian church must be. They must know that, when they fall, they've got a place where they can return and find people who love them in spite of everything that they have done (*A Song of Ascents*, 42).

We read earlier about Jones' nervous collapses in 1917 as he tried to resume his evangelistic work in India. Jones truly believed that he would have to leave the mission field. He recounted his experience as he knelt in prayer in the Lal Bagh church as follows: God said to him, "Are you yourself ready for the work to which I have called you?" His reply was, "No, Lord, I'm done for. I've reached the end of my resources, and I can't go on." He then heard God say, "If you'll turn the problem over to me, I'll take care of it." He replied, "Lord, I close the bargain right here." He arose from his knees knowing that he was a well man. (Jones, *A Song of Ascents*, 89) He had turned himself over to God. He had offered a complete surrender, and that made all the difference. Graham notes that Jones did not learn the secret of complete self surrender until he tried to live without it. (393)

SELF SURRENDER & CONVERSION: LIFE UPON THE WAY – THE MESSAGE FOR THE REST OF US

In the mid-1950s, Jones decided to write a book on Conversion. He felt that such a book was needed because only one-third of the church members knew what conversion was by first-hand experience. Jones solicited from his readers' instances of striking conversions that he used in his book and which are included in many of the sermons in Chapter 4 (Graham, 368)

Jones believed that Jesus divided all of humanity into two classes, the converted and the unconverted. This distinction according to Jones runs through time and eternity. (*Conversion*, 15) "The necessity of conversion is not imposed on life but emerges out of life. Life echoes Jesus' message, "You must be born again" (*Conversion*, 34). Jones writes that all of life is under the process of conversion.

> For example, photosynthesis is the process by which the energy of sunlight is used in transforming water and air into plant food. Without that basic conversion, life would perish. Where there is life there is conversion. Christian conversion is conversion to the Kingdom of God (*Conversion*, 36).

Jones asserts that the self in the Christian faith is to be surrendered. The action we take is self surrender; the process is termed "conversion." Jones believed strongly that together with the urgency (and inevitability) of conversion is the necessity of constant surrender to God:

> The urgency for conversion is to be found in the speed at which life is going to destruction and chaos. All the old timetables are out of date" (*Conversion*, 7).[5]

E. Stanley Jones noted repeatedly that modern man would not live with God and so now cannot live with himself. Jones was very psychologically minded and followed closely the early psychoanalytic movement and its successors. He commented that the helping professions such as psychiatry and social work were inadequate to meet the spiritual needs of modern man.[6]

---

5   This was Jones' comment in 1959 – surely it remains true today.

6   Jones quotes the eminent psychologist Stanley Hall, "If the church allows conversion to fossilize then psychology when it become truly biological will preach it" (Conversion, 250).

The doctor's offices are filled with disrupted people who are passing on the sicknesses of their minds and their souls to their bodies. The helping professions lose the battle at the place of their own lack of resources. Knowledge they have; inner resources they do not have. Pagan psychiatry has no way of getting to conversion for it has no purpose or method of self surrender to God. The patient is supposed to be cured by self knowledge, which is a fallacy. The unconverted can't convert the unconverted. The reasons (psychological) counseling has to be strung out interminably is usually because the counselor hasn't got any conversion to offer, therefore has to deal interminably with minor issues with the central issue untouched — the need of conversion *(Conversion,* 89).

Jones writes that it is irrelevant to try to lop off sin by sin and work harder to be good. Rather, he says, all sins are rooted in the un-surrendered self. Our sins cannot be removed by our efforts but only by this act of self surrender. The result of self surrender is conversion. This is not a change of label. It is not something that we earn, but something that we receive as a gift from God.[7] Jones testifies in his sermon "God's Search for Man," that we don't climb a ladder to God, but God comes to us. Jesus is God's redemptive invasion of us. We don't know how it happens, but we are transformed and taken up into the Kingdom of God. (127)

In conversion, Christianity asks us to take the one thing that we own (the self) and give it back to God. In surrendering

---

7   When Jones wrote about conversion, he was adamant that he was NOT talking about proselytism. Jones emphasizes that Jesus was opposed to proselytism: "You canvas land and sea to gain a proselyte, and when you gain him you make him twofold more a child of hell than yourselves" (Matt: 23:15). Proselytism, according to Jones, is the coming over from one group to another group without any necessary change in character or life. It is a change of label and not of life. Conversion is a profound change in character and life, followed by an outer change which corresponds to that inner change. It is the business of religion, the chief business, to produce conversion" (Jones, *Christ at the Round Table,* 136).

the self, we may naturally fear that nothing will be left. We wonder, according to Jones, about how we are to live without the self, which gives us identity, value, and worth in this world. The response sounds paradoxical, for it is in the total surrender of one's life that one finds the true meaning and joy in life: "Conversion is Life (Jesus) impinging on life, awakening it, unifying it, making it care, and making it love" (*Conversion*, 49). This surrendered self no longer accommodates to the pattern and values of this world for it has been liberated from the demands of the world and placed in the hands of Jesus. The self is now free![8]

According to Jones, an example of a truly surrendered and paradoxically "free" man is Paul in chains in the jail at Philippi. When we surrender ourselves, he says, the self is not canceled, but cleansed from self-centeredness and returned to us with a new focus – a focus on God. God is now the center of our universe. Jones would say that this self returned is now a *whole* and healthy self. He would often say that we are never so much ourselves than when we are most God's. (Sermon entitled "Self Surrender")

In his sermon, *"How Are We To Be Changed?"* Jones spells out the process (which can be gradual or sudden) of conversion. He identifies three components:

♦ Mental conflict

♦ Emotional crisis

♦ Resolution of the conflict

And four stages:

♦ The stage of drawing near when you put "yourself in the way of being found by God."

♦ The stage of decision, when you inwardly decide to be His.

8 Jones' sermon on "Self Surrender" contains more detail on this process and many illustrations.

♦ The stage of implementation when you surrender your life to Christ. You affirm that you belong to Christ.

♦ The stage of receptivity when you accept from Christ forgiveness, grace, love – you accept everything from Him! (Jones, *Conversion* 190)

Jones would never leave this matter of "self surrender and conversion" to chance. In case the reader misses any of the steps or the processes of this experience, he spells it out again and again. Here is another variant on the steps to conversion:

♦ Turn toward yourself and your past; review your life.

♦ Turn from your past ways of behaving; that is repentance.

♦ Turn yourself and your sins over to Christ; that is surrender.

♦ Turn toward all your relationships and change them; that is restitution.

♦ Turn with Him and face life and its future; that is life committal (Jones, *Conversion* 198).

According to Jones, the fruits of conversion are the most beneficial and regenerative to the individual and to society of anything that has ever happened to the human race. (Jones, *Conversion* 129). Conversion produces, according to Jones, an "altered relationship with God, which produces an altered relationship with yourself, with your neighbor, with nature, and with the universe. You are no longer working against the grain of the universe – you are working with it" (*Conversion* 131).

Jones maintains that we don't earn or inherit conversion. For example, in his sermon on "Transformation," Jones notes that God has no "grandchildren" and that in spite of Jacob's famous religious genealogy, Jacob has to surrender to God, i.e., give up his old name as "Jacob the supplanter" - to be given his new name — "Israel," (striver with God)." In conversion, Jones says, we are given a new name and a new nature. The old self has been transformed, not sent away or wiped out, but changed. Jones, who was always eager to find another theologian to reinforce his convictions, quotes Paul Tillich on this transformation:

> The New Being is not something that simply takes the place of the Old Being. But it is a renewal of the Old which has been corrupted, distorted, split and almost destroyed. Salvation does not destroy creation; but it transforms the Old Creation into a New One. Therefore, we can speak of the New in terms of a renewal (20).

According to Jones, there is no substitute for conversion. If the Church loses its power to convert, it has lost its right to be called Christian (Jones, *Conversion* 253). Jones once wrote that, throughout his life, he had been in search of a vocabulary to express adequately the fact that he had been converted. The type of spirituality he championed was one which was both inwardly nourishing and outwardly active, and one which transcended what he perceived to be narrowly conceived traditional categories of knowing God. This type of spirituality is broadly appealing today and it has profound relevance to a new view of missions where the Christian may give as well as receive from the non-Christian world.

Jones concludes his book, *Christ of the Roundtable,* by turning to the last chapter of the book of Revelation, "Come forward, you who are thirsty" (Revelation 22:17). "What does this amazing verse mean?" Jones asks, "Apparently this, after God has done everything as described in the whole book of Scripture there is nothing else to be done, for he has done it all – nothing else, for us who follow him except to say, **Come!**" (*Christ of the Roundtable* ,145).

IV

PRESENTATION OF
SERMONS

AS I transcribed many of the more than one hundred sermons that were available to me on audio tape, I wondered just how they might be organized into a coherent framework for this book. I selected fifteen which seemed to be representative of Jones' thinking on self surrender and conversion. However, an organizing principle was missing. I was searching for a larger framework. Serendipitously I happened upon a sermon entitled, *My Life's Convictions* (1952) and as I laid out these twelve convictions, I found that my fourteen remaining sermons sorted easily under each of these Life Convictions. They simply fell into place. It was astonishing that my framework was right in front of me all the time. Perhaps E. Stanley Jones laid it out for me. These convictions have been noted previously on page 55 and are now linked to each of the sermons presented in this section.

Life Conviction	Sermon
We live in a moral universe.	Two Approaches to Life: Faith and Science (1961)
God is behind this moral universe and is Love.	Gods Search for Man (1950)
Jesus is incarnate God.	But Who Do You Say that I Am? (1953)
The center of the incarnation is the Cross.	Self Surrender (1961)
The *Way* to live is by grace and receptivity.	How Are We To Be Changed? (1954) & Transformation (1950)
The Way of Christ is written into me and into the nature of reality, and The Christian Way is the natural way of life.	The Christian Faith & the Body (NA).
The gift of the Holy Spirit is the birthright of all Christians.	The Holy Spirit – 2 sermons (1960 & 1961)
The Kingdom of God is God's total answer to man's total need.	The Kingdom of God (1950)
The Way to meet unmerited suffering and injustice is to use it.	Christ & Human Suffering (NA)

Love is the strongest force in the universe and will win.	The New Birth on the Pattern of Jesus (1957)
Jesus is Lord!	The Word Became Flesh (1961)
Jesus is the one perfect gift that we have to give the world.	The Marks of the Christian Church (1953).

Each sermon is presented virtually as it was preached and is introduced to set the context, clarify the message, and highlight the various presentations of the themes of self surrender, conversion, and the Christian **Way** to live. Many examples in the commentary come directly from the subject sermon. These sermons, often delivered more than a half century ago, remain contemporary and timely. According to Mathews,

> These messages are not interesting as "period pieces" but deal with the deeper matters of the meaning of Christ in our world, the necessity of conversion, the meaning of discipleship, the reality of the kingdom of God, and the role of the church. The themes are not outdated, for in many instances the church has yet to catch up to many of Jones' perspectives (Mathews 14-15).

And now to the sermons themselves...

I. MY LIFE'S CONVICTIONS

COMMENTARY

BY the time E. Stanley Jones delivered the sermon "My Life's Convictions," he had been a Christian for more than 50 years. He shares with his audience the twelve convictions that provide the infrastructure (for these convictions hold him) and the beliefs to which he has committed his life. While these comments will summarize this particular sermon, each of these twelve convictions will be illustrated in subsequent chapters by one or more sermon that deals directly with each of Jones' life convictions.

These convictions emerged over the course of E. Stanley Jones' life as an evangelist devoted to sharing the Good News of Jesus Christ around the world. Jones is not one for half answers or convenient truths; he was committed to knowing reality, and for him, reality was convincingly and assuredly Jesus, the incarnate God. Jones would commit his life to living along Christ's Way.

A comment in Jones' autobiography, *A Song of Ascents,* illustrates his profound commitment and joy in serving Christ as an evangelist:

> My son-in-law, Bishop James Mathews, when I returned from a six months' evangelistic tour in the East, said: 'I've left a book open on your desk with a marked passage. It reminded me of you.' The passage was from John Wesley at eighty-two: 'Matthew Henry says that he sometimes gets tired in the Lord's work, but never of the Lord's work.' By the grace of God, I can go one better. I never tire of the Lord's work and I never tire in the Lord's work. I do not

know what weariness means. I never tire of traveling, or speaking, or writing, and am just as fresh at the end as at the beginning. Thus is it with me today, and I take no thought for the morrow.' At eighty-two I could honestly say Amen to that; no credit to myself — grace! (334)

The necessity for self surrender and conversion is a component part of each of Jones' convictions. Jones asserts that in following Jesus we are set upon the "**Way**" to live. For example, his conviction that "Jesus is Incarnate God" – God reaching down to mankind to redeem us requires a response to Christ's offer, "Come unto me. I am the way, the truth and the life." Man's response is self surrender. Regarding the conviction that "The Way to live is by grace and receptivity," Jones maintains that God comes to us, and all we have to do is surrender ourselves and accept the gift. The struggles of life stop and life can be lived by relaxed receptivity: *"Relaxed receptivity is a taking of the gift of God all the time and leaning heavily upon grace for everything you need"* (83). Jones was firm in his conviction that the "Way" of Christ was written not only in the Bible, but in us and in the nature of reality. Jones recalls the moment that the implications of the revelation, "Without him, Christ, was not anything made that was made," dawned on him, He affirms that this means that the touch of Christ is on all creation, and that everything is made to work in his way. When it does so, it works harmoniously, but when it works in some other way, it works to its own ruin.

Jones bet his life on Christ and believed that Jesus is the perfect gift of God to mankind. He concludes this sermon with these lines:

If Jesus is not the answer, there is no answer. If this is not it, there is no it. It is all a vast blank and a vast illusion. But how could this man have been an illusion who talked truth? How could this be unreal when every syllable was reality? And so I bet my life on Jesus. The deepest and profoundest fact is that I belong to him. I don't know what the future holds, but I know who holds the future (93).

73

MY LIFE'S CONVICTIONS

SERMON

IN my studies with you I gave you a list of some of my life's convictions, since then I thought about the matter a great deal and I have been speaking on it considerably. My first thought was that I would bypass that this year, but I have not been able to get away from it. Probably a handful of you were here at that time. Even so, I have considerably modified my statement of my life convictions and I am going to share them with you tonight. I sat in a train some time ago and said to myself, "You have been a Christian for 50 years; you walked with Christ for 50 years and you have faced life together. What have you learned? What has life taught you in these 50 years? What are the convictions which you hold, or deeper, which hold you?" and I jotted down in my notebook some of the convictions that I no longer hold, but which hold me. I find that there are twelve.

These convictions have not been arrived at easily. I have lived rather a stormy life, particularly in India where my faith is battered day after day, year after year. I take my faith and say to the non-Christians, "There it is. Break it if it can be broken. If it can be broken, it must be broken. I don't want to be in a paradise if it turns out to be a fool's paradise. If this isn't reality, I want to know it. For no matter what you say or I say, the last word will be with the facts." And so, if I hold a faith today, there are scars on that faith, but underneath those scars there are no essential doubts. Just the way to live. Marginal doubts — yes. Lots of things I don't understand but even my marginal doubts — my question marks — are being straightened out into exclamation points. And that's what He's doing with me all the time. Straightening out my question marks into exclamation points of certainty and realization. But I want to share with you as far as I've gone that life is an unfolding secret. But I suppose in a year hence I shall say "Well it's deeper than that, higher than that, more wide-sweeping than that," for there's a surprise around every corner in this whole business.

One would have thought that after talking about one subject (Jesus/Conversion) for over 50 years you'd be so tired of it you wouldn't want to look at it. I've talked about this for 50 straight years—morning, noon, and night. And in between times I've thought about it. Any other subject would have gone so thread bare and so stale, that you wouldn't want to even mention it again. But after 50 years it's as fresh as the morning dew— popping with novelty, bursting with surprise, the horizons breaking constantly and beckoning to further horizons. This is the only subject you could talk about 50 years straight and not get fed up. I am more eager today (to talk about this subject) than when I began. Therefore there must be some divine quality in this thing that doesn't fail you; that has the feel of the real and the eternal upon it. It's great to be able, at my age, not to have to recast your life when you face out to the coming beyond.

I say to myself all you have to do is to follow out what you got in Christ. An old Scotsman was dying. His daughter said, "Shall I read the scriptures to you?" "No, Lassie," he said, "I thatched my roof before the storm began. Let it blow." So it is great to be 68 and you don't have to feverishly set your house in order for any coming storm. All you have to do is walk straight up and out.

I want to share with you some of the convictions that now underlie my faith. **First of all, I believe that there is a moral universe which we don't produce but we discover.** I believe that the universe takes sides. It is not indifferent to your virtue or your vice. There is something built into the structure of things. It is not built up by mores and customs. It is built into the nature of reality. You don't break these laws, written into the nature of reality you break yourself upon them, and those laws are color blind, class blind and race blind and religion blind. Break them and you get broken. It is a world where you get results or consequences. If you work with the moral universe, you get results. It will back you, sustain you, and further you, but if you work against the moral universe you will be up against it frustrated. You get consequences. Some people go through life getting results, others get consequences. You get one or the other. And no one escapes. It is a dependable moral universe. It doesn't have a payday, every Saturday night or every month. But everybody pays, sooner or later. And you get away with nothing, for whatever you do registers itself in yourself and the payoff is in yourself. Anybody who thinks he can cheat a moral God in a moral universe is a moral imbecile — preachers included. The moral universe will not ask how many sermons you have preached. Break it and you get broken, like that. I know that. It is burned in me with many an experience. Sin is, has been and shall be ever the parent of misery and you can't make it the parent of happiness and joy.[1] It won't work.

The second conviction that has come upon me is that behind this moral universe, sustaining this moral universe, is God who stands to us in relationship of father and who loves us and cares for us and would redeem us. But revelation of this one God is progressive – it had to be. If he had revealed himself all at once to us at the beginning, we would have never understood it any more than a rabbit could understand higher mathematics. All the great philosophies in the world, India, China, Greece were completed just about the time of the coming of Christ. Philosophy had taken man as far as a man could go under philosophy and then after man had gone as far as he could go, God in the fullness of time revealed himself perfectly and finally in the person of Jesus of Nazareth. This Jesus of Nazareth stood and said that "I came not to destroy the law of the prophets. I came not to destroy but to fulfill."[2] Jesus didn't

---

1   Thomas Carlyle (1795 – 1881) was a Scottish essayist, satirist, and historian, whose work was hugely influential during the Victorian era. The quote is from his book *The French Revolution: A History, Book 1, Section VII.* <http://www.britannica.com/eb/article-1133>.

2   Matthew 5:17.

come to wipe out man's search for God either through the Hebrews, or the Hindus, Greeks, or the Chinese. He came to fulfill it and to perfect it in himself. The revelation that I get in Jesus is not an absolutely new, never heard of before newness. It is newness in the sense of completion, of perfection. The idea of goodness was always here for God has not left Himself without a witness in any nation. But we never saw Goodness with a capital **G** before. The idea of truth was here before but we never saw the Truth with a capital **T**. We saw life with a small l but one day Life with a capital **L** moved among us. All that man had longed for and searched for was manifested in Him.

Revelation was progressive, culminating in the final and complete and perfect revelation of God in Christ. But it is an unfolding revelation. We seem, in humanity, to get to a place where we discover an ultimate and that is the beginning point of progress. In the realm of mathematics we have made no discovery beyond the discovery that $2 + 2 = 4$. In multiplication, 2×2 do make 4. No matter how hard we try to improve on that fact — we try every time we go to school — but it won't work. We can't (improve on it), $2 + 2 = 4$. Does that stop mathematical progress? No, upon that fixed fact the vast mathematical calculations are built. The perfect becomes the progressive. In geometry things equal to the same thing are equal to each other. Does that stop the progress of geometry? No, it begins it because upon that fixed axiom, you build up your vast geometric calculations. They are adding no new notes to the musical scale. The musical scale is fixed but within that fixed scale there is infinite range. Vast symphonies have been born and will be born out of that fixed scale. The perfect become progressive.

There appeared upon our planet a man who turned to humanity one day and said, "If you want to know what the Father is like, look at me."[3] The ultimate revelation of God —

---

3 John 14:9.

the Father. Our hearts sing to themselves, "Is God like that?" If so, he is a good God and he is trustable. I could ask nothing higher and I could be content with nothing less. If God is like Christ, then I can believe that the universe is not only friendly, it is redemptive. It not only means well, it means to make me well. After 2000 years of progress in every realm of knowledge, we have not surpassed a character concept and found a higher character higher than Christ-likeness. The highest compliment that you can pay to God or man is to say that he is a Christ-like God or a Christ-like man. The highest descriptive of character in any language is the adjective Christ-like. If God is not like Christ in character then I am not interested in God. I would turn to Jesus of Nazareth and I would say, "You are the highest I know. Take my heart." A man lived among us for three years and you can take the characteristics of his character and transfer them to God without lowering your concept of God — lowering? No, you heighten it. For the doubt is not to the character of Jesus, the doubt is about the character of God. We say that if God is like Jesus, then he is all right. But we believe that Jesus is the revelation in time of what lies back in eternity.

That leads me to the third point, namely that Jesus is incarnate God. Jesus is not man become God, but God become man. He is not man reaching upward, rather He is God reaching downward. We could not get to God, so God came to us and came to us in the only form that we could understand him, namely in a human form. I am grateful that he did not just come to us in a book, to reveal himself through in a book. I can respect a book, and be loyal to a book, but I can't love a book. I must love a person. It does not say that the word became printers ink…a book. It does say the word – the divine word became flesh – a person. God had to reveal himself perfectly through a perfect person. If Jesus of Nazareth is not that perfect person, then I don't know where there is one. I have swept the horizon east and west for these past 45 years and if it is not Jesus, it is nothing. I cannot find any category into which I can put Jesus and keep him there as a mere human being. He breaks every human category. He is like me and unlike me. Like me in that he stands and faces life as I face life, a man. He calls on no power that is not at my disposal or yours for his own moral battles. He is so like me that he stands along side of me facing God praying. He is so like me that I can almost put my hand on his shoulder and say, "Brother Man." Yet when I am just about to do that I can't for he steps on the other side, on the side of God and confronts me with an offer that no man may dare offer another without blasphemy. He says, "Come unto me, I am the way, the truth and the life."[4] He is like me therefore my example, unlike me therefore my redeemer. I need somebody to show me how to live — an example, but deeper, somebody to dispose me to live after I have seen how to live. I need a redeemer.

When I turn to his birth and I see the same two things. He is like me and unlike me. He is like me in that he was born of a woman. He is unlike me in that he was born directly of God. So the likeness and unlikeness in his life and in his birth do not contradict, they coincide.

I see this man performing miracles and I am not scandalized in the age of science that he would do it. I say of course, for the central miracle is not the opening of the blind eyes or the unstopping of deaf ears, or making the lame to walk or the dead to rise. The central miracle is the Person. He rises in sinless grandeur above saint and sinner — a moral miracle, a miracle of being. Then being a miracle, would he perform miracles? The answer is that being a miracle, it would be a miracle if he did not perform miracles. I don't believe in Jesus because of the miracles. I believe in the miracles because of Jesus. He carries them. The central miracle is this miracle of the incarnation. God become man. Grant that central miracle and all the lesser miracles become credible in light of that central miracle. Upon that all the rest of them hang. And every one of His miracles shows not mere power but a redemptive act. If He had power to perform miracles, He had power to restrain Himself from

---

4   John 14:6.

performing miracles, for He performed no miracles for Himself nor to show His power or to satisfy curiosity. There is a quality about His miracles for they show the quality of His own character in everything that He did.

I believe then that this that I find in the Gospel is not man's search for God, but God's search for man. Religions are man's search for God and therefore there are many religions. But there is but one Gospel — God's search for man. I will repeat that sentence and I hope that you will remember it for it has done me a lot of good. There are many religions, there is but one Gospel. For religion is man's search for God. I believe that the Gospel is not man's search for God, but God's search for man. There is but one Gospel.

Jesus did not come to set a religion against other religions. He never used the word religion. He did not come to set up a religion against another, a little bit better, going a bit further. He came to set the Gospel over against all human need whether in this religion or that religion, the other religion or no religion. Jesus is incarnate God — God speaking a language I could understand, a human language that I can understand. God showing His character in the only place where I could understand it, in the stream of human history. When I say God, I think Jesus and I could not think anything higher of God than that he would be like Jesus. That is wonderful that after 2000 years that I could say that. If I were to sit down and try to think about the type of God that I would want to see in the universe, His lineaments would take on the character of Christ or He would not be good or trustable.

The center of this incarnation leads me to my fourth point, the cross. Here the identification was complete. He shared our toil for thirty years and was baptized into our toil at the baptism at the Jordan River and at the cross he was baptized into our sins. At the Jordan he took a baptism of repentance though he needed no repentance. He became a part of us, taking a baptism which we have to take but he does not. And then at the cross, the identification with man became so complete that he became sin for us—bore on his own body our sins on a tree.

He stood up one day and said, "I was hungry and you fed me. I was thirsty and you gave me drink. I was in prison and you came unto me."[5] And they said, "Lord, when?" Jesus said, "In as much as you have done it unto one of the least of these...you have done it unto me for I am hungry in their hunger and bound in their bondage."[6] For every man's hunger is his hunger. Everyman's imprisonment is his imprisonment. There is one thing that he left out. He could not say I was sinful in your sin. He was hungry in our hunger, he was bound in our imprisonment, but he was not sinful in our sins for that would be misunderstood. While he could not say that, he did that. He walked straight up to the cross and identified with us in the deepest place of our need—our sin. And (He) cried the cry that you would never have to cry, "My God, My God, why has thou forsaken me?"[7] The cry that we do cry when we sin, (is the cry of) feeling a separation from God. The identification was complete.

What does that mean then? If it means anything it means this—that God is searching for me and I do not have to find God. I have to allow God to find me. It also means that nobody is further than one step from God. It means that if you turn around right now, you'll be in the arms of redemptive love. The Way (is) Jesus, the Way comes right straight down beneath our feet; and if I turn around and begin to walk, I'm on the Way. If I'm in the hole, then that Way begins in the hole; if I'm in hell then that Way begins in hell if I turn around and begin to walk. All anybody has to do to get into the kingdom of God is to say one word—yes—provided that word carries with it your life. Yes. Jesus is God's yes to me and when I say my yes

---

5   Matthew 25:35-36.

6   Matthew 25:40.

7   Matthew 27:46.

in response, we are together forever. Too cheap you say? Oh no, for it is a gift but that when you take it you belong forever to the giver.

That leads me to my next point which is namely that the way to live is by grace and receptivity. I can't get to God so God comes to me and all I have to do to find Him is empty my hands and take the gift. It is absolutely free. I cannot offer the atonement of my own suffering, of my own blood to atone for my own sins; I can't. Since I can't offer my own blood, I accept His. He died to redeem me. Don't ask me to explain that. It is mystery all immortal guise. Before the shrine of the wonder that God gave Himself for me on the cross, I shall forever, forever explore and be grateful. All I know is that when I open my heart to it something, redemptive touches me and lifts me, changes me and makes me over. It is the most redemptive touch that ever came upon the framework of human life. The Way to live is by grace and receptivity. It is not by struggling and trying to be good but to let go and accept the gift. So many people are struggling so hard to be good. People come up to me after my address and say, "Thank you very much for that message, I will now try harder." I say, "Don't." *You* are trying harder. You don't come up to your wife and say, "Dear, I am trying hard to love you." What would she say? She would say, "Is it as bad as that?" You don't try hard to love somebody. Love meets you in a person and you surrender...it's got you. And then you go beyond the first, second, third mile anywhere for this love; it has got you! To live by grace is the answer. The levels of life are three: first, there is the level of instinct; second, the level of duty; and the third —the one above— is of grace. A great many people are trying to live on the level of duty. Religious people are trying hard to fulfill the laws of duty, to live at the level of duty. They are whipping up their wills. Christianity is not about the whipping up of the will, it is about the surrender of the will.

One of the most illuminating things that was said today was the fact that some of the elderly residents (of Old People's

Homes) say, "Now I am going to relax and enjoy myself for I have done my duty." It was very revealing, meaning that their religion was a religion of duty and when they no longer feel the lash of duty, religion fades out and dies out. They have never been on the level of grace. They know nothing about grace. Because if you have grace in your heart, you are forever driven by an impulsion that you can't control. You say fulfilled? "Were the whole realm of nature mine. That is an offering far too small. For love so amazing, so divine, demands my soul, my life my all—now and forever."

Life (can be lived) by relaxed receptivity. If you know how to take, then you know how to live. The first law of life is receptivity. The first thing that a child has to learn (to live) is to receive from its mother. Unless you know how to let go and let God – let God take hold of you then you don't know how to live. But if you know that you are always receiving, always receiving and the moment you do that, you find an impulse to give. For the moment that He took hold of me, I felt as if I wanted to put my arms around the world and share this (experience) with everybody. I still feel that way. People say to me, "why don't you settle down and why don't you enjoy life and have a home?" Well, first of all, I do enjoy life and my home is everywhere and I would rather put my arms around the world and share this with everybody than to be in heaven. For this is heaven right now. Relaxed receptivity is a taking of the gift of God all the time and leaning heavily upon grace for everything you need and therefore feeling adequate.

The sixth thing that has written itself upon me is that the way of Christ is not only written in the Bible but it is written into me and into the nature of reality. I remember when this discovery, this revelation came to me. I realized that the way of Christ was written in here yes, (pointing to the Bible) and in here, (pointing to himself). A number of passages in the New Testament say that God created the world through Christ.

---

8   John 1:1-3.

"Without him, Christ, was not anything made that was made, through who, Christ, God made the worlds, by whom and for whom (Christ) were all things created."[8] Passages like this "through whom he made the worlds..." Without Him – Christ—was not anything created?" What do these strange passages mean? Did God create the world through Christ? What does this mean? Does it mean that the touch of Christ is on all creation? That everything made is to work in His way? Does it mean that when it works in His way it works well – harmoniously – adjustably and happily and if it works some other way it works to its own ruin? Are we made by Christ and for Christ? And when we find Him do we find ourselves?

I believe that I'm predestined to be a Christian by my makeup. I believe that the way is not just written in the Bible it is written in my blood, my nerves, my tissues and my being. Every cell of my being is made by Him and for Him. I'm predestined to be a Christian. It's says in Romans 8:29, "For those whom he foreknew he also predestined to be conformed to the image of his Son." Am I predestined to be in the image of his Son? And is that destiny written, not in mere scripture, but in my blood, my nerves, my tissues? Strange that I who have my roots in Methodism am standing in this pulpit here preaching to you *predestination*. It is supposedly a Presbyterian doctrine. But I do preach it. I am predestined to be a Christian. I can live according to that destiny if I want to, but I can live against it if I want to. But if I live against it (that destiny), I will get hurt automatically. I can fulfill that destiny and when I do, then I go from harmony to harmony, and from rhythm to rhythm and from joy to joy in an unending series. I believe that there is a way to live and that way is Christ. That life will respond to no other way.

I was in a barbershop some time ago and the man who just had his hair cut and left the shop called back to the barber, "Well, be good." The barber called back, "I'll have to." Interesting...I say to a lot of people, I say you are destined to be good. You don't dare be resentful. For look what happens to you when you have resentments in you, you fall to pieces. You don't dare have fears in you; for look what happens to you, you break out all over. And you don't dare be a self centered person for you will be sand in the machinery of living. You are destined to be a Christian and so am I. I can live against that destiny but inevitably I will get hurt. Again and again I often say to myself, "Stanley Jones, this is the way to live, if you want to live some other way, you will get hurt." That is about all there is to it.

Anybody who tries another way is a fool and I could put an adjective to it and I would not be swearing. He is a "self-damned fool." We are made for what we find in Christ and for nothing else and when we find him we find ourselves. When I am most His, I am most my own. Bow to Him and I am freest. If I go against Him, I go against myself. If I revolt against God, I revolt against myself. He has got me hooked. I know exactly what happens when I go against Him, I will be in turmoil. In five minutes, disruption would spread through every portion of my being. If I revolt against Him that would follow automatically.

Out on the West Coast, in the State of Washington, I spoke on this subject that the Christian way is written within you, not merely in the Bible, but written in you. A little girl heard my lecture and as she was walking home with her mother that evening she said, "What Stanley Jones said this evening was common sense. And mother, he guarantees it." I don't guarantee it but the universe does and that is more important. When you are a Christian you have cosmic backing. You walk the earth as one who has got the universe behind him. You walk the earth without apology. I am afraid of nothing.

The next thing that I would suggest and follows as a corollary to the other is that the Christian way is the natural way to live. I do not believe that sin is natural—accustomed, yes, but not natural. If evil were natural, why would it disrupt me? It does disrupt me. I know exactly what happens when I commit a sin. It works with a mathematical precision. I am orphaned, estranged, out of sorts, furtive, underground and everything cries out within me, outraged and says, "This is not the way!" And then I know exactly what happens when I do the Christian thing, I am universalized; I am at home; I walk the earth a conqueror; I am afraid of nothing and the sum total of reality is behind me and everything cries out within me and says, "This is the way, now you got it!" I believe that goodness is my native land and that evil is alien. I gasp and die in an alien atmosphere — in evil.

Tertullian[9], the great church father said the soul is naturally Christian. Reinhold Niebuhr[10], the theologian, says that the soul is naturally pagan and Dr. Walter Horton[11] says the soul is half Christian and half pagan. You can take your choice. I vote with Tertullian. If the soul were naturally pagan, and I define paganism as living without the God reference, if the soul were naturally pagan, then the paganist ought to sin and be full of

---

9   Quintus Septimius Florens Tertullianus, anglicized as Tertullian, (ca. 200 AD) was a notable early Christian apologist. He was the first great writer of Latin Christianity, thus sometimes known as the "father of the Latin Church." He introduced the term Trinity, as the Latin trinitas, to the Christian vocabulary. <http://www.tertullian.org/readfirst.htm>

10 Karl Paul Reinhold Niebuhr (1892–1971) was one of the seminal religious thinkers of the 20th Century. As a theologian, ethicist and pastor, he worked to make the Christian world comprehensible to and responsible for the modern world. He promoted such ideas as. "God acts in history but is also hidden from history and cannot be known but by incomplete reason and completed faith." <The Columbia Encyclopedia 6th ed., s.v."Niebuhr, Helmut Richard" [database on-line]; available from Questia, http://www.questia.com/PM.qst?a=o&d=101261328; Internet; accessed 28 March 2007.>

11 Walter Marshall Horton (1895-1966) was an internationally known theologian and leader in the modern Ecumenical Movement. Through his sermons, radio broadcasts, lectures, and frequent world travels, Horton helped to develop an ecumenical Christian theology, to foster dialogue between theological liberals and conservatives, and to promote an active role for unitive Protestantism in the post-war world. < http://www.oberlin.edu/archive/holdings/finding/RG30/SG4/biography.html>

harmony. Is it? No, the pagans are sad. Paganism does not know how to be happy. Fundamentally paganism is unhappy. You say, aren't there people who are getting along well without Christ? I don't know anybody east or west who is getting along well without Christ. Can the heart get along without love, the lungs without air, and the eye without light? If so, then people can get along well without Jesus Christ. However, I don't believe that they can. I believe that paganism is sad. It jumps from thing, to thing, to thing. It does so to forget the central emptiness that God is gone. They have to invent more and more ways to keep life tolerable. Life has lost its savor. Pagans are infinitely unhappy.

There is more joy to the square inch to being a Christian than there is to the square mile outside; it is pure unadulterated joy and it is a joy without a hangover. I won't get up tomorrow morning and say, "Stanley Jones, why were you a Christian last night? What made you do it?" I won't wake up and kick myself around my room and say what in the world made you do it. Aren't you a fool? I will probably wake up with a grin. Some people wake up with a groan. I will rub my hands and say, "Good, another opening day. Grand." It is fun to be a Christian. It is fun. If it is not fun to be a Christian, then it is no fun at all. I don't try to have a good time, I just have it! It is fun to be a Christian.

I was up in Alaska writing on a book between meetings and I had to write before a mirror because there was no other place to write. I don't usually write my books in front of a mirror but I stopped my writing and looked into the looking glass and I saw myself and said, "Stanley Jones you are a very happy man aren't you?" I said, "Yes I am, very." And I said, "How did you get this way?" I said, "I don't know." "I walked across a field one day and I stubbed my toe and I said, "What is this is treasure?" I ran off and I sold everything I had and bought that field...I said, "I have been hugging myself ever since." All that self-loathing and self-rejection and self hate drops away. It is as bad to hate yourself is to hate somebody else. Self-hate is sin as other-hate is sin. Put yourself in His hands is no longer hating yourself for He accepts you and you accept yourself — He forgives you and you forgive yourself — He respects you and you respect yourself. You have no illusion of grandeur — you say, "yes I can do things but through His grace I can accomplish things but only inside of Him — I step out of him — I am impotent and powerless." The life I now live is not my life — for I am never so alive as when fully His, — but the life which Christ lives in me.

Being a Christian is the natural way to live. Sin has gone down into the human personality and depraved it. If it were natural, it would not deprave us. We should blossom and bloom under sin. The fact that sin depraves us shows that it is not the natural way to live. The Christian way is. All coming to Christ has the feeling of a homecoming upon it. It is like waking from an awful dream. It is like coming to my homeland and realizing that this is what I was born for. When I find him, I find myself. Chesterton[12] says, if the natural will not submit to the supernatural it becomes the unnatural. When I take my natural and submit it to the supernatural it becomes more natural than ever before. The Christian is the most natural person in the world. He has a natural joy and a natural gaiety and a natural laughter. Some of you look pretty gloomy but you will be smiling before the week is over. There is more joy to being a Christian in one minute than there is in a life time living otherwise. A saint said, if I could drop into hell the pure joy that I have in my heart, hell would turn into heaven. One drop would transform hell. It would. It is wonderful being a

---

12 Gilbert Keith Chesterton (1874–1936) was an influential English writer of the early 20th century. Chesterton has been called the "prince of paradox." The source of the idea attributed to Chesterton is most likely from Chesterton's book *The Everlasting Man*, the chapter on the Five Deaths of the Faith, but the exact quote or source is not known. The Columbia Encyclopedia 6th ed., s.v."Chesterton, G. K." [database on-line]; available from Questia, http://www.questia.com/PM.qst?a=o&d= 101237068; Internet; accessed 31 March 2007.>

Christian and I have never gotten over the wonder of it. I never expect to.

The eighth thing that I believe is that the gift of the Holy Spirit is the birthright of all Christians. After I was a Christian, I ran in the joy of that for some months and then I felt a deeper need and made a deeper surrender and made a deeper acceptance and found the greater fullness of the Holy Spirit. I found that if I would offer my all for His all that I could have that all of His in exchange for the all of mine. It is the best exchange in the world. (I will say more about the Holy Spirit later.)

The ninth conviction is that the Kingdom of God is God's total answer to man's total need. The Kingdom is the ultimate order. And, if I seek that first, everything else is added to me. I believe that Kingdom is man's total answer to man's total need. I will take up this subject tomorrow morning.

My next point is that the way to meet unmerited suffering and injustice is to use it. I remember when this issue was clarified in my mind. I was in India and understood the Hindu approach to unmerited suffering. The Hindu says that what happens (to you) is the result of a previous birth — so that whatever is — is just. If you are suffering now, then you were sinful then. "just as a calf will find its mother among a thousand cows — so your deeds will find you out among a thousand rebirths."[13] Accept it. It is yours. Whatever is — is just. A Hindu

---

13 r^shi (Seer, Sage) vyaasa and bhagawaan Ganesha, Mahaabhaarata (ca. 5000 B.C.E.). Mahaabhaarata is the largest epic in the history of mankind. it originates form bhaarata (India) - the land of king bharata, son of duushyanta and shakuntalaa. Mahaabhaarata is one of the two itihaasa (historical account) scriptures of sanaatana dharma (Hindu-dharma), the other being the raamaayaNa. It describes events that took place in ancient bhaarata around 5000 BCE. The main event was the appearance of Lord krishNa - the 8th avataara (incarnation) of Lord vishNu towards the end of dwaapara yuga (the penultimate age among the four ages in a mahaayuga which corresponds to a complete cycle of the earth's percession). < http://www.hindunet.org/mahabharata/>

said to me one day that Jesus must have been a terrible sinner in a previous life because he suffered so much in this life. According to the strict law of Karma he was right. But, I would suspect the premise which brought him to that conclusion. And then one day the whole thing clarified itself to me through a verse. In that verse I saw a vast possibility. It was during a time in India when I was puzzled. And then I read this verse. "And when they shall deliver you up before Kings and Governors for my namesake. They shall turn to you for a testimony."[14] "Oh," I said. "Can I turn everything – injustice – everything into a testimony? Can I use everything and can I bear witness to everything? Use it for Your purposes? Yes that is possible. I believe that the way to meet life is to take hold of whatever comes – pleasure, pain, compliments or criticism. To rescue out of the heart of every injustice, every evil – some good. Jesus didn't bear the cross, he used the cross. The cross was sin. He turned it into the healing of sin. The cross was man at his worst and Jesus showed through it God at his redemptive best. The cross was the worst thing that could happen to Jesus, and Jesus turned it into the best thing that could happen to the world. And when you can do that, you're invulnerable. That lighted up a whole area, I didn't have to explain injustice – I could use it. I did not have to explain why this that or the other thing happened. I could take hold of it and transmute it into something else. This turned me from the defensive to the offensive. I believed therefore I could rescue out of the heart of everything that happened to me something good. Everything furthers the Christian if he knows how to use it.

They put Jesus on a cross and there he was crucified, and then, and then, if the devil can turn pale, he must have turned as pale as death for he watched that man take that cross and

---

14 "But before all this occurs, they will arrest you and persecute you; they will hand you over to synagogues and prisons, and you will be brought before kings and governors because of my name. This will give you an opportunity to testify" (Luke 21:12-13).

turn it and turn it and turn it and turn it into redemption. He (the devil) must have sat back and said, "Well, I didn't get much out of that. I put him on a cross and he redeemed the world through it." Every thing furthers those who follow Christ. And so then, if you know that, you know how to live, if not on account of, then in spite of. And that has become a simple philosophy of life. It is a wonderful way to live—to rescue out of whatever happens something good. God is rescuing out of everything something good.

My Tenth conviction is that love is the strongest force in the universe and will win. In my short life, I have watched the dictators come and go. I have watched them have their brief and bloody days depending on force. At the end of every one of them disillusionment sets in. Disillusionment will toss us to Jesus because everything else breaks down. I used to believe in war. I supported it during the World War I, but I lost my faith in it. I found that it was a means out of harmony with the ends in view, and so I lost my faith in it. And now I am trying to do away with war by advocating world government. There can be no peace without justice, no justice without law, and no law without government and no government without power to enforce its laws and so world peace depends on world government I believe that and therefore I shall try to bring forth world government.

I believe that we that we have got to do away with war. No one will ever win another one. Another war would be the end of the race. We have come to the place where we have discovered atomic energy and God is saying now look you depended on force and here it is in the heart of an atom. But if we use it again—both sides will be ruined probably in twenty four hours. So, I shall try to depend on love and the forces of good will and I shall try to make a world where everyone will be safe, where everyone will be safe—realizing of course that there is something beyond world government and that is the Kingdom of God.

91

My 11th conviction is that Jesus is Lord and will finally conquer. The earliest Christian creed and the simplest one, I understand is, "Jesus is Lord." Did you know what that meant? This man who walked their dusty roads and was crucified dead and buried and had gone to the right hand of God was going to have the last word in every human event. He was at the throne of God and He would have the last word. The early Christians said…Jesus is Lord! Not this king or that king and not only a savior, but Lord! Jesus decides things in the end and everything must bow. Now I would like to reiterate my faith in that. Jesus is Lord! The kings and the captains will come and depart but Jesus will be Lord. Tyranny will grind people under their feet, but Jesus is Lord. The man that I obey is at the right hand of God the Father at the center of moral power. That gives me courage. I am optimistic because of the fact that there is something behind things that will have the last word. Perhaps not today or tomorrow but on the third day. Yes.

And then the last thing that I want to say is that Jesus is the one perfect gift that we have to give. It is the one perfect export that we have to export. It is the one thing that I can go to the nations of the world with — without apologies. When I go to the east I have to apologize for many things. I have to apologize for many things in my own country. I love my country. I love it deeply and profoundly. I love my country but I have to apologize for many things in my country for we in America are only partially Christian. I have to apologize for many things in the Christian church for the church too is only partially Christian. I have to apologize for many things in myself for I too am only a Christian in the making.

However, when it comes to Jesus Christ there are no apologies upon my lips for there are none in my heart. It is the one place where there is no stammering on my tongue and the one place where I have no apologies in my heart – that one place is in Jesus. It is great to have one place where you are sure that you are on solid ground.

An artist pictured the face of Christ. But around that face were dark and glowering clouds but that face was illumined right in the center of those dark clouds. There are many things that I cannot explain. There are dark clouds around him and many things are inscrutable, and I don't understand them. But that face..."that face that far from vanishes rather grows and becomes my universe that feels and knows." I say that I have one solid place in my universe that I could utterly put my whole weight down and that is the place of Christ.

If this is not the answer there is no answer. If this is not it, there is no it. It is all a vast blank and a vast illusion. But how could this man have been an illusion who talked truth? How could this be unreal when every syllable was reality and so I bet my life on Jesus. The deepest and profoundest fact is that I belong to him. I don't know what the future holds, but I know who holds the future.

Let us pray.

E. Stanley Jones in his early years in Lucknow, India

2. WE LIVE IN A MORAL UNIVERSE

COMMENTARY ON

"TWO APPROACHES TO LIFE: FAITH AND SCIENCE"

THIS sermon begins with a rather lengthy story of how Jones arrived "safely and on time" for the first Christian Ashram (1940) to be held in the United States. While this account might seem to be beside the point as an extended preface to a sermon, it is addressed to an Ashram audience which always seemed to enjoy anecdotes that pertained to his commitment to them. In addition, the story illustrates two things; the validity and power of E. Stanley Jones' "inner voice," and his conviction that when God guides, God provides in the practical as well as the spiritual arenas of our lives.

This address asserts that the Christian approach works from revelation down and from the facts (science) up to conclusions. E. Stanley Jones will make it clear that these two methods of understanding life do not come out at different points, but at the same place. He believes that life is rendering one verdict and that is the Christian verdict. If we work from revelation down or from the facts up, both ways will come out at the feet of Jesus. We live in a moral universe which is not man's creation but man's discovery. (Jones, *The Way*, 19)

In his book, *The Way*, Jones illustrates this belief that the approach of religion and science will coincide.

I was tapping my way down a very steep mountain path in pitch dark. A misstep on either side would bring disaster. It was a slow and tedious process. When I was about half way down, suddenly the lights came on. There was the pathway clear; I could abandon my tedious method of tapping my way and walk with confidence along a lighted way. My tapping in the dark was the way of science and experience; my assured walking in the light of a revelation of the paths' way was the Christian way. They were not contradictory; they were different approaches to the one Way (19).

Jones emphasizes these passages, "Without Him, Jesus, was not anything that was made." (Hebrews 1:1); "Through whom, Christ, he made the world." (Colossians); "By whom and for whom were all things created" - in heaven above, visible and invisible. Jones asks, "Is the message that all things were created by Him and for Him?" He answers, "Yes, and Jesus is the **Way**.

Some of the messages of this sermon are found in Jones' book *The Way*, which was one of his favorites. The Way is not just the way of salvation, but the **Way** to live. Jones will argue that because all things were created by Jesus and for Jesus; that there is both a Christ touch and a Christ purpose in creation, and that creation is made for Him. "Our human destiny is to be Christian and that destiny is written into the nature of reality. It is written both into our physical body and into our relationships. That destiny is written into all of life. The Christian way is not imposed on life, but is *inherent* in life" (Jones, *The Way* 8). Jones asks, "Is the Christian **Way** the **Way** we are made to work as well as the **Way** that God wants us to work?" He will answer in the affirmative.

Jones tells his audience that the **Way** has implications for all of life. "All life is of one piece. There are no dualisms, no compartmentalisms. Life is one, and the laws that govern life have one source – God" (*The Way*, 21). The right or moral thing in all spheres, economic, physical, social, political, educational, is always the healthy thing and it is always the Christian thing. It is always illustrated as the **Way**.

Jones shares illustration after illustration in this sermon to reinforce his core thesis that the Christian Way is the natural

Way to live life in a moral universe created by a loving (and orderly) God.

This is a universe where you get results or consequences. If you work with the moral, universe you get results. It will back you, sustain you and further you. You will get results. If you go against the moral universe, you get consequences. You will be up against it and be frustrated. Some people go through life getting results and others get consequences. You get one or the other. You don't break these laws. You break yourself upon them. These laws are color blind, class blind, race blind and religion blind. Break them and you get broken. If you jump out of a ten story building, you don't break the law of gravity you only illustrate it. You don't break these moral laws; you break yourself on them (105).

Evil, according to Jones is unnatural and is the word "live" spelled backwards! For example, in C.S. Lewis' *The Screw Tape Letters, a* senior devil is giving advice to a junior devil and says, "We work under a cruel handicap. Nothing is naturally on our side. Everything has to be twisted before it is of any use to us" (*The Way*, 32).

Christ will be repeatedly shown to be the **Way** and Jones closes his message with an invitation for his listeners to choose to follow Christ's Way. He will gently insist that once we recognize that Jesus is the Way, we must follow His Way.

If you work from Revelation down, and the facts up, you are coming out at His feet. That is the most exciting thing that I know of on this planet. I watched it with baited breath and I would like to stay around long enough to see how it all comes out. But what I say to you is true — tremendously true. A man, a non-Christian, said one night at the close of one of my addresses: "If what the speaker has said tonight isn't true, it doesn't matter. But, if it is true, then nothing else matters." A non-Christian said that! If Jesus is the Way, then we have to come to Him or else we are lost and out of the way. Every road that leads away from Jesus Christ has a precipice at the end of it. Every road that leads away from Him means you are sorrowful; you go away sorrowful. All coming to Jesus has a feeling of homecoming. When you come, you feel that you are out of your estrangement, your alienation. Now what conclusion must I come to? That the Christian way is the natural way to live. (112)

Jones would often close his sermons by telling his audience just how much fun it is to be a Christian. It is fun for Jones because he is living upon the Way of life and not a victim to impulse, whim or fancy. "The Christian way is life set to music; the unchristian way is life set to misery" (Jones, *The Way*, 38).

WE LIVE IN A MORAL UNIVERSE:
TWO APPROACHES TO LIFE

SERMON

I begin this sermon by telling you the story about the first Ashram held in the United States. It was to be held at Saugatuck, Michigan in the summer of 1940. However in May of that year preceding the American Ashram, I was at Sat Tal and I heard the inner voice say to me, "It's all right I will get you there safely and on time." I thought to myself, why should I be hearing that word of comfort now? I had everything fixed up; I was going to fly from Calcutta to Hong Kong and get a boat across the Pacific to get to Saugatuck, Michigan on time. But the voice kept saying, "It's all right; I will get you there safely and on time." Soon I saw why that voice told me that. Shortly after, everything fell to pieces along the proposed trip. I had a reservation to go through the Mediterranean on a Japanese boat, but the Mediterranean was closed because the war was on. Yet the voice kept saying, "It's all right; I will get you there safely and on time." And then I had a telegram from the American Express Office in Bombay telling me that there was an American boat going by way of South Africa to New York, would I take it? It was the only thing open so I said yes and wired that I would take that boat. But when I got to Bombay and asked when that boat would arrive in New York they told me it would get there ten days after the Ashram would begin. And yet my inner voice had said, that I would arrive "safe and on time." I decided that since there was nothing else open, I would have to take that boat. I finished up writing *Is the Kingdom of God Realism?* on board ship. When we got to South Africa, the captain said, "We have to stop somewhere and get water along the way to New York." They decided on Trinidad, in the West Indies. I looked the island up on a map and saw that it was on the route that Pan American Airlines was using on its flights to South America. I decided to get off the ship and fly from Trinidad to Miami. I caught a plane the next morning and arrived in Miami. I took the train the next day to Chicago. I was feeling a little sorry that I couldn't go by New York to settle up with the Methodist mission board secretary before I began my one year evangelistic campaign in the United States. However, when I got to Chicago all the mission board secretaries were there. They were holding a meeting in the hotel where I was staying so I was easily able to get my business with them accomplished. The next day a pastor said, "I have come to drive you out to Saugatuck, Michigan." I told him what had happened and that God had been performing miracles for 12,000 miles. Today was the very day the Ashram was to open. My driver said, "If God has brought you so far along I will take you the rest of the way." But when we were about twenty miles from Saugatuck the car began going this away and that away on a hill and my driver said, "My goodness! My brakes are gone." We went back and forth across that road and put up this side of disaster. He said, "I can't go on without brakes." So we went back five miles to where there was a garage and the mechanic worked on it for three hours. I watched the time as he did his work. Just as we approached the deadline for the opening of the Ashram, the man came out from under the car and he said, "It's fixed you can go." We went the twenty miles to the Ashram and as we pulled into the campground the bell was ringing for the opening of the Ashram—safely and on time—exactly on time.

I've heard wonderful reports of how you (Ashramites) have been getting along; its good news. It's the news that I wanted to hear and have heard with a great deal of satisfaction and gratitude. I'm tempted to tell a story about Bishop Pickett since I heard he told some about me. I went out to India before he did and he took the church—the Lucknow Church—which I had had as a pastor. I was off at evangelistic meetings in Madras and I sent a wire to him welcoming him to India. I said, "Welcome" and then I put in a passage of scripture; 2 Corinthians 8:8.[1] However, the telegraph system changed one of the numbers. Instead of 8:8, he got 1:8, which reads this way, "We do not want you to be ignorant concerning the affliction we experienced in Asia; for were so utterly, unbearably crushed that we despaired of life itself." Bishop Pickett must have asked himself, "What kind of welcome is this?" Some months later when I met him he asked me about the telegram and I had to explain.

I am going to talk to you this morning about the two great approaches to life. There is the Christian approach to life and then there is the scientific. The Christian approach works from Revelation down. We do not apologize from working from Revelation down, for Jesus is our starting point. He's the uncovering, we believe, of the authentic nature of God in

---

1   "I do not say this as a command, but I am testing the genuineness of your love against the earnestness of others. For you know the generous act of our Lord Jesus Christ, that though he was rich, yet for your sakes he became poor, so that by his poverty you might become rich. And in this matter I am giving my advice; it is appropriate for you who began last year not only to do something but even to desire to do something – now finish doing it, so that your eagerness may be matched by completing it according to your means" (2 Cor. 8:8-11).

understandable terms, human terms. So we do not apologize for working from Him down to life; we glory in it.

But there's this other method of working from the facts up and out to conclusions — the scientific method. The big question for religion and for science is this: do these two approaches come out to two places — rendering two verdicts on life? Or, do they come out to one place? Is life then rendering one verdict? The deepest conviction of my life is this: if you work from Christ down and from science up, if you go far enough with both, deep enough, you come out to a Christian verdict on life. Life is rendering one verdict and that is the Christian verdict. Whether you come from this way down or this way up, we are discovering that the God of grace and the God of nature are the same God.

Now I find myself re-emphasizing something that has been emphatic in my life as I have gone along. However, I am now beginning to re-emphasize some things that I put into the corner a bit. Somebody said to me, "Which of your books do you like the best?" And I said, "Please don't make me choose among my babies." But, if I were to pick out one (of the 23), the one message that I would like to give would be the message of *The Way*. Evidently my readers have not agreed with me, because it has not sold as the two other books have sold. *The Christ of the Indian Road* sold over a million copies and *Abundant Living* went further still — went beyond a million. But *The Way* did not sell as well. I must have said it very badly. But the thing I tried to say there was this: there are passages in the New Testament which I think the church has not taken seriously. The church has glanced at them but has never made them the working force in Christianity. They are passages such as the following: "Without Him, Jesus, was not anything that was made;"[2] "Through whom Christ he made the world;"[3] By whom and for whom were all things created - in heaven above,

2   John 1:3.
3   Hebrews 1:2-3.

visible – invisible."[4] Is the message that all things were created by Him and for Him?

What do these strange passages mean? Did God create the world through Christ? I thought the world was created before and Christ came 2000 years ago. Do these passages mean that the touch of Christ is upon all creation, and that everything that is made and in the inner structure of its' being is designed to work in the Christian way? If it works in the Christian way, does it work well; harmoniously, adjustably, happily, usefully, and creatively? If it works some other way, does it work to its own ruin? Is the Christian way written not merely in the Bible but in our blood? Not only in the texts of Scripture, but into the texture of our being, our organs, our relationships, and our everything? I believe so, and it's written supremely in Jesus – "I am the Way."[5] Is it written secondarily in us (as the Way)?

There are a number of passages in the Acts of the Apostles that speak of the Christian way as "the Way." Saul laid hold of those belonging to the Way. A commotion arose over the Way and then Felix having a more excellent knowledge of the Way.[6]

The Christian way is called "The Way." We usually phrase it that the Christian way is the way of salvation. It is, but Scripture doesn't say so. It says it's *the* Way – full stop, unqualified. Is the Christian way *the* Way—the way to do everything?—to think, to act, to feel, to be, under every circumstance, individual and collective? For God and man, are there just two things in life: the Way and not the way? Is the Christian way always *the* Way? Is the unchristian way always

---

4   Collosians 1:16.

5   John 14:6.

6   "Meanwhile Saul, still breathing threats and murder against the disciples of the Lord, went to the high priest and asked him for letters to the synagogues at Damascus, so that if he found any who belong to the Way, men or women, he might bring them bound to Jerusalem" (Acts 9:1-2). "When some stubbornly refused to believe and spoke evil of the Way before the congregation, he left them, taking the disciples with him, and argued daily in the lecture hall of Tyrannus" (Acts 19:9).

not the way? Are there no exceptions? Are we destined by our makeup to be Christians? It says in Romans 8: "Whom he did predestine to be conformed in the image of His Son."[7] Am I predestined to be conformed to the image of His son? Am I predestined to be a Christian? Is that destiny written in my blood, my nerves, my tissues, my organs, and my relationships? I can live against that destiny if I want to, but if I do, I get hurt – automatically. Nothing punishes me; I punish myself when I live against the Way.

Now we used to say that God predestined people in the inscrutable word of God. We can't accept that kind of predestination. But what about this: Am I destined by my makeup to live in His way? If I live in His way, am I rhythmical, harmonious, adjusted, happy and creative? If I live in some other way do I get hurt? An African Chief got up in a meeting in Africa and said, "I'm doomed to be a saint." I think he meant destined. Are you destined to be a Christian? Is that destiny written into the nature of things?

I was speaking in Sweden and a biologist came up to me at the close of my speaking along this line and he said, "You know this biological predestination to Christianity is the most exciting thing I have ever heard." Are we biologically predestined to be Christians? If that is true, that is tremendously true. If it isn't, forget it. Now I believe that you and I have something written within us. When God made you and me and the universe He stamped within us a way – this Way – the Way of Jesus. And if we live according to that way, we live. If we live some other way we get hurt.

I was talking to a great surgeon some time ago and he said, "You know I have discovered the Kingdom of God at the end of my scalpel – my operating knife." He said, "It's in the tissues."

I said, "Doctor go on, that's interesting."

---

7   Romans 8:29-30.

He said, "Well, the right thing morally, the Christian thing, is always the healthy thing physically."

I said, "Doctor, will you say that again."

"The right thing morally," he said, "the Christian thing, is always the healthy thing physically."

Then I said, "Doctor, morality is not only written in the Bible – it's written in our blood?"

He said, "Yes, it is there and it's inescapable."

I quoted that one day and a leading economist came up to me and said this, "I would like to put it this way; the right thing morally, the Christian thing, is always the healthy thing economically." Then I said, "There is a way to get along with material things and that is God's Way. If you try to get along on some basis other than God's basis, you won't. Your relationships will sour and break down."

He said, "Yes, you are right."

I said this in Sweden and a chemist came up to me at the close and said, "You are right about this in economics. In South Africa, they put up a great chemical plant that was going to undercut everything in the world. They put into it a hundred million pounds — pounds, not dollars — and they were going to undercut the world in chemical sales, because they had cheap African labor." He said, "For ten years they have tried to make that thing go but it won't work; it has never gotten off the ground." Why? Because the basis of it was an injustice — the inhumanity of man to man. They were going to exploit the African and keep its labor costs down. Therefore they were going to undercut the world. Then the moral law spoke. You don't break this moral law; you break yourself upon it.

This is a universe where you get results or consequences. If you work with the moral, universe you get results. It will back you, sustain you and further you. You will get results. If you go against the moral universe, you get consequences. You will be up against it and be frustrated. Some people go through life getting results and others get consequences. You get one or the other. You don't break these laws. You break yourself upon them. These laws are color blind, class blind, race blind and religion blind. Break them and you get broken. If you jump out of a ten story building, you don't break the law of gravity you only illustrate it. You don't break these moral laws; you break yourself on them. Here was a great nation breaking itself upon this moral law.

I went down into a gold mine in South Africa. I went down 8,000 feet into a shaft and in the mine saw an African miner working alone in the dark for 20 cents a day. The price of gold had doubled and all the white people received vast increases in their salary. But the African had not. He was not supposed to know about the increase in the value of gold. Now South Africa has become the most unhappy country in the world. Everyone is afraid of everyone else. Every home has to have two dogs, a big dog and a little dog…the little dog to wake up the big dog! Everyone is afraid of everybody. Why? They are trying to work life against the Way and it won't work.

Again I quoted this matter of the Way and a leading sociologist came up to me and said, "I would like to put it this way. The right thing morally and the Christian thing is always the healthy thing sociologically."

Then I said, "There is a way to get along with people — that's God way. And, if you try to get along with people on some basis other than God's basis, you won't. Your relationship will snarl up and break down." And he said, "You're right."

Then here was a great statesman, John Hay,[8] who said, "After trying various ways for nations to get along with each

---

8   John Milton Hay (1838–1905) was an American statesman, diplomat, author, journalist, and private secretary and assistant to Abraham Lincoln. He served as United States Secretary of State from 1898 to 1905 under presidents William McKinley and Theodore Roosevelt. <http://www.britannica.com/eb/article-9039635/John-Hay>

other, I have come to this conclusion: that the only possible way is to love your neighbor as you love yourself." But, that is Christian. Jesus said that 2000 years ago.

Now you come along and say that you must love your neighbor as you love yourself, and if you can't get along with yourself – you can't get along with your neighbor. You don't have to love your neighbor as you love yourself — but if you don't love your neighbor as yourself, you can't get along with your neighbor and you can't get along with yourself. God's got us hooked. So from the international down through the sociological on into the economic back into the physical straight on into the moral and spiritual – all up and down the line – the right thing morally – the Christian thing, is always the healthy thing in every situation. Is that true? Yes!

I was talking to a politician in India, trying to get him to give up a relationship he had with a woman. He was snarling up his own life, his family's, and another family. To ward off my appeal he told me about a British General who'd been challenged by the Oxford Group movement[9] with their four absolutes: absolute honesty, absolute purity, absolute unselfishness and absolute love. This British General was challenged by their four absolutes but wasn't prepared to put his life on them. So in order to ward off the appeal of the Oxford Group movement, this British General said he was going to organize another group movement – he said it half seriously and half humorously. He was going to organize the Cambridge

---

9   The Oxford Group was a Christian organization founded by American Christian missionary Dr. Frank Buchman. The group promoted a belief in divine guidance: one should wait for God to give direction in every aspect of life and surrender to that advice. Buchman's program emphasized acknowledgment of offenses against others, making restitution to those sinned against, and promoting the group to the public. The Oxford Group changed its name prior to WWII to Moral Re-Armament and believed that divine guidance would prevent WWII from breaking out. Moral Re-Armament would later change it's name to Initiatives of Change. <http://www.britannica.com/eb/article-9057830/Oxford-movement>

Group movement. They were going to have four absolutes too but the opposite: absolute dishonesty, absolute impurity, absolute selfishness, and absolute hate. This Indian politician told me that and waited for me to laugh.

I looked him straight in the face and I said, "Why not?" I said, "Why don't you organize a movement based on absolute dishonesty, absolute impurity, absolute selfishness, and absolute hate? If you believe in evil, why don't you go ahead and make it absolute? Why are you so tentative in sin? Why don't you sin with the stops out?"

He looked at me in surprise and said, "Oh no, I couldn't do that."

I said "Why not?"

He said, "You see it wouldn't work."

"Ah," I said "it wouldn't work. You've given away the case."

The only way you can keep evil going is to throw enough good around it to keep it going. Make it pure evil and it will destroy itself, for the word evil is the word live spelled backwards. It's an attempt to live life against itself and it can't be done. Therefore Carlyle says, "Sin is, has been, and shall ever be the parent of misery and nobody can make it the parent of happiness."[10] It won't work.

I said in a youth meeting some time ago, "Every self-centered person is an unhappy person. If you ever find a happy, self-centered person bring him to me. I have never seen one. They are grumpy; everybody is wrong; everything is wrong." At the close of the meeting a youth came up to me and said, "I'm your exception. I'm absolutely self-centered and I'm

---

10 Thomas Carlyle (1795 – 1881) was a Scottish essayist, satirist, and historian, whose work was hugely influential during the Victorian era. The quote is from his book The French Revolution: A History, Book 1, Section VII. <http://www.britannica.com/eb/article-1133>.

absolutely happy." Well I said, "Enjoy it for as long as you can. It won't last long." His knees buckled – literally right there in front of the pulpit.

I challenge you to build a society on absolute dishonesty. Nobody would trust another. On absolute impurity – it would rot. On absolute selfishness – nobody would think in terms of another. On absolute hate – it would be so mean-spirited that it wouldn't hold together. Then, what conclusion must I come to? This, that every dishonest man is a parasite upon the honesty of some honest man whose honesty holds together that situation long enough for him to be dishonest in it. Every impure man is a parasite upon the purity of some good man whose purity holds together that situation long enough for him to be impure in it. And every selfish man is a parasite upon the unselfishness of some unselfish man whose unselfishness holds together that situation long enough for him to be selfish in it. And every man of hate is a parasite upon the love of some good man whose love holds together that situation long enough for him to be hateful in it. There is a way to live and that way is not merely written in the Bible, text or Scripture, but into the texture of our being. It is therefore inescapable.

Some day the scientists are going to put it all down on the table. They are going to say this and this and this is the way to live, and not this way and not this way, and we are going to look at it and we are going to say, "Brother man, the way that you say is the way to live is the Christian way, and the way you say not to live is the unchristian way." They will say, "We don't know anything about that, but this is the way life works." I believe that some day the scientists are going to throw it all out on the table.

Dr. Adler,[11] the great psychiatrist, said, "I suppose all the ills of human personality can be traced back to one thing, not understanding the meaning of the phrase: 'it is more blessed

---

11 Alfred Adler (1870–1937) was an Austrian medical doctor and psychologist, founder of the school of individual psychology. He argued

to give than to receive.'" "But Dr. Adler," I said, "Jesus said that 2000 years ago and you come along and say if you don't understand that you don't know how to live." We are working from Revelation down and you are working from the facts up, are you coming out at the same place? Yes.

Somebody asked Dr. Kilpatrick, the great educator,[12] what he considered the greatest discovery of modern education, and without a moment's hesitation the great educator said, "The greatest discovery of modern education is: 'He that saves his life shall lose it and he that loses it for a cause shall find it again.'" "But Dr. Kilpatrick," I said, " that is not a discovery; that is a rediscovery. Jesus said that 2000 years ago." Five times he said it – save your life and you will lose it. Center yourself on yourself and you won't like yourself and nobody else will like you. Lose it in a cause, and the supreme cause is the Kingdom of God, outside of yourself and it (your life) will come back to yourself again—released, happy and free. Then

---

that human personality could be explained teleologically, separate strands dominated by the guiding purpose of the individual's unconscious self ideal to convert feelings of inferiority to superiority (or rather completeness). The desires of the self ideal were countered by social and ethical demands. If the corrective factors were disregarded and the individual over-compensated, then an inferiority complex would occur, fostering the danger of the individual becoming egocentric, power-hungry and a ggressive or worse. Adler took a holistic approach to human personality. The name of his teaching -"individual psychology" was chosen to reflect it. <http://www.britannica.com/eb/article-9003744/Alfred-Adler>

12 William Heard Kilpatrick (1871–1965) was a US American pedagogue and a pupil, a colleague and a successor of John Dewey. He first met John Dewey in 1898 and again met him in 1907. Kilpatrick decided to make philosophy of education his specialty and occupied all courses by Dewey. From this developed a co-operation, which persisted up to Dewey's death in 1952. The Columbia Encyclopedia 6th ed., s.v."Kilpatrick, William Heard" [database on-line]; available from Questia, http://www.questia.com/PM.qst?a=o&d=101253234; Internet; accessed 31 March 2007.

education comes along and says that is our greatest discovery. It isn't a discovery; it's a rediscovery.

Now I think that many people think that Jesus was a moralist – imposing a moral code upon humanity for which humanity is poorly made. Some have said that "Christianity is a set of scruples imposed upon the ordinary frame work of humanity, to keep it from functioning naturally and normally."[13] If that is true then we are in for trouble. But Jesus was not a moralist in that sense at all. He was the revealer of the nature of reality—first of God. He said, "If you want to know what God is like then look at me. He that has seen me has seen the Father."[14] And I say to myself, "Is God like you? Is the power back of the universe like this gentle heart that broke upon the cross for men?" If so He can have my heart without qualification or reservation. He revealed the nature of God in understandable terms—human terms. So when I say God, I think Jesus. I couldn't think of anything higher than that God should be like Jesus. When He lifted up the laws underlying the universe he seldom used the imperative,[15] almost never

---

13 Alexis-Charles-Henri Clérel de Tocqueville (1805–1859) was a French political thinker and historian best known for his Democracy in America (appearing in two volumes: 1835 and 1840) and The Old Regime and the Revolution (1856). In both of these works, he explored the effects of the rising equality of social conditions on both the individual and the state in western societies. Democracy in America (1835), his major work, published after his travels in the United States, is today considered an early work of sociology. An eminent representative of the liberal political tradition. The quote is from Democracy in America. < The Columbia Encyclopedia 6th ed., s.v."Tocqueville, Alexis De" [database on-line]; available from Questia, http://www.questia.com/PM.qst?a=o&d=101274809; Internet; accessed 28 March 2007.>

14 John 14:6-9.

15 The imperative is a mood that expresses an intention to influence the listener's/reader's behavior. <http://www.thefreedictionary.com/imperative>

the subjunctive[16], almost entirely the indicative.[17] He kept saying "This *is*, and you must come to terms with it."

When Jesus finished the Sermon on the Mount the people were astonished at his teaching, for he taught them not as their scribes but he taught them with authority. The word there "with authority" means literally "according to the nature of things." He taught them according to the nature of things. When the people heard it they said, "Oh, oh, oh, that is what I feel inside, self-verified." Dr. Boss, a famous psychiatrist, the head of the International Psychoanalytical Association of Europe and head of the Department of Psychotherapy at the University of Zurich — a great man — came out to India and spent six months in our Psychiatric Center training our staff, having seminars for six months. And, he did it without pay. I said. "Dr. Boss, you seem to put your Christianity and your psychiatry together, how do you do it?"

"Well" he said, "I had difficulty when I first began because I was a Freudian but the demands of human nature drove me back to the Christian position."

I said, "Dr. Boss will you say that again?"

He said, "The demands of human nature drove me back to the Christian position."

I said, "Dr. Boss that is the most important statement that has come out of psychiatry in this generation."

For what human nature demands for its fulfillment, Christianity offers in its Gospel; they fit each other. So the demands of my nature and the commands of Christ are one.

---

16 The subjunctive mood is used not to indicate that something is being asserted but that it is contrary to fact, supposed, doubted, feared or desired. < http://www.thefreedictionary.com/subjunctive>

17 The indicative is used to express an objective fact. < http://www.thefreedictionary.com/indicative+mood>

Therefore you are bound to come to Him if you are going to live.

In a moment we are going to lunch. I am going to say at the close of this meeting, "Go to lunch." In the first Epistle of John, it says, "his commandments are not burdensome."[18] I have often wondered how you could command someone to do something or other. For example, can you command someone to love? You can't stand over someone and say, "Love, or else." However, suppose His command and my inner demand are one? Suppose what He commands, my nature demands? Suppose I should say to you, "Go to lunch." Would that commandment be burdensome? No. You would say, "I want to do that, I need to go to lunch if I am to live." That is the way it works.

Now, what then must I believe? This—if you work from Revelation down, and the facts up, you are coming out at His feet. That is the most exciting thing that I know of on this planet. I watched it with baited breath and I would like to stay around long enough to see how it all comes out. But what I say to you is true—tremendously true. A man, a non-Christian, said one night at the close of one of my addresses: "If what the speaker has said tonight isn't true, it doesn't matter. But, if it is true, then nothing else matters." A non-Christian said that! If Jesus is the Way, then we have to come to Him or else we are lost and out of the way. Every road that leads away from Jesus Christ has a precipice at the end of it. Every road that leads away from Him means you are sorrowful; you go away sorrowful. All coming to Jesus has a feeling of homecoming. When you come, you feel that you are out of your estrangement, your alienation. Now what conclusion must I come to? That the Christian way is the natural way to live.

However, there are several passages in the Bible that seem to suggest that sin is the natural way. "The natural person does

---

18 1 John 5:3.

not accept the things of the Spirit of God, for they are folly to him, and he is not able to understand them because they are spiritually discerned."[19] But the Revised Standard Version[20] and Moffatt's translation[21] changed that *"natural man"* into "unspiritual. And, the Greek bears it out: "the unspiritual man receives not the spirit of God." It is not between the natural and the unnatural but between the spiritual and the unspiritual. Another passage which is brought up: "Jesus would not could not trust himself to men because he knew what was in man."[22] But that passage is neutral. We don't say that sin is not in man; it is. It has gone into man's nature and has corrupted man's nature—depraved man's nature. But if it (sin) were natural, why should it deprave him? If it were natural why shouldn't we bloom and blossom under sin? But I know and you know what happens when we sin. We are unhappy. Everything says, "this is not the Way." "All things betray thee who betrays me."[23] However, when I come to Jesus Christ I walk the earth with confidence, afraid of nothing. The sum total of reality is behind me and everything cries out and says

---

19 1 Corinthians 2:14. (RSV)

20 "The unspiritual man does not receive the gifts of the Spirit of God, for they are folly to him, and he is not able to understand them because they are spiritually discerned." RSV, 1 Corinthians 2:14.

21 "The unspiritual man rejects these truths of the Spirit of God; to him they are 'sheer folly,' he cannot understand them. Moffatt's Translation, 1 Corinthians 2:14. 22 John 2:23-25. "While he was in Jerusalem for Passover many gave their allegiance to hi when they saw the signs that he performed. But Jesus for his part would not trust himself to them. He knew men so well, all of them, that he needed no evidence from others about a man, for he himself could tell what was in a man."

23 From the poem The Hound of Heaven by Francis Thompson. < Francis Thompson, Poems of Francis Thompson, ed. Connolly, Terence L. [book on-line] (New York: D. Appleton-Century, 1934, accessed 28 March 2007), 77; available from Questia, http://www.questia.com/PM.qst?a=o&d =53691978; Internet.>

this is the Way. Now, I believe that sin is unnatural and that we are made for the good as the eye is made for light.

Tertullian,[24] the great church father, said, "The soul is naturally Christian." Dr. Reinhold Niebuhr[25] says, "The soul is naturally pagan." Dr. Walter Horton,[26] another modern theologian, says, "The soul is naturally half pagan and half Christian." You can make your choice. I vote with Tertullian. If the soul were naturally pagan, and I define paganism as living without the God reference, then when we are pagan we ought to be happy. Are the pagans happy? Not that I know of. They have to invent more and more ways to keep life tolerable. The Christian has a joy without a hangover.

One theologian said, "The Christian way is sense, common sense, and if we try some other way then you are a fool." He put a word beginning with D in front of it, and I am not swearing when I say it. That's right. If any man tries it any

24 Quintus Septimius Florens Tertullianus, anglicized as Tertullian, (ca. 155–230) was a church leader and prolific author of Early Christianity. He also was a notable early Christian apologist. He was the first great writer of Latin Christianity, thus sometimes known as the "father of the Latin Church."He introduced the term Trinity, (Theophilius to Autolycus - 115-181 - introduced the word Trinity in his Book 2, chapter 15 on the creation of the 4th day). as the Latin trinitas, to the Christian vocabulary. <http://www.tertullian.org/readfirst.htm>

25 Karl Paul Reinhold Niebuhr (1892–1971) was a Protestant theologian best known for his study of the task of relating the Christian faith to the reality of modern politics and diplomacy. <The Columbia Encyclopedia 6th ed., s.v."Niebuhr, Helmut Richard" [database on-line]; available from Questia, http://www.questia.com/PM.qst?a=o&d=101261328; Internet; accessed 28 March 2007.>

26 Walter Marshall Horton (1895-1966) was an internationally known theologian and leader in the modern Ecumenical Movement. Through his sermons, radio broadcasts, lectures, and frequent world travels, Horton helped to develop an ecumenical Christian theology, to foster dialogue between theological liberals and conservatives, and to promote an active role for unintuitive Protestantism in the post-war world. < http://www.oberlin.edu/archive/holdings/finding/RG30/SG4/biography.html>

other way, he's a fool. You can put in the other little word if you like, and you will be exactly describing it. The Christian way is the natural way to live; sin is the unnatural. "His yoke is easy and his burden is light"[27] for His burden is the same burden that wings are to a bird, that sails are to a ship, that love is to the heart. When you find His way, you find your own. Bound to Him, you walk the earth free. Low at His feet, you stand straight before everything. When you find Him, you find yourself. And so, the Christian way, is *the* Way.

Shall we pray? Dear Father, help us to take thy way, all out with no reservations, with complete self-giving. Every time we take some other way we get hurt. Everyday I find myself saying Stanley Jones if you want to live, this is the way. If you don't want to live, then live some other way and get hurt. It's working out that way and so help us to no longer to be tentative—yes, no or maybe—but all out, wholly thine— therefore wholly in ourselves. We ask thee for Jesus sake. Amen.

---

27 Matthew 11:30.

115

Jones at his Writing Table, South India 1968

3. GOD IS BEHIND THE MORAL UNIVERSE AND IS LOVE

COMMENTARY ON "GOD'S SEARCH FOR MAN"

JONES is spiritually transparent in this 1950 sermon on the well-known verse from John 3:16, "For God so loved the world that he gave his only begotten son that whosoever believes in him shall have eternal life." This particular passage is deeply personal to Jones, for it was with this Bible verse that he accepted his conversion at the age of 17.

> I remember when I was seeking Christ, kneeling at a Methodist altar, lad of 17; a friend knelt along side of me and repeated this verse, "God so loved the world." This friend, a schoolteacher, said, "Can't you put your name there, God so loved Stanley Jones that he gave his only begotten son that if Stanley Jones believes in Him he shall not perish but have everlasting life. Can you read it that way?" I said, "Yes, I think I can." And I repeated it, "God so loved Stanley Jones that he gave his only begotten son that if Stanley Jones believes in him, he shall not perish but have everlasting life." She said, "Don't you believe that?" I said, "Yes, I do." Then she said, "You're changed" (136).

Jones states that, while he feels inadequate to preach on this verse, he desperately wants to tell its story, for he believes that it contains the whole message of God's deep love for mankind. Jones sets his fears of inadequate expression aside and begins the sermon entitled, "God's Search for Man."

Religion, Jones asserts, is the cry for life turned qualitative. Religions are man's search for God. Christianity is unique among all religions for it offers the Gospel which tells the story of God's search for man. In his exposition, Jones breaks down the words in this famous New Testament verse, *"God so loved the world that he gave his only begotten Son that who so ever believes in Him shall not perish but have everlasting life."*

Jones begins with *"That God so loved the world...."* According to Jones, we are immediately struck by a unique characteristic of *this* God. The initiative begins with God. All other religions begin with man. He writes in his book, *Transformation*:

> The Hindu scriptures are filled with the accounts of men who by their austerities stormed the very citadel of God and disturbed His calm aloofness by their very insistence and persistence. God would occasionally respond only so His calm might not be further disturbed. They had to overcome God's reluctance to deal with man (121).

The Christian God, Jones states, is a God unlike the gods of Hinduism who do not act for fear of being caught up in the cycle of rebirths. This God has relationships, and this God loves. If God loves, then, according to Jones, the whole nature of the universe has at its heart *love*. There is no question of God's reluctance. God takes the initiative because he loves, and it is natural for a God who loves to seek an object for his love. That object is all of humanity. Jones continues that, if the world is the object of God's love, then it is also the object of his redemption *(How to be a Transformed Person,* 122) Jones asks, "How far does God's self giving love go?" It goes all the way to the cross, Jones affirms. According to Jones, this *love* can transform us:

> This transformation is the not the uplifting of ourselves by our bootstraps, not affirming your self into better living, not tinkering with human nature, with human hands and with human resources, but the exposing of ourselves to divine resources, opening of ourselves to what God has for

us. If we are to be transformed then there is a transformation that takes place on the part of God. Again—
takes place on the part of God. He becomes transformed in
order for our transformation. He stoops so that we might
rise. He becomes like us so that we might become like Him
and the initiative is in God. This gospel begins in God (124).

Jones next considers the phrase, *"That whosoever believes in
Him..."* The emphasis in this sentence is on the words
"whosoever" and "in." The invitation is open to all mankind,
not just the moral or the upright, but all![1] Jones continues as
follows:

I am amazed at that word "whosoever;" it's prodigal; it's
careless. It doesn't make distinctions, doesn't mark people
off into moral groups, but in the prodigal wave of His hand
He says, "Whosoever," and I gasp. I say, "My God, you are
prodigal in your giving, but you are just as prodigal in your
forgiving." Did you say, "Whosoever?" Without
distinction? I'm astonished at God's carelessness about
moral distinctions, and yet I know that whosoever will do
exactly what He says won't be the kind of person that he
was. He will be fundamentally and radically different. (135)

The second critical word in this passage is "in." We must
do more than simply believe, we must believe **in**. Jones tells us
that with his first conversion, he believed, but he did not believe
in: "I didn't believe enough to invest myself or to offer myself
to Christ as just I was...." It is no surprise that, before many

---

1   "A skeptic was heckling the Christians. "Do you believe that Jesus
turned water into wine?" he asked. "Well, I don't know," said one man,
"but this I do know, that in my home, He turned beer into furniture." The
miracle of changed lives is taking place today to the degree that it is being
tried. "Whosoever works wheresoever and by whomsoever it is really tried"
(Jones, *How to be a Transformed Person*, 124).

altar calls, Jones would ask the pianist to play the hymn, *Just As I Am.*[2]

---

2   Charlotte Elliott (1789-1871) who published her "Invalid's Hymn Book" in 1838 and "Hymns of Sorrow" two years later, was the author of about a hundred and fifty hymns, three of which have lived: "Christian, Seek Not Yet Repose": "My God, My Father, While I Stray" and "Just as I Am without One Plea." Miss Elliott was herself an invalid for about fifty years of her long life. Her hymns, like those of Anne Steele, are plaintive and sweet in tone, and expressive of warm and beautiful devotion. The powerful lyric "Just as I Am without One Plea" would have made her fame secure. Lines from other hymns show the mingled strength and delicacy of her style, the nobility and sweetness of her character, and the genuine value of her religion. < Jeremiah Bascom Reeves, The Hymn in History and Literature [book on-line] (New York: Century, 1924, accessed 30 March 2007), 285; available from Questia, http://www.questia.com/ PM.qst?a=o&d=3019618; Internet.>

> Just as I am, without one plea,
> But that Thy blood was shed for me,
> And that Thou bidst me come to Thee,
> O Lamb of God, I come, I come.
>
> Just as I am, and waiting not
> To rid my soul of one dark blot,
> To Thee whose blood can cleanse each spot,
> O Lamb of God, I come, I come.
>
> Just as I am, though tossed about
> With many a conflict, many a doubt,
> Fightings and fears within, without,
> O Lamb of God, I come, I come.
>
> Just as I am, poor, wretched, blind;
> Sight, riches, healing of the mind,
> Yea, all I need in Thee to find,
> O Lamb of God, I come, I come.
>
> Just as I am, Thou wilt receive,
> Wilt welcome, pardon, cleanse, relieve;
> Because Thy promise I believe,
> O Lamb of God, I come, I come.

In reflecting on the phrase, *"Should not perish...,"* Jones believes that, in evil, humanity does in fact perish.[3] He says we fall to pieces in our sin: "We see people outside of God perishing here and now, perishing from conflicts, fears, inhibitions, complexes, and guilt" (Jones, *How to be a Transformed Person* 125). God does not punish us for our sins; rather sin is its own punishment" (9). He continues as follows:

> We sometimes wonder about that word perishing, how much is involved. I can see how people perish now with evil. I can see them go to pieces under evil; they do perish. The personality goes to pieces—has no cement within it— it breaks down. If you project that out into eternity, then what will happen? If you keep it up long enough then the personality goes to pieces and perishes. Perhaps forever and they would suffer what the Bible calls eternal destruction, unfit to survive—lights out. Whether that is true or not, I don't know. It would seem to point in that direction. For people do perish now; evil is not the way to live. The word evil is the word live spelled backwards. God doesn't punish you for sin. Sin is its own punishment. You don't have to punish the eye for having sand in it, the body for having a cancer in it, the soul for having evil in it. For evil is its own punishment. He doesn't punish you for sin; sin is its own punishment—and therefore its destruction. You perish if you keep it up long enough; you are wiped out. The forces want to hold together for only in Jesus is

Just as I am, Thy love unknown
Hath broken every barrier down;
Now, to be Thine, yea, Thine alone,
O Lamb of God, I come, I come.

Just as I am, of that free love
The breadth, length, depth, and height to prove,
Here for a season, then above,
O Lamb of God, I come, I come!

3   Evil is the word live spelled backwards. Evil goes against the essence of life.

there sufficient cement. In Him all things cohere and hold together. (137)

Jones has an interesting interpretation of the words, "*Everlasting Life.*" He maintains that this is available to us now! He sees Eternal life as a quality of life, not necessarily as the duration of life. Eternal life is Christian life in the midst of time when we have Jesus in our lives. Eternal life is not something that we gain by what we *do*, but the result of who we *accept*. Today we can live, according to Jones, "as one who has a thousand unrealized possibilities in his heart" (*How to be a Transformed Person*, 126).

In summary, according to Jones, this well-known verse from the Gospel of John tells us that God took the initiative and came to us. In response, if we surrender ourselves, we will be transformed. Why does God demand self surrender? "Is he a despot?" Jones asks. "Of course he is not." Jones reminds us that God went first — God surrendered his son, and the cross is the sign of God's surrender. God transformed himself that we might be transformed. The fact of Jesus, the word become flesh, is the revelation of God's love.

GOD'S SEARCH FOR MAN

SERMON

OVER these many years I have looked at this verse — looked at it wistfully, wishing I had enough courage to speak on it. Each time I had to turn away with a feeling of inadequacy; it's too big. This summer I dared speak on it. Perhaps you know the verse — at least you have suspected what verse it would be. It is the biggest verse in Christian literature, or any literature I think. There is more packed into it than any other verse in all literature: "God so loved the world that He gave His only begotten Son that who so ever believeth in Him shall not perish but have everlasting life."[4]

I looked at that verse again and again and I said I know what will happen. If I try to expound on that and understand it, well it's like picking a rose to pieces to see its beauty. It's perfect just the way it is. And I know when I finish today I shall kneel (at least inwardly) and say, "I couldn't tell it." This word goes beyond my words — I cannot catch it in the web of my words. In the end I will have to kneel before the shrine of mystery embodied in these words. Remember the poet that said, "Little flower in the crannied walls, if I knew you root and all, and all in all, I would know what God and man is."[5] And I say, "Little verse of twenty five words if I knew you roots and all and all in all, I would know what God and man and life is."

Emerson[6] once preached a sermon, which was a masterpiece of diction and thought and expression. Afterwards, he said to a friend, a frank friend, "What did you think of my sermon?" And the friend said, "Well, Emerson, it was perfect. The diction

4   John 3:16.

5   Alfred Lord Tennyson, Flower in the Crannied Wall, 1869. < Paul Eldridge, "Hope," in Infidels and Heretics: An Agnostic's Anthology [book on-line] (Boston: Stratford, 1929, accessed 28 March 2007), 60; available from Questia, http://www.questia.com/PM.qst?a=o&d=272246; Internet.>

6   Ralph Waldo Emerson (1803-1882) was an American essayist, poet, and leader of the Transcendentalist movement in the early nineteenth century. Emerson was a Harvard Divinity School graduate and an ordained Unitarian minister. Emerson's most memorable and controversial sermon, known as the Divinity School Address, challenged formal religion by suggesting that Jesus was a great man and prophet but was not God. < The Columbia Encyclopedia 6th ed., s.v."Emerson, Ralph Waldo" [database on-line]; available from Questia, http://www.questia.com/PM.qst?a=o&d=101242651; Internet; accessed 28 March 2007. >

7   The friend was most likely Thomas Carlyle whom Emerson met in 1832 and became lifelong friends despite their different theological positions.

was perfect; the thoughts were sublime and the delivery was wonderful, but nobody would have ever been converted through that sermon anymore than any man could get drunk on buttermilk."[7]

The trouble with this verse is it goes through my head like wine. It intoxicates me when I just touch it. I say to myself: "Is this true? Does this verse mean what it says?" At the close of one of my addresses in India, a Hindu, chairman said, "If what the speaker has said tonight isn't true, then it doesn't matter. But, I tell you, if it is true, then nothing else matters." If the verse, which I have read to you this morning, isn't true then it doesn't matter. It's the result of a fevered imagination. But, if it is true, then nothing else matters. This is it. My verse begins with God. "God so loved the world."

I am going to speak to you in these meetings on how to be a transformed person. This morning I'd like to introduce to you, and myself, the resources that lie back of our transformation. This transformation is the not the uplifting of ourselves with our bootstraps, not affirming your self into better living, not tinkering with human nature, with human hands and with human resources, but the exposing of ourselves to divine resources, opening of ourselves to what God has for us. If we are to be transformed then there is a transformation that takes place on the part of God. Again—takes place on the part of God. He becomes transformed in order for our transformation. He stoops so that we might rise. He becomes like us so that we might become like Him and the initiative is in God. This gospel begins in God.

I say God, but I don't know what God is like until I see Him. So I don't begin at God and I don't begin at man. I begin at the God-man. From the God-man I work out to God, and from Him, I work down to man. I have got a starting point in my universe. I look up through Him to God and say, "If God is like that He's a good God and trustable." If the God that's back of the universe is like this God, whose heart broke upon the cross for men, He can have my heart without qualifications or reservation. If God is Christ-like, He can have my heart without qualification. If I were to try to think of the kind of God that I'd like to see in the universe, I couldn't think of Him as higher in character than Jesus of Nazareth. If God isn't Christ-like then I am not interested in Him.

I said that in India and a Hindu came up to me at the close and said, "That's devotion par excellence to think that you wouldn't be interested in God if He's not like Christ." I said, "No, I wouldn't, honestly." If Jesus isn't the revelation of the heart of the universe, He ought to be. And then if He isn't, then I would turn from the universe and say, well here, I got the highest that I know."

Dr. Coffin[8] says, "suppose Jesus would come back to us from the heavens and come back to us weeping, sobbing as if His heart would break. Suppose He would come back to humanity and say, "I'm sorry, I meant for you to believe that there was a Father back of everything—that somebody cared; somebody loved. But I searched the universe and there is no such Father; there's no heart there, nothing but impersonal law. There is no God and no Father. I'm sorry I misled you." What would I do? I would feel disappointment creep into every portion of my being. I know that. But in the midst of my disappointment, I would turn to Jesus and say, "Well, I've got you. The universe has let me down; disappointed me to the core, but I've got you." And then I could begin all over again.

A little missionary boy was asked what he wanted most on Christmas Day. He was in school and his parents were out in foreign lands and of course he felt their absence. The headmaster of this school said to the little fellow, "What would

8   Henry Sloane Coffin (1877 - 1954) was president of Union Theological Seminary from 1926-1945. The idea presented here is from Some Christian Convictions, published by Yale University Press in 1915. < The Columbia Encyclopedia 6th ed., s.v."Coffin, Henry Sloane" [database on-line]; available from Questia, http://www.questia.com/PM.qst?a=o&d =101238134; Internet; accessed 28 March 2007. >

you like most for Christmas?" The little fellow looked at the framed picture of his father on the desk and he said, "What I would like most would be that my father would step out of that frame." I think that is the cry of the human heart everywhere. It says: I wish God would step out of the frame of the universe and would become intimate and tender so that we could see him. Philip said, "Lord, show us the Father and it suffices us."[9] Then one day Jesus turned to us and said, "If you want to know what God is like look at me. He that has seen me has seen the Father."[10] Jesus is God stepping out of His frame — that personal approach from the unseen. It is God meeting us in our environment, showing us His character where your character and mine is wrought out namely in the stream of human history. When I say God, I think Jesus. So the gospel begins with God and comes down to us.

I've often said to the students in many parts of the world, that "Religion is the cry for life. In everything, from the lowest cell to the highest man, there is an urge after completion for a more abundant and fuller life." Everything says Tagore,[11] "Lifts up strong hands after perfection." I've said that religion is that cry for life turned qualitative. We want to live not merely fuller but better. The moment we say better we have standards, and the moment we have standards we have religion. For religion is the cry for life turned qualitative. As long as men will want

---

9   John 14:8.

10   John 14:7.

11   Rabindranath Tagore (1861 - 1941) was a Bengali poet, Brahmo Samaj (syncretic Hindu monotheist) philosopher, visual artist, playwright, novelist, and composer whose works reshaped Bengali literature and music in the late 19th and early 20th centuries. A cultural icon of Bengal and India, he became Asia's first Nobel laureate when he won the 1913 Nobel Prize in Literature. < The Columbia Encyclopedia 6th ed., s.v."Tagore, Sir Rabindranath" [database on-line]; available from Questia, http://www.questia.com/PM.qst?a=o&d=101273478; Internet; accessed 28 March 2007. >

to live fully and better, we will be religious. The forms of religion may come and go but the spirit of religion is deathless from age to age. But, when I have said that to students, I have known in my heart of hearts that I was only describing half of religion — that upward seeking urge. What about this downward seeking urge? If we cry for life does He not say, "I have come so that you might have life? And since He is that personal approach from the unseen coming to us with an offer of life with a capital L, then when my cry for life with a small L meets his offer of Life with a capital L and there we set up saving relationships. And I can draw on the resources of the divine for human living now, then real religion sets in.

I once heard a man in India, a visiting speaker from America, give a very elegant sermon on a man's search for God. A Scotch missionary came to me at the close and said, "Have you ever read *The Hound of Heaven?*"[12] As a young missionary I had to confess that I hadn't. He said, "Sell your coat and buy it." When I read it I knew what he meant. It wasn't mere man's search for God; it was God's search for man, like the hound of heaven pursuing us down the years; the foot falls, the constant pressure upon the heart that never lets us go. The moment we turn around, we are in the arms of redeeming love.

Religions are man's search for God; the Gospel is God's search for man. Therefore there are many religions; there's but one Gospel. If you forget everything I said, remember that. "Religions are man's search for God; the gospel is God's search for man. Therefore there are many religions; there's but one gospel." And so the Gospel starts from the heart of God. Jesus is God taking His heart and wrapping it in flesh and walking

---

12   Francis Thompson (1859 - 1907) was an English poet and ascetic. The Hound of Heaven," his most famous poem, describes the pursuit of the human soul by God. <Francis Thompson, Poems of Francis Thompson, ed. Connolly, Terence L. [book on-line] (New York: D. Appleton-Century, 1934, accessed 28 March 2007), 77; available from Questia, http://www.questia.com/PM.qst?a=o&d=53691978; Internet.>

among us to let us see the nature of the divine and the nature of the universe and Jesus is that key.

The account says, "That God loved." We get so used to that – that we scarcely see its' implications. The Vendantic Hindu would have never had said that. He would have said, "If God loved then God would get entangled in the round of rebirth for if God acts, he must get the result, the fruit of his action. And if he did so, it would come into the wheel of existence and the wheel of rebirth and that would be degrading." So God is in the nirvana state, being without relationships and without bonds – a state of pure being – the actionless, passionless Brahman.[13] He doesn't love. He's pure essence. In order to bring it into the state of relationships with bonds He comes into various incarnations, i.e., the Hindu gods. But God, the highest God, is without relationships and without bonds. And here Jesus reverses that whole conception and said, "God loves."

The Stoic didn't believe that the man who is superior should love. Because the moment you love, you let pity in your heart, and the moment you let in pity, you let in sorrow. So love and pity must both be kept out. You must keep a hard exterior against life that life may not get behind your armor. The Mohammedan[14] does not say God is love, he says God is

---

13   A Hindu concept of supreme being. Brahman is said to be eternal, genderless, omnipotent, omniscient, and omnipresent, and ultimately indescribable in the human language. It can be at best described as infinite Being, infinite Consciousness and infinite Bliss. Brahman is regarded as the source and essence of the material universe. It is pure being. <The Columbia Encyclopedia 6th ed., s.v."Brahman" [database on-line]; available from Questia, http://www.questia.com/PM.qst?a=o&d=101233970; Internet; accessed 28 March 2007. >

14   Mohammedan is a term used as both a noun and an adjective meaning belonging or relating to either the religion of Islam or to that of its last prophet Muhammad. The term is now largely superseded by Muslim, Moslem or Islamic but was commonly used in Western literature until at least the mid 1960s.

power. He commands and man obeys. The Old Testament Jehovah doesn't say God is love, he is a qualified partisan of Jews. And though Jesus flung back the curtain one day and said, "God loves" that has the biggest implications for life of anything that you can imagine. If God loves, and if God is love, then the nature of the universe and its heart is love. The universe is not only friendly, it not only cares, it is redemptive. It not only means well, it means to make me well. And all I have to do is consent to this divine initiative in order to be made well. That makes the universe an entirely different universe. It's (the universe) not vast indifference, it's a pulsating heart. It said, "God so loved the world." One would have thought that He would have chosen how He loved. He would have loved the good and sternly disapproved of the bad. He would correct the bad by isolation, aloofness and leaving them alone as the Pharisee of that day did. He (the Pharisee) thought he could correct evil by aloofness and by a frown, and by telling the wrong doers no. They thought that in that disapproval the people would come to goodness. Here is a breath taking statement: "God so loved the world" – as it is. That didn't mean that he approved of the world. You can love people of whom you do not approve.

A little fellow in a school where the standards were very high and conduct was very appropriate, kept breaking the rules. And the headmaster called him in and said, "Johnny, we like you, but we don't like what you do. We love you, but we don't love what you do." And that is something like God. God says, "I love you, but I don't necessarily approve of you. But I love you still." That meant that God could love us even in the midst of His disapproval of us.

A drunkard, a man bloated with his debauchery, sat as a pastor lashed him with a moral lecture. He deserved it; his face was bound up and his eyes were bleared and his lips were bloated. He was getting over a binge drinking episode. He sat there withering under the lashing that the pastor gave him. When the pastor was through the mother got up and without a word walked over and planted a kiss upon her son's bloated lips. He told me later, "I could stand what the pastor did; I deserved every word he said. But I couldn't stand my mother coming and kissing me. Something broke within me and I knew I belonged to goodness from that moment. I was a different life." And God leans over and does the same thing even though He doesn't approve of us. The love persists. Then it says, "God *so* loved the world" and I don't know how much is packed into that word *so*. He so loved the world that he gave his only begotten son.

Speaking to an Indian audience one day about God giving His son to redeem mankind. A non-Christian woman spoke up and said, "What kind of Father was He? He sent His son to die. Why didn't He come Himself?" This village woman had a rare insight. Is Jesus somebody else? Is He different from God? A little fellow said, "Well I love Jesus, but I hate God because God wanted to destroy the world but Jesus wouldn't let Him." Where did he get that? As I understand it God was in Christ reconciling the world unto himself and when Jesus came God came. He is the human life of God, that part of God that I can see. He is God meeting me where I am, to lift me where I want to be.

In one place Jesus was called "The Word." In the beginning it was the word and the word was with God and the word was God.[15] Why was he called "The Word?" I suppose He was called the word because the word is the revelation of the hidden thought. If I stand here without a word you cannot get my thought. Only as I put my thought into a word do you get it and say "Now I got his thought to that word." My word is the offspring of my thought, the son of my thought and my word and my thought are one. If the words are true words, the word and the thought are one. When you take hold of the word you say, "I've got his thought, they are one." But the unexpressed thought is greater than the expressed thought. When I put my

---

15   John 1:1.

thought into a word I have to limit it for you to get it. I say to myself, "I can't quite put my thought into these words." All expression is limitation. So the unexpressed thought is greater than the expressed thought. There is a sense that the thought and the words are one. There is a sense in which the thought is greater than the word because you have to live it and you put it into a word.

Jesus was called "The Word." Why? Because He's the revelation of the hidden God. Without Him I have to project my imagination into the universe, but with Jesus I don't have to project my imagination, for Jesus is God's interpretation of Himself. Jesus is God speaking the language that I can understand — the human language. Jesus is revealing His character where my character and yours is wrought out – namely in the stream of human history. Jesus is the revelation of the hidden God; He is the word, expressing the hidden thought. And when you take hold of that word, you say I've got his thought. When you take hold of Jesus you take of God projected onto you. God simplified, God become available. Jesus is not somebody, a third something stepping between you and God, He's a mediator only in the sense that He mediates God to you and me. When you take hold of Him you take hold the very self of God. I don't argue, I only testify. The more I deepen the Christ consciousness, the more I deepen the God consciousness. I can't tell where Jesus ends and God begins. In my experience, they are one. The thought and the word are one, but Jesus said, "I and the Father are one," but in another place it said, "the Father is greater than I" and He is. The unexpressed God is greater than the expressed God, for when God came down to live among us and show us His heart, He had to limit himself. It was a real limitation. He became man, in a real sense, so the expressed God is less than the unexpressed God because there is self-limitation there. But they're one.

How far does this self giving go? Did He sit on a cloud and say, "I've got to redeem you?" Did He walk our way and say, 'I am going to show you an example?' Did He sit on a hillside and say, 'I am going to be your teacher?'" How far did He go? How far does that soul go? The identification was so deep that it was breath taking. One day Jesus stood up and said, "I was hungered and you fed me, I was thirsty and you gave me drink and I was sick and you visited me, in prison and you came unto me, I was naked and clothed me, a stranger and you took me in."[16] They looked at Him and said, "Lord, when did we see you hungry and fed thee and thirsty and gave thee drink?[17] We never saw you this way. And the master said, "In as much as you have done it unto one of the least of these you've done it unto me."[18] For I'm hungry in their hunger; I'm bound in their imprisonment; I'm lonely in their being a stranger. Every man's hunger is mine and every man's bondage is mine, and every man's loneliness is mine. I'm identified with it. Here was complete identification. There was one thing He couldn't say; it would be misunderstood. He couldn't say "I am sinful in your sin." That would be misunderstood, but one day He walked straight up to a cross and died between two malefactors – a thief on this side and a thief on that side. And He died as one of them. What was He doing? He couldn't say it. He was *doing* and it was this, He was becoming identified with our sin. The writer of the 1st letter of Peter puts it, "He became sin for us. Bearing in His own body our sins upon a tree."[19] Did He love us so? If that is true, that is the ultimate revelation. Here I stop and my knees bend instinctively and I say, this is it and God couldn't go further than that - to be sin for me.

Amy Wilson Carmichael[20] is an authentic saint in India. She worked with girls in a home, girls that came from temple

---

16   Matthew 25:35-36.

17   Matthew 25:37-39.

18   Matthew 25:40.

19   1 Peter 2:24.

20   Amy Beatrice (a.k.a. Wilson) Carmichael (1867-1951) was a Protestant Christian missionary in India, who opened an orphanage and founded a mission in Dohnavur. The organization she founded was known as the

prostitution. The institution is radiant with the love of God. However, one girl wouldn't respond to Ms. Carmichael's love and instruction. She was a hard and unassimilated knot. One day Ms. Carmichael called her in and she bared her arm and took a needle and she said, "I am going to thrust this needle into my arm."

The girl looked at her in surprise and said, "that will hurt you."

"Yes," she said, "it will, but it will hurt me nothing to what you're doing is hurting me. And to let you see how what you're doing is hurting me – I'll let you see with this outer sign."

So she thrust the needle into her arm and as the blood began to trickle down the girl burst into tears and flung her arms around Ms. Carmichael's neck and said, "I didn't know you loved me like that." And from that moment that girl was changed. She looked up through that blood, past the blood, into the soul of Ms. Carmichael and saw that there was a cross of pain on the heart of Ms. Carmichael because of what she was doing. And she was saved as it were by that blood.

Did something like that happen in history? When love meets sin in the loved one – pure love meets sin in the loved one – what happens? At the junction of pure love of that sin – a cross of pain is set up—inevitably. For it is the nature of love to insinuate itself into the sins and sorrows of the loved one. It can't help it. If it's love, it gets in. If it gets in, it bleeds. All love has the doom of bleeding upon it if there is sin in the loved

Dohnavur Fellowship. The fellowship would become a place of sanctuary for more than one thousand children who would otherwise have faced a bleak future. In an effort to respect Indian culture, members of the organization wore Indian dress and the children were given Indian names. She herself dressed in Indian clothes, dyed her skin with coffee, and often traveled long distances on India's hot, dusty roads to save just one child from suffering. <http://www.heroesofhistory.com/page49.html>

LIVING UPON THE WAY

one. And the deeper the love the more poignant the pain. Suppose God is love and if God isn't love, I'm not interested.

He that made the eye, shall He not see? He that made the ear, shall He not hear? He that made love, shall He not love? He that put the impulse to sacrifice in the heart of the best, shall He not give Himself? If God is love, then when that love meets sin, you and me, the loved ones at the junction of that love and that sin, is a cross of pain that will be set up inevitably. For it is the nature of love to take upon itself that which would fall upon the loved one. Can't help it. How would I know that? I'm bounded my senses; I'm sunk in them. How would I know that there is a cross of pain in the heart of God except that He showed me. How could He show me? Only in human history. Only by an outer cross upon a hilltop. He lifted up an outer cross that I could go look through that cross and beyond that cross back into the universe and see that there is an unseen cross upon the heart of God. I look at these wounds of Jesus, to this blood of Jesus, and I see that the nature of the universe is redemptive. That God wears on His heart a cross – and I am saved by that blood.

A hunch back boy in the school which was self governing was caught stealing another boy's lunch. The rules of the school were that any boy that was caught stealing had to be publicly flogged. They made the rules themselves. The school was called together the boy was called forward. And the master said to him, "Take off your coat."

And the hunch back boy looked at him and said, "Sir, please oh no not that." He never wanted to take off his coat before other boys because of the disfigurement. He said, "Please sir, not that."

There was a terrible silence and a big boy, the boy from whom the lunch had been stolen, rose and said, "Sir, is there anything in the rules that would keep one boy from taking the punishment of another boy?"

The master thought a moment and said, "Why, no."

Then he said, "Sir, I would like to take it." He came forward and he took what would have fallen upon the hunch back boy.

The hunchback boy telling about it in later years said, "I saw through that the cross. I saw that God took upon Himself what would have fallen upon me, and through what that boy did for me, I saw the cross and became a Christian." And that hunchback boy is preaching in Texas today, redeemed by the cross in miniature. I suppose that is an echo of the soul. "So loved the world that He gave His only begotten son that whosoever...." I am amazed at that word "whosoever;" it's prodigal; it's careless. It doesn't make distinctions, doesn't mark people off into moral groups, but in the prodigal wave of His hand He says, "Whosoever" and I gasp. I say, "My God, you are prodigal in your giving, but you are just as prodigal in your forgiving." Did you say, "whosoever?" Without distinction? I'm astonished at God's carelessness about moral distinctions and yet I know that whosoever will do exactly what He says won't be the kind of person that he was. He will be fundamentally and radically different. And that reaches down to the lowest depth of human need and puts His arms around every one of us, no matter what we've done or been.

A pastor of a very fashionable church was awakened one night by the rapping on the door. He opened the door to a little girl dressed poorly and she said to him, "Sir, my mother asked me to get you to come to get her in." The pastor was puzzled about these words ... "get her in." Then he took the little girl's hand and went down through the streets of the city and into a slum section, up the rickety stairway and into an un-kempt room. The surroundings obviously were those of a dying prostitute — dying with consumption. And he sat down along side her bed to try to "get her in" because she was dying. He told her about Jesus as the teacher and how beautifully he taught. She listened avidly and then shook her head and said, "That's not for the likes of me." And then he told about Jesus the example, how He walked and talked and everything that He did was right and how He never missed His step and she listened. Then she shook her head sadly and said, "That's not for the likes of me." Then the preacher was about at the end of his resources and then he reached back into his past where he used to know something that he had laid aside and he brought it back. He talked about one that went to the cross for us, to die, to redeem us. And as he talked about that she began to shake her head, "Yes, that's it – that's for the likes of me." In telling about it later, he said, "you know, we got her in." Then he added, "And I got in too." Both of them knelt at the foot of the cross and found the same thing. "Whosoever" –Whosoever believes in Him shall not perish but have everlasting life. Whosoever believes, not merely believe, but believe in. A lot of us believe, but we don't believe in.

I remember when I was seeking Christ, kneeling at a Methodist altar a lad of 17, A friend knelt along side of me and repeated this verse, "God so loved the world." This friend, a schoolteacher, said, "Can't you put your name there? God so loved Stanley Jones that He gave His only begotten son that if Stanley Jones believes in Him he shall not perish but have everlasting life. Can you read it that way?"

I said, "Yes, I think I can." And I repeated it, "God so loved Stanley Jones that He gave his only begotten son that if Stanley Jones believes in Him, He shall not perish but have everlasting life."

She said, "Don't you believe that?"

I said, "Yes, I do."

Then she said, "You're changed."

And I said, "No I'm not."

I was believing it, but I didn't believe *in* it. I didn't believe in it so much that I said, "Well here I am – take me as I am." I didn't believe in it enough to invest myself, I believed it, but the next day in a moment of complete surrender I passed from believing; to believing in. I said, "Take me as I am, I believe in." That moment light broke. I passed from believing, to believing in, and that believing in meant that I believed in it so much that I surrendered myself to it. I said, "You've got me just as I am." And the moment I said, "You got me" it was done.

I shall never forget the occasion. I was in my room on the third story of my home, and I knew that I would go to that place of prayer that night. I had been twice—no light—I knew I would go again, for I was pressing hard on the gates of life; I wanted something. I knelt beside my bed and I said, "Oh God, please save me tonight." And a ray of light broke into my heart; a tiny ray pierced the darkness. I got to my feet and I said, "Oh, He's going to do it." I found myself running the mile to the church, the eagerness of my soul got into my body, and I found myself running the mile to the church. I look back on it and I felt myself as pilgrim running from the city of destruction to the city of God. And I thought if I could only get to that altar of prayer and I would find God—I thought that is were you found him. I came into the church and went straight to the front seat; I had never done a thing like that before in my life. I wanted the preacher to stop preaching so that I could get to that altar. I said, "if I could just get there – I know I could find Jesus." He scarcely finished and I was the first one there. I had scarcely bent my knees when heaven broke into my spirit. I was reconciled. I took hold of the man along side of man and I said, "I've got it." It – what did I mean? Everything I wanted and more. Reconciliation with God, reconciliation with myself, reconciliation with life. I believed in — He had me to my depths.

"Should not perish..." We sometimes wonder about that word *perishing*, how much is involved. I can see how people perish now with evil. I can see them go to pieces under evil; they do perish. The personality goes to pieces—has no cement within it—it breaks down. If you project that out into eternity, then what will happen? If you keep it up long enough then the personality goes to pieces and perishes. Perhaps forever and they would suffer what the Bible calls eternal destruction, unfit to survive—lights out. Whether that is true or not, I don't know. It would seem to point in that direction. For people do perish now; evil is not the way to live. The word evil is the word live spelled backwards. God doesn't punish you for sin. Sin is it's own punishment. You don't have to punish the eye for having sand in it, the body for having a cancer in it, the soul for having evil in it. For evil is its own punishment. He doesn't punish you for sin, sin is its own punishment — and therefore its destruction. You perish if you keep it up long enough; you are wiped out. The forces want to hold together for only in Jesus is there sufficient cement. In Him all things cohere — hold together — should not perish but have everlasting life.

Everlasting life, you can have now. Eternal life is a quality of life, not a "duration." A Harvard professor gave a lecture on the question - "Is eternal existence desirable?" And he came to the conclusion that it wasn't. George Bernard Shaw, affirmed the same thing when he said, "I wouldn't want to live with George Bernard Shaw forever." Well, I don't know if I would have liked to live with Stanley Jones forever — the Stanley Jones I was before I met Christ. But now I think I would like to live with him forever. Now it seems to me that life is essentially and fundamentally good and that right now eternal life is in the midst of time. If there is no future, I say well, "I've got it — if I get to the end of this life and I look out and I see that there is no future life, I say well I don't repent. It is a better way to live. The universe has let me down, I'm sorry. You weren't as good as I thought you were. But I have no regrets. This is the better way to live." Like the old lady who said, "If I ever get up to heaven and they wouldn't let me in the gate, I would shout all around the walls and say — well, thank God, I had a wonderful time coming."

We've got eternal life now in the midst of time when we got Him. Now I know how you feel and I know how I feel. You say, "Brother Stanley you have offered the tribute of your words, but you never really said it." I know. But by Eternal God, I shall try forever to tell it. Even though I know with Paul that its an unspeakable gift and yet you can't speak it. I've been introduced in many ways, one I shall never forget. A Parsee in India, a professor in Bombay, introduced me in these words, "The speaker is an author but doesn't care to be called an author. He's a lecturer but doesn't care to be called a lecturer. He prefers to be called an Evangelist. An Evangelist is the bearer of good news. The evangelist will now bring us his good news." Wasn't that lovely? As I rose I said to myself, "Stanley Jones are you bringing good views, a philosophy about life, or good news? In my heart of hearts I answered and said, if I bring Christ it is good news." I have brought you the good news tonight!

The basis on which your transformation can take place…and this *way* that He brings (to us) runs right straight down to the lowest depths of human need. It runs right straight down to hell. He descended in hell and the *Way* runs right there and if you turn around your feet are on the *Way*. That's all. Nobody is further than one step from God. And that one step is – yes! And if you'll take it this morning – then you are on the way. Shall we bow our heads in prayer?

PRAYER:

Oh God we are in thy presence. We worship at the shrine of the wonder of the divine act and we reach out our soiled hands and take the gift. That thou knowest that when we take the gift that we belong forever to the giver. You've got us and forever. We thank thee for it, in Jesus name. Amen.

4. JESUS IS INCARNATE GOD

COMMENTARY ON

"BUT WHO DO YOU SAY I AM?" (1953)

THIS sermon conveys what for Jones is the essence of Jesus Christ's ministry. Jones talks about Jesus' living in the mode of obedience and self-surrender while his disciples were living in the illusory world of self-saving. Even after the transfiguration, the disciples could not grasp that Jesus was about self-surrender. They were not. A series of blunders on the part of the disciples would ensue. Only finally did the disciples understand what Jesus was so clearly telling them. Once they grasped his message and surrendered themselves, they forgot them selves into immortality.

The lengthy text that begins this sermon focuses primarily on the words, *"But who do you say that I am?"* Jesus asks Peter his perception of him, and Peter responds; "The Messiah of God," which Jones calls the greatest confession in human history:

> When it finally dawned upon the people to whom Jesus had come that this was not a man who came into life in an ordinary way or who had an ordinary man's touch upon life, they saw through the veil of flesh the outcroppings of the Divine, and they saw that Jesus was the Son of God (150).

Jones suggests that we would have thought that Peter's confession that Jesus is the Messiah of God would have resulted in a dramatic change of purpose and commitment for the disciples. However, the rest of the passage suggests that Peter is not quite so sure what the implications would be when he said, "Jesus is the Messiah of God." It soon becomes clear that he and the other disciples were not prepared to follow Jesus if it meant a life in poverty, myriad difficulties, and particularly if it meant death on a cross. "Their failure to understand Jesus' prediction of his suffering and their refusal to ask him about it shows how little they have grasped. The disciples clearly have much to learn as they follow Jesus on the road" (Oxford Bible Commentary, 940). Jones notes, *"The fact of the matter is that nothing was done right in the rest of the chapter. Everything single thing that they did was a blunder, but why? (150).*

In some detail, Jones provides an explanation for the component parts of this lengthy preaching text. He emphasizes the serious of blunders and miscommunications on the part of his disciples. These false steps occur because of their unwillingness and inability to understand that the *cross* would be a part of Jesus' Messiahship. It must have been terribly difficult for them to fathom that the Messiah of God would die rather than rule. One would have assumed that such a Messiah would at least assert his power **before** he surrendered it to a cross. Jesus would do neither. He would not respond in the manner that the disciples anticipated. Jones suggests that Jesus is saying to these uncomprehending followers:

> At the center of my being the Son of God is the cross; and at the center of your being followers of mine, will also be a cross. You have to lose your life too. You will be crucified followers of a crucified Lord. And he said: "For those who want to save their life will lose it, and those who lose their life for my sake will save it" (151).

However, according to Jones, it was not simply that the disciples could not understand what Jesus was saying because it was counterintuitive — they could not understand because they were living un-surrendered lives. They had not yet surrendered **themselves** to follow him: *"They thought that they had given up everything to follow Jesus – they had – except themselves"(153).* For example, the man who wanted to bury his father first or the man who wanted to say good bye to his family before departing gave what could be thought of as reasonable and conventional excuses. However, there would be nothing conventional about the radical demand to follow Jesus and there could be no "excuses." Jones tells us that the lack of self-surrender is the central problem in the Christian life:

> What is the central problem of our Christian life? Jesus put his finger on it: "If any man would come after me let him leave father, mother, brother, house, and lands and yea his own self also" – why [the self] last? Because that is the last thing that we ever give up. We are ready to give up brother, father, sister, and lands to go; but the self is un-surrendered. (154)

The lack of self surrender is illustrated in the disciples' reaction to Jesus' identity as the Son of God. According to Jones, their reactions reflect a range of clashes that include various common human egotisms including individual against individual, group against group, and race against race. The unsurrendered self is always being hurt and it is always in the way:

> I see many a layman come into the Christian movement and give up everything to be a Christian, except the layman. You don't give the layman sufficient position and place and power and see what happens; he goes back into his "tent" to sulk (154).

Another of Jones' comments about the problems of the "unsurrendered self" is this succinct illustration: "One man put it this way, 'Wherever I go, I go too and I spoil everything" (158).

Jones was convinced that the egotism of the unsurrendered self was behind much of the racial discrimination that he observed in America. It is worth underscoring Jones' deep commitment to efforts to erase discriminatory practices in the United States. He often spoke out about "race egotism" in both his books and sermons, and according to Graham, Jones was sensitive to issues of race from the inception of his ministry:

He was one of the very first American evangelists to include African Americans in his public meetings. In fact, he refused to hold meetings where African Americans or any other racial or ethnic group was excluded (Graham 355).

Graham describes Jones' views on the scourge of race egotism:

The failure of the League of Nations to confront racism, Jones would insist, was one of the primary causes of Japanese militarism and of the outbreak of World War II in the Pacific. Moreover, racism was also a major problem in the United States, as a hesitation of American democracy to fulfill its divine potential as a nation. Indeed, throughout his long public career, there is no other political question on which Jones spoke out more frequently and more passionately than the issue of racial prejudice (174).

The exact date of this sermon, *Who Do You Say I Am?*, is unknown. However, it was probably preached in the late 1950s or early 1960s. It provides an illustration of Jones' prescient views on the profoundly negative effects of segregation in America and Apartheid in South Africa. He believed that it was God's will that all racial egotisms would be swept away. This belief is consistent with how Jones supported India's efforts for independence from British rule and his efforts to have Christianity become "indigenous" in India and elsewhere.[1]

---

1   In 1904 Jones wrote a letter to his childhood teacher, Miss Nellie Logan where he described the anticipated presence of a Black preacher to speak at Asbury College, only to then say that the minister's visit was summarily canceled. Jones writes, "The Mason and Dixon line is not yet erased from the minds of some! Oh, Lord have mercy!" (Graham 40). In 1942, Jones would write an even stronger letter on this subject. In the course of holding interracial meetings, a Methodist pastor wrote that Jones "tends dangerously toward social equality between all races." He wrote; "You ask why I should come to the South. I was born in the South and educated there – may I not visit my home land? You say that I am guilty of an "outspoken advocacy of bitter opposition to the Jim Crow law here — if

In regard to Jones' personal efforts on behalf of racial equality, Jones tells a fascinating story about his relationship and influence on Martin Luther King in his autobiography, *A Song of Ascents*. He writes:

> I thought that my book *Mahatma Gandhi, an Interpretation* was a failure. It did not seem to dent the Western world with its emphasis on armaments. But when I saw Dr. Martin Luther King, he said: "It was your book on Gandhi that gave me my first inkling of non-violent non-cooperation. Here I said to myself, is the way for the Negro to achieve his freedom. We will turn this whole movement from violence to nonviolence. We will match our capacity to suffer against the other's capacity to inflict suffering, our soul force against his physical force; and we will wear our opponents down with goodwill." Then my book was not a failure, I replied. "No, if we can keep the movement non-violent," he answered (*A Song of Ascents*, 260).

Self surrender, the focus of this sermon, makes racial superiority and race egotisms irrelevant and obsolete. "Every man is a man for whom Christ died," is a phrase often used by Jones. The multiple "blunders" of the disciples were "stumblings" over the un-surrendered self. Jones reminds us that *"Your life will be a series of blunders from now until you drop into the grave unless you get that self off your own hands into the hands of God. Your self in your own hands is a problem and a pain,*

---

that is a crime then I plead guilty. If to ask for equal rights for citizens of the American democracy is a crime, then I'm guilty of that crime. You say "He tends dangerously toward social equality between all races." If to do so is a crime against democracy and Christianity then again I plead guilty and glory in that guilt. The crime it seems to me is to be on the other side. It is treason against Democracy and against the Christian faith to advocate inequality of treatment of races. If I should be kept back from India permanently, which God forbid, then I should consider seriously giving the balance of my working days to help the Negroes of America to an equal status in our democracy and to their fullest development as a people for the color question has become a world question (Graham 282).

your self in the hands of God is a possibility and a power" (163). Jones repeatedly maintained that the central thing we all need to let go of is the self. That is our only problem: *"I don't believe that any of us have any problems at all except that. Solve that and you can face the world and all the other problems because you are now clear with God and yourself"* (164). The disciples finally let go of that unsurrendered self. God then received them and transformed them:

> He took them and flung them against the world's problems and the world's needs and shook the world with them. It was only possible when they got themselves off their own hands into God's hands (164).

Jones makes it clear to his audience that this same transformation can occur for them if they come forward to the altar and surrender themselves to God. Many would surely do so.

JESUS IS GOD INCARNATE
"BUT WHO DO YOU SAY I AM?"

SERMON

And it happened that while He was praying alone, the disciples were with Him, and He questioned them, saying, "Who do the people say that I am?" They answered and said, "John the Baptist, and others say Elijah; but others, that one of the prophets of old has risen again." And He said to them, "But who do you say that I am?" And Peter answered and said, "The Christ of God."

But He warned them and instructed them not to tell this to anyone, saying, "The Son of Man must suffer many things and be rejected by the elders and chief priests and scribes, and be killed and be raised up on the third day."

146

He was saying to them all, "If anyone wishes to come after Me, he must deny himself, and take up his cross daily and follow Me. "For whoever wishes to save his life will lose it, but whoever loses his life for My sake, he is the one who will save it. "For what is a man profited if he gains the whole world, and loses or forfeits himself? "For whoever is ashamed of Me and My words, the Son of Man will be ashamed of him when He comes in His glory, and the glory of the Father and of the holy angels. "But I say to you truthfully, there are some of those standing here who will not taste death until they see the kingdom of God."

Some eight days after these sayings, He took along Peter and John and James, and went up on the mountain to pray. And while He was praying, the appearance of His face became different, and His clothing became white and gleaming. And behold, two men were talking with Him; and they were Moses and Elijah, who, appearing in glory, were speaking of His departure which He was about to accomplish at Jerusalem. Now Peter and his companions had been overcome with sleep; but when they were fully awake, they saw His glory and the two men standing with Him. And as these were leaving Him, Peter said to Jesus, "Master, it is good for us to be here; let us make three tabernacles: one for You, and one for Moses, and one for Elijah" — not realizing what he was saying.

While he was saying this, a cloud formed and began to overshadow them; and they were afraid as they entered the cloud. Then a voice came out of the cloud, saying, "This is My Son, My Chosen One; listen to Him!" And when the voice had spoken, Jesus was found alone. And they kept silent, and reported to no one in those days any of the things which they had seen.

On the next day, when they came down from the mountain, a large crowd met Him. And a man from the crowd shouted, saying, "Teacher, I beg You to look at my son, for he is my only boy, and a spirit seizes him, and he suddenly screams, and it throws him into a convulsion with foaming at the mouth; and only with difficulty does it leave him, mauling him as it leaves. "I begged Your disciples to cast it out, and they could not." And Jesus answered and said, "You unbelieving and perverted generation, how long shall I be with you and put up with you? Bring your son here." While he was still approaching, the demon slammed him to the ground and threw him into a convulsion. But Jesus rebuked the unclean spirit, and healed the boy and gave him back to his father. And they were all amazed at the greatness of God.

But while everyone was marveling at all that He was doing, He said to His disciples, "Let these words sink into your ears; for the Son of Man is going to be delivered into the hands of men." But they did not understand this statement, and it was concealed from them so that they would not perceive it; and they were afraid to ask Him about this statement.

An argument started among them as to which of them might be the greatest. But Jesus, knowing what they were thinking in their heart, took a child and stood him by His side, and said to them, "Whoever receives this child in My name receives Me, and whoever receives Me receives Him who sent Me; for the one who is least among all of you, this is the one who is great."

John answered and said, "Master, we saw someone casting out demons in Your name; and we tried to prevent him because he does not follow along with us." But Jesus said to him, "Do not hinder him; for he who is not against you is for you."

When the days were approaching for His ascension, He was determined to go to Jerusalem; and He sent messengers on ahead of Him, and they went and entered a village of the Samaritans to make arrangements for Him. But they did not receive Him, because He was traveling toward Jerusalem. When His disciples James and John saw this, they said, "Lord, do You want us to command fire to come down from heaven and consume them?" But He turned and rebuked them, and said, "You do not know what kind of spirit you are of; for the

Son of Man did not come to destroy men's lives, but to save them." And they went on to another village.

As they were going along the road, someone said to Him, "I will follow You wherever You go." And Jesus said to him, "The foxes have holes and the birds of the air have nests, but the Son of Man has nowhere to lay His head." And He said to another, "Follow Me." But he said, "Lord, permit me first to go and bury my father." But He said to him, "Allow the dead to bury their own dead; but as for you, go and proclaim everywhere the kingdom of God." Another also said, "I will follow You, Lord; but first permit me to say good-bye to those at home." But Jesus said to him, "No one, after putting his hand to the plow and looking back, is fit for the kingdom of God."[2]

I read this lengthy passage to you but I want to put my finger upon one portion of the text [**Who do you say that I am?**] that I will speak about this evening.

The disciples did not really understand what Jesus was saying and they were afraid to ask him. The background of this chapter is of course in the opening verses – the setting is this. Jesus went down to Philippi where there was a white grotto with an image of Caesar, who was worshipped as a God. In that setting where Caesar was worshipped as God, Jesus turned to them and said, "Who do you think that I am?" They had followed Him on the basis that he was a good man, perhaps the best of men, but a man, a prophet. They had watched Him for three years, night and day. Then He turned to them in the midst of it and said, "Who do you think that I am?"

Jesus waited until this prayer hour to speak to his disciples. Jesus was praying, and prayer is the most abject thing that a person can do. A person says: "I am not sufficient in myself; I kneel to another and ask for a light to guide the way." So, when He was in prayer, Jesus turned (to his disciples) and said,

---

2   Luke 9:18-62.

"Who do you think that I am *now*?" Suppose He had asked them this when the winds and the sea were calmed before His voice or when He raised Lazarus from the dead or performed a miracle here and there? Asking them at those times, would have coerced their minds. Asking the question at those moments would have forced them into saying: "Well, you are certainly not a man if you can do a thing like this." But Jesus was very much a man when He prayed, and yet He turned to them in the moment of prayer and said: "Who do you think that I am?" And upon the trembling lips of Peter was the great confession — the greatest moment perhaps in human history — when it dawned upon the people to whom Jesus had come, that this was not a man who came into life in an ordinary way or who had an ordinary man's touch upon life. They saw through the veil of flesh, the outcroppings of the Divine and they saw that Jesus was the Son of God.

When that dawned upon their minds, one would have thought that the whole of the rest of their lives would be fitted into that fact and everything would become rhythmical and harmonious because they had come to the supreme knowledge that Jesus was the son of God, not man become God, but God become man. You would have thought that everything would have gone right from that moment on. Up to that moment, they were having a lot of trouble with themselves and others; they were spotty in their following of Jesus. Now we would have thought that everything would have come together and that everything would have gone on gloriously. The fact of the matter is that *nothing* was done right in the rest of the chapter. Every single thing that they did was a blunder. Why?

In a moment, we will put our finger on the reason. Jesus tried to get them to see, in the light of what He was seeing, the reasons. The moment He revealed himself as the Son of God and they understood it (caught it), He began to put content into (the fact of) His being the Son of God. Jesus said that the Son of Man is to be delivered into the hands of men and the third day he would rise from the dead. Jesus began to say that in the center of His being as the Son of God, is the cross. For immediately Jesus began to talk about the cross. As soon as they found out who He was, He wanted to put the content of the cross into the center of their understanding of Him. *"He sternly ordered and commanded them not to tell anyone, saying: The Son of Man must undergo great suffering, and be rejected by the elders, chief priest and scribes, and be killed, and on the third day be raised."*[3]

In other words, He was saying that at the center of His being, the Son of God is the self-giving of God at the cross. They thought that at the center (of Jesus' being) would be self-assertion upon the throne. That is why James and John came to Him and said, "Lord, give us seats one at your right and left in your kingdom."[4] They thought that He was going to Jerusalem to set up His kingdom. They thought that He was going to be a self-asserting Christ now. He had been humble up to this moment but from now on He would assert Himself and conquer His enemies and stand on top of things. On the contrary, He tells them that at the center of His being the Son of God is self-giving. Then it began to dawn on them what He meant by the following verse. *"Then he said to them all, "If any want to become my followers, let them deny themselves and take up their cross daily and follow me."*[5]

At the center of my being the Son of God is the cross; and at the center of your being followers of mine, will also be a cross. You have to lose your life too. You will be crucified followers of a crucified Lord. And he said: *"For those who want to save their life will lose it, and those who lose their life for my sake will save it."*[6]

---

3   Luke 9:21-22.

4   Mark 10:37.

5   Luke 9:23.

6   Luke 9:24.

Then the account goes on and we read the account of the transfiguration. This was a stunning blow to them to know that the whole thing was going to end at the cross and they were to follow Him as crucified followers of a crucified Lord. Jesus then began to give them some reassurance—that there was a dark side here but a glory side as well. So He went up to a mountain and in the act of prayer His garments became luminous and His whole appearance became unearthly white and there appeared with Him Moses and Elijah—Moses representing the law and Elijah the prophets. They were talking to Him. What were they talking about? They were talking about Jesus' departure that He was to accomplish at Jerusalem. In other words, they were talking about His death. They called it *departure*. Heaven was interested in this matter of Jesus' death and the divine self-giving, so emissaries came from heaven—Moses and Elijah—and talked with Him about that departure. For that was the focal point of the whole business—His death. In other words, heaven was interested for it was to be the greatest point in all of Christ's life.

Peter, seeing Moses and Elijah (representing the law and the prophets) and Jesus, said: "Let's make three tabernacles, one for you, one for Moses and one for Elijah, one each." Peter symbolically wanted to put them on the same level: Moses representing the law and Elijah the prophets and Jesus the new order. He thought, let's put them all together. The Jewish heart of Peter wanted to hold onto all three. As he spoke, the account says, a cloud overshadowed them. That was a cloud that cleared their thinking. Sometimes a cloud has to come over us to clear our thinking and that cloud cleared their thinking and their attitudes. They feared as they entered the cloud and a voice came out of the cloud saying, "This is my son, hear him!"[7] Moses was fulfilled in Him. Elijah has been fulfilled in Him. You can't put them on the same level now. He stands out; hear Him. And they lifted up their eyes and saw no man save only Jesus.

---

7   Luke 9:35.

He occupied their horizon. He charged them to not tell anyone about this occurrence.

On the next day, when they had come down from the mountain, a great crowd came to meet Him. Remember a man came out of the crowd and said: *"Teacher, I brought my son who was with an unclean spirit and I asked your disciples to cast out this unclear spirit, but they could not, please help me." Jesus answered: "Oh faithless and perverse generation, how long must I still be with you and bear with you? Fetch your son here."*[8] Jesus checked the unclean spirit, cured the boy and handed him back to his father. The crowd said this is the majesty of God — power over death, nature, demons and sickness. This is the majesty of God.

While they were all marveling at all that He did, Jesus said to his disciples: "Let these words sink into your ears:" [get this if you miss everything else] "The Son of man is to be delivered into the hands of men."[9] Jesus was going to the Cross. They did not understand the saying and they were afraid to ask. They could not grasp the idea that He would go to a cross to lay down His life. They thought that He would assert His life into power, and here He was surrendering it into redemption.

Now from that moment on there is a series of mistakes and blunders. Everything they (the disciples) did was wrong. What was the center of their difficulty? The center of their difficulty was this: while Jesus was in the realm of self-surrender, the disciples were in another realm, the realm of self-assertion. They had not passed from self-assertion to self-surrender. They were still thinking in terms of: what are we going to get? Peter said, Lord we have left everything and then what shall we get?[10] They left everything to follow Jesus except themselves. They left fishing boats, nets, settled occupations, parents and home — everything to follow Him, except themselves.

---

8   Luke 9:37-42.

9   Luke 9:44.

10   Mark 10:28-30.

The fact of the matter is here they revealed the center of all our spiritual and moral problems. We are ready to give up everything to follow Jesus *except ourselves*. I have seen many a missionary give up home, loved ones and friends, business and occupation and prospects, to become a missionary, everything except the missionary. You touch him and he is still touchy. The self is un surrendered. I have seen many a minister go into the ministry and give up everything to be a minister, prospects of riches, this, that and the other thing to go into the ministry. They give up everything except the minister. The self is still there, watchful of its position, place and power. I see many a layman come into the Christian movement and give up everything to be a Christian, except the layman. You don't give the layman sufficient position and place and power and see what happens; he goes back into his "tent" to sulk.

What is the central problem of our Christian life? Jesus put his finger on it: "If any man would come after me let him leave father, mother, brother, house, and lands and yea his own self also"[11] – why [the self] last? Because that is the last thing that we ever give up. We are ready to give up brother, father, sister, and lands to go; but the self is unsurrendered.

Mohammed Ali Jinnah, a Muslim patriot in India[12], said: "For the sake of my country, I am willing to sacrifice my own

---

11 Mark 10: 29-30.

12 Muhammad Ali Jinnah (1876–1948) was an Indian Muslim politician and leader of the All India Muslim League who founded Pakistan and served as its first Governor-General. He is commonly known in Pakistan as Quaid-e-Azam. Jinnah rose to prominence in the Indian National Congress expounding ideas of Hindu-Muslim unity and helping shape the 1916 Lucknow Pact with the Muslim League. Differences with Mahatma Gandhi led Jinnah to quit the Congress and take charge of the Muslim League. He proposed a fourteen-point constitutional reform plan to safeguard the political rights of Muslims in a self-governing India. His proposals failed amid the League's disunity. Disillusioned by the failure to build coalitions with the Congress, Jinnah embraced the goal of creating a separate state for Muslims as in the Lahore Resolution. The League won

mother, and yes, I am willing to sacrifice my children, and yes, then if need be, I am willing to sacrifice myself." But the self was last. He was ready to let the mother and the children go first, but the self was still there. Now the center of our spiritual difficulties is a lack of self-surrender. All other things are marginal.

Now I want to clarify what I mean with an illustration. A great many people think that Christianity means world surrender; that you have to turn your back on the world if you are going to be a Christian. Out on the west coast I met a woman who was the head of sixty five charm schools across the country on which she received significant royalties. She lived in a mansion. She had a radio program with ten million listeners. She was clearly exceedingly wealthy. In the midst of this wealth, she had an experience of dissatisfaction. She did not know what was the trouble was. She was financially and professionally on top of the world, but in internal tumult so she thought that reading some history might help her. So she got a book on what she thought was the history of the pilgrims of New England, but she picked up *Pilgrims Progress* instead and read it and was converted. She believed that Christianity was world renunciation and that you have to reduce life to complete physical emptiness. She walked out of her home, abandoned her charm schools and moved into a trailer with her two children. She renounced everything that had to do with the world. I saw her at this time and said, "Do you know that you are running away from the world? You seem to think that Christianity demands world surrender. It doesn't; it demands something much deeper than world surrender; it

---

most Muslim seats in the elections of 1946, and Jinnah launched the Direct Action campaign of strikes and protests to achieve "Pakistan", which degenerated into communal violence across India. The failure of the Congress-League coalition to govern the country prompted both parties and the British to agree to partition. As Governor-General of Pakistan, Jinnah led efforts to rehabilitate millions of refugees, and to frame national policies on foreign affairs, security and economic development. < http://www.pakistan.gov.pk/Quaid/index.htm>

demands self surrender. The moment you surrender your self and give your self to Him, He turns to us and says, now all things belong to you; the world, life, death, the present and the future. It all belongs to you, since you belong to Christ." Christianity demands more than world surrender, it demands self surrender and when you surrender yourself, the world comes back to you. It (the world) is yours; you can walk into it emancipated but it is all yours. Its beauty, its art, its relationships, is all yours. "Oh, I can see what I have been doing," she said, "I have been reducing life to that of a vegetable and calling it victory." She believed that if you become a Christian, it is life surrender — you have to deny this thing called life. But Jesus said, "I come that you might have life and that you might have it more abundantly."[13] Is Christianity designed to reduce life? No, it raises life to the nth degree, until you tingle with life at every pore. Then what does Christianity demand? It demands something deeper than the surrender of the world or life, it demands the surrender of the self. The one thing that you own He asks you to pass back to Him, and say "Jesus, you created it, take it back." The one thing you give to me, I give it back to you. It is yours do with it what you will. He cleanses it from a thousand contradictions and its egoisms and then and hands it back to us and says now it is yours. It (your life) never was yours until you handed it over to Him. Now life is yours; you are free. You have lost your life and now you have found it.

Now, there is the center of the disciples' problem; they had given up everything except themselves and then everything went wrong. Let's see what these "errors" were. First, an argument arose among them. Who would be the *greatest*. You see that the unsurrendered self began to clash with their colleagues, each wanting to be first. The "self" wanting to climb up on top. Peter said: "I made that confession, didn't I?" Andrew said: "Who brought you here?" And John said, "Don't I lean on his bosom" and Judas said, "Who pays all the bills?" They

---

13 John 10:10.

went around fighting with each other, trying to be the greatest. They were trying to be big by [making] big assertions. They were never so small as when they were most trying to be big. If that is all we knew of the disciples, I would have put my handkerchief over them and said, "Goodbye, I don't want to look at you any more. You are too much like me." As they tried to be big they sunk lower and lower. Jesus set a child in the midst and said, "…if you want to be *great*, be like this child; *and if you want to be the greatest of all, become the servant of all.*"[14]

There is a place for ambitious people in the Christian faith. Three different groups can emerge. He said: "He that would be greatest among you, let him be the servant; and he would be first, he would be the slave of all."[15] The Son of man who gives His life as ransom for many is at the top. At the top because of the degree of His self-giving.

There are three groups, the great, the first and the Son of Man. These three groups are designated because of the degree of self giving. The lowest degree was the servant of all, the next degree was the slave of all who goes further in his self giving and the highest of all was the Son of Man who gave His life as a ransom for many. There is a place for ambitious people but the way up is the way down, and you must lose your life and you will find it coming back (to you) to the degree that you lose it and find it again. Now an argument arose among them about who was the greatest. Here was the ego assertion clashing with others. They were trying to get along with each but they could not because the self of each of them was asserting itself against every other self. The result was confusion all because of a lack of self surrender.

Across the years, I have seen one cause for difficulties in a church or mission situation. It is always one thing, namely someone asserting himself against the others and the whole

---

14 Mark 9:35.

15 Matthew 20:26-27.

thing is caused by a lack of self surrender. We can't get along with each other because we can't get along with ourselves and we can't get along with God because the self is in the way. One man put it this way, "Wherever I go, I go too, and I spoil everything."

How are we going to get along with each other? There is only one way to get along with each other and that is to surrender to Christ and then you can afford to surrender to other people having surrendered to Him. Having surrendered to Him you can afford to surrender to other people. That verse in Ephesians 5:21 "Submit yourselves one to another out of reverence for Christ." Having submitted yourself to Him out of reverence for Him, now you can afford to submit to each other without losing your self respect. You can say, "I have submitted to Him, therefore I dare submit to you because in submitting to you I do it for His sake and for His love and I do it out of reverence for Him." That takes the sting out of self surrender. I have already submitted to Him and now for His sake, I submit to you. Out of love for Him, I do this for you, and then you can't be hurt because you have hurt yourself with the supreme hurt and therefore you can't be hurt by other people. But if you have an un-surrendered self it is always being hurt and it is always in the way. That was the first clash and it was the clash of personal egotism.

Then we see another group. John said, "We saw a man casting out demons in your name and we forbade him because he is not following with us."[16] Here is the second clash. A group of disciples against a group of disciples. John saw some people casting out demons in Jesus' name and he forbade them because he was not following John and his disciples. He was willing for those demons to stay in if his group could not get them out. And a lot of us are willing for people to be lost if their denomination can't save them. It was self-assertion that was now evolving into the group self assertions. We not only

---

16 Luke 9:49.

want our selves to be first, but we want our group to be first. I saw a sign on a billboard near a church which read: "This church is the ONLY church in the world authorized by God to represent Jesus Christ in the world." How is that for humility?

In a local hymnbook are these words: "I'd rather be a Baptist and wear a smiling face, than be a dirty Methodist and fall away from grace. I'd rather be a Methodist and talk about free grace, than be a hard-shelled Calvinist and damn near half the race." They set it to music and sang it. Now here was group egotism – there is such a thing among the denominations now, (i.e., denominational envy). There is jealousy and envy.

Jesus rebuked them, and said: "He who is not against you is for you."[17] You are not the issue, but I am (Jesus) the issue. If you are not with me, you are against me. Following this group or that group is not the issue; following Jesus is the issue.

The third clash: *"When the days drew near for him to be taken up, he set his face to go to Jerusalem. And he sent messengers ahead of him. On their way they entered a village of the Samaritans to make ready for him; but they did not receive him, because his face was set toward Jerusalem. When his disciples James and John saw it, they said, "Lord do you want us to command fire to come down from heaven and consume them?" But he turned and rebuked them. Then they went on to another village."*[18]

Here is the third clash: [remember that] *the first was individual against individual; then group against group; and now we see race egotism, or race against race.* James and John showed racial prejudice. There is one thing that is troubling our people in American at the present time. We put all kinds of alibis around the central thing—it is race egotism. We don't want the Blacks to rise because it hurts our pride not to have someone beneath us, and we want to be on top. We analyze it here and rationalize there, but, down underneath, the problem is a false

17 Luke 9:50.

18 Luke 9:51-56.

belief in the racial superiority of white people. There is the un-surrendered race-self. As we do live in that un-surrendered race-self, we are losing ourselves by the moment. I come from the Southland and I love it, but the south is losing itself because of racial segregation. I told my friends in the southland the other day that as we segregate Blacks, we are segregating ourselves from national leadership. You cannot elect to the Presidency of the United States any man who holds these views (segregation). In segregating the Blacks, we only succeed in segregating ourselves from national leadership. The laws of God are at work and the laws of God are color blind. We will fight it (integration) and we will try to circumvent it, but in the end, it (integration) is going to get it. The bell is tolling and the tide is rolling in and you cannot push it back any more than you can turn back the tides of Hampton Roads with your two hands. Man is rising and it is God's will that man should rise and racial egotisms are going to be swept away.

For example, South Africa is a country with 2 million white people trying to hold down 8 million Africans in South Africa and behind them 150 million Africans in the rest of the continent. There are two million whites trying to hold a line against 150 million Africans. If the white South Africans would take them in and make them a part of their civilization and lift everyone in sight then they would all rise. However, now the white South Africans think that they are saving their lives (by Apartheid policies). However, they are going to lose them, and they are losing them by the moment. South Africa is the most unhappy country in the world because their consciences are troubled; they are breaking themselves up on the laws of God.[19]

---

19 In 1969, while I was traveling with Jones in Africa, we needed to pass through Johannesburg, South Africa on our way to Zimbabwe, then Rhodesia. It was clear to the immigration authorities that Jones was an outspoken critic of Apartheid and we were carefully monitored during our transit stay. He was in fact not permitted to travel in South Africa during that time. Evidence of separate facilities for blacks and whites was present even in the International transit lounge of that country's airport.

You can't put another man down without staying down with him. The scientist, Booker T. Washington, has said: "The only way to keep a man down in the gutter is to stay down with him."[20] But you say, "Look where they have come from; they were slaves." I know. But look where we have come from. At the time of the Roman ascendancy, Servius a Roman[21] said, "The stupidest and the ugliest slaves in the market place are those from Britain." However, someone else with the eyes of a Christian, looked on those stupid and ugly slaves and said: "Angels, Angels, if they could be Christian, they would be angels." So we are not angels, but we are no longer stupid and ugly slaves. I don't care where a man has come from, I am only interested in where he is going. I don't care where you have come from, I want to know your destination.

James and John were never so small as when they tried to assert themselves and call divine fire down from heaven...and if that had happened it would have been the end of James and

---

20 Booker Taliaferro Washington (1856–1915) was an American political leader, educator and author. He was the dominant figure in the African American community in the United States from 1890 to 1915. Washington played a dominant role in black politics, winning wide support in the black community and among more liberal whites (especially rich northern whites). He gained access to top national leaders in politics, philanthropy and education. In addition to the substantial contributions in the field of education, Dr. Washington did much to improve the overall friendship and working relationship between the races in the United States. His autobiography, Up From Slavery, first published in 1901, is still widely read today. The exact quote is "One man cannot hold another man down in the ditch without remaining down in the ditch with him."<James D. Anderson, "Black Rural Communities and the Struggle for Education During the Age of Booker T. Washington, 1877-1915," PJE. Peabody Journal of Education 67, no. 4 (1990): 46. [database on-line]; available from Questia, http://www.questia.com/PM.qst?a=o&d=95840010; Internet; accessed 28 March 2007.>

21 Servius Tullius was the sixth legendary king of ancient Rome, and the second king of the Etruscan dynasty. The traditional dates of his reign are 578-535 BC. He was murdered by Tarquin the Proud. < http://encyclopedia.jrank.org/SCY_SHA/SERVIUS_TULLIUS.html>

John.[22] We would never have looked at them again. We would have said they are just like the rest of us. But Jesus turned and rebuked them and they went to another village.

Now here are some more miscellaneous mistakes that were made by individuals. As Jesus was going along the road, a man said that he would follow Jesus wherever he went. But Jesus said, *"Foxes have holes, and birds of the air have nests; but the Son of Man has nowhere to lay his head.[23]"* You are looking for a soft spot and I have nothing to offer you. The man wanted comfort and that is the quest of the modern day; we are looking for gadgets that will make us comfortable.

Jesus said to another, "Follow me." But the man said, let me first of all bury my father." I don't think that the father was lying dead at home, I think that he wanted to go home and wait until his father did die. Jesus said, *"Let the dead bury their own dead; but as for you, go and proclaim the Kingdom of God."[24]*

Another said "I will follow you; Lord, but let me first say farewell to those at my home."[25] This man was someone who worshipped custom he did not want to break any of the conventions so that anyone would say that he did not say goodbye before he left. They are the people who are bound by the grave clothes of convention. Jesus said, *"No one who puts a hand to the plow and looks back is fit for the kingdom of God."[26]*

You see that every single thing that was done in the rest of the chapter was done wrong. Why? There was only one reason. Every single time they stumbled over the un-surrendered self. Your life will be a series of blunders from now until you drop

---

22 Luke 9:54.

23 Luke 9:58.

24 Luke 9:60.

25 Luke 9:61.

26 Luke 9:62.

into the grave unless you get that self off your own hands and into the hands of God. Your self in your own hands is a problem and a pain. Your self in the hands of God is a possibility and a power. When you get your troublesome, self-asserting self off of your hands and into the hands of God, then something is going to happen to you.

A doctor was called to see a patient who was apparently quite ill. Strangely enough, the doctor could not find any physical basis for his illness. The doctor said to the man, "Is something troubling you?"

The man said, "No, I am a member of the church, everything is fine. No, nothing is troubling me." The doctor went away puzzled.

The next day the man sent for the doctor and said, "I have been thinking about what you said all night and I have been talking to God. There is something troubling me. I looked at the ceiling last night and I could see nothing but 'Seek first the Kingdom of God.' When I looked at the floor, I could see nothing but 'Seek first the Kingdom of God.' When I looked at the walls, I could see nothing but this phrase, 'Seek first the Kingdom of God.' Now, Doctor, I have not been seeking first the Kingdom of God. I have been seeking first the Kingdom of John Brown." He said, "I pushed myself up in my organization and I have gotten to the top. But I have done it ruthlessly, caring little for those who I may have pushed aside. Now I am going to seek first the kingdom of God no matter what happens to myself, my business or anything else and I am at peace with myself this morning for I have made my surrender."

The doctor said, "I went away from there this morning with tears rolling down my face for I had seen the birth of a soul."

A successful executive came to visit a doctor and the doctor gave him a thorough examination. He was upset and nervous and clashing with himself and his employees. The doctor told him that he needed a new philosophy of life and handed him a bill for $3000. The doctor knew that if he charged him a small amount of money, the man would not pay any attention to the doctor's advice. The man was furious to be charged $3000. He went to the pastor and complained and the pastor said, "It is true. You do need a new philosophy of life." The pastor gave him my book *Abundant Living* and he began to read it and he saw that the trouble was in himself. He saw that the trouble within himself was just himself. He had never given up that and he gave it up and became a new man and then new relationships with himself and others and life and came out of it. That is the central thing that we have to let go.

You may ask, "How do I find a new philosophy of life? How do we find that the trouble is within our selves?" We can (find a new philosophy of life) and when we do, we become a new person and have new relationships with our self and others. The central thing that we have to let go is the self. The disciples did finally let go of that self. They surrendered themselves. For ten days they waited and waited until they got to the end of themselves. Then God said: "You are now at the beginning of me. You are at the end of your rope and I am reaching down my hand." He took them and flung them against the world's problems and the world's needs and shook the world with them. It was only possible when they got themselves off their own hands into God's hands.

Now is that our problem? I don't believe that any of us have any problems at all except that. Solve that and you can face then the world and all the other problems because you are now clear with God and yourself.

Now tonight, we are going to let you have an opportunity to get this self of yours off your own hands and into the hands of God. We will have counsel and prayer with you personally. It would be easy for me to dismiss you now and say that you may go. That would not be fair to raise you to this point and then just dismiss you. You say, "I see what it is and I want my seeing to turn into seeking." You are saying, "I want to do business with God." We are going to have a prayer. Those who wish to go, may go. Others who may say, "I want to find what you are talking about and I want to get my self off my hands and into the hands of God. I want to stop all my religious wanderings. I want to be born again," can come forward for prayer.

PRAYER:

Dear Father bless those who would like to go, and bless those who stay and may your spirit rest upon us as we stay or as we go and grant that something may happen to us here together that makes us forever and forever new. We ask it in Jesus' name, Amen.

5. THE CENTER OF THE INCARNATION IS THE CROSS

COMMENTARY ON "SELF SURRENDER"

I have been crucified with Christ; the life I live is not my life, but the life which Christ lives in me. And my present bodily life is lived by faith and the Son of God who loved me and sacrificed himself for me. I will not nullify the grace of God."(Galatians 2:20-21)

THE text for this sermon on "Self-Surrender" is taken from Galatians. Paul is writing to explain his method of preaching the Gospel to the Gentiles and to distinguish it from the Gospel preached by Jewish Christians, which emphasized the strict observation of the Mosaic Law. Paul is making the point that, when Gentiles are justified (saved) by Christ, they do not need to take any preliminary steps such as participating in adult circumcisism. Paul emphasizes that, if justification were solely available through the law, there would have been no reason for Christ, "for if justification comes through the law, then Christ died for nothing" (Galatians 2:21) Paul confesses that he once lived by the law, which resulted in the persecution of Christians, but since his dramatic conversion, he has died to the law and now lives in Christ. While this particular passage is most often used as an illustration of Paul's view on "justification by faith," Jones emphasizes this passage for its message on the importance of self surrender.

This sermon focuses on the phrase, "The life I live is not my life, but the life which Christ lives in me." According to Jones, this verse describes the transformation from being self-centered to Christ-centered that occurs at the moment of conversion. It is this insistence on the importance of self-surrender rather than justification by faith that is Jones' 'perspective' on these well-known verses.

E. Stanley Jones had a sophisticated understanding of religious and psychological viewpoints on the nature and the importance of the "self," that part of our being which has awareness and reflects on that awareness. Jones understood well that many experience the "self" as a problem and a pain. He often used the following sentence, to emphasize the difficulties that the un-surrendered self can present to the sorry soul who "houses" this problematic being: "Everywhere I go, I go too, and I spoil everything."

As Jones sets up the Christian answer to the "self," he takes time to explain the various non-Christian religions' perspectives on the "self." Hinduism and Buddhism are world weary and self weary, he says. They focus on self renunciation and self transcendence for the self is a burden to be rid of.

Psychiatry, according to Jones, holds virtually the opposite view in that it focuses intently on the "self" but does not provide a better answer to the *problem* of the self. Jones notes that while psychiatry places "value" on "self-realization," that is, those moments when we come to know, accept, and express ourselves, we are still left with the "self" as the "false" center of an individual's life. Jones rejects both the Eastern view of the self and the views of modern psychiatry.

Alternatively, Christianity, according to Jones, has the most radical answer to the question of "what to do with the self." The self is to be surrendered, not denied and discarded or narcissistically over-valued and cultivated, but surrendered. Jones emphasizes again and again that the "answer" to the question of the "self" is not self- realization as if the answers can be found within the self, but self surrender to Christ who holds the ultimate answers:

> Christianity points an arrow straight at the heart of our problem — the un-surrendered self — and it says let go of

the one thing you've got. But then you say anxiously "my self is gone; the one thing that I own is gone" (177).

When we give back to God the one thing we own – the self — we can now fulfill the destiny to which God intended, for the Christian faith teaches that we are a child of God, and our destiny is to be made into the likeness of the Son of God. When you surrender yourself, you can then fully know yourself as a child of God. You are then under that unfolding destiny that God has for you. The self is clearly not wiped out; rather, you are living under a future that is unfolding with the grace of God. You are living under an unfolding plan of redemption. According to Jones, Christianity would reverse the order proposed by psychiatry[1] and begin with "surrender yourself." Then you can accept yourself, and then you can express yourself:

> It is a paradox. I can't explain it. But when you lose your life and find it, you are never so much your own as when you are most His. Belonging to Him, you belong to yourself. I don't argue this point (179).

Jones readily admits that self surrender is often extraordinarily difficult. Intuitively, we believe that we cannot give up the one thing that we own. It is a severe demand for we think that we cannot live without the self:

> Now the last thing in the world that we ever give up is ourselves. We give up here, here, here and here. Many a man who goes into the ministry gives up everything to be a minister except the minister. Many a missionary goes out across the seas and gives up everything to be a missionary – everything except the missionary. The self is still there watchful of its position, place and power (176).

This (un-surrendered) self is placed as the focus of our lives and ties up our energy *and* our lives. Instead, Jones says, that center belongs to God. Problems ensue until the self stops trying to be God! Jones asks that we consider closely the passage from

---

1   (Know yourself, accept yourself and express yourself.)

Galatians, "I have been crucified with Christ" (178). Once "crucified" with Christ, you in fact can *live* and have meaning and purpose in your life. Jones states emphatically, *"If you are not crucified with Christ voluntarily and with set purpose then you will be crucified on the cross of your own contradictions and your own conflicts. It isn't a question of if you would rather be crucified or not. You will be crucified"* (178). However, if you accept being crucified with Christ, you can now focus on a new center which has been cleansed, and you can cultivate yourself around that surrendered self.[2] In this sermon Jones raises a series of paradoxes; I am dead, nevertheless I live, I am alive now and yet not I, but Christ lives in me and the life that I now live is with the Son of God. You are dead and then alive, you don't exist but then you do. You lose your life and it comes back to you. (180) Jones admits that this is a paradox that he cannot explain; he can only testify to that "experiential fact" (180):

> I only testify that his bondage is freedom, his imprisonment makes you walk the earth a conqueror. Bound to him – you walk the earth afraid of nothing.[2] You are his and his forever! Now you can accept that self – Christianity teaches self-love and teaches that the self is not to be canceled (179).

To illustrate *bondage as freedom*, Jones' refers to a passage from his book, *Christ and Human Suffering*, where he tells Tagore's story of the violin string:

> A violin string lies on the table. It is under no constraint. We might think that it is free. But is this mute thing free? Put the string in its place on the violin. It is bound. When set in motion it gives out dull sounds. But draw it tighter, tighter. Stretch it up to key. Let it be swept by Kreisler's bow. Now it is free. It sings (116-117).

---

2   His yoke is easy because his yoke is my yearning. When I surrender to him, it is the same surrender which paint makes when it surrenders to an artist: mere color becomes a living picture, and which ink makes when it surrenders to a writer (Jones, *A Song of Ascents*, 302).

Jones will say again and again, "Self-surrender is the only remedy. I cannot go down any road on anything with anybody who has problems without running straight into the necessity of self-surrender. All else is marginal, this is central. I only have one remedy, for I find only one disease – self at the center, self trying to be God" (Jones, *Victory Through Surrender*, 8):

> The unsurrendered self is the root. The unsurrendered self is the disease. Don't deal with the symptoms – go to the root, go to the unsurrendered self and say, you got me and I am surrendering now" (to Jesus) (185).

Jones concludes as he ends most of his sermons with a call to his audience to get on their knees and surrender their broken selves – not their problems but their selves. In so doing, they can take on a new life and affirm, *"The life I now live is not my life, but the life which Christ lives in me"* (181).

THE CENTER OF THE INCARNATION IS THE CROSS "SELF SURRENDER" (1961)

SERMON

I am going to read to you a passage from the 2nd Chapter of Galatians verses 20 and 21:

> *"I have been crucified with Christ; the life I now live is not my life, but the life which Christ lives in me; and my present bodily life is lived by faith in the Son of God, who loved me and sacrificed himself for me. I will not nullify the grace of God…"*

Recently a publisher of scientific/medical books said in the Open Heart something like this, "I don't know what to do with myself, I alternate between two views of myself. One…that the self is to be cultivated and the other that the self is a cancer. And I don't know whether to look on myself as something to

be cultivated or myself as a cancer that ought to be cut out."
This man is a highly intelligent man and was ultimately
converted. While he is highly intelligent and deeply changed
he didn't know what to do with this business of the self. He
alternated between believing that the self is something that
ought to be cultivated or something to be cut out. Now
obviously if he's that confused then a great many of us are
confused as to what attitude we should take toward ourselves.
The most important thing that we have is ourselves. The only
thing we have really, the only thing we will take out with us
into the next life. We won't take our houses, our lands, our
bank accounts, our cars, but we will take one thing out … our
selves. It is the only thing we will take out for it's the only
thing we've got. Many people are confused as to what attitude
they should take toward this — the most precious thing they've
got. However, some people don't like the possession that they
have – they don't like the self. One brilliant man said, "I
wouldn't want to live with myself forever." Evidently the self
that he lived with was not a nice self. One man said,
"Everywhere I go, I go too, and I spoil everything."[3] What is to
be done with this self?

Now in the verses read above, Paul says, "I do not nullify
the grace of God." Grace planned things out a glorious future
for him, as only grace could do. And then we come along and
cancel it out and nullify it. No, I don't want that; I want
something else. The biggest place of nullification is at the place
of the unsurrendered self. That nullifies the grace of God more
than anything I know, because it moves in and says, "I'm God.
I don't take the grace of God; I'm God, and I'm the center."
This self gathers attention, gathers loyalty, and gathers
everything to itself and tries to make itself God. That's the
supreme nullification of the grace of God. Now Sister Mary
talked this afternoon about the sacrifice and mentioned that
you only sing as you sacrifice.[4] And then she mentioned giving

---

3   Samuel Hoffenstein from his book of poetry titled Pencil in the Air.

up this, and this, and this, and this, and almost all were some precious, prized possessions. She cleared the way for me to talk about the supreme letting go, letting go of the center — the self.

Now the differing theories of the self speak about what should be done to the self and they come up with different answers. On the whole, India is personality weary and world-weary. They are tired of this weary round of coming back, birth after birth, after birth, after birth … re-birth. And so they want to get out of the world and get out of the burden of the self.

We learn that Buddha sat under the Bodhi tree and pondered long and deep on the problems of suffering and pain and came to the conclusion that existence and suffering are one. As long as you are in existence, you are in suffering. You will be in existence as long as you are in action, for it is action that makes the wheel of existence turn around. The wheel of existence is one of re-birth. The only way to get rid of action is to get rid of desire, for it is desire that brings forth action. If you cut the root of desire — even for life — and become a desire-less person then action will stop which will stop the wheel of existence turning round which will allow you to go out into that actionless, passionless state called Nirvana. Nirvana is literally the state of a snuffed out candle. If it isn't the end of being, it is certainly the end of becoming.

I asked a Buddhist monk in Ceylon, "Is there any existence in Nirvana?" He said, "There is no suffering how can there be any existence?" So Buddha would get rid of the problems of life by getting rid of life. He would get rid of our headaches by getting rid of our heads. Buddhism is weary of this thing called personality and proposed to snuff it out like a snuffed candle. Hinduism does much the same, it says that we should merge

---

4   Mary Webster met E. Stanley Jones in 1950 at an Evangelistic meeting and was later trained as a Lay Evangelist and often accompanied Brother Stanley along with others as a part time secretary. She was a powerful witness for Christ and a delightful and engaging speaker.

our personality into the impersonal. So the practicing Hindu sits with his attention concentrated upon the point of his nose dreaming himself out into that actionless, passionless essence called Nirvana. Just as a drop of water is lost in the ocean, so the separate individual personalities are lost in the sea of existence. You are gone. The impersonal is all. And in the Bhakti cults[5], Bhakti means devotion, they try to merge themselves into the image of the divine, the one whom they obey.

A man came to one of our Ashrams at Sat Tal. I said, "where did you come from?"

He said, "Ram, Ram." Ram is one of the names of their Gods.

I said, "Where are you going to?"

He said, "Ram, Ram."

I said, "what do you want?"

He said, "Ram, Ram."

I said, "What is your name?"

He said, "Ram, Ram." His answer to everything that I asked him was "Ram, Ram." He had merged himself into the object of his devotion. He apparently didn't want to be himself any longer.

Now, you come to the modern day and you find the reverse of that, the reverse of not wanting to know yourself. Psychiatry, modern psychiatry, says three things; first, *know yourself;* second,

5   Bhakti (loving devotion) or Bhakti School, adoration of a particular god, a cult that became a presiding force in medieval times. Unlike Buddhism and Jainism where there is no place for the Supreme Being (God), the Bhakti School, and other religious teachers taught differently: They preached loving devotion to a personal God. The Bhakti cult of early Vedic times worshipped Varuna, the sovereign god of the Vedic phase of Hindu mythology. Later, the worship of Vishnu and Shiva was included. One of the leading exponents of the Bhakti School was the 16th century Mewar Princess MIRA BAI, who wrote exquisite love songs to Lord KRISHNA. <http://www.mewarindia.com/ency/bhai.html>

accept yourself; and third, *express yourself.* What's missing there? Something that is vital and very important from the Christian standpoint is missing.

First, *know yourself.* Psychiatry thought that if you just know yourself then you could cure yourself of all your ills. If you could have insight into yourself, then that insight would cure you. Now, cure by insight has just about had its day. It's made its contribution. It helps you marginally here and there. However, our psychiatric institutions are filled with people who have insight into what's the matter with them, but they are still hospitalized. Why? The question is deeper and insight doesn't necessarily cure you.

Second, *accept yourself.* A psychiatrist says, you just need to accept yourself. However, how can you accept an unacceptable self? A self full of conflicts, full of everything that is wrong and you are asked to accept yourself. How can you? You cannot accept the unacceptable.

And third, *express yourself.* Now if you get a dozen people in one place, all of whom want to express themselves, then you have the stage set for clash and confusion and jealousy and anger and strife. For instance, we have in our churches classes for training members in leadership skills. We say to our young people, "go out and become leaders." You get a dozen people together all of whom want to be leaders, then what? I said that in a meeting one day and a Baptist minister spoke up after I said, "what have you got?" He said, "You've got a Baptist church." He might have said it about any other denomination. When you are in the mission field you have young people who have been trained to be leaders and you put them in one mission station, say a dozen of them. They act as leaders and imply, "I'm a leader; fall in behind me." You have self assertion and these leaders express themselves. These are not leaders but rather fussy managers of other people. These are not leaders.

I look to see what is missing here. The missing thing is what Christians would introduce. Their emphasis is a terribly radical concept that cuts across many of our modern emphases. The Christian would say, "Yes, know yourself, but he would add, surrender yourself." Then you can accept yourself and then you can express yourself. Why? Because as Paul says, "I have been crucified with Christ." The Christian then has the most radical attitude toward the self. It says to *surrender the self*, not to cultivate it. If you try to cultivate an unsurrendered self, then you have to sit on the lid all the time. That unsurrendered self just won't be cultivated and then it begins to explode.

However, if you change the center and surrender yourself to Christ and focus on that new center, then around that new center you can cultivate the surrendered self. But only when Christ has got it (that self) and it is no longer trying to be God but is surrendered to God. Now the last thing in the world that we ever give up is ourselves. We give up here, here, here and here. Many a man who goes into the ministry gives up everything to be a minister except the minister. Many a missionary goes out across the seas and gives up everything to be a missionary — everything except the missionary. The self is still there, watchful of its position, place and power.

I was talking to a missionary about to be sent home from the Congo. I said to her, "As you look at yourself, what do you think is your trouble?"

She said, "I am sitting on a lid."

I said, "What's under the lid?"

She said, "Two people: one who doesn't want to be a missionary and the other who is afraid that if she isn't the missionary she will be lost."

I said, "You don't want to be either one of those people, do you?" You see neither one had surrendered itself.

Peter said, "Lord we have left everything to follow thee what do we get?"[6] The fact that he asked "what do we get" showed he hadn't left everything. He had left his fishing boats, father, mother, brothers and sisters, occupation — everything except the self. What do we get? Jesus said, "if any man would come after me let him leave father, mother, brother, sisters, houses and lands – yea and his own self also."[7] Why did He put that last? "Yea and his own self also…" Because that is the last thing we ever give up — houses and lands, and occupation, mother, father, brother, sister, everything goes. But the un-surrendered self is the last thing we ever give up. And we are constantly tripping over that un-surrendered self.

A man was converted in one of our meetings. He was a cancer research doctor and he was tremendously excited over this business of being a Christian. He had given himself to Christ. He said, "You know I am going into the biggest mission field in the world." He said, "I am going to go back to try to convert the greatest pagans of the world."

I said, "Who are they?"

He said, "Cancer cells for cancer cells are cells turned selfish; they won't contribute. They demand that everybody contribute to them. Rather than give themselves for the sake of the rest, they demand that the rest give them selves for the sake of the cancer so that cancer cells are cells turned selfish. And they eat their way through to their own death and the death of the organism that they feed on." He said, "I am going back to convert them if I can."

A self that is centered on itself is a cancerous self. It demands that the rest serve them; it is selfish and the only thing to be done is to surrender that self.

Christianity points an arrow straight at the heart of our problem — the un-surrendered self — and it says let go of the one thing you've got. But then you say anxiously "my self is

---

6   Mark 10:28.

7   Mark 10:29-30.

gone; the one thing that I own is gone." You may believe that you are afraid to do this and will be bereft of everything. It does look as though you will be bereft. You might think that "I haven't a thing now that I have emptied my hands of the one thing I own—myself. I have laid it at the feet of another. Am I canceled out?" It would seem so for a moment. For you come to your knees and you die. You literally die.

Paul said, "I'm crucified with Christ." Note there that he said, "with Christ." If you're not crucified with Christ voluntarily and with set purpose then you will be crucified on the cross of your own contradictions and your own conflicts. It isn't the question of *if* you would rather be crucified or not. You will be crucified. The question is *if* you will be crucified with Christ; you will have purpose in it, meaning in it, goal in it, resurrection in it and the future in it! Or, would you rather be crucified like the impenitent thief upon the cross—a crucifixion that has no meaning except deeper and deeper darkness. So we are all hanging on a cross—some with Christ, some on the cross of their own conflicts and their own inherent unhappiness. So don't think that you will escape the cross. But here is a cross—which when you take it—has life in it.

"I am crucified with Christ," and the old version says, "Never-the-less I live." Is the self canceled out? Oh no, no, no! When we surrender it to Him, He cleanses it of a thousand contradictions and hands our life back to us—never-the-less, I live. Now I live—to my fingertips—to the roots of my hair—I live! You lose your life; you find it again and now you can accept yourself because that self is under redemption. It is an acceptable self; it is not perfect but it is a good self for it is being redeemed. It is in the process of redemption. God has got a hold of your life. The account says, "He taketh hold of the seed of Abraham, the children of Abraham."[8] He takes hold and they are under the process of redemption. Now that is an acceptable self, and now I can accept that self because He accepts it. Now I can love it because He loves it. Now I can respect it

8   Hebrews 2:16-17.

178

because He respects it. In other words, when you obey the deepest law of the universe, you lose your life and you find it again.

It is a paradox. I can't explain it. But when you lose your life and find it, you are never so much your own as when you are most His. Belonging to Him, you belong to yourself. I don't argue this point. I only testify that His bondage is freedom; His imprisonment makes you walk the earth a conqueror. Bound to Him, you walk the earth afraid of nothing. You are His and His forever! Now you can accept that self. Christianity teaches self-love and teaches that the self is not to be canceled. There is a lovely song that we sing. It's a beautiful song but completely untrue. The last line of the first verse says, "all of self and none of thee." The next verse to the last line says, "some self and some of thee," and the last line says, "none of self and all of thee."[9] That none of self is just wrong. You can't get rid of yourself. You put yourself out of the door and it will come back in the window, probably dressed up in religious garments. It is the same old self.

They taught a dog to play dead, and it was an amazing performance. They'd say, "Rover you are dead." Rover would fall on the floor and stick out his legs stiff, open his jaws, eyes rolling, rolled up, practically stiff. Rover was the perfect picture of a dead dog except at the end of his tail, it was wagging, meaning—am I not playing the part very well? Am I not a wonderful dead dog? Well, in people who say they have no self that tail begins to wag. You can see the self; it sticks out. No, you've got a self and you can't get rid of it. It is a part of you; it's you and by no known means can you get rid of it!

However, when you give yourself to Jesus in full surrender, you can now love yourself because you love something more than yourself. You love Jesus more than yourself, therefore,

---

9 From the hymn "None of Self and All of Thee" by Theodore Monod and James McGranahan. < http://library.timelesstruths.org/music/None_of_Self_and_All_of_Thee/>

you can love yourself in Him. Out of Him, you cannot love yourself. You are not a lovable self. Out of Him, you can't respect yourself; you don't like yourself. Out of Him, you cannot accept yourself, because your self is not acceptable. But, in Him, you can accept yourself; you can love yourself. You can rather like yourself. You find that you are a rather decent self because it is under redemption. It was this today and you will get better all the time. You were this today. You are better tomorrow, better the second day and better the third day. You are on the way — on the way up, up, up. You are under the upward call of God in Christ. You can now accept that self and rather love it. You can say, "I don't care where it has come from. I only care where it is going." Christianity teaches self-love — you shall love thy neighbor as thy self. Not more, not less but as yourself, for if you don't love yourself, then you probably can't love your neighbor or anybody else. However now you can get along with yourself and you live with yourself and other people can live with you.

Rufus Mosley used to say, (and he had a wonderful self), "I like to talk to myself because I like to listen to an intelligent person talk." And if you had a self like his you would like to talk to it. (I don't blame some people for not talking to themselves...) You can accept yourself realistically. One woman said, "I ain't what I want to be and I ain't what I expect to be, but I certainly ain't what I was. I am on the way up!" So you *can* love yourself. And all that hypocrisy about not having a self is not true. I do have a self but I do know my limitations, and I know who has got me. And, if I step out of Him, I know what will happen to me.

One woman said, "If it were not for the Holy Spirit, Stanley Jones would be a mess." She was profoundly right. Everyone of us is a mess outside of Jesus, and inside of Jesus, every one of us is a message. You then have destiny, meaning, goal. You will be on the way and then you can express yourself. You say, "Yes, I am expressing myself because it a self that He has got. For I am expressing Him in my expressions." Listen to what this verse says… "*the life I now live is not my life, but the life which Christ lives in me.*" I am still there *and* He is living His life in me and through me and we are on a cooperative plan. I supply willingness and He supplies power and we get along wonderfully together. There is no hypocrisy. The self is still there. It is still there but as long as Jesus has that helm and He's Lord and the self is subservient, it is wonderful.

I was up in Alaska writing on a book between meetings and I had to write before a mirror because there was no other place to write. I don't usually write my books in front of a mirror but I stopped my writing and looked into the looking glass. And I saw myself and said, "Stanley Jones you are a very happy man aren't you?" I said, "Yes I am very [happy]." And I said, "How did you get this way?" I said, "I don't know. I walked across a field one day and I stubbed my toe and said, 'What is this is treasure?'" I ran off and sold everything I had and bought that field. I have been hugging myself ever since. All that self-loathing and self-rejection and self hate drops away. It is as bad to hate yourself as to hate somebody else. Self-hate is sin just as other hate is sin. Putting yourself in His hands is no longer hating yourself for He accepts you and you accept yourself. He forgives you and you forgive yourself. He respects you and you respect yourself. You have no illusions of grandeur. You say, "yes I can do things but through His grace I can accomplish things but only inside of Him. I step out of him and I am impotent and powerless." The life I now live is not my life, for I am never so alive as when I am fully His for the life which Christ lives in me.

A college president said to me some time ago, "Do you remember writing a letter twenty years ago to a young minister who said his father had disgraced the family name and he felt terribly inferior?" Strangely enough I did, even after twenty years. I remembered what I wrote to him. I wrote, "Do you remember the genealogy of Jesus? The genealogy of Jesus includes Solomon who was born of David by Bathsheba, Uriah's wife. Did that fact break Jesus because he had that disgrace back there? NO. Because Jesus was more conscious of this (other) heredity, which came from the Father." I told this college president, "You have a new heredity—from God your Father. You have a blood transfusion from the Son of God. It has been given to you now, and you now have that heredity which cancels your earth-bound heredity. You are not inferior if you're a child of God and you needn't despise yourself if you are a child of God."

He said, "You know when I got that letter it did something for me, and I said I am a child of God and not inferior. I am in His grace." He said, "You see what has happened? I am the president of this college now, and when you wrote that letter I had a sense of inferiority. I was beaten by my "bad" heredity because my father disgraced our family name. Christ lives in me and if Christ lives in me I am respectable."

Why would you believe that you are inferior if you are a child of God? Put your shoulders back and march on unafraid. Realize that your *present bodily life* is lived by faith in the Son of God because this is not the word became word—it is the word became flesh. Then you don't despise your body any longer.

Do you remember what St. Francis used to call his body? Brother Ass.[10] When he was about to die, he turned to his body and said, "Brother Ass, I haven't treated you very well have I? I have been hard on you." We need to each accept our body and talk to it nicely. It is amazing what the body will do if you talk to it nicely. It will do wonderful things for you.

---

10 St. Francis of Assisi was said to have received the stigmata, painful wounds like those of Jesus Christ. He is said to have asked pardon to his body, which he called Brother Ass, for the severe self-afflicted penances he had done: vigils, fasts, frequent flagellations and the use of a hairshirt. < The Columbia Encyclopedia 6th ed., s.v."Francis, Saint" [database online]; available from Questia, http://www.questia.com/PM.qst?a=o&d =101244860; Internet; accessed 30 March 2007.>

When I was in Cairo and about to climb the Pyramids there was a pastor, a very eloquent man, who would only think about his own health and had his finger on his pulse all the time to see if something was the matter with him—and there always was. I said to him one day, "I am going over to climb the pyramids."

He looked at me and said, "Can your heart and your arteries stand it?"

I said, "I have not asked them and I don't intend to." I knew what my heart and my arteries would say, "Oh go ahead, Stanley, we'll stand with you. Sometimes you are a fool but you're a blessed fool. Go on."

Who loved me? Who loved me? And if He loved me, I can love myself too. I can love myself for loving Him. I can say, "You are a sensible man. You have put your faith in the central place in the Son of God. You are wise in that you chose the highest. You have done the only sensible thing that was ever done when you laid yourself at His feet and said, here I am. Take me as I am and make me over." He gave Himself for me and sacrificed Himself for me. The cross puts value in me. If I were the only person in the world, would Jesus come to die for me? Knowing Him as I do, I think He would say, "Yes, he's worth it." I love Him and I will give myself for Him. Doesn't that put dignity into your self? Of course it does! For you are a child of the heavenly Father, and you are on the way to be made into His likeness from one degree of glory to another. Now, have we surrendered ourselves? Has the self has gone up into that sacred flame and died as God—to live now as the Son of God—no longer itself but belonging to Him? Have you surrendered that one thing?

In the Midwest a pastor told me this story. He said, "I was very bitter and resentful against the Bishop and the Superintendent. I felt that they weren't giving me appointments big enough for me, and I was bitter and resentful. So

183

one day I said to one of my parishioners, "The Bishop and the cabinet are crucifying me; I am hanging on the cross."

And the parishioner, a very wise person, said, "Yes pastor you are hanging on the cross but you have never died. You are still wriggling with resentments."

He [the Pastor] said, "That is exactly what I needed. And I went off to my knees and I died. I died to the little man that I was — resentful, bitter, jealous, and envious. Out of the ashes of that hour came a new man — God's man — wanting nothing — afraid of nothing." He continued, "Two hundred and eighty-five people were converted in my church that year — a church which I thought was too small for me. I was really too small for it." And he said, "There hasn't been a Sunday since then that somebody hasn't come to God."

He died and was born again. I hope that there will be a lot of "graves" on this hillside where a man can point and say, this is where I died, and I put a "no resurrection" sign over it. There is no resurrection for that self. It has died.

A man came up to me one day and said, "Do you know me?" I have more difficulty with the truth at that place, more than any other place that I know. I meet a lot of people in my time and I hate to say that I don't know you. The nearest to truth I could come was this, "Well I do and I don't." It was something about him that I knew but I didn't really know him.

He said, "I am the man that came to see you in that hotel in Oklahoma."

I said, "You are not that man."

He said, "Yes, I am."

I said, "But you are different."

He said, "of course I am different."

I remember how he came into the room in the hotel and without any preliminaries threw himself down in the chair and said, "I'm trying to live a Christian life, but I'm having a terrible time of it. I said, "What's the matter?"

But he said, "I don't know but I say to myself, I'll give up this and I'll give up that and I'll compromise here and there, but please let me stay at the center."

Well, I said, "My brother that is very simple then, isn't it? That's why you're having a terrible time of it. You're God. But you're not God; God's God. And things don't add up when you're God. You have to surrender yourself to God and make him God. You've got to lose your life and it'll come back to you again. Will you'll do it?"

He said, "Is that what I've got to do?"

I said, "Yes, you've got to get yourself off your own hands and into the hands of God." We knelt and prayed.

And he simply said, "God please take me over and, oh God, make me over just as I am." And he turned that self-centered, festering self over to God and said, "Take me as I am" and He did. He shook my hand and went away. I didn't see him again until this occasion. And on that occasion his wife came to me and she said, "Thank you for giving my husband back to me." I said, "I didn't give him back to you. He gave himself to God and then God gave him back to himself and then to you and everybody else."

A woman said to me, "It is very comfortable to get yourself off your own hands." It is comfortable because that is where we belong—in His hands. He is the creator and the re- creator of that recalcitrant self and the redeemer. But, He does not cancel it; He cleanses it and then hands it back to us again. Now just as my fingers are rooted in the palm of my hands, all the sins that we deal with are rooted in the un-surrendered self. Why do we lie? Because the self thinks it will get the advantage. Why are we envious and jealous? Because the self doesn't want anybody to get ahead of it. Why are we bad tempered? Because of the un-surrendered self. Why are we

185

impure? Because the self thinks it will get some enjoyment. Why are we gloomy? Because the self is pouting. These things are the fruit; the un-surrendered self is the root. These are symptoms. The un-surrendered self is the disease. Don't deal with the symptoms. Go to the root. Go to the un-surrendered self and say, "You've got me I am surrendering now."

Jesus said you can't spoil a man's goods unless you bind the strong man then you can spoil his goods.[11] Who is that strong man? It is the un-surrendered self here. Then you can spoil his goods; the root of our difficulties is the un-surrendered self.

A man wrote me the other day saying, "you wrote about my daughter in one of your books. I want to tell you that she died a few weeks ago a lovely, lovely girl and we are grateful for what you said about her." She was in one of our first Ashrams in Blue Ridge and she went out on a mountain side over a rustic bridge under which a stream was flowing, a mountain stream. There she made her decision for Christ. She picked up a chip of wood and threw it into the stream and she said, 'there goes my pride' and watched it float away. She picked up another chip and threw it in and said, 'there goes my fear' and watched it float away. She picked a third and said, 'there goes my resentment' and watched it float away. Then she picked up the real one—she knew this was it—and she threw it in and she said, 'there goes my self' and watched it float away. That girl came back to the Ashram on wings. "Oh," she said, "it has gone." But had it gone? It came back again, radiant, beautiful, effective, lovable and creative. That self wasn't canceled; it was cleansed. It was now consecrated and fruitful for it was now wholly His and in Christ's hands.

Now I believe we would like to close this meeting on our knees wouldn't we? I believe we would. I was going to get us some blankets for us to kneel on, but why should we have blankets? Boards are befitting aren't they? Hard boards—very

---

11 Matthew 12:29.

befitting. Shouldn't we kneel right on hard boards and surrender ourselves to Jesus? There were no cushions at the cross; there were nails.

We are going to close this meeting, I don't know what you feel and you may ask, "Is this done once and for all or do you have to do it daily?" It is both. You give yourself once and for *all*. But there are little "alls" that you have to surrender daily. I believe I gave Him my all, but I find a lot of little alls I have got to let Him have. Whether it is the once and for all — the big all that you have to surrender — or for these little alls, I don't know but I think you would like to end this meeting on yours knees, wouldn't you? Would you like to come then? Those who want to surrender themselves, would you come and meet me here at this place of prayer and we will have a prayer together and close the meeting on our knees. Will you come?

187

6. THE WAY TO LIVE IS BY GRACE AND RECEPTIVITY

COMMENTARY ON

"HOW ARE WE TO BE CHANGED?"

THE text for "How Are We to be Changed?" is from 2 Corinthians 3:18:"*And all of us, with unveiled faces, seeing the glory of the Lord as though reflected in a mirror, are being transformed into the same image from one degree of glory to another; for this comes from the Lord, the Spirit.*" This text refers to the idea that those who believe in Christ will become increasingly transformed into his image. Therefore, salvation involves increasing conformity with Christ. (*Oxford Bible Commentary*, 1138).

This is a very practical sermon. It tells us the "how" of conversion. The title emerged from a comment that Jones heard from a man who came up to him at the close of a luncheon address. This attorney grabbed his hand and said, "Man, how?" (Jones, *The Way*, viii) Jones will answer that question in this sermon. The focus of the homily assumes that the listeners believe that Christianity is true, but don't really know how to gain an *experience* of Christ in their lives. The sermon answers the questions, "How do you get converted? How do we change?" Jones spells it out for us.

According to Jones, as we prepare for conversion, it will matter on *what* we focus our attention. We need to center our attention on the right place, and that is on Jesus. If we concentrate on something else, say ourselves, or evil, we become like that at what we habitually gaze. We become self-centered when we pay attention to ourselves and sinful when we pay attention to evil. When our attention is focused on God, this is called "the stage of drawing near to God."

We also need to pay attention to *where* we focus our attention. If we center our attention on the past, we can be drawn back into past mistakes or errors. When you look back, according to Jones, you go back! Jones tells his listeners not to pay attention to the sins and failures of others. Jesus repeatedly uses this phrase; *"What is it to thee? follow thou me"* (John 21:22-23) and Jones inserts it frequently in this sermon. No matter what distracts us or inconsequential event engages our attention, we are to ignore all interruptions and follow Jesus. Jones tell us that instead of looking to your past or looking at the failures of others, place your eyes on Christ. *"Place your eyes on Jesus, the Lord. There you have a place where you can let your whole weight down on something that is absolutely trustable."* Even if things are going wrong all around you, be assured that *in Christ* you have something that is trustable and something that you can count on.

If we really want to be converted, we need to be honest with ourselves and with God. We need to see Jesus "with an unveiled face." We need to take off our masks of deceit and dishonesty. There must be nothing between you and God when you make your full surrender. God is not intending to take us over but to make us over. According to Jones, God's will has your highest interest in mind: *"The will of God is your highest interest in every single situation there is. God could not will anything except your highest interest."* Jones reassures his audience that self surrender is nothing to fear:

> I surrender to the glory of the Lord. Then what happens? It says, "We are changed into his likeness." You don't have to change yourself. You become like that at which you gaze — with unveiled face. It is effortless. A flower gazes at the sun and unfolds with the very touch of the sun, and so if you look into the face of Jesus, you are being changed into

190

that same image. How do you become like him, by struggling and trying? No, but by just looking at him and offering an inner surrender (202).

According to Jones, if you can state with conviction "*Jesus is Lord*," you are on your way to conversion! Early Christianity reduced all religion to these three words. Jones is convinced that the simplicity in this three word statement conveys its truth. He tells us that all great discoveries are a reduction from complexity to simplicity, and the verse, "Jesus is Lord," is the greatest example!

As you draw near to conversion, you may find yourself, according to Jones, a bit upset. You may think that you are not worthy and may experience an emotional crisis. (Jones, *Conversion*, 197) You need to remind yourself that Jesus has not come to call the righteous but sinners. God offers us salvation He does not demand it, but God is seeking us. This should reassure you.

The next stage is when you inwardly decide to surrender yourself and implement your decision. You simply say, "I belong to Jesus." You have decided that the only thing that you own – *yourself* – belongs to another – to Jesus. Your conflicts and your crises have been resolved. You have taken a new direction in your life. (Jones, *Conversion*, 190).

Once you have surrendered yourself to Christ, you belong to Him, and "you are emboldened to take from Him forgiveness, grace, power, love, and everything" (Jones, *Conversion* 191). You have both a new spirit in your life and a new sphere of living. Jones asks, "Can we verify this promise that when you belong to Christ, all things belongs to you? How do we really know?" Jones reminds us of the specific Biblical promise in 1 Corinthians 3:21-23: "So let no one boast about human leaders. For all things are yours, whether Paul or Apollos or Cephas or the world or life or death or the present or the future – all belong to you, and you belong to Christ and Christ belongs to God." Jones notes that there are thirty-three

LIVING UPON THE WAY

thousand promises in the Bible that assure us of God's constancy (Jones, *Conversion*, 192). We have much to reassure ourselves.

According to Jones, Christian conversion is unlike any other religious transformation for it is a type all its own: "In Christian conversion you are given a new nature, hence a new name; a new desire, hence a new direction; a new sphere of living, hence a new quality of living We become new creations...and all of our human urges, instincts, and behaviors have become new and transformed" (Jones, *Conversion*, 42).

When you confess Jesus is Lord, you are *bound* to him, for the first thing in life, according to Jones, is not freedom but bondage. This may sound counter intuitive, but it is true: *"We need to find out what to obey and where to bend the knee."* When we are "bound" to Christ, we are most free. True freedom comes out of belonging. Christianity, according to Jones, is attuned to what the psychologists tell us are the three elemental needs of humanity — to belong, to have significance, and to have reasonable security (200). Jones believes that belonging to Jesus is true belonging and that it provides us with significance, certainty, and security for it means that we belong to the Son of God.

Jones concludes this sermon with an invitation for all who are in attendance to come forward and give themselves to Christ. His closing call reminds his audience that conversion comes from the Lord and is freely available to all. If Paul could put his arms around the Corinthians, who were thought to be the most depraved in a depraved world, in his invitation, then all are invited. If the Corinthians can "get in," then you can too!

THE WAY TO LIVE IS BY GRACE AND RECEPTIVITY
"HOW ARE WE TO BE CHANGED?" (1954)

SERMON

And all of us, with unveiled faces, seeing the glory of the Lord as though reflected in a mirror, are being transformed into the same image from one degree of glory to another; for this comes from the Lord, the Spirit. (2 Cor: 3:18)

HOW? That is the thing that people want to know. They are more or less convinced that it (Christianity) is true, but how do you get it? A woman who had only been a Christian for a few years sat in the dining car of a train. It was late and she could not find a place to sit in the coach, so she went to the dining car. She sat down next to a man who offered her a cigarette. She said, "No thank you, don't need it."

He offered her a drink. Again she said, "No thank you, I don't need it."

He responded, "What do you mean, you don't need it?"

"Well," she said, "I don't need it, I have something better."

He asked her, "Where have you been?"

She responded, "Chicago."

"What were you doing there?"

"Speaking."

"On what?"

"On Religion."

And with he and his seat mates covered their glasses with their papers.

She said, "You need not do that. It (alcohol) has nothing to do with what I am talking about."

"All right" they said, "go ahead and talk to us about what you have."

And she began. For two and one half hours the whole dining car was gathered around her listening, including the waiter and no one ordered a drink. One man said to her, "Where did you get this?"

She replied, "At the foot of the cross."

"How did you get to the foot of the cross?"

"At the end of my rope."

Then for two and one half hours, the whole dining car listened to this young woman describe the "how" of Christianity. That is what people want to know.

My text is this, "And all of us, with unveiled faces, seeing the glory of the Lord as though reflected in a mirror, are being transformed into the same image from one degree of glory to another; for this comes from the Lord, the Spirit."[1]

Now in being changed you have to place the focus of your attention at the right place. For whatever gets your attention, gets you. You become like that at whom you habitually gaze, so getting your eyes on the right place is everything.

I was speaking in Dr. Weatherhead's[2] church at City Temple, London and he said to me, "Will you say something to my elders that might encourage them? I have just preached for ten weeks on how to avoid a nervous breakdown and I ended

---

1   2 Corinthians 3:18.

2   Leslie Dixon Weatherhead (1893-1976) was an EnglishChristian theologian in the liberal Protestant tradition. Renowned as one of Britain's finest preachers in his day, Weatherhead achieved notoriety for his preaching ministry at City Temple in London and for his books, including The Will of God and The Christian Agnostic. < D. W. Bebbington,

up with one and my elders are upset." Now Weatherhead is a good psychologist and a great preacher but I think that he missed his psychological step. If you concentrate for ten weeks on how to avoid a nervous breakdown, you will probably end up having one. He had his attention concentrated on a nervous breakdown and whatever gets you attention gets you. He should have turned to the positive side and talked about how to live victoriously. If he had done so, the victory side of life would have had his attention.

I saw an announcement in the paper that a certain preacher was going to preach for eight weeks on the devil. If you concentrate for eight weeks on the devil, at the end, the devil will probably have you!

A man in Florida announced the topic for his Sunday evening service, "The Mistakes of Stanley Jones." If he had come to me, I could have told him a lot of mistakes he didn't know anything about for I knew many more than he would ever know. The next day I saw him in the Preachers' meeting which I was addressing. I came up to him and I asked him, "I saw where you preached on my mistakes last night. How many of your audience were converted while you were preaching on the mistakes of Stanley Jones?" He looked a little confused. I said, "While you were preaching on my mistakes, I was preaching on the wonder of Jesus and we had twenty-five people converted. How many did you get?" He said, "Well, I have to fight the devil." I said, "My brother, be careful when you fight the devil. Take care that he does not invade you." This preacher looked at the mistakes of other people and lived on them. That is a poor diet. For when you are denouncing others you are not announcing, and when you are on the prosecutor's stand, you are not on the witness stand. Whatever gets your attention gets you!

Evangelicalism in Modern Britain: A History from the 1730s to the 1980s [book on-line] (London: Routledge, 1993, accessed 31 March 2007), v; available from Questia, http://www.questia.com/PM.qst?a=o&d =109064142; Internet.>

Now, where are we to fasten our attention? Some people fasten their attention on their past mistakes. They say, "Look what I have done." They are gripped and held captive by their own failures and mistakes. That is a mistake. Don't look back, for if you look back, you go back.

Others fashion their attention on the sins and failures of other people. Peter said to Jesus one day, speaking about John, "Lord, and what should this man do?" And Jesus said to him, "What is that to thee? Follow thou me."[3] But there are people who stay outside of the church and outside of Christ because they see some weakness in some disciple of Jesus and they live on that weakness. Yet Jesus is saying, "What is that to thee? Follow thou me."

General Feng,[4] the great Christian general in China was at one time a marvelous Christian. He led a bible class every morning attended by six hundred officers – every man with his bible. But then the General became bitter and resentful and slipped away from Christianity. I saw him at that time. He began to berate General Chiang Kai-shek[5] and other Chinese Christian leaders. I said to him, "Marshall Feng, I am afraid that I must quote a passage of scripture to you." Peter said to

---

3   John 21.22-23.

4   General Feng Yü-hsiang (1882–1948), held various military positions under the Ch'ing dynasty. Feng's conversion to Methodism in 1914 gained him the sobriquet the Christian General. From 1920 to 1926 he struggled with Wu P'ei-fu and Chang Tso-lin for the control of N China and Manchuria. He then threw his support to the Nationalists, and he became minister of war and vice chairman of the Executive Yüan at Nanjing in 1928. By 1930 he had broken with Chiang Kai-shek and had launched an unsuccessful military campaign against him. From 1931 he held office in the Nationalist government, but he never again wielded power. In 1947, while in the United States on an official mission, he denounced the government of Chiang Kai-shek. <The Columbia Encyclopedia 6th ed., s.v."Feng YÜ-Hsiang" [database on-line]; available from Questia, http://www.questia.com/PM.qst?a=o&d=101243857; Internet; accessed 30 March 2007.>

Jesus one day, speaking about John, "Lord, and what should this man do?" And Jesus said to him, "What is that to thee? Follow thou me."[6] The General looked at me quizzically and then went on and was more bitter than ever. I stopped him again and I said that I must quote this passage of scripture again. "What is that to thee? follow thou me." General Feng pounded his big fist and hit himself on his knee and said, "Good, you've got my attention."

You cannot live on somebody else's mistakes. And, if you place your eyes upon the hypocrites of the church, you will become one. People tell me that there are hypocrites in the church and I say, "Come on in brother, we can have one more!" You must not dwell on your resentments. One woman said that all she does during the Quiet Time[7] is chew on her resentments. Some focus on resentments, others focus on their fears, or some their negative attitude. They say, "I can't do this

---

5   Chiang Kai-shek (1887–1975) was a Chinese military and political leader who assumed the leadership of the Kuomintang (KMT) after the 1925 death of Sun Yat-sen. He led the national government of the Republic of China from 1928 to 1975. Chiang Kai-shek served in the Imperial Japanese Army from 1909 to 1911. He commanded the Northern Expedition to unify China against the warlords and emerged victorious in 1928 as the overall leader of the Republic of China. Chiang led China in the Second Sino-Japanese War, during which Chiang's stature within China weakened but his international prominence grew. During the Chinese Civil War, Chiang attempted to eradicate the Chinese Communists, but ultimately failed, forcing his government to retreat to Taiwan, where he continued serving as the President of the Republic of China and Director-General of the KMT for the remainder of his life. < The Columbia Encyclopedia 6th ed., s.v."Chiang Kai-Shek" [database on-line]; available from Questia, http://www.questia.com/PM.qst?a=o&d=101237102; Internet; accessed 30 March 2007.>

6   John 21:22-23.

7   In the Ashram meetings, the quiet time is from 10 pm until after the morning devotions. In *A Song of Ascents,* Jones described this as a time of quiet listening where God speaks directly to us through the framing of words within the mind, without being audible.

or that and am afraid of this and that." When that happens, you then become negative.

Where are you then to place the focus of your eyes? The passage is clear as crystal. "Beholding the glory of the Lord."[8] Place your eyes on Jesus, the Lord. There you have a place where you can let your whole weight down on something that is absolutely trustable. When every thing else goes to pieces around you, you can say, "Here is one spot that will not let me down." Place your eyes on Christ. Don't look back or in or around. Look at Jesus. The center of the Christian faith is Christ. We don't begin with God or man; we begin with Jesus. If you begin with God, you don't begin with God; you begin with your ideas about God, and that is not God. You don't begin with man for, if you do, you will begin with the problems of man, and, if you begin with a problem, you will probably end with a problem and, in the meantime, will probably become a problem.

One modern minister said, "Without a problem spake he not unto them." We are a problem obsessed people and we are problems dealing with problems. I spoke to a group of social workers one day and said, "Aren't you cases dealing with cases?" They laughed as if to say, how did you know us?

We don't begin with God and we don't begin with man; we begin with the God-Man. Not our ideas of God, but God's idea of Himself—not a verbal word but a vital word. Jesus is God simplified. Someone asked some children what they thought of Jesus. One little boy said, "Jesus was the best photograph that God ever had took." Was he? Yes. Jesus is the express image of God's person. And if God in character is like Jesus, He is a good God and trustable.

Another child when asked about God said that "Jesus is the one who gave God a good reputation." Jesus is God's heart wrapped in flesh and blood and we see the heart of God through Jesus. We start with Jesus and it matters what kind of a Jesus

---

8   2 Corinthians 3:18.

we start with. Some start with a pallid and pale type of Jesus, a Jesus of ecclesiasticism. I was in a courtroom where they used to try cases in the Inquisition. On the judge's bench was a wooden figure of Christ and, whenever the ecclesiastical judge would announce a sentence against any heretic, the head of Jesus would nod in affirmation. However, underneath the bench was a cord which the judge pulled and the head of Jesus nodded at the pull of the string of the Judge. That was a Jesus taken captive by ecclesiasticism. That is not the Jesus that I am talking about.

I said to you on several occasions that the earliest Christian creed was three words, "Jesus is Lord." "If thou will confess with thy mouth that Jesus is Lord, thou shall be saved."[9] "No man can say Jesus is Lord except by the Holy Spirit."[10] In both cases those words are in quotation marks showing that they were used as an early Christian creed. The Christians had reduced their religion into three words. *Jesus is Lord* — not will be but is Lord now! Jesus sits at the right hand of final authority and final absolute authority. Whoever has the first word will have the last word in all human affairs. He is on the throne. He is Lord. That was important. So the early Christians reduced all religion to three words.

They tell me that all great discoveries are a reduction from complexity to simplicity. The false hypothesis is always very complex. The truth is always simple. If you tell lies, you have to have a very good memory to remember what you said and the more lies you tell the better memory you must have. A woman sat at a missionary's table in Japan and said, "Well, suppose I tell them this and that." The missionary responded, "Why not tell them the truth?" and she said, "Why, that's an idea. I had not thought of that." She tried to build up a false world and it would not hold together. Of all the reductions

9   Romans 10:9.

10   1 Corinthians 12:3.

from complexity to simplicity, this is the greatest—these three words—Jesus is Lord!

I read an article today that said the greatest thing in life is *freedom*. I believe in freedom for everybody everywhere for I am bound in every man's bondage and I am free in every man's freedom. However, the first thing in life is not freedom, the first thing in life is bondage. We need to find out what to obey and where to bend the knee. If you make freedom — your personal freedom the first thing in life, the most important thing in life — it will be a freedom to tie yourself in knots. You will have the freedom to become a problem to yourself and others. Rather the first thing humans need to find out is what to obey.

The psychologists tell us that there are three needs in human nature; the first to belong; the second to have significance; and the third to have reasonable security.[11] The first need is the need to belong. We need to belong to something (meaningful or significant), to someone that we can honor and obey. My freedom comes out of that belonging. The aviator is free to fly as long as he obeys the laws of aviation and I am free to live as long as I obey (the laws of God). The first thing to do is to find the Lord. Place your eyes on Jesus—not Jesus as a nice teacher and a beautiful doer—but the Jesus who is Lord. Put your eyes on that kind of Jesus, and if you do anything can happen. Put your eyes on Jesus. Cease looking at yourself. Cease looking around at others or your past failure. Put your eyes on Jesus as

---

11 B. R. Hergenhahn, *An Introduction to the History of Psychology, Third Edition* (Pacific Grove: California, 1997) 522-7. The reference is from Maslow's Hiearchy of Needs. The theory contends that as humans meet 'basic needs', they seek to satisfy successively 'higher needs' that occupy a set hierarchy. Maslow's hierarchy of needs is often depicted as a pyramid consisting of five levels: physiological, safety, love/belonging, esteem, self actualization. The basic concept is that the higher needs in this hierarchy only come into focus once all the needs that are lower down in the pyramid are mainly or entirely satisfied. The three needs mentioned here fit into love/belonging, esteem, and physiological.

Lord and things begin to happen thick and fast. Wonderful things happen—transforming things.

But you have to not merely see Jesus and see Jesus as Lord; you have to see Him with *unveiled face* — that is you must take off your mask. You have to take off the mask. Stop being dishonest with yourself and others and God. Turn real; come clean with God. Your first step is complete honesty. Pull down your veils. Cease that play acting – that making of yourself what you are not and come clean with God. Say to God, "Here I am as I am; I am taking down my veils." Are you prepared to do that?

The Oxford Group has four absolutes: absolute honesty; absolute purity; absolute unselfishness; and absolute love.[12] They are quite correct in saying that the first absolute is absolute honesty. You have to be honest with yourself and God or you don't get anywhere. What are some of the other veils that we need to take down? They are fears, resentments, denominational pride and self-centeredness. Stand before Jesus as you are. Say, "Here I am; I take down all my veils." There must be nothing between you and Him. You must make a full surrender. There are a great many people who are afraid of a full surrender. I was talking to a woman one day who was a bundle of misery. I said, "My sister, surrender your will to God." She looked at me frightened, and said, "If I did that I would be at God's mercy." She thought that God was looking

---

12 The Oxford Group was a Christian organization founded by American Christian missionary Dr. Frank Buchman. The group promoted a belief in divine guidance: one should wait for God to give direction in every aspect of life and surrender to that advice. Buchman's program emphasized acknowledgment of offenses against others, making restitution to those sinned against, and promoting the group to the public. The Oxford Group changed its name prior to WWII to Moral Re-Armament and believed that divine guidance would prevent WWII from breaking out. Moral Re-Armament would later change it's name to Initiatives of Change. Many of the principles espoused by the Oxford Group because the foundation for the "Steps" in the Alcoholics Anonymous movement. <http://www.britannica.com/eb/article-9057830/Oxford-movement>

for a chance to make her miserable. When it was her will against God's will that had landed her where she was in abundant misery. God's will is always your highest interest! The will of God is your highest interest in every single situation there is. God could not will anything except your highest interest.

The will of God says Jesus is my nourishment. I am nourished when I do the will of God. My poison is to place my will against God and ignore His will (for me). When I do that, I poison my happiness, my joy, my effectiveness — my everything. But God's will is my nourishment. It is the thing I am made for as the eye is made for light and when I do His will, I do my own deepest will.

Surrender then is getting life back to where it ought to be in the hands of God. He gave us life and now we turn it back and say to God, "It is yours." Then God says, "All right, you lose it and I will let you find it again and your life will come back to you cleansed of a thousand contradictions and sin." And now having lost your life you find it again. I am never so much my own as when I am most His. I am never so free as when I am bound to Him. I walk the earth a conqueror. I stand straight when I am low at His feet. With unveiled face I see that glory of the Lord. I surrender to the glory of the Lord. Then what happens? It says "we are changed into his likeness." You don't have to change yourself. You become like that at which you gaze with unveiled face. It is effortless. A flower gazes at the sun and unfolds with the very touch of the sun and so if you look into the face of Jesus you are being changed into that same image. How do you become like Him? By struggling and trying? No, but by just looking at Him and offering an inner surrender.

Do you know that when you surrender to Christ you are then being made in His likeness? If you are surrendered to Him you are being made in the likeness of the greatest thing this planet has ever seen — the face of Jesus Christ. To be made like Him makes everything else trivial — of no account. You are beginning a new type of personality. By gazing at the right person, you are being changed into that image.

A man wrote me some time ago and said, "I feel inferior. My father has disgraced the family and brought shame upon our name. I can't lift up my head and I am inferior." I wrote back to him and I said, "Well now look at the genealogy of Jesus and see what you find there. Note that Solomon was born of David by Uriah's wife."[13] I said that relationship was in the genealogy of Jesus but did that stop Jesus? No, Jesus created a new genealogy and gave man a blood transfusion from the Son of God. When you come to Jesus, you receive a blood transfusion of the Son of God. You are grafted into the Divine Nature. The man wrote back, "Your letter wiped out all inferiority and I didn't have to look back to my heredity and I looked up and I had a new heredity from God." Suppose that your ancestors have disappointed you and let you down. You can begin a new heredity with a blood transfusion from the Son of God or an engraftment from the Divine nature. When that happens, you are being made into that image. That is a high destiny.

Now how does conversion come about? Perhaps you have an initial upset. You come up to the moment of conversion but you hate like the dickens to change your life. You have got to reverse all your values and you have to say that I am wrong and that is not an easy thing to do, for an ego to say. It is difficult to say, "I am just wrong." It is upsetting and you are upset and that is why people are initially upset when they come to these meetings. We don't apologize for upsetting people. For the purpose is not to upset them but to set them up (for conversion). There is an initial upset in order for an eternal set up. You have to then make a decision and then comes what we call conversion. There is an experience of a rapid climb and then life is lived on a higher level. However, as you live life at that higher level, you find that it is still up and down. You experience

13 2 Samuel 12:24.

victory but then defeat and then you come to the necessity of finding a deeper cleansing and a deeper filling of the spirit. You can't go further until you go deeper. And then there is your full surrender to God and you receive the Holy Spirit. Life climbs again and is lived forever on a higher plateau!

Sometime ago I went through the Panama Canal. We ran into a great lock. The gates were closed upon us and we seemed to be completely helpless. We could not go anywhere except up. We were shut in but as the great sluices were open down beneath and the great bubbling water filled the space, in just seven minutes our huge vessel rose thirty five feet. It felt effortless. We sailed on at a new level for a time. Then we went into another lock and again the gates were shut and again we felt helpless; we were shut in and helpless. We had to surrender to our experience. And then again, from beneath the boat, the bubbling water began to fill the lock and we rose thirty five more feet. We rose seventy feet in all. When we finished going through the locks, we went out onto Lake Gotham.

This is an analogous illustration of what happens in conversion. We are shut in with God. We can't go back; we can't go forward. We feel frustrated and all we can do is let go and let God and then His grace takes hold of us and lifts us up and up and up. And the thing that we strove to find, we find effortlessly. We are now up on a higher level. The gates are then opened and we go out on that new level. However, then we are shut in with God again. We can't go back. We can't go forward. Again, if you let go and let God you will be taken to a higher level. The bubbling from beneath will raise you up and then as the gates open you will find that you live life on a permanently higher level.

We are changed into the same image from one degree of glory to another. But you say, "Yes, that is very beautiful but I can't do it." You don't have to do it. The account says, "But this comes from the Lord, who is the spirit." That is strange. The Lord out there? Yes, on the throne. But it also says spirit, for the Lord's spirit moved in on the inside. He has chiseled you into the same image from within and all you have to do is surrender and accept His grace.

Conversion comes from the Lord, who is spirit. You could not do that. But God does it. You cooperate and the thing that seems impossible to you is now possible. You can walk up to your temptations and struggles and sins and everything and in His name conquer them. You may say, "That is all well and good but conversion is not for me because I am not one of the mystic types." I want to read to you again from Paul, "*And all of us, with unveiled faces, seeing the glory of the Lord as though reflected in a mirror, are being transformed into the same image from one degree of glory to another; for this comes from the Lord, the Spirit.*"[14] Paul writes that this experience is for *all of us.* Who are included in the word *all*? The Corinthians were included. Who were they? In that day the morality of Corinthians was very loose. The most derogatory thing that could be said of a person was that "He lives like a Corinthian." In a depraved world, the Corinthians were thought to be the worst. Paul put his arms around that group (the Corinthians) and said *all.* And Paul included that type of person. If they can get in, you and I can get in. Everyone can get in. And these are the steps.

We, with unveiled face, beholding the glory of the Lord, are being changed into the same image from one degree of glory to another. This comes from the Lord who is a spirit and when you surrender to him he takes you over and makes you over. That is the good news.

Now each night I have given you a chance to come and be changed. Many of you have come forward. Some of you ought to come here tonight. You are not yet a Christian. You have not yet made a decision. You have been on the edge of this thing called conversion, but you have never given yourself to Christ. I am going to give you an opportunity tonight just as somebody gave me an opportunity one night. I will never,

---

14   2 Corinthians 3:18.

never cease to be thankful that I had that opportunity and that I came forward and knelt. What somebody did for me, I am going to do for you. I am going to let you come forward and kneel.

The second group is for those of you who are in the churches. Many of you are in the churches. For you Christ has become a name—not a reality and your faith has grown stale. Your heart is ashes and there is no kindling fire within your heart. There is nothing contagious about your Christian experience. You are outwardly a Christian but inwardly the fires are nearly gone out and you are inwardly dead. I would like you to come too.

And then some of you who are inside the Churches, who say yes, "I am a Christian but I am afraid that I am not a full Christian. I do not witness; I want to make a full surrender to Christ. I want to be wholly His. I want to be one hundred percent a Christian or nothing."

I am going to give you an invitation that whatever is on your heart that you come and lay it at the feet of Christ. I believe that something will happen to you here tonight that will make life forever anew. I am going to dim the lights so that you can be alone with God as it were. And I am going to ask you who would like to come and meet me at this place of prayer to do so. I believe that you won't need any urging from me. I believe that the spirit of God is here and He is doing the urging and you are going to listen to His urging and to your own inner urges and I believe that you will come. We'll come and stay long enough to lay what is on our hearts at His feet and make a full surrender and let Him have us. And then we will come and go in prayer. We will make this whole place an altar of prayer tonight. I would not be ashamed to come; I would be ashamed not to come if I should come. If I am hungry, I am not ashamed to come to the table. If I am ignorant, I am not afraid to go to the library. And, if I need God, then I will seek Him. Come.

THE WAY TO LIVE IS BY GRACE AND RECEPTIVITY

COMMENTARY ON "TRANSFORMATION"

THIS sermon predates the publication of Jones' book, *How to Be a Transformed Person,* which includes this same story in more detail and extended over a series of daily devotional readings.[15] Jones typically developed ideas for a new book and then would flesh them out first in a series of sermons. After all the details had been worked out, he would then move to write the book on that particular topic or theme. This sermon and others are practical and describe the HOW by showing the WAY. According to Jones, Jesus was short on exhortation but long on exhibition. This sermon is an exhibition on the promise of *transformation.*

The Biblical context of this sermon is the story of Jacob's (whose name means the *supplanter*) struggle with the angel in Genesis 32.

That night he, Jacob, arose took his two wives, two maidservants and his eleven children and crossed the ford of the Jabbok. He took them and made them cross the stream along with all that he had.

Jacob was left alone and a man (Angel) struggled with him until the break of day, when the man found he could not master him, he struck the hollow of his thigh, so that Jacob's thigh was sprained in the wrestle. Then he said, "Let me go, for the day is breaking." "I will not," said Jacob, "unless you bless me." "What is your name?" said the man. "Jacob," he answered. "Then your name shall be called Jacob no longer," said the man, "but Israel (striver with God) for you have struggled with God and men and won." "Tell me what is your name," said Jacob. "Why ask my name?" He answered and

---

15 A more detailed version of this sermon can be found on pages 71-78 in *How To Be a Transformed Person* by E. Stanley Jones.

blessed him on the spot. Jacob called the spot "Peniel, (God's face)" saying "I have seen God face to face yet I am alive." The sun rose upon him as he passed Peniel.

This sermon, with its Hebrew bible text, pursues the theme of redemption in the transformation (*conversion*) of Jacob. Jones makes a point of this conversion story from the Hebrew Bible because Jacob's conversion would impact a whole nation – the children of Israel. Jacob *had* to undergo a personal transformation in order to assume his significant role in the life of the Hebrew people. His conversion could not be "handed down" – through extension, the result of his lineage from Abraham and Isaac. That would be a "second hand" conversion. According to Jones, there are no "conversion waivers" granted because of our parents, or grandparents, for God requires each of us to accomplish this task of self surrender. It is the job of each generation to be converted. Jones draws an analogy to the evangelical revivals that have occurred in the United States where vast groups were converted only to find the effect diluted in subsequent generations of Christians. Conversion is a solitary choice and act whose transformative benefits are not inherited.

We see that Jacob had a number of moral failings beginning with the tricking of his father and brother Esau for a birthright. While Jacob obtained the inheritance, he also secured the hatred of his brother. Jacob's behavior would result in a series of "expected" consequences for we live in a moral world where we get "results or consequences." "We reap what we sow – inevitably. There are no exceptions" (Jones, *How To Be A Transformed Person*, 73). As Jacob's story unfolds, we witness that, in spite of his self-centered and morally despicable behaviors, he is slowly moving toward transformation. God wants Jacob in spite of Jacob.

The story in Genesis 28 of Jacob's dream of a ladder going up to heaven illustrates, according to Jones, Jacob's "half conversion." When he awoke, Jacob affirmed that he would make God his God and offered Him one tenth of his resources.

208

As Jones sees it, Jacob essentially says, *"If God will be with me and will prosper me on my journey, then God will be my God and I will give Him a tenth of everything that he gives me." Jacob would tithe"* (216). According to Jones, this modest offer of wealth suggests that Jacob is surely not fully converted and that he would continue to sin with false "religiosity." Jacob is still Jacob! Jacob has surrendered ten percent of his assets, but not himself. Jacob remains duplicitous and becomes increasingly fearful that others will cheat him, which they indeed try to do. Jacob continues to receive the consequences for his immoral actions. Jacob may have wanted to escape the outcomes of his sins, but he did not want to escape the real sin — himself.

Jones believes that God – in spite of Jacob — was patiently waiting to transform this son of Israel. God delayed until Jacob was alone, anxious, and ready. Jones notes that these states are often the emotional precursors of conversion. Jacob's all night struggle with the angel is his conversion moment: "where like the Hound of Heaven, God pursued Jacob down through the years, awaiting this hour when he would acknowledge that he was beaten and would ask for a true blessing from God" *(How To Be A Transformed Person,* 75). Jacob would confess his name – "I am Jacob – the supplanter – the cheater; the one who takes advantage of others; who tricks them and takes their resources for my own benefit." This honest confession revealed the "soul-naked" man before God.

God then did bless Jacob and gave him a new name, Israel, (striver with God) which corresponded to his now changed character. According to Jones, the transformation of Jacob was so outstanding that it changed the life of a whole nation *(How To Be A Transformed Person,* 71). If God can even work with a trickster such as Jacob, then there is hope for the Jacobs of this world, and there is clearly hope for all of us. God does not care, according to Jones, where we have come from; rather he cares about where we are going. God forgives us our pasts, for he wants us to have a future, a future doing his work.

"So where does this all leave us?" Jones asks. "Who are we? What is our name? What is our character? What do we display before God? Is our name representative of negative internal emotions such as fear, resentment, anger, or guilt? Or is our name a damaging personal characterization such as thief, hypocrite, or scoundrel?"

> Some of us would say my name is ego; that's my name. I am a self-centered person. My name is resentment. My name is fear. My name is impurity. My name is hypocrite; I am two people. I long to whisper that into the ear of God. God says, 'All right, thank you. I have another name on my tongue. I'll give you my own new name for you – it would be the opposite of the others' (224).

When we tell God our real name, the real truth about our identity, God responds by giving us a new name, a name that defines our transformed character. The schemes and false selves we create for ourselves, as Jacob did, are not the way to live. The only way to live is by truth which is God's way. We have to surrender ourselves to God to really live, and we have to get ourselves off of our hands and into the hands of God. When we speak the truth – and tell God who we are and surrender to him —redemption sets in, and a new name is given to us out of God's love. Our names which have been fear-associated are now faith-committed. These new names imply a new transformed nature (Jones, *How To Be A Transformed Person* 76).

Jones believes that he will not need to persuade his listeners to be transformed. The facts about their lives will necessitate it: *"There is only one way to live and that is God's way. You can't live against God without living against yourself"* (225). We all know (and love) persons who are living with a sense of failure and futility, of defeat and disaster, of conflict and division, of fears and resentments. These persons, according to Jones, cry out for some sort of transformation. They have to get themselves off of their own hands and into the hands of God. God will convert them and give them new names, transforming their fear into faith:

You've got to get yourself off your own hands and into the hands of God. He that saves his life shall lose it. If anybody who has ever lost his life by saving it as Jacob did until he hit bottom. That lonely midnight hour was the zero hour for Jacob, when the self-centered way of life came to the end of the road, a dead end. The moment we say our name, redemption sets in. A new name is given and that's good news. You can be a transformed person, completely and utterly (226).

THE WAY TO LIVE IS BY GRACE AND RECEPTIVITY "TRANSFORMATION" (1950)

SERMON

I will read to you some verses from the 32nd Chapter of Genesis beginning with the 22nd verse (Moffatt's translation):

That night he, Jacob, arose took his two wives, two maidservants and his eleven children and crossed the ford of the Jabbok. He took them and made them cross the stream along with all that he had.

Jacob was left alone and a man struggled with him until the break of day. When the man found he could not master him, he struck the hollow of his thigh so that Jacob's thigh was sprained in the wrestle. Then he said, "Let me go, for the day is breaking." "I will not," said Jacob, "unless you bless me." "What is your name?" said the man. "Jacob," he answered. "Then your name shall be called Jacob no longer," said the man, "but Israel (striver with God) for you have struggled with God and men and won." "Tell me what is your name," said Jacob. "Why ask my name?" he answered and blessed him on the spot. Jacob called the spot "Peniel (God's face)" saying, "I have seen God face to face yet I am alive." The sun rose upon him as he passed Peniel.

I'm going to talk to you tonight about the transformation of Jacob. We have been talking in these night meetings about how to be a transformed person. And I want to pick out of the pages of the Old Testament a living illustration of transformation. Jacob desperately needed it. His crookedness was a byword. Jeremiah says in the ninth chapter "...for a brother will cheat like a Jacob."[16] How is that for a reputation to be passed on? And yet, the very next chapter says, "...for He whom formed the universe is Jacob's God."[17] I'm surprised at that. God calls himself the God of Isaac, and Abraham and Jacob.[18] I can understand how He can be the God of Abraham and Isaac, but Jacob? Maybe it means that He is the God of the crooked man made straight—the person transformed.

That word **Jacob** is full of redemption. It is the same with humanity. If Jacob can be made straight, then so can everybody. You remember in one place God is called, according to Moffatt's translation, "The God of Abraham - The Awe of Isaac," Awe with a capital A. Why the change? The God of Abraham – The Awe of Isaac. I suppose the reason was something like this: In Abraham, God was first-hand, living and vital—creative. Under the touch of God, Abraham went out and founded a great people, walked out of a great civilization not knowing where he was going to found a new nation.

However, when it came to Isaac, Isaac was one step removed from reality. He lived on a second-hand faith, on the afterglow of his father's faith. Still he lived in *awe* of his father's God. He was the awe of Isaac, but it (his faith) was fading, getting dimmer and that's dangerous.

Now we see what happens in the third generation. The fading out in Isaac resulted in moral crookedness and decay in Jacob. Jacob had no basis of morals except his own self-interest.

---

16 Jeremiah 9:4.

17 Jeremiah 10:16.

18 Exodus 3:14-15.

When God went, the moral universe went and Jacob became god — a man who looked after number one, a completely self-centered man. That is very dangerous.

In America we've gone through in many ways the same three stages. When the evangelical revival[19] swept across our country it left a deposit of changed characters. With all its faults it converted men. Then came the second generation; that second generation kept up the contacts with their father's God. They lived in *awe* of their fathers' God and kept up the contacts with the churches. Many of them held official positions, but it was dimmer. They were living in an afterglow of their fathers' faith. It (their faith) was one step removed from reality – dim. Now we have come to the third generation and we're getting the results of that in moral decay. For when God goes, your moral

---

19 It's unclear which revival movement Jones is referring to here. There are thought to be six great revivals. First Great Awakening (1727) included influential figures such as Jonathan Edwards, George Whitefield and John Wesley. The Second Great Awakening (1801) in the United States involved a series of camp meetings, the best known occurring in Cane Ridge, Kentucky. Figures vary on attendance, but scholars of revival consider it a key moment in the Revival movement. Several Christian denominations resulted from this event. The Third Awakening or maybe "resurgence", from 1830, was largely influential in America and many countries worldwide including India and Ceylon. The Plymouth Brethren started with John Nelson Darby at this time, a result of disillusionment with denominationalism and clerical hierarchy. The next Great Awakening (sometimes called the Third Great Awakening) began from 1857 onwards in Canada and spread throughout the world including America and Australia. The next Awakening (1880 - 1903) has been described as "a period of unusual evangelistic effort and success," and again sometimes more of a "resurgence" of the previous wave. Moody, Sankey and Spurgeon are again notable names. Others included Sam Jones, J. Wilber Chapman and Billy Sunday in North America. The final Great Awakening (1904) had its roots in the Holiness movement which had developed in the late 19C. The Pentecostal revival movement began, out of a passion for more power and a greater outpouring of the Spirit. < The Columbia Encyclopedia 6th ed., s.v."Great Awakening" [database on-line]; available from Questia, http://www.questia.com/PM.qst?a=o&d =101247123; Internet; accessed 31 March 2007.>

universe goes; it becomes convenience and man himself becomes God. His (man's) desires become dominant with a capital D and for all intents and purposes the man becomes God. Then he begins to build up, as Jacob did, a universe surrounding this—a universe full of conflict and ultimately misery and unhappiness.

Now let's look at how Jacob got himself into trouble by his self-centered activity. First of all he supplanted his brother, his twin Esau – at birth he supplanted him — that's why he was called the heel-grabber.[20] Then you remember when they grew up, Jacob took advantage of his brother's hunger and when he came in exhausted and asked for some of Jacob's porridge. Jacob caught him off balance at a weak moment and he said, "Give me your birth-right and I will, (give you some porridge)."[21] He (Esau) sold his birth-right for a mess of porridge. It was a mean trick to take advantage of his brother's hunger, but Jacob was the man of the main chance, always looking after number one.

Then you'll remember when Rebekah, his mother, overheard a conversation between Isaac and Esau. She went and reported it to Jacob. Isaac, the father, was talking to his son Esau, his firstborn, "Go out and get me some venison – the kind that I like and cook me a savory dish and then I'll bless you. I will give you the blessing of the first-born (which carried with it a property right.)"[22] Rebekah heard that and Rebekah loved Jacob but didn't care for Esau. When you get a situation in the home where a parent favors one child over another child you are in for trouble—when one becomes the pet of the parent. So Rebekah called Jacob and said: "Look here, you do exactly what I tell you ... go out quickly and kill two kids (young goats) and we will cook a savory dish and give it to your father. Then go in (he is nearly blind and can't see) and you tell him you

---

20 Genesis 25:23-26.

21 Genesis 25:29-34.

22 Genesis 27.1-4.

214

brought the dish and get his blessing."[23] Jacob objected and said, "My brother is a hairy man and I'm smooth." She said, "Leave that to me." She took the skin of the kids and put it over his arms and around his neck. So Jacob went in and the old man was suspicious; he said "It's the voice of Jacob, but the hands are the hands of Esau." And he blessed him and gave him the blessing of the firstborn.[24] He (Jacob) came back and told his mother and they were rejoicing over the cleverness of their trick. They had their way, but he got the blessing "plus" and the "plus" was he got his brother's hatred. Esau had a hatred of Jacob on account of the blessing that he had gotten from his father. Esau muttered, "It will soon be time to mourn for my father and then I will murder my brother Jacob."[25]

You can get your way in the universe "plus." You can get results or consequences in this moral universe. Some people go through life getting *results*; the moral universe backs them. Others get *consequences* and Jacob began getting consequences. Then now look what happens then to Rebekah. After she got her way through the clever trick she played on her husband and on her elder son, she began to be ill at ease with herself. Then Rebekah said to Isaac, "These Hittite women tire me to death, if Jacob marries a Hittite like these women, some native girl, what good is life to me?" Now Rebekah was in a conflict with herself over what she had done; she had to live in the state of self-justification. While always trying to put a good fix on the thing that she had done, that produced a conflict within Rebekah, and so she projected that conflict out into her environment. She said, "These Hittite women tire me to death." Meaning, "I bore myself to death. I don't like myself therefore I don't like these people."

You see Rebekah got her consequences too. She was inwardly bored with herself and became bored with her

23 Genesis 27:8-10.

24 Genesis 27:11-30.

25 Genesis 27:41.

environment and then she hit on another plan. She saw that Jacob was in league with the elder brother and the elder brother was dangerous. So she said: "You better go off and go to my father's house and there find a wife among your own people. Go to Paddan-aram (to the house of Bethuel) and there you'll find a wife and come back."[26] It was partly to find a wife and partly to get away from the mess that Jacob had made at home. He'd cheated his brother, cheated himself out of his own peace and contributed to making his mother an unhappy woman.

So he tried to get away from the mess that he had made — partly to get a wife but partly to get away; it was an escape. And on the way he had a vision of a ladder with angels of God descending and ascending upon that ladder.[27] When Jacob arose in the morning, he made a vow: "So Jacob rose in the morning and, taking his stone he had put under his head, he erected it as a pillar, pouring oil upon it. He called the place Bethel – God's dwelling. Then Jacob made a vow: If God will be with me and guard me on this journey, giving me food to eat and clothes to wear, so that I return to my father's house safe and sound, then the Eternal shall be my God and this stone which I erected as a pillar shall be God's dwelling, and I will give thee faithfully a tenth in all thou has given me."[28]

At first sight that looks lovely, but it was one of those half-conversions that left the essential Jacob intact. He said, "If God will be with me and will prosper me on my journey then God will be my God and I will give Him a tenth of everything He gives me." Jacob would tithe. He would give everything except one thing, Jacob. And Jacob was still there; the surfaces had been converted but the depths had not been converted and Jacob was still Jacob. Religious perhaps, but Jacob still perceived

---

26 Genesis 28:1-2.

27 "And he dreamed that there was a ladder set up on the earth, the top of it reaching to heaven; and the angels of God were ascending and descending on it" (Gen.28:12).

28 Genesis 28:18-22.

that Jacob was intact, untouched, unconverted. He had been horizontally converted but not vertically. It was one of those half-conversions.

Then he went, you remember, and found Laban, in the country he was going to. And you remember he served Laban for seven years in order to marry Rachel. He'd fallen in love with Rachel. He'd served Laban for seven years and then he was to marry Rachel but Laban cheated him. He woke up in the morning and found that the woman he got was not Rachel but Leah, her sister, the elder sister.

The cheater was now being cheated. Jacob had supplanted the elder brother, and now the elder sister supplanted her sister. The universe was giving Jacob "consequences." But Jacob said "All right I'll go on." He served seven more years for Rachel, for he really loved Rachel. But in the midst of it he began to scheme about how he could get hold of his father-in-law's flocks for himself. Jacob continued to assert how righteous he was. A dishonest man talking about his honesty! He had to keep up that front to live with himself. Jacob made a scheme by which the weaker lambs fell to Laban and the stronger to Jacob. And the account says he grew exceedingly rich with large flocks, male and female slaves, camels and asses; he got everything. But he heard Laban's sons muttering, "Jacob has got a hold of all our father's property; he's acquired all of his wealth from what our father had." Jacob also saw that Laban's glances were not so friendly as they were before.[29] Jacob got Laban's money; he got his property. Plus he got the hatred of the sons of Laban and the unfriendliness of his father-in-law.

Jacob is doing exactly here what he did back home — making a mess — creating difficulty for himself but all the time he was asserting that God was helping him. He said "However, the God of my father has always been with me." I'm prosperous; he must be with me. Look what God has given to me. How did he get it? And then he said: "God has taken the stock from

29 Genesis 31.1-2.

your father and given it to me." Jacob played the trick in which he got the stronger; his father-in-law got the weaker "but God did it." When he sinned he sinned "religiously."

And then the payoff began to come; it always does. Jacob said: "I have to get out of here – it is getting too warm, too uncomfortable." Then Jacob started to put his sons and his wife on camels, driving all of his cattle and all of his stock he'd gathered in order to return to his father Isaac in the land of Canaan. While Laban was away sheep sheering, Rachel stole the household gods that belonged to her father. Jacob once again outwitted Laban, the Aramean, never letting him know that he had fled. Jacob just stole away. He fled. Three days later Laban was told that Jacob had fled, so he took his kinsmen and pursued him for seven days overtaking him in the hill country of Gilead. And when Laban overtook him he said, "Why did you do a thing like this?" Jacob answered, "I fled secretly because I was afraid. I thought you would take your daughters from me by force."[30] He had fled from his home (of his birth) in Canaan because of the fear of Isaac, and now he was fleeing from Laban's home because the fear of his father-in-law. Sin always has a payoff. It creates fears. You get your way and you don't like it and that's what happened to Jacob.

But finally they patched up a truce, a truce between his father-in-law and himself. And the account says Laban took a boulder and erected it as a pillar. Jacob said to his men, "gather stones" and Laban said to his men, "gather stones." And they set up a pillar, a kind of a cairn[31] as they call it or a watch post, a Mizpah.

---

30 Genesis 31:25-32.

31 A cairn is a non-naturally occurring pile of stones erected by a person or persons. They are built for several purposes: To mark a burial site, and/or to memorialize the dead; To mark the summit of a mountain; to indicate a path across stony or barren terrain or across glaciers; to help mariners locate themselves. Additionally cairns have been used to commemorate any sort of event, from the site of a battle to a place where a cart has tipped

Now we usually use that word Mizpah in a lovely way. We inscribe it on wedding rings, "May the Lord watch between me and thee while we are absent one from the other."[32] It's rather lovely, and I dislike taking that beauty out it, but I'm afraid I must. That watch post or Mizpah was really saying: "may the Eternal keep a watchful eye upon us while we are out of each other's sight." May the Lord keep his eye on you! Both needed watching. So they patched up the truce and parted, but each saying: I hope the Lord will watch you, for you need watching.

And then when Jacob got free from his father-in-law he wasn't free yet and he began to think in terms of Esau. What am I do when I get back there? I'm getting out of this frying pan and going into a worse fire. So Jacob made a scheme. Jacob sent messages ahead to his brother Esau in the land of Seir, the country of Edom, with these instructions:

"You shall say to my lord Esau: 'Your servant Jacob says: I have been residing with Laban until now. I have oxen, asses, flocks and slaves both male and female, that I hereby send to tell my lord, in the hope of finding favor with you." The messengers came back to Jacob reporting that they had gone to his brother Esau who was already on the way to meet him with 400 hundred men. Jacob was terrified and anxious. He divided his party with the flocks and herds and camels into two companies, thinking that if Esau attacked and overpowered one company, the surviving company might escape. Then Jacob prayed, "Oh save me from the power of my brother, from Esau, I am afraid of him; he may come and kill us all." He didn't ask to be saved from his sin—from Jacob, but he asked to be saved from the consequences of his sins. "Oh save me from the power of my brother for I am afraid that he is going to attack me."

---

over. < The Columbia Encyclopedia 6th ed., s.v."Cairn" [database on-line]; available from Questia, http://www.questia.com/PM.qst?a=o&d=101235110; Internet; accessed 30 March 2007.>

32 Genesis 31:49-50.

You see he had not 'struck bottom' yet. He wanted to escape the consequences of his sins, but he didn't want to escape the real sin — himself. So he selected some presents and sent them with the companies, one company here, and one company behind. He thought that maybe they could appease Esau in that way. Each one was to say that "they belong to your servant Jacob; they are a present for my lord Esau." He thought to himself: I will appease him with the present in front, and then if I can get access to his presence perhaps he will receive me. So the company moved ahead of him while he passed the night in the tent. And now here was Jacob caught between two consequences — his brother Esau and his father-in-law, Laban. And these consequences were closing in on him like a vice.

And then came that dreadful night, that crisis night. "That night he arose he took his two wives, his two maidservants and his eleven children and crossed the ford of the Jabbok. He took them and made them cross the stream with all that he had and then Jacob was left alone — with Jacob. It's a terrible thing when all of your armor is struck off you, and you stand there naked in the presence of God. You are alone in the presence of God. It's a terrible hour. Jacob was terribly alone. He hadn't a support in the universe. He couldn't look to God because he knew he had offended God. He couldn't look around himself because he had messed up every situation he'd been in. There was no support and he was left alone. It was midnight, terribly dark in that hour. It is an awful moment when all your armor is stripped away from you and you stand facing the consequences of what you've done. Does divine grace leave us in that awful loneliness? Is that what is meant by the phrase, "Orphanage of spirit?"

Then an angel wrestled with him, a divine messenger who represented the love of God that wouldn't let him go. This God could not interfere until Jacob hit bottom. Now Jacob had hit bottom. There he was terrified at midnight, lonely and beaten. And then began the struggle, symbolic of the struggle that takes place in man's soul between good and evil. At midnight they wrestled. The angel said, "Let me go for the day is breaking" and Jacob clung to him and said, "I will not let thee go except thou bless me." Why did he ask for the blessing? Well he had one blessing that turned out cursed. He received his father's blessing and that turned out to be a curse. Everything that he touched turned out cursed except this request for a blessing. "I want one blessing that will be a blessing." He was tired; he had been searching for fool's gold. Jacob said, "I won't let you go till you bless me." And then the angel asked him a question. Everything was gathered up in that awful question that he asked Jacob. It was very simple but it went straight to the point. He said to Jacob, "What is your name?" And how Jacob hated to say that name. He must have sobbed upon the angel's shoulder and said: "It's Jacob. I've been supplanting everybody I could; I'm sorry. But my name is Jacob." He finally got that name out. "Then your name shall be called Jacob no longer" said the angel, "but Israel" — a striver with God or a prince with God - "for thou has striven with God and men and won." The moment he said his old name, really said it from the depths, God said, "I will give you a new one." You won't have to face it — that word Jacob all your life. I will give you another one - Israel, a prince with God.

And the moment we get our own name, when we say what our name really is, and then God says, "All right, I'll give you a new one." Then Jacob asked the angel his name, "Please tell me your name." "Why ask my name?" the angel answered and then blessed him on the spot. And what a blessing! Jacob named the spot Peniel, which means God's face. "I've seen God face to face and yet I'm alive." Jacob saw God face to face when he saw himself face to face. When he saw what kind of man he really was, without any veneer or facade, he saw that he was Jacob. He now saw God face to face because he'd seen himself face to face and acknowledged what kind of person he was. And the account says, "the sun rose upon him as he past Peniel." This was a sunrise experience. The sun arose upon a new man as he walked out of that morning hour a changed Jacob; now the word Israel was his new name.

LIVING UPON THE WAY

The next verse says, "When Jacob looked up there was Esau coming with four hundred men! (Moffatt's translation had an exclamation behind it.) So he assigned the children to Leah and Rachel and to the two maids, putting the maids and their children in front and Leah and her children and Rachel and Joseph in the rear. He passed on before them bowing seven times to the earth to reach his brother, and Esau ran to meet him and embraced him falling on his neck and kissing him, while they wept together."[33]

Of all things! Talk about drama. We expected Jacob to be butchered, but when Esau looked on Jacob's face, he said: "This is not my brother; he's different; he's a changed man." And when something changed in Jacob, something changed in Esau and the first thing we know they are weeping on each other's shoulders, embracing each other and crying. What does this mean? Apparently this — that when you get changed, the world around you changes. The moment you get reconciled with God, you begin to get reconciled with your brother. Reconciliation begins to take place.

I know a man and his wife who are always squabbling over the radio — he wanted the news and she wanted the music. The squabbling would go on all evening. One day he was converted and he came home and when the radio hour came he walked to the radio and turned on the music. She looked at him with surprise. She said, "It's the news hour." "Yes," he said, "I know, but I thought you'd like the music." She looked at him in surprise and walked straight over to the radio and turned on the news. Now isn't that simple? From that moment on they were friends. When one changed the other was changed.

Jacob found a solution. Jacob changed the attitude of Esau. Look at what happened. Esau said, "What are all these presents for?" And Jacob said it was "for my lord's favor." He told him at once what they were for. But Esau said, "I have plenty, keep

---

33 Genesis 33:4.

what you have, my brother." But Jacob answered, "No, if I've found favor with you, pray accept my presents for I have had access to the presence of God himself and found a welcome." So he urged him and so Esau took the gifts. Then Esau said, "Let us travel on our way and I will march in front." He had come down there to wipe out Jacob and now he was his (Jacob's) escort. "I will get my 400 men and we will march in front." They traveled together. Jacob said to his household and all his people, "Put away your foreign gods; wash yourself clean, change your clothing. Let us move up to Bethel where I shall make an altar to the God that answered me in the hour of my distress and accompanied me on my journey. Then they handed over to Jacob all their foreign gods with their amulets and earrings and Jacob buried them below the single oak at Shechem.

A revival, a morally cleansing revival went through that company. Now before this change, suppose Jacob had made that suggestion? Put away your foreign gods clean yourselves up and let's go up there and worship God. You know what the family would have done? They would have burst out laughing. They would have said: Why doesn't the old man begin with himself? Why doesn't he clean up? They saw he had cleaned up, saw that he was going straight and they took their amulets and earrings and everything else and buried them at the sacred oak. The revival began and a cleansing impulse went down the life of the Hebrew people. If Jacob had been unchanged he would have left a deposit of corruption in the life of these great people and it would be a question if God could have used such a people to bring Christ into the world through them. But that wrestling at midnight on Jabbok's banks sent a moral cleansing down through the life of the nation. They saw that a crooked man could become straight, bad men could become good, and weak men could become strong. That did something for the life of the people. And God could say, "I'm the God of Abraham, Isaac and especially Jacob." For I am the God of the crooked man made straight. And Jesus could say, they could come from the east and the west and they should sit down at the Kingdom of God with Abraham, Isaac and Jacob. Jacob was to get in too.

That means that there is hope for us all. I don't care where you come from. I'm only interested in where you're going. I don't care how crooked you've been or what you've done or what you've been. I ask one question: Where are you going? What are you going to do? You can look back on that past and it will be a forgiven past. If God forgives it, you can forgive yourself, because you say that I am not that same person. I belong to another person. Jacob could say, "I'm Israel." And when they founded the nation in Palestine, they called it not Jacob but Israel. The crooked man was made straight—the prince with God.

Now let's come down in these last moments and ask this question, what about us? The crux of the whole thing is: What is your name? The name in those days stood for character. When the man's character changed, they changed the name. Jesus gave the name Boanerges to James and John in the beginning because they were tempestuous, "sons of thunder."[34] The tempestuous nature had to have a name that would fit it them so he called it Boanerges. You remember when Joseph was "changed?" His name was changed into Barnabas. Joseph means "one more." I suppose he belonged to a large family and when they got down to him they ran out of names and they said let's name him Joseph.

After Joseph had laid his all upon the altar of Christ then you remember they said …"we've got to change his name; his name isn't Joseph any longer, it's Barnabas (which means son of encouragement)." They changed his name to fit his character. So the important thing is: what is your name? Meaning, what is your real character. And that's the crux of the matter. Now before we go on we have to tell God our name. Some of us would say my name is ego; that's my name. I'm a self-centered person. My name is resentment. My name is fear. My name is

---

34 Mark 3:17.

impurity. My name is hypocrite; I'm two people. My name is Legion; there are many of us. My name is pride. My name is tied up. My name is guilt. I long to whisper that into the ear of God. God says all right, thank you. I've got another name on my tongue. I'll give you my own new name for you—it would be the opposite of the other.

Some of us have come here to learn our names. One teacher of psychology in a college, after I had spoken about this at another Ashram, came up to me and said, "I have learned one thing—at last I know my name." The moment she told God her name, God gave her another—just like that. And some of us are going to whisper our name to God tonight, to tell him the whole truth. And God's going to immediately say, Good. Now we can do business; I will give you another one, the opposite of your old, and that's good news. And when the morning will come the sun will rise on a new person, rise on a new life and you will be a different person. What about Rebekah. Poor Rebekah schemed for her son, made all these schemes for her son and then when she sent him off in that country she never saw him again, for he didn't come back for twenty years. By that time she was dead. All our schemes that we build up go down in ashes. There is only one way to live and that is God's way. You can't live against God without living against yourself.

I was in a city in Oklahoma some time ago and a man came up to me at the close of a meeting and said, "Do you know me?"

I have difficulty at that place; I come the nearest to lying at that place of any place I know. I hate to say to a man, "No, I am sorry, I don't know you." So I said to him, it was the nearest I could get to the truth, "I do and I don't." There was something familiar about him, but I didn't know him.

"Oh, I'm that man that came to see you down in that hotel in that city in Oklahoma."

"Oh" I said, "you're not that man."

He said, "Yes I am"

"But", I said, "You're different"

He said, "Yes, of course I'm different."

I remember how he came into the room in the hotel and without any preliminaries threw himself down in the chair and said, "I'm trying to live a Christian life, but I'm having a terrible time of it.

I said, "What's the matter?"

But he said, "I don't know but I say to myself, I'll give up this and I'll give up that and I'll compromise here and there, but please let me stay at the center."

Well, I said, "My brother that is very simple then, isn't it? That's why you're having a terrible time of it. You're God. But you're not God; God's God. And things don't add up when you're God. You have to surrender yourself to God and make him God. You've got to lose your life and it'll come back to you again. Will you'll do it?"

He said, "Is that what I've got to do?"

I said, "Yes, you've got to get yourself off your own hands and into the hands of God." We knelt and prayed.

And he simply said, "God please take me over and, oh God, make me over just as I am." And he turned that self-centered, festering self over to God and said, "Take me as I am" and He did. He shook my hand and went away. I didn't see him again until this occasion. And on that occasion his wife came to me and she said, "Thank you for giving my husband back to me." I said, "I didn't give him back to you. He gave himself to God and then God gave him back to himself and then to you and everybody else." And it was as simple as that. You've got to get yourself off your own hands and into the hands of God. He that saves his life shall lose it. If anybody who has ever lost his life by saving it as Jacob did until he hit bottom. That lonely midnight hour was the zero hour for Jacob, when the self-centered way of life came to the end of the road, a dead end. The moment we say our name, redemption sets in. A new name is given and that's good news. You can be a transformed person, completely and utterly. Shall we pray?

E. Stanley Jones teaching at the Sat Tal Christian Ashram

7. THE CHRISTIAN WAY IS THE NATURE OF REALITY

COMMENTARY ON "THE CHRISTIAN FAITH AND THE BODY"

THIS sermon addresses the significant matter of the relationship of the Christian faith to the body and presents Jones' view of healing in the Christian tradition. Jones makes it clear that he is not a faith healer. He states unequivocally that Christianity is not a healing cult, for the center of Christianity is not us or our body, but Jesus, the Christ. When we focus on physical healing, that makes us the center. God becomes our servant, to heal us and keep us in good repair. Christians must focus rather on offering themselves (self-surrender) to Christ and on maintaining a reconciling relationship with the son of God. When we are reconciled to God, we are reconciled to ourselves, and our bodies and some illnesses fade away (Jones, *A Song of Ascents*, 331).

Sickness is not the will of God. However, Jones states that he is no absolutist in regard to the healing of disease. He is opposed to those who believe that all diseases must be cured in this life or else there is sin or lack of faith: "That position leaves a lot of wreckage behind" (Jones, *A Song of Ascents*, 330). God will cure some diseases during this earthly life, but others await the final cure in the resurrection. Christianity, however, shows us how we can use disease and suffering for the glory of God, and death according to Jones is "but an anesthetic which God gives in changing bodies" (Jones, *A Song of Ascents*, 229).

229

The text for this sermon is John 5:2-9, the story of the Sabbath healing of the paralytic lying by the Bethzatha fountain in Jerusalem. According to Jones, the healing of this invalid was the result of pure grace and did not necessitate a demonstration of faith on the part of the invalid or his friends. Jesus simply asked if the man wished to be made whole/healed. In this sermon, Jones tackles head on the issue that some persons do not want to be healed. They do not really want their lives to change. They do not wish to accept responsibility for their lives and their choices. For some, illness provides "secondary gain."[1] These persons receive care and attention from their inabilities rather than for their abilities. Jesus asks the paralytic a pointed question, "Do you want to be healed?" That was a pertinent question, for the healing of Jesus in this instance complemented the desire on the part of the man to be healed.

Jones often used as illustrations persons who were alcoholic and who dramatically gave up drinking after they were converted.[2] He was involved in the creation of Alcoholics

---

1   Secondary gain is a psychiatric term meaning that a person has a hidden reason for holding onto an undesirable condition, such as illness or injury. There are times when the disability, such as chronic pain, lasts far longer than expected for the ailment to be healed. However, the patient continues to receive care and attention and may be (unconsciously most often) unwilling to give up the illness for fear of loosing the attentive concern of others.

2   Jones was apparently personally impacted by alcohol. He did not speak or write often about his family; however in 1948 at the close of an address, he spoke about his father, Albin Davis Jones. "I don't believe I have ever mentioned it in public but the reason for my fierce hatred for this abomination, (alcohol) this curse, is that my own family was struck by it. It struck my own father. Our family lost everything. My father, having fallen a hopeless victim to the habit, finally stopped at nothing to satisfy his awful appetite. He sold our furniture, even our chairs and beds. He was a terrible victim. He and his wife and his children suffered unspeakably. Now, you see why I hate it and why I'll fight it with every breath until I die" (Graham 34).

Anonymous, (AA). One of AA's founders, Dr. Bob studied *Abundant Living* and *Living Victoriously*.[3] Both books are often cited in the history of the Alcoholics Anonymous movement.[4] For example, **Step #3, Surrender,** and **Step #11, Necessity for a Quiet Time,** from *AA's Twelve Steps to Sobriety* sound strikingly similar to Jones emphasis on *conversion* and the *maintenance of a daily spiritual discipline*. These two "steps" are the primary subjects of the two books mentioned above.[5]

Jones tells this remarkable story of a conversion both saving and sobering an alcoholic:

In my student days I stood in the open square by the courthouse on a soapbox and preached. Just in front of me was a drunk who was being held up partly by a peeled stick he had in his hand. He kept commenting on what I was saying: 'That young fellow make me feel like crying.' I preached with one hand on his shoulder, to keep him quiet. At the close I invited those who wanted to be converted to come to the mission. Among others, this man came. "Do you want to be saved?' I asked. 'Yes, but I am drunk.' 'I know that you are drunk,' I replied, 'but he can save you.' 'If you say so it must be so,'he replied, and we got on our knees. I prayed, and then he prayed, and in the midst of it he opened his eyes, looked around surprised: "Why he has saved me! And I am not drunk too!' He got up, took a whisky bottle out of his pocket, and gave it to me: 'I won't need that anymore.' He handed me the stick and said, 'I won't need that anymore, either.' He walked down that aisle not only saved, but sober. Conversion had saved and had sobered him at the same moment. A miracle? Yes, of course (*Conversion*, 97).

3   Jones, E. Stanley. Abundant Living. New York: Abingdon-Cokesbury Press, 1942. Jones, E. Stanley, Victorious Living. New York: Abingdon Press, 1936.

4   <http://alcoholism.about.com/library/blmitch7.htm>

5   THE TWELVE STEPS

1.   We admitted we were powerless over alcohol — that our lives had become unmanageable.

2.   Came to believe that a Power greater than ourselves could restore us to sanity.

3.   Made a decision to turn our will and our lives over to the care of God as we understood Him.

Jones was progressive in his view that spirit, mind, and body are a whole: *"There used to be a time when we would hand the body over to the doctor, the mind to the psychiatrist and the soul to the minister"* (242). Instead, they are all bound up together, and when the mind is ill, that illness can be passed on to the body, and illnesses of the body can affect the mind as well. Spiritual unease can impact both the body and the mind. Human beings are units, not pieces.

In the late 1940s Jones began his plans to open up a "sanatorium" in Lucknow, India. According to Graham, "It would provide both psychiatric treatment and spiritual healing for missionaries and others. No doubt Jones was influenced by this plan to start a psychiatric hospital by the memories of his own experience of emotional distress earlier in his career." The Nur Manzil Psychiatric Center in Lucknow, India opened by Jones in the late 1950s remains in existence and continues to

---

4. Made a searching and fearless moral inventory of ourselves.

5. Admitted to God, to ourselves, and to another human being the exact nature of our wrongs.

6. Were entirely ready to have God remove all these defects of character.

7. Humbly asked Him to remove our shortcomings

8. Made a list of all persons we had harmed, and became willing to make amends to them all.

9. Made direct amends to such people wherever possible, except when to do so would injure them or others.

10. Continued to take personal inventory and when we were wrong promptly admitted it.

11. Sought through prayer and meditation to improve our conscious contact with God as we understood Him, praying only for knowledge of His will for us and the power to carry that out.

12. Having had a spiritual awakening as the result of these steps, we tried to carry this message to alcoholics, and to practice these principles in all our affairs.

respond to patients' psychological, social, and spiritual needs. It is commonplace now to make the mind/body connection, and Jones affirmed it almost fifty years ago.

In this sermon, Jones tells us that God can touch us directly and heal us, *and* he can also touch us indirectly by removing the causes of many diseases. Resentments and stress, for example, can contribute to physical conditions such as heart disease and allergies. Anger and resentment don't really hurt others, although that may be how we intend it to be; instead they hurt us. These negative emotions preoccupy us with pessimistic thoughts and feelings. The basis of all resentment, according to Jones, is the *un-surrendered self.* Jones will make the case again and again that we (our body, mind, and spirit) are made for positive good will and purpose. When we surrender ourselves to Christ, we can experience healing, but self surrender always comes first.

While not addressed in this sermon, Jones experienced personal healing such as the healing at the Lucknow Church in India and the curing of the majority of the negative consequences of his adult onset diabetes.[6] This 1917 healing is described in detail in an archived Methodist document:[7]

> After his first eight years of service in India, Jones suffered a complete nervous breakdown. Broken both mentally and physically, he was forced to take a furlough back home to the United States. His doctors held out little hope that he could ever return to India and resume his mission work

---

6   In the early 1950s, Jones was diagnosed with diabetes. There was a question whether or not he could continue on his evangelistic travels and intense speaking schedule. However, his inner voice said, "You go. In me you are well and whole." Jones learned how to control his diabetes by diet – even while moving from place to place. (In fact in the three months following his diagnosis of diabetes, he traveled to seventy-three cities.) By the third month, Jones found that his diabetes was completely under control. He maintained this same non-sugar diet for the rest of his life (Jones, *A Song of Ascents* 336).

7   We have read it in Jones' own words on page 22 in Chapter I.

again. With that prognosis, Jones' dreams were dashed. He had been 17 when he had experienced a conversion to Christianity and then studied at Asbury College in Wilmore, KY. While there he had been "flooded by the spirit" for four days and felt a distinct call to missionary service. He had left for India in 1907, arriving at Lucknow.

Of his breakdown he wrote, "I was suffering so severely from brain fatigue and nervous exhaustion that I collapsed, not once but several times." Reluctantly, he boarded a ship to take him home. Even while conducting services on the ship taking him back to America, Jones collapsed again. The ship's doctor put him to bed, ordering him to remain there for the duration of the trip.

After a year of rest in the United States he returned to India but first stopped in the Philippines to hold evangelistic meetings with university students in Manila. During those services, Jones again collapsed. This time, doctors urgently warned him that returning to India and resuming his rigorous schedule could worsen his condition or even kill him. Nevertheless, he traveled to India, but went "with a deepening cloud upon me. When I arrived in Bombay, I was so broken that I went straight to the hills for another long rest. Again, I descended to the plains, and again I was shocked and crushed to discover that I couldn't take it. I was exhausted mentally, nervously and physically. I was completely at the end of my resources."

This was an ominous and devastating blow to Jones, who had just returned after a year of rest and furlough in the United States. "I realized that I would have to give up my missionary career, go back to America, and work on a farm to try to regain my health. It was one of my darkest hours."

While conducting evangelistic meetings in Lucknow, Jones was praying one evening when an event transpired that completely transformed his life. While in prayer he heard a voice speak to him asking, "Are you yourself ready for this work to which I have called you?" He replied, "No, Lord, I am done for. I have reached the end of my resources." The same voice responded, "If you will turn that over to me and not worry about it, I will take care of it." Jones quickly answered, "Lord, I close the bargain right there." He arose from my knees knowing that he was a well man.

Immediately, Jones experienced God's healing grace. "A great peace settled into my heart and pervaded my whole being. I knew it was done! Life — abundant life — had taken possession of me." He walked home that evening as a man renewed mentally, physically and spiritually. Jones said he began preaching, teaching, counseling, writing — often working from early morning until far into the night — all without the slightest trace of weariness or exhaustion. "I seemed possessed by life and peace and rest — by Christ Himself.

This was not a temporary cure. Jones, recalling that time, wrote, "More than a score of the most strenuous years of my life have gone by since then, but the old trouble has never returned. I have never had such health. But it was more than a physical touch. I seemed to have tapped new life for body, mind and spirit. After that experience, life for me functioned on a permanently higher level. And I had done nothing but take it![8]

---

8   In his book, *Growing Spiritually,* Jones tells of an intriguing sequel to the story of his healing. "Pauline Grandstrand, a very saintly woman of prayer, was on furlough in America at the time, and the Voice of God said to her: "Give up everything and to go to pray for Stanley Jones." The Voice persisted and she canceled her engagements, shut herself up in her room in the hotel for a whole day, and prayed. By evening the burden had lifted. When we went over the matter and compared times we found that at the very time she was on her knees in American the release was coming to me in India. But she knew nothing of what was the matter with me. She only knew the Voice called and she obeyed. And in that obeying she helped release me from a very real bondage and set me free for these years of service - untrammeled" (283).

We see here again a powerful illustration of Jones' overriding theme and the conviction of his life; **it is not until we surrender our all to God that we can be healed:**

> It was when Jones was finally utterly helpless and turning completely to God that he received his healing and the direction of the Holy Spirit to continue his work as a missionary evangelist (Graham 110).

Jones' life-changing experience should be of great encouragement to all who feel at the end of their resources. He strongly believed that the grace of God that flowed to E. Stanley Jones can flow into other broken lives.

Near the end of his life, Jones suffered a devastating stroke and would write,

> I never dreamed that a stroke that leaves you helpless would be a call to present a Divine Yes, the universal Yes which meets a universal need.[9] My means of locomotion were shattered, and I could not recognize my own voice on a Dictaphone. The only hopeful thing was that my intelligence was unaffected. Everything else had been changed. But I said to myself, "Nothing has changed! I'm the same person that I was. By prayer, I am still communicating with the same person. I belong to the same unshakable Kingdom and the same unchanging person. The glorious thing was that my faith was not shattered. I was not holding it; it was holding me. Jesus is Lord! I can honestly say that I wasn't asking, "My God, why?" I could and I can face the future with him. If it is hard for me to preach a sermon now; why not be one?" (Jones, *The Divine Yes*, 26).

Jones became that sermon for the last thirteen months of his life as he lived the affirmation of the Divine Yes. His daughter helped put Jones' last book together after his death

---

9   *The Divine Yes* has at last sounded in him, for in him is the yes that affirms all the promises of God. (2 Cor: 1: 19-20).

(see footnote 22, page 36) and wrote in the introduction that she hoped that this book would be of particular help to many kinds of people: "Among these are the seriously or chronically ill, the discouraged, those who feel themselves badly used of life, or those whose lives seem to have caved in on them" (Ibid., 10). Jones would consistently affirm that:

> Disease is not the will of God. And God will either cure you now in one of these ways or give you power to use it until the final cure in the resurrection (Ibid, 9).

In his own suffering, Jones had the power to use the profound disabilities created by his stroke to glorify God and to show a workable way to live to others – to be thrown back on grace (Ibid., 116):

> Could I, in a lesser way, face this cross and help redeem a world in however small a way. Could, I even I, add my small yes of response to the Divine Yes which stands behind the whole universe? (Ibid., 116).

Jones would affirm that **Divine Yes.**

THE CHRISTIAN WAY IS THE NATURE OF REALITY: "THE CHRISTIAN FAITH AND THE BODY"

SERMON

Now in Jerusalem there is a bath by the sheep-pool, which is called in Hebrew Bethzatha; it has five porticoes, where a crowd of invalids used to lie, the blind, the lame, and folk with shriveled limbs waiting for the water to bubble. For an angel used to descend from time to time into the bath, and disturb the water; where upon the first person who stepped in after the water was disturbed was restored to health, no matter what disease he had been afflicted with. Now one man was

237

there who had been ill for thirty-eight years. Jesus saw him lying, and knowing he had been ill for a long while he said to him, "Do you want your health restored?" The invalid replied, "Sir, I have nobody to put me into the bath, when the water is disturbed; and while I am getting down myself, someone else gets in before me." Jesus said to him, "Get up, lift your mat and walk." And instantly the man got well, lifted his mat, and started to walk. (Moffatt's Translation, John 5:2-9)

Tonight, I am going to speak to you on Christianity and health and healing. One night during these ashrams, we consider the question of the relationship of the Christian faith to the body.

First of all, let me tell you that what I believe. I do not believe that the Christian faith is a healing cult. Its primary business is not to heal the body and keep it in repair. If that were its primary business, it would make us the center and God would be serving us. We would be the center. And when we are the center, we are off center. God is the center and the primary business of the Christian faith is to reconcile us with God. Reconciled with God, we are reconciled with ourselves and hence with our bodies and hence with our neighbors and hence with nature.

The primary business of the Christian faith is to right your relationship with God. He is the center. We serve him. The second thing that I would like to say before I go into my subject is that I don't believe that all diseases are cured in this life, no matter how much faith we have. This is a mortal world and the body breaks down sometimes. We were never intended to be immortal in a mortal world. Therefore all diseases are not cured in this life. Some will have to wait for the final cure in the resurrection. Paul evidently had a disease. We read that he had a "thorn in the flesh." What was that thorn in the flesh? He said to the Galatians, "You know because of an infirmity of the flesh, I preached the gospel at first to you and I bear you witness that you treated me as an angel of God and did not despise my infirmity of the flesh, but would have plucked out

238

your very eyes and given them to me."[10] Evidently Paul had bad eyes, which were a sore trial to him as a public speaker. Three times he asked God to take this infliction away and God said, "No, but my grace is sufficient for you, my strength is made perfect in my weakness."[11] Then Paul rose up and said then, "I glory in my infirmities, for when I am weak, then am I strong."[12] Now I believe that God gave him power to use that infirmity until the final cure in the resurrection. Paul was not asked to bear it but take it up into the purpose of his life and transmute it and do something with it and use it. When his eyesight went bad, his insight went better! And because he was shut off from many of the outer sights, he was shut in with God.

Now having put those two provisos, let me hasten to say, that I don't believe that sickness is the will of God. I believe that it is an enemy to be destroyed, and God will cure those diseases in some of the ways that I will mention. Or, he will give us power to use illness until the final cure in the resurrection. But disease is not the will of God.

I come now to my text. *Now there is in Jerusalem by the sheep-gate a pool, in Hebrew called Bethzatha, which has five porticoes. In these lay a multitude of invalids, blind, lame and paralyzed. One man was there who had been ill for thirty-eight years. When Jesus saw him and knew that he had been lying there for a long time, he said to him, "Do you want to be healed? The sick man answered, "Sir, I have no man to put me into the pool when the water is troubled, and while I am going another steps down before me." Jesus said to him, "Rise, take up your pallet and walk." And at once the man was healed, and he took up his pallet and walked.*[13]

---

10 Galatians 4:13-15.

11 2 Corinthians 12:9.

12 2 Corinthians 12:10.

13 John 5:2-9. (RSV)

The older version says, "Do you want to be made whole?" The newer translation says, do you want to be healed? Now this was a pertinent question because a great many people don't want to be healed. They use illness as a strategy out of responsibility. If I were well, I could do this, but I am not well, therefore I don't have to do it.

Jung, the famous psychiatrist, says there was a difference between his psychiatry and that of Freud. Freud finds the basis of neurosis in childhood. Something happened back in childhood that laid the basis of this neurosis now. Jung said, I find it in the present. I ask, what is the responsibility that this patient will not assume?[14] Why is he dodging out into illness, into this neurosis? To escape responsibility?

Very often we do that. For we are not willing to face up to life and so we develop this, that or the other to keep from the necessity of doing so. At our Sat Tal Ashram, there was an adolescent girl who wanted attention and so she invented methods of getting attention — one was by the method of a bandage. She would come down with a bandage here, there and everywhere. One day I saw a big bandage on her hand and I said, "may I see what has happened?" And without leave, I unfolded it to see what was happening, and there was not a thing wrong. But she got attention through illness. A lot of people do that. They can't gain attention by their accomplishments or what they do, so they get attention by their illnesses — by recounting their illnesses. I have some cousins who live by recounting to each other their various ailments. They talked disease; they thought disease and they were disease. And every time I went there, I felt diseased. It was their strategy to gain sympathy and attention. They did not want to be well.

Dr. Shirkey, a pastor in Washington, D.C. and a prince of a man, told this story and said that I could tell it, so I am not doing it without his leave. He said, "When I was a boy I had

14 Carl Jung (1875-1961).

240

sensitive finger tips and so my mother gave me permission to grow long fingernails to protect those sensitive finger tips. My teacher not knowing that, called me out before the school and made me cut my finger nails before everyone. It so set me against school. I hated it and I began to invent ways to avoid going to school. One way was to invent a pain in the hip and I said it so much that I did have a pain and it got worse. The doctor said that the hip would have to be put in a cast. I was on the way to have the hip put in the cast when I broke down and told my mother the truth. We never had the hip put in a cast and we turned around and went home." He could have been an invalid. He could have escaped out of health into invalidism. Today he is a prince of man and found his way around it.

In India, we have a very wonderful and lovely soul; we call her Sister Leila the Greek. She does massage. I say that she gives a message in her massage. She rubs the love of God into you. She can tell by looking at your body what kind of soul is on the inside. That is rather disconcerting. She has been down among the lepers, massaging the lepers. It is one thing to deal with the lepers and give them medicine, and to deal with them at some distance, but it is another thing to touch them, to massage their open wounds. She did it. I knew she would never become infected because she was inoculated by the love of God. They tell me that 90% of the disease germs that fall on healthy skin die in 10 minutes and I knew that she would kill every disease germ that came near her by the love of God. She spent the winter massaging lepers and she said we can heal up their wounds. But almost all of those who were in this leper colony, when they got to the place when their wounds were almost healed, they would open them up again and keep them open. For if their wounds were healed, they would have to go out into the world and face responsibilities. And they prefer to stay in the shelter of the home where they were fed and cared for. Only those people who came in from homes and took the treatment and then returned home would allow their wounds to heal up so that they could go out and accept responsibility.

So when Jesus said, do you want to be healed? Do you want to be well? It was a very pertinent question. We had an alcoholic in one of our previous Ashrams and told me that she had fought against alcoholism for years but failed. One day she was on her way to a class reunion of her college. She was about to take the train but stopped at a tavern and ended up drunk and never went to the class reunion. When she came out from under the night of intoxication, she said, I have been blaming everyone for my alcoholism — my parents, my circumstances — just everyone for my condition. This is one time that I can't blame anybody. Nobody compelled me to go into the tavern and escape that reunion. I was responsible and for the first time I acknowledged my responsibility for what I was. And then she said, "I knelt down and really asked God to cure me and it happened just like that. It passed away and I never wanted a drink since, it was gone." When she really wanted to be well, well enough to accept her responsibility for being what she was and well enough to ask God without condition. She wanted to be well, the moment she did she was a well person.

Now somebody has defined these Ashrams as healing love for mind, spirit and body. In that order! First of all — the mind; we get a wrong idea, a wrong notion and that sends us on the wrong track. The first thing is to correct the wrong thinking and then that (correction) goes into the spirit and gets into the body. There was a time when we used to hand the body over to the doctor, the mind to the psychiatrist or the educator and the soul to the minister and we used to say "Take care of each." Now we know that we can't do that – they are all bound up together. Sometimes the mind and the soul get sick and pass on their sickness to the body. Sometimes the body gets sick and passes on its sickness to the mind and the soul.

The American Medical Association says that it is about 50/50. Fifty percent of diseases are rooted in the mental and spiritual and 50% are rooted in the physical. I said that one day and a doctor came up to me and said, "50/50 nothing, it is more like 75% of those who come to me don't need medicine.

They are passing on the sickness of their minds and souls to their bodies. They will never be well until they change their attitudes." A member of the Mayo clinic said to me, "We can deal with 25% of the people who come to us with the instruments of science, but 75% we don't know what to do with. You cannot touch them with the instruments of science. They need to change their attitudes of mind and spirit before they will be well." The British Medical Association says that there is not a single cell of the body that is not totally removed from the influence of mind and emotion...for good or for ill. It reaches clear down to every cell of the body. So when you say, I feel it in my bones, you do!

We have sayings in our language, "Oh, that man is a headache." Why? Because you think of him with anger and resentment and you get a headache. Or you say, that woman is a pain in the neck. You think of her and you get a pain in the neck because you think of her with anger. "Oh, he makes me sick," and he does. One woman said "Whenever I think of that woman, my stomach turns over." One doctor said that whenever he got angry, he pulled his car along side of the road and would not drive because he could not see straight and he was afraid that he would have an accident. Your state of mind and emotion affect every cell of your body for good or ill.

Now, healing is of two types. One is the direct type where God touches the body directly and heals it by the touch of God. I've seen that happen. I've seen it happen not only in functional diseases. I've seen it happen in structural diseases. I've seen cancers cured by the touch of God. I remember a girl had a cancer on her tongue that had been burned out and cut out ten times. I was praying for her and in the midst of praying for her she gave herself to Christ and then I said to her, "Don't you believe God can cure you of this cancer?" She opened her eyes and said, "He has!" and I knew he had for I too had faith.

My brother was a doctor and was going past the house the next day and I called him in. I said "We'd like you to examine her," but we didn't tell him what had happened. He looked at her and said "she is well" He'd seen her in the hospital, and he examined her a year later and said that's she had a perfect cure. He said, "that's a perfect cure, she's well," I've seen that happen.

And I have also seen Him touch functional disease. I have seen Him take away the causes and cure the disease. Sometimes it's direct, and sometimes it's indirect. Now we usually think of healing as just a direct touch. God would perform a miracle without our cooperation. We now see that that's a weak way to face the whole thing. I am now in the process of reading a book entitled *Prayer Can Change Your Life*.[15] It's the story of an experiment by a professor in the Redlands University in California, with three groups — one who used nothing but psychiatry, another group used nothing but prayer, and a third group that used prayer and psychiatry. Those who used prayer alone were helped very little. Those who used psychiatry alone were helped about 50%, but those who used prayer and therapy together were cured about 71% of the time. What do they mean by that? In the prayer therapy combination, they, while praying for riddance of the disease, they went down to see why they were ill; and went down to the roots of the thing to deal with those roots. They began to cooperate with God, and they had amazing healings, but they dealt with physical causes and added prayer.

Now, I've never wanted to be called a healer or looked on as a healer. I wanted to be an evangelist to try and get man reconciled with God. I still believe that's our primary purpose. Jesus did heal people but He asked them to keep it quiet about the healings — lest His presentation of the gospel should be smothered by the demands of the people wanting healing — and putting aside the central thing he came to do, which was to reconcile man with God. Jesus wanted to inject the gospel

---

15 William Parker and Elaine St. Johns, *Prayer Can Change Your Life: Experiments in Prayer Therapy*. (New Jersey: Simon & Schuster, 1972).

into humanity and healing is often a part of that process. I have not been able to run away from the fact that healing does occur. And we've seen some very remarkable things happen, but I know how it has happened. Only when you put yourself at the disposal of Christ does anything happen. And you don't do it! He does it through you! And that's all there is. He does the healing.

Now I believe that God can touch us directly and heal us. I've watched it happen again, again, and again. But then He also touches us indirectly, through removing the causes of many diseases. For instance, there are certain attitudes of mind and emotion that create disease. What are they? One is resentment. If you are going to be a well person you cannot harbor resentment because resentment is sand in the machinery of human living. There was a man who had high blood pressure and a bad heart and for ten years he was an invalid, he couldn't work, and functioned as a semi invalid. One day the doctor, out of the blue skies said to him, "Against who have you a resentment?"

The man looked at him in surprise and said, "It's against my nephew."

The doctor said "You and I better go and see that nephew."

And they went and saw that nephew and talked over the whole thing and buried the whole business. He came back and his blood pressure came straight down and his heart ceased to act up and a few days later he was back at his work — he had been an invalid for 10 years because of his resentments.

There was a woman at one of our Ashrams who told me that she had 35 allergies and that she could not eat this or touch that. If you have to live with 35 allergies, you are in trouble. Then one day she realized that she had a resentment against a member of her family. She decided that she needed to give up the resentment and surrender it and she did and every single one of those 35 allergies dropped away. She said, "Ragweed, I can go to bed with it now. Strawberries — I can eat them by the

245

quart. Peaches — I used to think that the acid was in the peaches but I found out that it (the acid) was in me." The resentments had upset the rhythm of the body and created all of these allergies.

You have got to let go of all your resentments. I was recently visiting a pastor in the hospital. He was the pastor of a large church. He had had a heart attack. The basis of it was that his church secretary dominated him. She dominated everybody and he got a heart attack dealing with her. And he was in the hospital when I saw him. I said to him, "You have got to surrender all resentments and then you have to surrender all anxieties and fears."

Some people have a fear of this, that or the other thing. A Canadian woman came to one of our Ashrams. She was so fearful that she had to change her place of employment. She was afraid that she would be at a tea party and drop her cup of tea in front of everybody. So, she changed from religious education and became a nurse. She said "If I am a nurse, I will not have to go to tea parties. " I saw that it was a real fear. She came to the Ashram and they announced one day that they were going to have a tea party. I said, "Sister Ruth, you and I are going to go to that tea party and you and I are both going to drop our cups right in front of everybody." She went into a panic, "Oh no," she said. I saw that she was frightened. I went to the Tea Party, but she was not there. I could see that she was running away. But during the last five minutes of the Tea Party, she showed up and she was standing in a group with a cup in her hand and I walked up behind her and took the cup out of her hand and let it drop — in front of everybody. She walked off laughing and I knew that the operation was successful. Now she is a minister's wife and goes to lots of tea parties.

There was a woman who said that several doctors diagnosed her physical condition as a serious illness and confined her to her hospital bed for a long time. She said, "I didn't think that I would ever recover if it were not for your book, *Abundant Living*. I was placed in the hospital for several weeks, diagnosed with nervous exhaustion and for several weeks the nurse would bring me sleeping pills and sedatives but they had no effect what ever. I saw through reading *Abundant Living* that my real illness was fear. After reading a portion of *Abundant Living* I would take the sedatives and sleeping pills the nurse would bring and hide them under a pillow or throw them under the bed and I found that I had no trouble falling off to sleep. The nurse found several of the pills under the bed one morning and gave me a good bawling out, but I told her that I had found something much more powerful and the peace of mind that I needed." Can that happen? Yes, it does happen.

I know a woman who dedicated her son to the ministry and was very glad indeed when he went into the ministry but then he got married and everything changed. She was willing to give him to God, but she was not willing to give him to another woman. And a conflict set up and she had a heart attack, and one day her son sat along side of her. "Mother, you dedicated me to God and now you must dedicate me to my wife. And now you must not only give me to God but to her as well. And you must let us live our lives." The woman saw her essential selfishness and surrendered the conflict by surrendering her self. The moment she did that she was a converted woman and was well. You have got to surrender the self to God.

A woman rose in one of our meetings and told how she had nearly choked herself to death by unsurrendered resentments. Her husband was a pastor and he thought that they should change churches—that they should go for another appointment in the Conference, but she thought that they should stay and finish their work. He went to the conference and arranged with the bishop for a transfer and did not tell her anything about it until it was all arranged. He then called her and told her about the transfer, and then he stayed away and let her pack up the house. She said, "I was boiling with resentments. I could not sleep and I was choking myself to

247

death. I went to the next appointment sick and was prepared to be an invalid." She said one day a woman sat along side her bed and said, "You took your husband for better or worse, didn't you? If he turns out worse, you had still better take him." She said, "I saw that I was acting badly and foolishly and so I surrendered the whole thing to God. The moment I did my breathing became normal again and you see that I can talk." And she could. She came here choking herself to death with resentments. God will heal you directly or he will heal you indirectly.

I have a photograph taken at one of the Ashrams with three women who were healed in three different ways. One woman had a rye neck, and her face was twisted and she could not look straight ahead and she needed to have an operation. She said to me, "can we have prayer together? I want you to pray for me." I went into the chapel and prayed for her and with her. I put my hands on her head explaining that I had no healing power, but it may be that that the love of God will use my hands but that it would be God who heals. We prayed together. The next morning she arose and said the "pull" is gone and in 2-3 days her face was straight. That is one way—God touched her directly and healed her.

The second woman had everything wrong with her. She was under weight and in poor health. She came to the healing service among others. I laid my hands on her. She went home that night and as she sat in her room in the Ashram, she reached for a cigarette as she had done for all of her adult life. She said, "I don't want it now, but later." The later never came. She had struggled with the habit of 2-3 packs of cigarettes a day for more than 20 years, and she could not give it up. But to her amazement, it was gone. She did not struggle; she did not fight with it; it was gone! Now that is the second type of healing. God did not touch her directly, but he touched the cause and her body bounded back into health.

The third type of healing was a woman who was going to have an operation for a cyst and she came to the healing service and we laid hands on her and nothing happened – nothing of the kind. And then she became interested in the Holy Spirit. She wanted to receive the gift of the Holy Spirit. She forgot all about her healing and began to seek the Holy Spirit and in a communion service, she found Him. She gloriously and wondrously found the filling of the Holy Spirit. That afternoon she was telling about this wonderful thing that had happened to her and she suddenly said the cyst was gone and it was. She went back to her doctor and the doctor said there will be no operation because there is no cyst. That was another method of healing. This time God gave her kind of healing that Paul speaks about when he says in Romans 8:11, "If the Spirit of him who raised Jesus from the dead dwells in you, he who raised Christ Jesus from the dead will also give life to your mortal bodies through his Spirit who dwells in you." The spirit that dwelt within her quickens her mortal body into health and that, I believe, is a type of healing – for the spirit of God to dwell within you and quicken you into health.

Disease is not the will of God. And God will either cure you now in one of these ways or give you power to use it until the final cure in the resurrection.

First World Ashram Congress, Jerusalem, July 1972, with E. Stanley Jones turning the Ashram movement over to the world

8. THE GIFT OF THE HOLY SPIRIT IS THE BIRTHRIGHT OF ALL CHRISTIANS

COMMENTARY ON TWO SERMONS ON THE HOLY SPIRIT

In these two sermons, Jones is explaining the purpose and function of the Holy Spirit — the birthright of all Christians. The Holy Spirit is God's effort to be as close to his children as possible. We can experience God as father — in relationship *to* us, but separate from us, as Son who is *with* us, an even closer relationship, and as the Holy Spirit who dwells *in* us. Jones emphasizes the active progression of God's relationship with us. The presence of the Holy Spirit *in* us is the culmination of God's seeking to be as close to us as possible: *"The Holy Spirit is the applied edge of redemption — redemption applied where it counts, on the inside of me. It is redemption* applied" (260). This redemption is now universalized and available to all.

The presence of the Holy Spirit *in* us is what enables us to do as Christ asks. Jones states that it would be impossible to "turn the other cheek, go the second mile and love our enemies" without the resources of the Holy Spirit in us. Jones affirms that, *"If you take the Holy Spirit out of the New Testament, you have a beautiful body of doctrine and teaching but incapable of being put into action"* (276).

Jones felt strongly that the church had missed its step in not sufficiently emphasizing the gift of the Holy Spirit at Pentecost. He writes in *The Christ of Every Road*:

The church is living between Easter and Pentecost. Easter stands for life wrought out, offered; Pentecost stands for life appropriated, lived to its fullest, unafraid and clearly and powerfully witnessing to an adequate way of human living. The church stands hesitant between the two (25).

According to Jones, it is as if a final fact about Jesus has been ignored. Jesus lived, died, rose from the dead, *and* then lives in us through the gift of the Holy Spirit. He comments:

To take the first three, but to stop short of the fourth, is the supreme tragedy of present-day Christian living. We emphasize his life, his death, and his resurrection. The consequence is that we have an objective gospel. It lies in history – not in us. And because it lies in history and is objective, the characteristic of Christian living is dimness, a sense of faraway-ness and unreality (Jones, *Christ of Every Road*, 91).

Sadly, according to Jones, the Church has not helped its members take the final step in incorporating the reality of Jesus **in** us. In another passage he asserts, "There is in Christianity, a lost chord, and that lost chord haunts us. Until we get it back our spiritual lives will be more wistful than winsome, more plaintive than passionate. That lost chord is Pentecost" (*Christ of Every Road*, 47).

In these two sermons on the Holy Spirit, Jones describes in detail the role of the Holy Spirit in our lives. **The Holy Spirit convicts us, converts us, cleanses us, consecrates us, commissions us, and finally conforms us to the mind of Jesus. (264)** He draws on a verse from Corinthians to summarize this transformation: "And all of us, with unveiled faces, seeing the glory of the Lord as though reflected in a mirror, are being transformed into the same image from one degree of glory to another; for this comes from the Lord, the Spirit" (2 Cor: 3:18). In that process of transformation/conversion, the Holy Spirit moves into the subconscious mind and redeems it, for according to Jones, the work of the Holy Spirit is largely in the

252

subconscious mind. He points up this conviction in *Abundant Living*: "The Holy Spirit not only fathoms the depths of man; He refashions the depths of man and unifies man at the center, so that the conscious and the subconscious speak the same language, understand each other, drive for the same goals, and own a common Lord" (152).

Jones explains in considerable detail the impact of the Holy Spirit in the lives of the apostles. Pentecost was a decisive event in their lives, and it was decisive because of the presence of the Holy Spirit:

> Draw a line through the New Testament and on one side is spiritual fumbling, hesitancy, inadequacy, defeat, and on the other side is certainty, courage, adequacy, victory. That lines runs straight through Pentecost. When we read the Acts of the Apostles, which is taken up with the doings of the apostles after Pentecost, we are struck with the incongruity between the apostles and their acts. Here were very ordinary men doing extraordinary things, thinking in an extraordinary way, leaving an extraordinary effect in the changed lives of men and society. The very temper and spirit of their lives was extraordinary. They seemed to have found a power by which to live. And far from being rampant emotionalism, the striking thing is their amazing balance and sanity. They burned with zeal, but they met issues and crises of the most far-reaching consequences and met them with poise and insight. They picked their way through intellectual and moral bogs and quagmires and marked out paths which we today tread with safety and salvation. And more than that, they brought to bear upon life a power that redeemed men and made them immediately God conscious (*Christ of Every Road*, 94-95).

Jones understood that the Holy Spirit was often a cause of considerable discomfort on the part of his listeners. Some were frightened by the Holy Spirit; others relished certain of the special gifts such as speaking in tongues, which Jones did not believe were a primary or necessary gift of the Holy Spirit.

Jones helps his listeners distinguish the difference between the *gifts* of the Spirit and the *gift* of the Holy Spirit. He stated that the gifts of the Holy Spirit were the virtues of Christ. Christ had the Holy Spirit but did not speak in unknown tongues, and it was therefore not required that his followers speak in tongues to demonstrate that they had gifts of the Holy Spirit.

As the birthright of every Christian, these sermons emphasize the gift of the Holy Spirit, rather than the separate gifts of prophecy, speaking in tongues, and the others. Here we see Jones' manner of handling the matter of speaking in tongues, which is often a contentious and divisive issue among many Christians. He did not judge those who would speak in tongues, but simply asked that the words should either be interpreted to the hearers or that speaking in an unknown language be done silently or in private. Jones did not believe that speaking in tongues was a part of the emphasis of the early church. (*Divine Yes*, 77) Rather, a special miracle occurred at Pentecost – God was using all languages and thereby "universalizing" the Christian message. Those who listened to God's message heard it in their own language. Paul said, "If you haven't got an interpreter — don't speak an unknown language."[1] Is speaking in tongues, then, an exclusive sign of the Holy Spirit? Jones would suggest, "No."

> Some people say the sign that you have the Holy Spirit is that you can speak in tongues. If you had the gift of tongues then you had the gift of the Spirit. If you haven't, you haven't. Now why did the gift of tongues come in the early days at Pentecost? I believe it was because the Jewish mold had to be broken. God broke that pattern in the very beginning. At Pentecost, people from all over that ancient world were present and began to hear in his own language the wonderful works of God. What did that mean? It meant

---

1   "If anyone speaks in a tongue, let there be only two or at most three, and each in turn; and let one interpret. But if there is no one to interpret, let them be silent in church and speak to themselves and to God" (1 Cor. 14:27-28).

that every language and every culture was to be a vehicle of the divine — that God was going to use all languages and all cultures. The Jewish mold was broken. I believe that was a special miracle for a special purpose, and I am persuaded that that miracle does *not* happen today. There was another type of tongues in Corinth — an unknown tongue that needed an interpreter, but at Pentecost they did not need an interpreter (288).

Jones' profound experience of the presence of the Holy Spirit while at Asbury College did not include speaking in tongues. In his autobiography, *A Song of Ascents*, he notes that everything that happened to the disciples at Pentecost was identical to what happened to Jones and the Wilmore, Kentucky community except for one thing. No one spoke in tongues. He writes, "Certainly God had a chance to give us the gift of tongues if he had wanted to. We were open for anything. The emphasis was on the gift of the Spirit, instead of on the "gifts of the Spirit." Had the emphasis been upon the "gifts" especially the gift of tongues, it would have left us with two groups – "tongues" and "non tongues". It would have left us divided. Instead we were one — one in the Holy Spirit" (70). In Jones' last book, *The Divine Yes*, he re emphasizes his views on the subject of speaking in tongues:

> The genius of the Christian faith is seeing today that, wherever the use of tongues is made as a sign of the gift of the Holy Spirit, you will find inevitable division. It did so then, and it does so now. The fruits of the Spirit do not divide; they unite (80).

Jones virtually never gives a sermon without specifying just *how* the listeners are to make use of what they have heard. He concludes these two sermons on the Holy Spirit with the method that we are to draw on if we wish to receive the Holy Spirit. The steps are as follows:

♦ Believe it is the divine intention for you to receive the Holy Spirit.

♦ Make sure that receiving the Holy Spirit is your intention.

♦ Bring the matter to a crisis.

♦ Remember the price you are to pay – **yourself**.

♦ Then pay the price of a complete **surrender.**

♦ Accept the gift of the spirit.

♦ Share His gift with others.

♦ Make the surrender once and for all and yet continuous.[2]

Receiving the gift of the Holy Spirit necessitates a complete self surrender (conversion). Jones maintains that, "The Holy Spirit surrenders to us when he comes in. Imagine the divine audacity to be willing to come down and live within me — next to everything I think, and say and am. He must love me to be willing to do that. He gives his all to come within me – can I give less than my all? No, it is an exchange: my little all for his all and what an exchange!" (*271*).

As the birthright of every Christian, the Holy Spirit is the normal and natural presence of God in our lives. We can all be baptized with the presence of the Holy Spirit in our lives. Jones ends these two sermons with an altar call offering his listeners the opportunity to have the presence of the Holy Spirit in their lives. He tells his congregation that Jesus Christ is present in the hall tonight and all they need to do is seek him.

A young minister went into a church. He was beaten. He saw a sign, which said "Jesus Christ is in this place. Anything can happen here." But he was frustrated and defeated, and he said to himself, "If anything can happen here, I better go in." And he went in and he knelt, and something happened to him. Today he is a pastor on fire

---

2   *Abundant Living,* pages 156-158 spells out the details of this process of receiving the Holy Spirit.

for God. Jesus Christ is in this place. Anything can happen here, and He is here to give us the Holy Spirit (296).

"THE GIFT OF THE HOLY SPIRIT IS THE BIRTHRIGHT OF ALL CHRISTIANS" THE HOLY SPIRIT (1960)

SERMON

IN the 4th chapter of Ephesians are these familiar words, "One Lord, one faith, one baptism."[3] I am going to talk to you tonight about the Holy Spirit. Who is he? What does he do? How can I find him? The Holy Spirit is a distinctly Christian conception with a distinctly Christian content. The phrase, the Holy Spirit, is not found in the Old Testament. In the Old Testament we find the word *spirit*, God's spirit, the spirit of the Lord, but not the Holy Spirit. "Take not thy holy spirit" but "thy holy" modifies spirit. "The Holy Spirit," the account says, "could not be given until Jesus had been glorified." Why? Because Jesus had to live, speak, die, rise again and go to the right hand of the Father before *content* could be put into the Holy Spirit — God's content, the content of Jesus — because people had strange ideas of what constitutes divine power.

I sat in a train in India and the people came and sat at the feet of a Sadhu in my compartment, a holy man. At every station people would come on board to sit at his feet. I asked one of his disciples, "Who is he?" He said, "He's God." But I could see that he was a spastic—no doubt suffering with cerebral palsy. He could not speak plainly without great effort, and they took the abnormality (of his physical condition) for

---

3   "There is one body and one Spirit, just as you were called to the one hope of your calling, one Lord, one faith, one baptism, one God and father of all, who is above all and through all and in all" (Eph.4:4-6).

257

God. Anything that was different was God. His disciple said to me, "He could tell you anything." So I asked him a question, but he said, "My head is tired now." If he had been physically normal the people would not have looked at him twice; however, he was abnormal and therefore judged to be divine. This is an example of the strange ideas men have held about what constitutes divine power.

The Old Testament said that the spirit of the Lord came upon Samson and Samson went out and slew a thousand men. Put that in the pages of the Acts of the Apostles and it would read something like this, "The Spirit of the Lord came upon the hundred and twenty in the upper room and they went out and slew a thousand people who had slain Jesus." You would shudder and you would think, "Would we do that with the spirit of Jesus?" "No." When you look into the face of Jesus and you've seen what divine power is like — it's a Christ-like type of power. Our previous views of the *power* of the spirit would have to be amended. The type of power that you would get in the Holy Spirit is the power that was in Jesus. He said: "I am going to give you another comforter, something like me." The Holy Spirit then is a Christ-like spirit.

An Ashram member (Brother Boyce) commented about the Holy Spirit. "You know when you talk about the Holy Spirit cold chills go up and down my spine."

I said, "Why?"

He said, "I am afraid of it."

I said, "What are you afraid of?"

He said, "I am afraid of rampant emotionalism — an off-centered oddness."

I said, "But my brother, the power that was in Jesus was the Holy Spirit and Jesus was the most balanced character that ever moved down the pages of human history. Every virtue balanced by its opposite virtue. He went off into no visions and no dreams. From his guidance, through prayer, you and I get our guidance and are in possession of all his faculties. Are you afraid of being made like Christ? There was nothing psychopathic about him."

"That changes the picture," he said. He took me by the lapel of the coat and he said, "Come out here and sit down and talk to me about it."

I sat down and quoted this passage of scripture, "If you then who are evil know how to give good gifts unto your children, how much more will your heavenly father give the Holy Spirit to those who ask him."[4] I said, "My Brother, let's ask him." And I started to pray, I hadn't prayed two sentences when he grabbed my arm and said, "You need not pray he's already come." I never finished my prayer. He went from resistance to receptivity in two minutes. This Brother worked fast! When he understood the conception that the Holy Spirit was a Christ-like spirit, then he could take it with both hands and open arms.

We're afraid of the Holy Spirit. But why should we be afraid? I believe that the receiving of the Holy Spirit at Pentecost is normal Christianity. But most of us are subnormal and you know when you are subnormal disease germs rush and take you over. But some people in the name of Pentecost have gone above normal into fever and because some people have gone into fever it has scared most of us into anemic condition! I don't want to be above normal or below normal. I'd like to be normal. The Holy Spirit is my birthright as a Christian. The Holy Spirit is not an influence or an energy, or merely an impersonal kind of power. Jesus says "He shall guide you into all truths."[5] Jesus makes Him (the Holy Spirit) a person.

The general name for God is God the Father. When God comes to redeem us where we are, we say God the Son. When God abides in our hearts, we say God the Holy Spirit. The Father is God up there, the Son is God back here, and the Holy

4   Luke 11:13.
5   John 16:13.

Spirit is God *in us* — here. When the rupture came between man and God the divine lover, God the divine lover wanted to get back again in contact with man. For *love* seeks out an object for its love. God's first step toward renewed contact with His people was when God came upon the smoking mountain and thundered the *Ten Commandments*, the law — "thou shall and thou shall not." That was His first approach. Then He came in a movable tabernacle then in a fixed temple where he dwelt in the Shekinah.[6] God then came closer, in the incarnation, Emmanuel means *God with us*. But it was "with" and with is still not close enough. So Jesus said, "The Spirit of truth is with you and shall be *in* you."[7] It's the *in* that God is driving at. The Holy Spirit is the applied edge of redemption – redemption applied where it counts, on the inside of me. It is redemption *applied*.

Now Jesus said to his disciples, "Don't leave Jerusalem until you be imbued with power on high."[8] Their tendency, of course, would be to get out of Jerusalem — they caved in at Jerusalem; they had all forsaken him and fled. If they could get rid of those bitter memories by distance they would take it. And so I suppose they would say, "Let's go to Galilee and get away." Jesus said, "Don't — stay right where you have been a failure and I am going to make you a success. Where you caved in I am going to give you power to face that situation." And that did something for the apostles. Suppose they had received the Holy Spirit in Galilee in a quiet mountain, they would have said, "Yes it works here in a quiet mountain, but it won't work up there, (in Jerusalem)." They would have always had an

---

6 Shekinah is the presence of God on earth or a symbol or manifestation of His presence.

7 "This is the Spirit of truth, whom the world cannot receive, because it neither sees him nor knows him. You know him, because he abides with you, and he will be in you" (John 14:17).

8 "While staying with them, he ordered them not to leave Jerusalem, but to wait there for the promise of the Father" (Acts 1:4).

apprehension about Jerusalem, so Jesus said, "Stay right where you have been a failure and I will make you a success." They stayed and when the Holy Spirit came upon them — *in them* — they turned and faced Jerusalem without blinking an eye. They called Jerusalem to repentance: "You killed the Lord of glory, open the gates of repentance and salvation."[9] The people then poured into the city by the thousands. They conquered Jerusalem. All sense of inferiority and escapism and runawayism had gone. They were now marching up to the worst (of their experiences/challenges) and conquering them.

Now my text says, "One Lord, one faith, one baptism."[10] The one Lord, of course, is the Lord Jesus. It is interesting that those early disciples said, "Jesus is Lord" — not will be –but *is*. How did they come to that conclusion? How could they believe that a man who was born in one of our stables, worked at one of our carpenter's benches, walked our dusty roads, slept upon our hillsides, died upon one of our trees, and was laid in one of our rock tombs, that that man was at the right hand of final authority and would have the last word in human affairs? How did they believe that? Not easily, I imagine. Their characteristic affirmation regarding God was, "Hear Oh Israel, the Lord our God is one Lord." God was Lord. Here they were saying Jesus *is* Lord. How did they come to that conclusion? Not lightly. They were forced to it; they saw that his touch upon life was the touch of God. He was doing something that only God could do and from their almost unwilling lips came the confession, "Jesus is Lord." They believed in one Lord and one faith. One faith in that one Lord and that was the thing that unified them.

If I were to say to this audience tonight, "What do you believe?" You'd go that way and this way — no two believing exactly alike; but suppose I say, "Whom do you trust?" and you'd come together with one name upon your lips, one loyalty

---

9 Acts 1:23.

10 Ephesians 4:5.

in your heart, Jesus! Around Him we are one. We have one faith in the one Lord.

And then there is one baptism. Now the usual interpretation is that it is baptism by water, I have nothing derogatory to say about water baptism for I have given it many times and in many lands and in many modes. But it would seem a disappointment if it were one Lord, one faith and then one baptism by water. What was this one baptism, which this one Lord gave? The account tells us that John says, "I baptize you with water, but he that cometh after me he shall baptize you with the Holy Spirit and with fire."[11] That was his one baptism and Jesus said, "John truly baptized you with water, but ye shall be baptized with the Holy Spirit, not many days hence." Jesus never baptized with water, although his disciples did. Why didn't he baptize with water? Because Jesus saved himself to give the one baptism — the baptism of the Holy Spirit. The account says in Acts that he has ascended to the father and receiving the gift of the Holy Spirit he poured forth this, which you now see and hear.[12] Now that was his baptism, the baptism of the Holy Spirit.

Now if the Holy Spirit comes upon us, what happens? I am going to lift out of the scriptures as much as I can certain things that the Holy Spirit does and then we will see at the end how we can find him. First, he *convicts*. You remember it says, "He shall convict the world of sin."[13] The Holy Spirit upsets us in the beginning. It does so to set us up on a higher level. It is a divine upsetting and some people that come into our Ashrams find that in the first few days that they are upset. We do not apologize for that upsetting because I think that it is a good

---

11 Matthew 3:11.

12 "This Jesus God raised up, and of that all of us are witnesses. Being therefore exalted at the right hand of God, and having received from the Father the promise of the Holy Spirit, he has poured out this that you both see and hear" (Acts 2:32-33).

13 John 16:8.

upsetting. One woman said, "I'm going to leave (the Ashram)." She said, "I came here for comfort and I didn't get it." She wanted sympathy. She had lost her husband ten years before and she wanted us to sit and hold her hand and tell her how sorry we were. We didn't. We told her she could be adequate to face her husband's death and everything else with joy and victory.

In Canada a woman stood up at one of our meeting and she said, "I've lived for ten years under a shadow of a grief. My husband died ten years ago and I used to go out in the morning to listen to a bird that came up in the tree to sympathize with me. It used to say, "Poor Helen." (That was her name). 'Poor Helen, Poor Helen.' It added to my self pity." And then she said, "I came here to this Ashram and Brother Stanley standing by the lakeside giving his addresses would have his sentences punctuated by a deep-throated bullfrog which kept saying, 'So what, so what, so what.' Now, she said, "I have been listening to the gospel according to that bird — poor Helen — pity, self-pity. Now I am going to listen to the gospel according to that bullfrog - I have lost my husband - so what; I've had sorrow - so what; I've had grief, yes, every one has had it. I am going to use my sorrow and make something out of it." Her Calvary turned to an Easter morning.

A woman, in the midst of our Open Heart,[14] sent a note to me and said, "Why do we sit here and blame ourselves this way? Why don't we talk positively?" I said, "My sister this is the morning of the Open Heart and also the morning of the Upset Heart. You can't get rid of things unless you upset your heart and turn it over - spill it over." She didn't want to face the facts and get victory. She wanted comfort. The Holy Spirit doesn't bring comfort; He brings a divine uneasiness. This woman didn't leave the Ashram but stayed and she walked

14 Each Ashram opens with the experience of the Morning of the Open Heart where the participants respond to a series of questions: "Why have you come? What do you want? What do you really need?" (Jones, *A Song of Ascents*, 224).

out of that Ashram with adequacy to face her husband's death and everything else. So the Holy Spirit convicts us and if you felt badly then that is all right. It's an upset to set you up on a higher level.

The second thing that the Holy Spirit does is to *convert*. If He convicts, He converts. Jesus said, "Except ye be converted and become like little children you cannot enter the Kingdom of God."[15] There are three things there: "except ye be converted." Here I am going the wrong direction, away from God, so the first step is to turn around – reversal. So I reverse myself; I turn around and go in a new direction. I come to Jesus and He gives me a new spirit – the spirit of a child. "Except you be converted and become as little children." When you have the spirit of a child, you have a fresh beginning, a new simplicity and a new openness and a new receptivity. I can turn around, but I cannot give myself a new spirit. God must do that. He must reach down and change this basic human nature of mine. Then I enter the Kingdom of God – a new sphere of living, a new direction. And, in that new sphere of living – the Kingdom of God – Jesus and I work out things together. I supply willingness and He supplies power. He converts us. We are born of the spirit. It's a mystery and a miracle. I can't explain it, but I know it.

The third thing that the Holy Spirit does is that he *cleanses*. The Holy Spirit **convicts, He converts and He cleanses.** Usually there is a period separating conversion and cleansing; it was that way with me. After I was converted I walked under cloudless skies for a year, the sun of my happiness had apparently risen in the sky to stay there forever. The day after I was converted I walked out and I had never seen the universe like this. I walked up to an old chum of mine and slapped him

---

15 "At that time the disciples came to Jesus and asked, "Who is the greatest in the Kingdom of heaven? He called a child, whom he put among them, and said, 'Truly I tell you, unless you change (be converted) and become like children, you will never enter the kingdom of heaven'" (Matt 18:1-4).

on the back and I said, "My, this is a D-fine (damned fine) day isn't it," using the old vocabulary to express my newfound joy. I think the angels must have smiled and must have said to each other, "He is trying to say Hallelujah but he doesn't know the language." They said, "Let him alone he will learn." I said to myself, "I can't do that again, I have been converted." So it (my inappropriate language) dropped off. But if I didn't say something the stones would have cried out; the hard bare facts of life would have cried out. But after about a year, I found things coming out of my subconscious. I didn't know about the subconscious then, but out of the depths of me came tempers, ugliness, and grumpiness — emotions that I hadn't known before. I said, "What's the matter here?" And I was appalled because I thought everything was straight; but everything apparently wasn't clean.

At that period I got a hold of a little book called, *The Christian's Secret To A Happy Life* by a Quaker woman, Hannah Whithall Smith.[16] I began to read it. I got to the forty-second page when something, a voice within me, spoke and said, "Now is the time to receive the Holy Spirit." I said, "I don't know what I want. This book is telling me, let me read it; and I tried to read on. At the close, I'll begin to seek, but not now, for I don't know what it is all about." But the voice was persistent, "Now is the time to get it." But I said, "I don't know what I want. Let me read this book and then I will seek." I tried to read on but the words were literally blurred, so I saw that I was in a controversy. I dropped on my knees beside my

---

16 Whithall-Smith, Hannah. *The Christian's Secret to a Happy Life,* Christian Witness Co.,1875. Hannah Tatum Whitall Smith (1832–1911) was a lay speaker and author in the Holiness movement in the United Statesand the Higher Life movement in the United Kingdom of Great Britain and Ireland. She was also active in the Women's Suffrage movement and the Temperance movement. < Smith, Hannah Whitall." Encyclopædia Britannica. 2007. Encyclopædia Britannica Online. 31 Mar. 2007 <http://www.britannica.com/eb/article-9125976> The Asbury Theological Seminary's Archives in Wilmore has a great collection on Hannah Whithall-Smith.

bed and I said, "Lord what shall I do?" And He said to me, "Will you give me your all?" I thought a moment and I said, "Why, yes. I will. I will lay it all on your altar." "Well" he said, "Take my all. And the altar sanctifies that gift." I said, "Yes, I believe that and I arose from my knees." And I said, "Yes, it's done." I walked around the room pushing my hands this way and that way as though I was pushing doubt away. I did that for I don't know how many minutes when suddenly I was filled – wave after wave – of divine fire seemed to be going through my being – purging, cleansing. I could only walk the floor with tears of joy flowing down my cheeks, in praise. He had moved in. And then life seemed to be unified at a deeper level. I didn't seem to be at war with myself as I had been before.

I now see that He moved into the subconscious. We know that in conversion the conscious mind is converted. A new loyalty and a new love is introduced into the conscious mind. But what about the subconscious mind? The psychologists have lifted the lids from the subconscious and what they show is not very beautiful. We see driving urges, which have come down from a long history of humanity. These urges have a disposition toward evil, and what they describe is strangely like original sin. Can the subconscious mind be redeemed? These driving urges of self, sex and the herd reside in the subconscious. Can they be redeemed? If not then the 7th chapter of Romans is the best that we can have… "Oh wretched man that I am, I want to do this and can't and I don't want to do this and I do it."[17] And some people think that that is Paul's gospel – if that were Paul's gospel, we would have never have heard of Paul again. There is no gospel in it. It is defeat. The 8th (of Romans) chapter is Christianity where the Holy Spirit, the spirit of life in Christ Jesus, had made him free from the law, sin and death. He sings his way down to that 8th chapter, free. Can the subconscious mind be redeemed? I look at the disciples before Pentecost and I find that they are inconsistent in their

17 Romans 7:24.

spiritual life; they were capable of great heights and great depths. They seem to go up and down in their spiritual life.

At the Santa Claus Ashram in Indiana[18] I would swim across the lake — it isn't too far across — and when I would land on the other bank my feet would go down into the mud and ooze and bubbles would arise to the surface — not from my standing but from the decaying vegetable matter at the bottom of the lake. These were the gases that were coming up in the form of bubbles. You can see the bubbles arising from the depths of the subconscious in the apostles that told that there were decaying things down underneath and that their subconscious had not been redeemed.

I want you to reflect on the source of these bubbles, that is to think about what was going on in the subconscious mind of the apostles. I will illustrate each of these forces or drives of the subconscious.

1. *Selfish egoism* – the apostles quarreled over who was in first place.

2. *Self-righteousness* – "Although they all deny thee, yet not will I."[19] They took a they/I relationship.

3. *Resentment* – "Shall we bid fire to come down from heaven to consume them."[20] The apostles wanted to bring it (resentment) down from heaven to give it a religious tinge. But it was just pure resentment.

---

18 Santa Claus is the oldest United Methodist campground in the state of Indiana (located in Spencer County) and the first permanent campground ever established for that purpose here. Started in 1851 by John G. Lukemeyer, a minister for the German ME Church, the camp meeting was held annually until 1955, when it was replaced by Ashram. Presently it is owned by the Santa Claus Campground Trust, a private corporation formed in 1989, which operates a full summer schedule of youth camps and a May camp for senior adults. http://www.depauw.edu/library/archives/methinventories/santa_claus_campground.htm>

19 Mark 14:29-31.

4. *Spiritual impotence* – "why could we not cast it out?"

5. *Criticism* – "why this waste?"

6. *Group bigotry* – "we forbade them for they follow not us."

7. *Race/Prejudice*, "Send her, a Syrophoenician women, away for she cries after us."[21]

8. *Selfish-acquisitiveness*, "we have left all to follow thee, then what do we get?

9. *A dislike of self sacrifice*, "be it far from thee, this shall never be."

10. *Fear* - They were behind closed doors after Easter morning and before Pentecost.

The apostles were between Easter and Pentecost and they were behind closed doors. That is about where the church is today. It believes in the resurrection, yes. If you ask the church that question, it says, "Yes," we believe in the resurrection, He's alive." Yet we are behind closed doors, all shut up within ourselves, afraid and in the grip of elemental fears.

These are the ten forces that came up out of the sub-conscious mind of the apostles. Can the subconscious mind be redeemed? The good news is this: Yes! For the area of the work of the Holy Spirit is largely, if not entirely, in the subconscious mind. If we will turn over to Him all we know, the conscious, and all we don't know, i.e., the subconscious, He will move into depths that we cannot control and cannot order and He will take over these urges/drives. He will not erase them, but He will cleanse them. For example, the self, He will cleanse from selfishness and give it back to us again. The herd urge He'll cleanse from subservience to the herd and fasten it on the Kingdom of God – he gives it back to us again. And then

20 Luke 9:54.

21 Matthew 15:23.

the conscious mind and the subconscious mind are now under one control – the control of the Holy Spirit.

Then the fourth thing that the Holy Spirit does is that he *consecrates*, "who through the eternal spirits offered himself to God."[22] Through the eternal spirit He offered Himself. Is the Holy Spirit the spirit of consecration? Yes. A good many people have the idea that you have to consecrate yourself and you have to stand at the altar and keep your things on the altar. You may have the experience of trying to keep everything under control. You don't. Rather you turn it over to him and say, "You've got me and you've got to keep my powers under control." And so the Holy Spirit keeps your drives on the altar and keeps them consecrated.

Then He *commissions* us. The Holy Spirit said to the group at Antioch, "Separate me Barnabas and Saul for work to which I have called them."[23] They laid hands on them and were sent forth thus by the Holy Spirit. The Holy Spirit then sends us forth; he is the spirit of commission. He commissions us. Everything takes on meaning and value. Laymen and minister both feel a commission when they receive the Holy Spirit.

And finally, the Holy Spirit *conforms* us to the mind of Jesus, "But we all with unveiled face beholding the glory of the Lord are changed into the same likeness from one degree of glory into another, but this comes from the Lord who is the spirit."[24] And then he makes us creative in its power.

An Indian woman said to me one day, "Most people are problem conscious instead of power conscious." And that Indian woman taught me something very, very important – we should not be problem conscious but power conscious. The

---

22 Hebrews 9:14.

23 Acts 13:2.

24 2 Corinthians 3:18.

Holy Spirit recreates us and then makes us creative. It says in the Old Testament ... "His Holy Spirit who calls his glorious arm to go at the right hand of Moses."[25] His Holy Spirit calls his glorious arm to go at the right hand of Moses; God's glorious arm was going at the right hand of Moses. When Moses lifted up his right hand, God's right hand went with it too. That came from the spirit, so he makes you creative and makes it possible for you to do anything you have to do.

Two laymen were discussing two ministers. They said, "We can't understand these two men. One is a man with half the powers of the other but he produces twice the result. The other man has twice the power but produces half the result. What's the difference?" They came to the conclusion that when the man with twice the power stood up, he stood up alone and projected himself and his power into the situation, but he was alone. But when the other man with half the power stood up he was not alone, there was Another. And everything that he said and did was heightened by Another – the Holy Spirit.

A missionary in India was treating someone who said, "You only have a third-class medical education." And this missionary said, "Yes, but I've got a first-class God." Some people have a first-class education and a third-class God. God is a weak influence in their lives. But some people with half the education do twice as much as other people because God has their powers. They are not working in the energy of the flesh but in the power of the spirit.

How do we receive the Holy Spirit? I am going to give you the steps:

1. First, it is God's intention to give you the Holy Spirit, "But this spake he of the spirit that they that believed on him were to receive."[26] Note the phrase, "...were to receive." It was God intention to give them the Holy Spirit. And to whom? To those who believe in Him. If you believe in Him

---

25 Isaiah 63:12.

then it is your birthright to receive the gift of the Holy Spirit. It is God's intention to give you the Holy Spirit. You don't have to overcome his reluctance; you simply have to lay hold on His highest willingness.

2. Make it your intention, not your vagrant wish nor will, but your intention to get your birthright. You as a child of God now have a right to reserve your right to that birthright. The Bible says, "The house of Jacob shall possess it's possessions."[27] Go and possess your possessions for it's yours but you haven't taken it.

3. Offer a complete self-surrender. The Holy Spirit surrenders to us when He comes in. Imagine the divine audacity to be willing to come down and live within me next to everything I think and say and am. He must love me to be willing to do that. He gives His all to come within me. Can I give less than my all? No, it is an exchange — my little all for His all and what an exchange!

4. We receive the gift of the Holy Spirit by faith. Faith is welcoming that which you believe in. You believe in it; now welcome it, and make it your own. Faith is pure receptivity. For example, I was about to take over the prayer vigil from a woman. As I walked up the aisle of the little chapel where she was seated with her back toward me I tapped her on the shoulder and I said, "I'm taking over." She was so engaged in seeking the gift of the Holy Spirit that when I said "I'm taking over" (and she transferred that message to the now presence of the Holy Spirit) and looked up into my face and her face was a sunrise. She said, "Oh, *He* has taken over!" Right then her faith took hold and victory came and He had taken over. The next year she showed me her watch and on the inside of her watch she had engraved these initials — I T O. I'm Taking Over.

---

26 John 7:39.

27 Obadiah 1:17.

In India, I was up in the Himalayan mountains and a British official — the highest official of the district, was going to visit the mission station that day and we were waiting anxiously for him. I looked up and saw him coming around the mountainside with his retinue and I turned to the missionary lady and I said, "He's come." She had been seeking the Holy Spirit and she looked at me and said, "He has come." My saying, "He's come," just turned the tide of her faith. It took hold; it was hers.

Praying Hyde was one of our greatest missionaries in India. They called him Praying Hyde. He was a Presbyterian missionary — United Presbyterian. When he went out to India for first time, he went by ship. When he got on board ship he found a letter from three ladies which said, "We are praying for you that you might receive the Holy Spirit." It made him peeved and he crumpled the letter and threw it down on the deck of the vessel. He said, "I am going now to India. If I haven't got the Holy Spirit, then what spirit do I have? And why should they presume to pray that I might receive the Holy Spirit?" But afterwards he thought better of it and took that crumpled letter and straightened it out and as he looked at it he got down on his knees and received the Holy Spirit. Well, I had that man in my home for three days in Lucknow, India, and I give you my word of honor – he never touched the bed for three days. The bed was *never* touched for three days. For three days and for three nights he was in the prayer room. He was praying for an outpouring spirit of God upon India and upon Lucknow. I went into the prayer room from time-to-time and I remember when I came in I felt like crawling under a rug. He'd been there for three days and three nights and I stepped into it fresh, but he had power. But it was the Holy Spirit that was praying within him.

I have spoken before about a happening that took place a year after I was converted. Just before I was called to the mission field an experience came to me, which I think I might recount. It was so unprovoked, even unsought, and I couldn't understand why it happened. It was the greatest spiritual experience that I ever witnessed in any land. A group of us, three or four of us young men in college, were in a young man's room praying about 10:00 o'clock at night. I remember that I was rather drowsy and I had my head on the side of the bed. As I knelt beside the bed, suddenly we were all swept off our feet by the Holy Spirit. We never slept the balance of the night. I could only walk the floor and praise Him.

Brother Pickett came up about 2:00 or 3:00 in the morning and said, "Stanley, He giveth his beloved — sleep." I said, "Yes, Brother Pickett, but I can't sleep." The next morning we went to the chapel service but there wasn't any chapel service. Nobody preached but everybody was under the power of the Holy Spirit. For four days there was no preaching — only people down on their faces, prone, praying for pardon, for release and then they would get it. This spread out into the surrounding country side and people came to Asbury.[28] When they would come inside the college compound they would fall under the power of the Spirit before they even got to the chapel. Some came to me and said, "Come out. There are people out here seeking God." Every classroom was turned into a prayer meeting. There were no classes for three days, and at the end there was probably not an unconverted person in that whole school. I wondered what it meant, but I saw later what it meant. From that moment I was ready to go anywhere, do anything and God said, "all right – I want you to be a missionary." That experience of the Holy Spirit created the climate. I said, "All right I am ready to go anywhere." I thought it was to be in Africa but it turned out to be India. (I will tell that story some other time.)[29] I saw the resources that are behind a person when the Holy Spirit is present. You don't have to work in the energy of the flesh but you can work in the power of the spirit, and

---

28 Asbury College is in Wilmore, Kentucky.

273

you can take everything you have and make something else out of it. By *faith* — you receive the gift of the Holy Spirit.

Let me quote my passage again, the passage that was thrown across the chasm when Brother Boyce walked across into the promised land of the experience of the Holy Spirit. "If ye then being evil know how to give good gifts unto your children, how much more should your heavenly father give the Holy Spirit to those who ask him?"[30] God's highest gift can be had for the asking when you ask Him with your life.

Now there is only one thing to do after we've talked about the Holy Spirit and that is to seek Him. And that is why we have put down these rugs, these blankets and created an improvised altar and this is what we are going to do. Some will come to find the birth of the Spirit. You say that, "I'm not sure if I am born of the Spirit and I would like to know — to have the experience that I am really born of the Spirit."

Some will say that I believe I am born of the Spirit but I am not filled with the Spirit. If you are a half filled vessel but with

---

29 "I thought I was to go to Africa, but when I graduated from college, I had a letter from the President of Asbury saying; "It is the will of the faculty, the student body, the townspeople, and we believe it is the will of God, for you to come and teach in this college." At the same time I had a letter from a very trusted friend saying: "I believe that it is the will of God for you to go into evangelistic work here in America." At that very time I had a letter from the Methodist Mission Board saying: "It is our will to send you to India." Here was a perfect traffic jam of wills! I had to have a clear way out. Other peoples' interpretation of the will of God for me would not do. I would have to know for myself and choose for myself. So I took the letter from the Mission Board, went into my room, spread it out on a chair, knelt beside the chair, and said: "Dear Father, I've got to answer this letter, and to do so may decide my life work. I am willing to go anywhere and do anything you want me to do. Tell me and I'll obey. What is it?" Very clearly the voice spoke: "It's India." I arose from my knees and said: "It's India." (Jones, *A Song of Ascents*).

30 Matthew 7:11.

not enough to over flow, come forward and ask to be filled with the Spirit.

Some will come to lay a resentment at His feet, others to lay a fear, others to lay an un-surrendered self, others will come to lay a guilt, others will come to lay an inferiority, and some will come to lay sheer emptiness. But whatever the need is we are going to come here and pray until we get ourselves off our own hands and into the hands of God. And then we will go back to our seats and others will come and take our places. And we will come and go while our pianist will play three or four verses of: *"Just As I Am;" "My Faith Looks Up To Thee;" "When I Survey the Wondrous Cross;"and "There is A Fountain Filled With Blood."* Three or four verses each of these and if they are still coming, she will start again.

We are all going to be in prayer both at the altar and while you are in your seats. A nurse said to me one night and said, "thank you very much for giving us the opportunity to get to our knees, for that is where we belong." That is where we do belong, I am going to be here with you and you just come. I need not urge you to come, your own urges will urge you to come and you will want to come. We will come and go and we will pray until we get ourselves off of our own hands and into the hands of God and then we'll go back to our seats. Others will come and take our places. We will come and go and we believe that the Spirit of God is going to work mightily here tonight for everybody. Now our sister will play and you will come. God bless you and I will meet you here.

"THE GIFT OF THE HOLY SPIRIT IS
THE BIRTHRIGHT OF ALL CHRISTIANS"
THE HOLY SPIRIT (1961)

SERMON

I have often said that I thought the Negro spirituals were the most triumphant religious music of the world. It's pain set to music — pain become healing — "nobody knows the trouble I've seen, glory hallelujah."[31] Anybody who starts there and ends there has got something.[32] Thank you. Shall we bow our heads for a moment of silent prayer? – Amen

In the 7th chapter in the gospel of John the 37th verse down thru the 39th we read these words, "On the last day of the feast, the great day, Jesus stood up and proclaimed, "If anyone thirst, let him come unto me and drink." He who believes in me as the scripture has said, out of his heart shall flow rivers of living water. Now this he said about the Spirit, which those who believed in him were to receive for (the Spirit) had not yet been given because Jesus had not yet been glorified."[33]

One night during the Ashram I speak upon the Holy Spirit for the Christian faith without the Holy Spirit is a *Council of Perfection*. It is asking you to do things that we can't do, turn the other cheek, go the second mile, love your enemies. It is

---

31 Henry T. Burleigh, Nobody Knows de Trouble I've Seen. New York, 1917.

32 "It is good to tell the Negro that he has produced in the Negro spirituals the most triumphant religious music the world has ever seen, because he has set his disabilities to music; but to leave the matter there and not give ourselves to doing away with those disabilities is to make religion an opiate" (Jones, *Christ and Human Suffering* 184).

33 John 7:37-39.

impossible unless there is a divine reinforcement and the Holy Spirit is the applied edge of redemption. It is redemption where it counts, down amidst the driving urges. If you take the Holy Spirit out of the New Testament you have a beautiful body of doctrine, teaching, beautiful life, but incapable of being put into action.

A woman cultured and refined came into a group, she had been a churchwoman all her life and she said, "I have been in the church all my life, but I haven't the slightest idea what they mean by the Holy Spirit." You take the Holy Spirit out and it's hard to catch/seize the beat (of Christianity). But here were men in the Acts of the Apostles doing things they couldn't do. They were reversing all the values of antiquity, turning the stream of history into new channels and doing it without effort. They weren't doing it. You could see the difference between the coming of the Holy Spirit and before He came.

You can see it at Ephesus. There were twelve men there in Ephesus, 19th chapter of Acts, but they lost or never had initiative. They were huddled together for protective purposes, but they had no initiative. And Paul came down there and saw that there was something lacking, definitely lacking. He put his finger upon the pulse of these people and said, "Did you receive the Holy Spirit?" They looked confused and said, "We've never heard anything about it, whether there will be any Holy Spirit?"[34] Then Paul instructed them about the matter and they received the gift of the Holy Spirit. What happened? Immediately they were on the offensive. Immediately the same thing that happened with the other twelve began to happen with this twelve. They went on the offensive and all Ephesus was shaken to its' depths and the people came and burned

---

34 While Apollos was in Corinth, Paul passed through the interior regions and came to Ephesus, where he found some disciples. He said to them, "Did you receive the Holy Spirit when you became believers?" They replied, "No, we have not even heard that there is a Holy Spirit." (Acts 19:1-7).

their books of magic. And the account ends up by saying, "So the word of God grew mightily and prevailed"[35]

However, before the coming of the Holy Spirit they had a very popular pastor, Apollos. He was a very eloquent and learned in the scriptures. He had everything except the Holy Spirit and the consequence was that the Christians that were produced didn't have that creative something that comes with the Holy Spirit for the Holy Spirit is the Spirit of creation.

Now Jesus stood up on that last great day of the feast, after they had gotten everything they could from the highest revelation that had been given to them that day – the highest morality. He said, "If you still thirst come unto me and drink." That was an amazing thing to say. Buddha pointed to the Eight Fold Noble Path..."Follow that."[36] Confucius said, "Take my teaching."[37] Socrates pointed to his philosophy. Moses pointed to the law – Muhammad to the Qur'an. Only Jesus could say, "Come unto me." Here infinite authority or infinite arrogance — speaks. How dare one man say to another — "Come unto me and drink?"

All of us have to point beyond ourselves to truth, to the way, to the life. Only Jesus had the sacred task of pointing to

---

35 Acts 19:20.

36 The Eight-Fold Path is the fourth of the Four Noble Truths - the first of the Buddha's teachings. All the teachings flow from this foundation. The Noble Truth of the Path that leads to Awakening. The path is a process to help you remove or move beyond the conditioned responses that obscure your true nature. In this sense the Path is ultimately about unlearning rather than learning — another paradox. We learn so we can unlearn and uncover. < http://www.buddhanet.net/e-learning/8foldpath.htm>

37 Confucius (551–479 BC) was a famous Chinese thinker and social philosopher. His philosophy emphasized personal and governmental morality, correctness of social relationships, justice and sincerity. These values gained prominence in China over other doctrines, such as Legalism or Daoism during the Han Dynasty. < Confucius." Encyclopædia Britannica. 2007. Encyclopædia Britannica Online. 31 Mar. 2007 <http://www.britannica.com/eb/article-9361385>

himself and saying, "I'm the way, I'm the truth, I'm the life and I'm the fountain that you have been thirsting for."[38] There is no half way to mark between the two. Either he is God or he is not god. Is it not blasphemy for one to say, "Come unto me." How dare one man say that to another? If he is not the incarnate God, then he is incarnate blasphemy. I choose the other hypothesis.

Now he said, "When you get the best you can get from the best – your best is not good enough. You still need me." And so not merely the down and out (need Him) but the up and on top need him too. And he said, "Your deepest need is to receive the gift of the Holy Spirit."

In Finland in the Open Heart[39] — a pastor got up and said, "My wife sent me here." She said, "You've got to go." She said, "The fact of the matter is you have run dry as a pastor." That is serious when a wife tells you that. And so he said, "I've come because my fountain has run dry." One woman sat up in one of our meetings and said, "My body has been wrung dry of all power to resist disease."

Do you remember the man who before he began to preach put his hands this way and then this way and somebody said to him, "Why did you do that before you preached?" And he said, "Well what I was going to say would be in quotation marks." Preaching in quotation marks doesn't win people (for Christ). It might be brilliant and it might be scintillating and it might be wonderful, but it isn't from the heart and so doesn't reach the heart. And the demons jumped on them and said, "Paul we know, Jesus we know, but who are you?" They jumped all over second hand preaching.

---

38 John 14:6.

39 Each Ashram opens with the experience of the Morning of the Open Heart where the participants respond to a series of questions: "Why have you come?What do you want? What do you really need?" (Jones, *A Song of Ascents*, 224).

A man in England, a rector, was a rector for 56 years in one church in the Anglican Communion and the account said that he never preached an original sermon in 56 years. He read somebody else's sermons for 56 years maybe that's why they stood him. Jesus said, "If you are thirsty come." Now I have no message for the un-thirsty, if you are thirsty, deep down thirsty – then I have a message for you tonight because it is not mine. I am going to repeat his words. He said, "Come unto me and drink."[40] Not only come to me, but come unto me and drink – receive. Many come to Him and they drink but don't receive. They are always giving, always giving, always giving. They say, "I'm consecrating. I'm going to do this; I'm going to do that; I'm going to do the other." But they never learned that gentle art of lowly receptivity. "Come unto me and drink" – take. Instead of taking we set the promises of God to music and sing them.

One man was given a check; he was so grateful for the check that he framed it and put it on his wall. You go look in your house and see if you haven't got any framed checks… that were countersigned in the blood of Jesus and you just put them on the wall instead of cashing them. Drink – learn how to take it if he says so — take it. I suppose that is the greatest disappointment of Jesus — they don't take Him.

Do you remember the proud, strong Jesus on his way to the house of Jairus and the woman reached up through the crowd and touched the hem of his garment and Jesus said, "Who touched me?" And Peter said, "Why Lord, the multitudes are thronging you and why do you ask who touched me?" And Jesus said, "Somebody touched me."[41] Is there a difference between thronging and touching? Yes. We throng Jesus every Sunday morning with our thoughts and our worship and our everything. But few touch Him. Few deliberately say, "I want you for my needs and I touch you." We are all thronging Him

---

40 John 7:37.

41 Mark 5:21-31.

here. We hope everybody will touch Him—that you will deliberately accept the gift of God — "come unto me and drink."

I go to the Shenandoah Valley — to the Ashram there — it's on a sort of pilgrimage for me. I should go there in shame and confusion because I have made perhaps my biggest blunder as an Evangelist, as a young evangelist, at one of those camp meetings. I started to say, "Those of you who want this blessing." I thought I would get them to stand, and then I thought no I will get them to put up their feet. Oops, I let the cat out of the bag. I thought I would get them to put up their hands but I got it mixed. So I said, "Everybody who wants this blessing, put up your feet." And a very pious Evangelist on the platform, a lady, tried to save the situation said, "The Lord help us!"

Now you might think that I shouldn't go the Shenandoah Valley again, but something else happened there that changed my life. I was very tense as a young evangelist and the people at this camp meeting were not very responsive and I was out of patience with them. I felt as though I could beat them over the head with a cudgel and beat them into the Kingdom of God. After one of these futile meetings I went out and lay down exhausted under an apple tree. As I lay there, Jesus came to me and said, "Stanley - you're tired aren't you?"

I said, "Yes I am and I have a right to be; I have worked hard."

And He said, "You are out of patience aren't you?"

I said, "Yes, I have a right to be because these people are very unresponsive."

And He said to me, "It isn't doing you any good is it?"

I said, "No."

"It isn't doing them any good?"

I said, "No"

"Well," he said, "Do you see how this apple tree brings forth fruit? Does it get into a frenzy of desire and say, 'I will bring forth fruit?' Does it get itself into a stew to bring forth fruit?"

I said, "No"

Then He said, "What does it do?"

I said, "Well, it takes from the earth, air and the sun and keeps the channels open and let's the life drain down into the apple and it brings forth fruit effortlessly."

And he said, "That's all you have to do, my son. Take my resources — it's all yours. Learn to receive and then keep the channels open - no blocks. Then I'll bring forth fruit to you and you will do it effortlessly."

I jumped up as though a revelation had come — "Oh I see, I can work effortlessly, I needn't wear myself out. I needn't get upset with this, that and the other. I can pace the gift of God, keep the channels open and He will give me fruit, more fruit than I can manage. It was an epiphany when I learned to drink.

Now it says here that this drink turns into rivers. If you drink, then rivers of living water shall flow from you. If you know how to receive, then you know how to give in abundance. The Old Testament speaks of the cup of salvation. Jesus spoke of the well of salvation. But here it's turned the Spirit's dispensation into rivers — rivers of living water.

There is a passage that's been redeemed for me, recently. The New English Bible says ... "for he giveth not the Spirit by measure."[42] Now the King James Version says, "for He, (God) giveth not the Spirit by measure to Him," (meaning Jesus). But according to this translation it could read — for He, (Jesus) ... giveth not the Spirit by measure. To whom? To us.

---

42 John 3:34 (NEB).

Now many of us have a measured gift of the Spirit. We have been born again and we are grateful for that birth, the birth of the Spirit. But it is very measured. Our joy is measured and it dries up when pain comes along. Our peace is measured; it dries up when trouble begins. And our love is measured against the unlovely and it dries up. But here it speaks of a *measureless* coming of the Spirit — is that possible? I believe it is possible because I see it actually at work in these apostles. They had a measureless joy, and a measureless vitality. Here was Paul dragged out of a city one day, stoned as if he were dead. Dead and dragged out of the city and the disciples stood around bemoaning him and Paul rose up and the account says ... "walked into the city."[43] (We would have had an ambulance and three or four doctors.) Paul walked into the city and the account says that he went the next day to Derbe. Paul had vitality, a measureless vitality. He threw it off (the stoning) as you'd throw blinding rain off your eyes.

Now the account says, "But this spoke ye about the spirit, which they that believed in him were receive — for the spirit was not yet given because Jesus was not yet glorified."[44] Why couldn't the spirit be given? It could not be given "because Jesus was not glorified." The type of power in the Holy Spirit had to be fixed in the person of Jesus.

Now there is a great deal of controversy in theology about where we ought to begin in understanding the Trinity. Some say our understanding should begin with God, but Dr. Van Dusen, President of Union Theological Seminary in New York City, has written a book, *Spirit, Son and Father*,[45] and he says, "The place that we are to begin is with the Holy Spirit." He says, "There we can begin and we can become one in the Holy Spirit. You don't have to bring up the controversial figure of

---

43 Acts 14:19-20.

44 John 7:39.

45 Henry P. Van Dusen, *Spirit, Son and Father*. New York, 1958.

Jesus – in the Spirit you are one." On the other hand, there are others who say you are to begin with God. And Paul Tillich the great modern theologian said, after traveling around the world, he said that "you must begin with Christ."

Now we here at this Ashram, for right or wrong, say that we must begin with the incarnation — with Jesus. We begin there because we know little or nothing about God apart from Jesus and what you know is probably wrong. We begin with the incarnation and from Him we work out to God and from Him work down to man. In His life we see Life — the word became flesh. We know little about God - apart from Jesus and we know little about the Holy Spirit or rather nothing apart from Jesus and the content of divine power.

I was in a train in India – the people were falling at the feet of a man at every station, a holy man. He was in the same compartment that I was in and I turned to one of his disciples and I said, "Who is he?" "Oh" he said, "He's God — he can tell you anything." I could tell he was had cerebral palsy and when he spoke he would twist and go into contortions but the very going into contortions meant that he was divinity. Were those movements not present, he would be just a man. This is an example of the strange ideas men have held about what constitutes divine power.

The Old Testament said that the spirit of the Lord came upon Samson and Samson went out and slew a thousand men.[46] Put that in the pages of the Acts of the Apostles and make it read something like this ... "the Spirit of the Lord came upon the hundred and twenty in the upper room and they went out and slew a thousand people who had slain Jesus." You would shudder. You would shudder and think, "Would we do that with the spirit of Jesus?" No, when you look into the face of Jesus and you've seen what divine power is like — it's a Christ-like type of power. Jesus was a man who lived and taught and died and rose again. And now we see what divine power is.

---

46 Judges 15:14.

Jesus never performed a miracle for himself — never extricated himself out of any difficulty due a miracle. Rather His miracles were always on behalf of some human need. And so Jesus had to live and die and rise again from the dead before the Holy Spirit could be given and his would be a Christ-like type of power. Our previous views of the *power* of the Spirit would have to be amended. The type of power that you would get in the Holy Spirit is the power that was in Jesus. He said: "I am going to give you another comforter, something like me."[47] The Holy Spirit then is a Christ-like spirit.

An Ashram member (Brother Boyce) commented about the Holy Spirit. "You know when you talk about the Holy Spirit cold chills go up and down my spine."

I said, "Why?"

He said, "I am afraid of it."

I said, "What are you afraid of?"

He said, "I am afraid of rampant emotionalism and off-centered oddness."

I said, "But my brother, the power that was in Jesus was the Holy Spirit and Jesus was the most balanced character that ever moved down the pages of human history. Every virtue was balanced by its opposite virtue. He went off into no visions and no dreams. From his guidance, through prayer, you and I get our guidance and are in possession of all his faculties. Are you afraid of being made like Christ? There was nothing psychopathic about him." If he was infinite sanctity he was infinite sanity.

"That changes the picture," he said. He took me by the lapel of the coat and he said, "Come out here and sit down and talk to me about it."

I sat down and quoted this passage of scripture, "If you then who are evil know how to give good gifts unto your

47 John 14:15-17.

children, how much more will your heavenly father give the Holy Spirit to those who ask him."[48] I said, "My Brother, let's ask him." And I started to pray, I hadn't prayed two sentences when he grabbed my arm and said, "You need not pray he's already come." I never finished my prayer. He went from resistance to receptivity in two minutes. This Brother worked fast! When he understood the conception that the Holy Spirit was a Christ-like spirit, then he could take it with both hands and open arms.

The pattern was set and now with the pattern set God can give us the Holy Spirit with two hands. In the Old Testament giving was with two fingers — enough to let people know He was there. But now He said, "I can give with both hands, all out without measure, if the pattern of Jesus is before you. I can give you everything. You are going to let me make you like Him. It is the measureless coming of the Holy Spirit. Now we begin then with Jesus the incarnate. From Him we work out to God and from Him then down to man and from Him we take the pattern of the power that is going to come from the Holy Spirit and we believe that is the safe place to begin.

Now the account says, "Out of him shall flow rivers of living water."[49] The statement is as psychologically a sound statement as you can get a hold of — the phrase "out of" rather than "into." People go into a tailspin when they center upon themselves.

But the Holy Spirit reverses that whole trend and turns you out and makes you begin to think in terms of others – that is the most healing thing that could possibly come to a personality — to get you interested in other people. I remember the moment I was converted. I rose from my knees and I wanted to put my arms around the world and share this with everybody. Five minutes before, I was a self-centered person – thinking only about myself. One touch of the Holy Spirit and I felt that wanted to put my arms around the world and share

48 Luke 11:13.

49 John 7:38.

this with everybody. Sixty years has gone by since then and I have never gotten over the impulse to put my arms around the world and share this with everybody. The spirit was there. The creative spirit and I hope that my last gasp will be the words of John Wesley, "I commend my Savior to you."[50]

When I get up to heaven I am going to ask for twenty-four hours of rest. I think twenty four hours will do the trick. I find that down here 8 hours – 8 good hours a night– will do it, (the trick) but to be on the safe side, I am going to ask for 24. And then I am going to ask for 24 hours to look around heaven, meet some of you – I hope all of you. Do you know what I would like to do then? I would go up to Jesus and say, "Oh, Jesus this is wonderful!" And I would let him know how grateful I am to be in heaven. I might say something like this, "I am not worthy to be here, but I am grateful that I am here. But, haven't you got some world that is fallen that needs an evangelist? Please send me." Honestly, I would like to do that.

Returning to the New Testament passage, which is my text today, the account says "… out of his heart"[51] (…will flow rivers of living water.). Evidently the translators have had difficulty in regards to where those rivers of living water come from. You remember the King James Version says, "…Out of his belly…"[52] and the other one says, "… out of his innermost being…" and here it says, " … heart. Evidently, they are trying to say something that is difficult to say. I wonder if they aren't trying to say, "Out of his subconscious." Yes, out of the depths of his being. Not the surface, but out of the depths of his being shall flow these rivers of living water — out of his subconscious.

Now Freud has given a bad name to the subconscious – he has said we are determined from the subconscious by dark,

50 John Wesley, "O let me commend my Saviour to you." The title of a sermon delivered in Chester, England outside the gates of St. John's Church on July 20, 1752. < http://www.ccel.org/ccel/wesley/journal.html>

51 John 7:38. (NKJ)

52 John 7:38. (KJ)

unfeeling forces.[53] Forces that have come down through a long racial history and we are determined by those dark depths, those unfeeling depths. But it would be strange if God would have created the subconscious and then couldn't or wouldn't redeem it. Can the subconscious mind be redeemed? The conscious mind can be redeemed — yes. Expose it (the conscious mind) to Jesus and miracles of conversion take place. But what about the subconscious? Can that be redeemed? Yes. I believe that the area of the work of the Holy Spirit is largely if not entirely in the subconscious mind and if you surrender all you know — the conscious, and all you don't know — the subconscious, the Holy Spirit will move into the subconscious mind and take over these driving urges – self, sex and the herd. The Holy Spirit will cleanse them, consecrate them, coordinate them and turn their energy out into creation. Out of them shall flow rivers of living water — that is the picture of a Christian.

What are these rivers? Some people say the sign that you have the Holy Spirit is that you can speak in tongues. If you had the gift of tongues then you had the gift of the Spirit. If you haven't, you haven't. Now why did the gift of tongues come in the early days at Pentecost? I believe it was because the Jewish mold had to be broken.

They had said that you had to be a Jew in order to be a Christian. You have to learn our culture and our language and

---

53 Sigmund Freud (1856-1939) was the father of psychoanalysis. In his description of the unconscious mind, he said it obeys the principle of psychic determinism. Unconscious experiences, according to Freud, are not subject to the same logic characteristic of conscious experience. Unconscious ideas, images, thoughts, and feelings can be condensed or dramatized in the form of abstract concepts and imagery. Often the relationship between the original experience and the unconscious symbolic representation can seem obscure. In Freudian psychoanalysis, the unconscious can be understood through free association, the interpretation of dreams, hypnotic suggestion and transference. < Bartlett H. Stoodley, The Concepts of Sigmund Freud [book on-line] (Glencoe, IL: Free Press, 1959, accessed 31 March 2007), iii; available from Questia, http:// www.questia.com/PM.qst?a=o&d=11760122; Internet.>

that it (Christianity) should all come through the Jewish channels but God broke that pattern in the very beginning. People (at Pentecost) were there from all over that ancient world and everybody began to hear in his own language the wonderful works of God. What did that mean? It meant that every language and every culture was to be a vehicle of the divine – that God was going to use all languages and all cultures. The Jewish mold was broken. I believe that was a special miracle for a special purpose and I am persuaded that that miracle does not happen today. There was another type of tongue in Corinth - an unknown tongue that needed an interpreter. But at Pentecost they did not need an interpreter for God spoke directly in the language of the people who heard. In Corinth there was a type of tongues that needed an interpreter and Paul said, "if you haven't got an interpreter – don't use it."

Now many people come to India hoping the miracle of Pentecost will be repeated – that they will be able to speak directly in the language of the people who hear them without an interpreter and without learning the language. The wreckage of those hopes are strewn across India. It has never happened. What then is the sign of the Holy Spirit? Is it speaking in tongues?

There are three passages of scriptures where they speak of the gifts of the Holy Spirit. One is in Romans 12:4-8 "For as in one body we have many members, and not all the members have the same function, so we, who are many, are one body in Christ, and individually we are members of one another. We have gifts that differ according to the grace given to us: prophecy, in proportion to faith; ministry in ministering; the teacher, in teaching; the exhorter, in exhortation; the giver, in generosity; the leader, in diligence; the compassionate, in cheerfulness." That is one list of the gifts of the Holy Spirit, but the gifts of tongues is not mentioned there. And another one is found in Ephesians 4:7-14. It says, "... and His gifts were that they should be apostles, some prophets, some evangelists, some pastors, some teachers to equip God's people for the work of the ministry, for the building up the body of the Christ until we obtain the unity of faith and knowledge of the Son of God to a mature manhood to the measure of the stature of the fullness of Christ." The gifts of the Holy Spirit are mentioned again but there is no mention of the gift of tongues. Now there is one place where he raised this gift of tongues and that is the 12th chapter of Corinthians. That is the only place that Paul mentioned it. But you say that there is another place — at the end of the Gospel of Mark, the 16th chapter — and it says, "...and these signs will accompany those who believe. In my name they will cast out demons; they will speak in new tongues; they will pick up serpents; and if they drink any deadly thing, it will not hurt them; they will lay their hands on the sick and they will recover." Now this that I have quoted is not a part of the Gospel of Mark. The gospel is broken off at the 8th verse and second century attempts were made to fill it out. All the versions say that — that it was broken off at the 8th verse and this is not a part of the original gospel.[54]

You would expect man that when he filled it out (completing the Gospel of Mark) without divine inspiration would name the kind of things that were named. Not one of them is a moral quality. Look at them. "My name will cast out demons; they will speak in new tongues; they will pick up serpents; and if they drink any deadly thing it will not hurt them; they will lay hands on their sick and they will recover."

---

54 There is much debate about the ending of Mark and many textual problems — there are nine different endings (or combinations of endings) known — but most of the debate focuses around the so-called 'longer' ending (16:9-20). There is evidence that these verses are not part of the original document, but rather an ancient 'completion' of it. Many scholars believe the ending is a compilation of resurrection stories from Luke, John, Matthew and Acts. < Frederick C. Grant, The Earliest Gospel: Studies of the Evangelic Tradition at Its Point of Crystallization in Writing [book on-line] (New York: Abingdon-Cokesbury Press, 1943, accessed 31 March 2007), 34; available from Questia, http://www.questia.com/PM.qst?a=o&d=4527567; Internet.>

But not one of them is a moral quality. They are all of them outer signs. And if that had been a sign of a Christian, Christianity would have perished. It would have died out as one of the cults. It would have not been a moral movement – morally cleansing and spiritually remaking humanity – it would have been a religion of signs and wonders – tossing off miracles. That would be exactly how man would have filled it out- if man filled it out and he did.

There is a gospel according to Thomas discovered in Egypt.[55] It has created quite a sensation. The last chapter of it reads something like this ... Peter said to Jesus, "Send Mary away, it is not befitting that a woman should inherit eternal life along with the men." And Jesus said, "No let her stay and I will turn her into a male and therefore she can stay with us and inherit eternal life with us."[56] That is the end of the gospel. That is what man would do to a Gospel if he got a hold of it. I never believed in divine inspiration so much as when I have seen these human attempts to complete the gospel.

Now what are the authentic signs of the Holy Spirit? I believe that there are nine and every one of them is a moral quality. And these I will read to you – it says. "But the fruit of the spirit is love."[57] Love is the first thing that Jesus did. Then Paul does it here (in this passage) and John did it. They put love first. Love, joy, peace, patience, kindness, goodness, faithfulness, gentleness and self-control are the fruits of the

---

55 The Gospel of Thomas is a New Testament -era apocryphon that was discovered in 1945 at Nag Hammadi, Egypt. The work comprises 114 sayings attributed to Jesus. Some of these sayings resemble those found in the four canonical Gospels (Matthew, Mark, Luke, and John). < The Columbia Encyclopedia 6th ed., s.v."Thomas, Gospel Of" [database on-line]; available from Questia, http://www.questia.com/PM.qst?a=o&d=101274388; Internet; accessed 31 March 2007.>

56 Gospel of Thomas, 114 "Simon Peter said to them, "Make Mary leave us, for females do not deserve life." Jesus said, "Look, I will guide her to make her male, so that she too may become a living spirit resembling you males. For every female who makes herself male will enter the kingdom of Heaven."

spirit. He said, "These are the fruit of the Spirit" and all of them are moral qualities. They are qualities of being and if you get the Holy Spirit it will begin in love and end in self-control. We would have put the self-control first – control yourself. No. It says spirit control (of our life) and ends in self control and you will give out love and in the process you will be controlled by love which will be the best self control. And so the rivers (of the Holy Spirit) are nine and they begin with love and end up with self-control.

Do you want those qualities of being? I don't see how I can get along without them. They are absolutely necessary and absolutely authentic. Now even when Paul mentioned the gift of tongues as one of the gifts of the Spirit, he said, "Yet, show I thee a more excellent way,"[58] and then Paul spoke of love and then he said, "Make love your aim and seek after the best gifts – love and prophecy."[59] Prophecy is not foretelling – foretelling human events, but forth telling the Good News. Love and forth telling the Good News – these are authentic signs of the Holy Spirit.

To those who say you can't have the Holy Spirit without the gift of tongues, the answer is simple. Did Jesus have the Holy Spirit? Yes. Did he speak in tongues? No. If he didn't speak in tongues, then I don't have to. All I want is to use the tongue I got. And suppose the authentic sign that the Holy Spirit was that you talked in an unknown tongue that the Christian didn't know it and nobody else knew it. What kind of God would that reveal? You'd say, Is God the God of the unknown – the unknown language? Is that God? What revelation does that give of God?

---

57 Galatians 5:22-23.

58 1 Corinthians 12:31.

59 1 Corinthians 14:1.

One woman got up in our meeting in El Paso, Texas at the Overflowing Heart[60] and she said, "I speak in tongues, but God only gives it to me when I am in the company of those who also speak in tongues, because He doesn't want to embarrass other people." I said, "Good gracious, is it an embarrassment? Does it embarrass people?" I thought it would redeem them. What good is it if it embarrasses them?

The greatest Spiritual awakening I ever saw was in Asbury College. A group of us were having a prayer meeting in a boy's room at about 10:00 at night. I was nearly asleep but as I knelt suddenly we were all swept off our feet. None of us slept the rest of the night. All we could do was to praise Him, praise Him, and praise Him. The next morning when we came to the chapel service there was no chapel service. People were seeking God. The classes were not held for three days because they were turned into prayer meetings. It was noised (sic) about the country that this great spiritual awakening had broken out and the people came, but they would be converted before they got into the building. They would fall on their knees outside in the hall, nobody speaking to them, struck down by the Holy Spirit. When it was over, every single student had been converted and the hand of God was on me to be a missionary. That is what I got out of it—that I was to be a missionary. But nobody ever spoke in tongues. Why? Because we were not expecting it; we weren't taught it. However, we changed character, we were cleansed, purified, empowered to speak the word of God so the fruits (of the Holy Spirit) came out of that and we must keep the movement morally sound and in channels that are redemptive, not just mystifying.

---

60 "The morning of the Overflowing Heart occurred at the end of each Ashram and was the time when the participants told how the internal and external barriers in their lives had been broken and how their relationships to God, to themselves, and to others were forever changed" (Graham 350).

Now I close by saying, "but this think ye of the Spirit which they who believe on him were to receive,"[61] – note the steps – "were to receive." It was God's purpose to give you the Holy Spirit. First, it is in his intention. Fix that in your mind. You don't have to over come His reluctance; you have lay hold of His highest willingness. It is His intention to give you the Holy Spirit. Second, make it your intention—not your vague wish— to find Him—but your intention. Say, "I am going to get my birthright." Third, surrender yourself. For the Holy Spirit is God giving Himself to us – if He gives His all, we can do no less than give our all and the whole thing is an exchange of my all for His all. Fourth accept the gift of the Holy Spirit by faith. Faith is welcoming that in what you believe in. Faith is saying yes to God's yes.

In Texas they were having the prayer vigil and my turn came (to take over the prayer vigil) and I tapped a woman on the shoulder and I said that I am taking over. She evidently was so wrapped up in her seeking the Holy Spirit – that when I said "I was taking over," – her face became a sunrise. Oh she said, "He has taken over." And that moment she was filled with the Holy Spirit. She later had inscribed in the back of her watch, three letters **I-T-O** – I'm Taking Over. When that occurs, you are to give yourself as a channel of the Holy Spirit because the Holy Spirit is like electricity in that He will not come in where He cannot get out. You are to be His channel— a relaxed, released channel of God's grace and of God's power. And that is open to everybody here.

We had a man in India who was called Praying Hyde. I had him in my home for three days and I know he didn't touch the bed for three nights. He was in the prayer room all the time. He was a man of very great prayer, but when he went out to India some woman gave him a letter to read on board ship and he read it on the deck of the ship. And when he saw what it contained he crumbled it up and threw it down angrily. These

---

61 John 7:39.

women said, "We are going to pray that you may receive the Holy Spirit." He said, "Haven't I got the Holy Spirit; I'm a missionary." But his anger died down in a little while and the spirit said, "You better take that letter," and he took the letter and he smoothed it out and the Spirit spoke to him and said, "You'd better let me come in." He surrendered himself and was filled with the Holy Spirit and became a tower of strength of prayer. Tory and Alexander were having a series of meetings in England as Hyde went through, but there were very little results. Hyde went to his room, shut the door and said, "I am going to stay here until something happens." Tory speaking of it afterwards said, "The moment when Hyde went to his knees things began to break and a great spiritual awakening took place from the power of that man's prayer."

Now the Holy Spirit is here and He is here. You don't have to beg Him to come, just take down the barriers and He will automatically come. He might come as gently as the dew on the morning hay; He may come like a rushing, mighty wind, but you will know He's there and He will bring his own evidence with Him and you will know that you know and you will be sure that you are sure and it will be satisfactory to you.

Last night I spoke to you about self-surrender, but self-surrender is not creating a vacuum. I've given myself; I've got nothing. Self-surrender is in order that He might give you everything. Self-surrender is in order that He might give you the Holy Spirit. The end is not your giving – the end is your taking. The taking is of the gift of the Holy Spirit and so tonight I am going to give you a chance to come to this place of prayer.

This is what we are going to do. I am going to ask the pianist to play softly – three or four verses of *"Just As I Am," "My Faith Looks Up to Thee," "When I Survey The Wondrous Cross," "There Is A Fountain Filled With Blood," "All To Jesus I Surrender,"* – three or four verses of each softly.

And we will come to this altar of prayer and stay here long enough to get us off our hands and into the hands of God. Some will come for the birth of the Spirit, you are not sure if you have been born again. You will come for the birth of the Spirit. Some will come and say, "Yes I am born of the Spirit, but now I want my birthright." In conversion there is a rapid climb and you're on a high plateau and then it becomes undulating, up and down, victory and defeat and then you are driven to the necessity of finding a deeper spiritual life – you have to go deeper before you can go further. And that leads you to come to Him to find the gift of Holy Spirit. It is fullness, cleansing and empowering.

Some will come for the baptism of the Holy Spirit and some will come to lay a resentment, a fear, a guilt at His feet—an emptiness, a half-wayness, a frustration. You are going to let Him have it all and you can stay here as long as it takes to get what is on your heart into His hands. Then you will go back to your seat and others will come and take your place and we will come and go. I needn't urge you to come. I think your own urges will urge you to come. You will want to come. One Presbyterian minister said, "I didn't like altar services because I am a Presbyterian, but when I saw you come along with us, I said 'if he needs it, then I need it too,'" and he found what he wanted.

I don't care how it's done. This seems to be the way that commits people, but you can be in prayer right where you are until your turn comes. But we will all be in prayer whether we are here at the altar or out there. We are going to turn this whole place into an altar of prayer and we will come and go and the Spirit will meet us here tonight, I am sure of it – He is here.

A young minister went into a church. He was beaten. He saw a sign, which said this, "Jesus Christ is in this place anything can happen here." But he was frustrated and defeated and he said to himself, "If anything can happen here I better go in." And he went in and he knelt and something happened to him. Today he is a pastor on fire for God. Jesus Christ is in this place anything can happen here and He is here to give us the Holy Spirit.

Now our sister will play and we will come. "If any man thirst let him come unto me and drink"[62] – will you come?

---

62 John 7:37.

9. THE KINGDOM OF GOD IS GOD'S TOTAL ANSWER TO MAN'S TOTAL NEED

COMMENTARY ON "THE KINGDOM OF GOD"

THE text for this sermon is from Luke 13:18. *"He said therefore, "What is the kingdom of God like? And to what should I compare it? It is like a mustard seed that someone took and sowed in the garden; it grew and became a tree, and the birds of the air made nests in its branches."*

The Kingdom of God was a major emphasis in Jones' preaching and evangelism. He first discussed this topic in the late 1920s and it would thereafter become a consistent motif in his sermons and books. In his 1928 book, *Christ at the Roundtable* Jones wrote, "The Kingdom of God was the most radical conception ever presented to the human race" (90). Jones wanted to understand how this phrase — the Kingdom of God - that Jesus used more than 100 times could have applicability and relevance now. Was the Kingdom of God something that Jesus merely talked about 2,000 years ago, or does it have current significance? Jones believed that the Church had mostly missed the import of the Kingdom of God. The apostles failed to see its significance and either reduced it to the manageable or relegated it to the life hereafter and the church has not done much better. In his book *A Song of Ascents*, Jones writes,

> The Kingdom of God had been pushed to the margin as inner mystical experience now, and then pushed beyond the borders of this life to heaven as collective experience. The minimization of the impact of the Kingdom leaves

vast areas of life unredeemed — the social, political and economic (154).

This sermon conveys the powerful message that the Kingdom of God is built into the nature of the universe (reality) and into the nature of humanity. Jones affirms that, when we find the Kingdom of God, we find life, and that Christianity, because it is built into the nature of reality is, in fact, the Way to live. "I see now as I have never seen before the eternal fitness of the gospel - it fits the soul like a glove fits the hand. They are made for each other and it fits the body and the mind in the same fashion" (Jones *Is The Kingdom of God Realism?* 7).

Jones would emphasize again and again the implications (and the gift) of the kingdom of God:

> Jesus believed in life and its redemption. Not only was the soul to be saved - the whole of life was to be redeemed. The kingdom of God coming on earth is the expression of that collective redemption. The entrance to the kingdom of God is by *personal conversion*, but the nature of that kingdom is social. The kingdom of God is the most astonishingly radical proposal ever presented to the human race. It means nothing less than the replacing of the present world order by the kingdom of God. It is the endeavor to call men back from the present unnatural, unworkable world order to a new one based on new principles, embodying a new spirit and led by a new person (Bundy, 8).

How is God to make known this reality of the Kingdom? According to Jones, there were two possible ways of revealing the nature of the Kingdom:

> One is to inaugurate it with a fanfare of physical accompaniment that would impose that rule with thunder and lightning and earthquakes which would say to quivering man: "Obey or else." That would create not men, but slaves. The other way would be for God to hide the Kingdom in the facts of nature and life and gradually reveal it as man developed sufficiently to see that Kingdom and

adopt it as his own. Then in the fullness of time, when God could find a people or nation most likely to be the people to accept that Kingdom and make it their own, he would reveal the nature and the implications of that Kingdom in understandable form — human form and in human relationships (Jones, *The Unshakable Kingdom and the Unchanging Person* 15).

God elected the relational revelation. He would unveil the nature of the Kingdom through a person. In the person of Jesus, the Kingdom has arrived. This is a "totalitarian" kingdom — for nothing would be exempt from God's love and rule!

It was a trip to Russia in 1934 that inspired Jones to write *Is the Kingdom of God Realism?* While there Jones witnessed a man-made totalitarianism and began to use the word *totalitarian* in conjunction with his writing and preaching on the Kingdom.[1] According to Graham:

> Jones chose this word totalitarian expressly both for its potentially provocative impact on Christians and to distinguish the Kingdom from the earth bound totalitarians such as communism, Nazism and fascism. The totality of the Kingdom of God for Jones embraces every human characteristic of body, soul, and spirit, and every human and personal and institutional relationship. However, unlike other forms of Totalitarianisms, the kingdom of God draws its inspiration and strength from God and is thus able to effect total and permanent change in all of these human characteristics and relationships (226).

Jones was not the only person elated by the reality of the Kingdom of God on earth. In a book written shortly before he died, Jones tells this intriguing story about H.G. Wells,

---

1 "Doing the will of God on earth as it is done in heaven is totalitarian because it comprehends every aspect of human life; no part of man's life on earth is exempt from the command to be submitted to the will of God" (Graham, *The Totalitarian Kingdom of God* 9).

...who when fumbling through history in search of the relevant came across the fact of the kingdom of God and was shocked as by an electric shock: Why here is the most radical proposal every presented to the mind of man, the proposal to replace the present world order with God's order, the kingdom of God' (Jones, *The Divine Yes*, 11).

This radical proposal comes with an offer – the offer of the Kingdom of God which we receive through conversion. We must be converted. We must make a conscious decision because a claim on our total life is involved. This new birth has profound social implications and in fact cosmic implications, according to Jones. The new relationship that we have with Christ after the surrender of the self is de facto a relationship with this new order, the Kingdom of God. (Jones, *A Song of Ascents* 385) "While the entrance to the kingdom is personal, the implications and nature of the kingdom are social. According to Jones, "we enter it personally but we live in it corporately" (*A Song of Ascents*, 386).[2]

Jones finishes this sermon with his conviction that we all have access to this "Unshakable Kingdom and an Unchanging Person." The Kingdom and the Person have coalesced for him:

> *Now I have an Unshakable Kingdom – the Kingdom of God embodied in an Unchanging Person, Christ. I don't know what the future holds but I know who holds the future. The Kingdom is not going to be shaken. Jesus is not going to change. He is the same yesterday, today and forever. (318)*

Once Jones believed that he understood and embraced the implications of the Kingdom of God (on earth), he believed that he had a divine entrustment to reintroduce the Kingdom

---

2 "The kingdom of God is the most radical conception ever presented to the human race and it is the most secular. It meant nothing less than the replacement of the present unworkable world order, founded on greed and selfishness and exploitation, with God's order founded on love and service and mutual aid (Jones, *Reconstruction of the Church, After What Pattern?* 12).

to Christianity.[3] (Graham, 242) Graham writes that, as a result of Jones' conviction that the Kingdom of God was reality:

> Jones lived in a different world. He saw and heard things that others did not, or saw and heard only indistinctly. The kingdom of God was not, for Jones, merely a theological concept or simply a lifestyle choice, although it embraced both theology and how he lived his Christian life. The kingdom of God, which was so utterly unrealistic to most people and even to many Christians, was, in fact, more realistic than the empirical world of sensible and tangible facts (263).

Jones will share with his listeners the reality of the Kingdom of God for them – and for them now!

THE KINGDOM OF GOD
"THE KINGDOM OF GOD IS GOD'S TOTAL ANSWER TO MAN'S TOTAL NEED"

SERMON

I will read to you a few verses from Luke 13:18. Then Jesus asked, "What is the Kingdom of God like? To what shall I compare it? It is like a grain of mustard seed, which a man took and put into his orchard where it grew up and became a

---

3   Graham emphasizes in rather dramatic language the import of Jones' revelation of the significance of the Kingdom of God: "In the later 1930s, on an apocalyptic world stage looming with everything fearful and gruesome, warring and wicked, and in cooperation with Stanley Jones, surely one of Jesus' most reliable, sold out apprentices, the Holy Spirit "launched a torpedo," the kingdom of God – Jesus' program on earth that the church has yet to grasp, to appreciate, to embrace, and to celebrate (242).

tree and the birds of the air made nests in its branches." He added, "To what shall I compare the Kingdom of God? It is like yeast that a woman took and mixed in with three measures of flour until all of it was leavened."

This morning I want to think with you about the central message, which these two parables are trying to teach. The central thing that Jesus was trying to put across in the parables was obviously one thing — *The Kingdom of God*. It was his central message. He went out preaching the Gospel of the Kingdom of God. It was the only thing that he called *his* Gospel. When he sent his disciples out he sent them out to preach the gospel of the Kingdom. He said this Gospel, the Kingdom, shall be preached in all the world, until the end comes.

What did he mean by this? It's been one of the most puzzling things in the whole of the New Testament. Jesus speaks of the *open secret* of the Kingdom of God. (Moffat's translation) It is a secret, yet it is open but not too obvious, lest we exhaust it too quickly.

I once watched a crow in India train it's young to forage for food. The crow for a while would put things straight into the mouth of the young crow. Then I saw her get hold of a morsel of food and then fly up on the roof, stick it under the palm leaves, the matting of the roof—tucked it away, hid it away— then flew up on the ridge to see what would happen. The young crow flew up and began to explore under those leaves, found the morsel and ate it, as the mother crow flapped her wings as much as to say, "Good - you're learning."

Now God could feed us directly without any mystery - just straight into our mouths. If He did that, mystery would go from the universe and development and exploration would go. So, He has hidden away His meanings — sufficient for us to begin to explore for them — to try to get them. He has packed them away so that in the finding of them we would be developed...in the finding. It's taken the human race — I think — 2000 years to begin to see the full implications or the fuller implication of the meaning of the Kingdom of God. It was too big for that generation. They didn't know what quite to do with the Kingdom. They reduced it to terms understandable for them.

Remember when Jesus came into Jerusalem? On his triumphal entry, the people cried out and said, "Blessed be the coming kingdom...the kingdom of our father David."[4] You see what they did there? They didn't reject that kingdom, but they reduced it to national proportions. It was to be the kingdom of their father David. They said "it's going to be David's reign again." They jammed the Kingdom into a nationalistic mold.

Jesus, however, was giving us a universal kingdom that would break all molds. However, like the early followers, we have been trying to reduce the impact of the Kingdom. From that day to this we have been doing the same thing with the Kingdom of God—not rejecting it but reducing it; making it innocuous; it was the most radical conception ever presented to the mind of man. H. G. Wells thumbing through history as a historian came across this conception of the Kingdom of God and he said: "This is the most radical conception ever presented to the mind of man."[5]

Again I ask: what did Jesus mean by it? We get some clues here and there. One was when he said: "When you pray, say 'Our Father – may thy kingdom come and may thy will be done on earth as it is in heaven.'"[6] The second phrase explains the first — the coming of the Kingdom of God was the doing of the will of God on earth as it was in heaven. Then how is the will of God done in heaven? In the individual role? Yes. In the collective role? Yes. In the total social arrangements of heaven?

---

4   Mark 11:1-11.

5   H. G. Wells, *The Outline of History*, 1920, Chapter 28, "The doctrine of the Kingdom of Heaven, which was the main teaching of Jesus, is certainly one of the most revolutionary doctrines that ever stirred and changed human thought."

Yes. "Thy kingdom come, thy will be done on earth as it is in heaven." As heaven is organized around the will of God — that would be the Kingdom. So earth was to be organized around the will of God and that would be the *Kingdom of God on earth.* But that Kingdom makes a total demand upon the total life; it demands that the whole of life come under one sway — one obedience to the will of God. It's a completely totalitarian order, demanding a total obedience of the total life. It goes into the innermost thought — the innermost thought cannot be thought without the approval or disapproval of the Kingdom. It goes out to the outermost rim of human relationships — the nation was to embody it: "The Kingdom of God should be taken away from you and given to a nation that shall bring forth the fruits thereof."[7] Just as the individual world was to embody it, the collective will is to embody it as well.

I read this morning in my devotions where Jesus said "Woe unto you Corazion — woe unto you Bethsaida — woe unto you — Capernaum."[8] Why did he speak these words of woe to this collection of cities? Did he expect the cities in their organized capacities to be the instrument of the Kingdom of God? Yes. And when they didn't, woe was pronounced upon them. So the individual, the smaller collective group, the total national group were to be the instruments of the Kingdom of God and the agent of its coming. It was to be a completely totalitarian demand upon the total life — for total obedience.

Then you say "That is total bondage — we're getting rid of totalitarianisms now and you introduce us to another?" Yes, and more total. This is total! You can't think a thought, aspire for a thing, do an act, or take an attitude, without the Kingdom demanding that it (the thought, aspiration, action or attitude) harmonizes with the kingdom or you get hurt. "But," you say,

---

6   Luke 11:2-4.

7   Matthew 21:43.

8   Matthew 11:21-21; Luke 10:13-15.

"That is total bondage." Strangely enough, it is not, for I find that when I do God's will I do my own. When I am most bound to him, I'm freest. When I am lowest at his feet, I stand straightest before everything. Bound to him, I walk the earth free. So that when I find Him, I find myself. Here is a completely totalitarian demand which when you totally obey it, you find total freedom. Is that what we are looking for? Or are we looking only to the half answers? The half answers are, for example, the totalitarianisms of Nazism and Fascism and Communism and if you totally obey them you'll find total bondage. The difference between these earth-bound totalitarianisms and the Kingdom of God is that when you totally obey the Kingdom of God, you find total freedom. Only God could have thought that out — that to lay a total demand on you, which when you obey it you find complete and total freedom.

Now that was presented to the early church as the gospel of the Kingdom. But before Jesus was through He seemed to have shifted His emphasis a bit. He started out preaching a new order. He ended up by preaching Himself. "I am the way" — come unto me; "I am the truth and the Life."[9] Which is it? Is it the gospel of a new order or is it the gospel of the Person — capital P. Which is it?

There seems to be some confusion; or, did He really mean for these two concepts to coincide and come together? I think that He meant that those two concepts should come together and coincide — for He used interchangeably the words "for my sake" and "for the Kingdom's sake." Relationship *with him* meant relationship *with this new order* — embodied in him. Did He then intend that He and the order should be one, and a relationship with Him determined your relationship with the new order — God's order — the order of the Kingdom? Was He the Kingdom embodied? Is the message neither the Kingdom alone, nor the person alone, but both?

---

9   John 14:6.

This new order (the Kingdom of God) and the absolute person come together. If that be true then what does that do for religion? It does two things to my mind. First of all, it makes religion very tender and personal for I have a relationship with a person and that person is Christ. My religion is then the religion of a personal relationship. I'm grateful I don't have relationships merely with a *principle* even if it started with a capital P. Imagine a child crying and you come to the child and say, "My child please don't cry. I am going to give you the principle of motherhood." What would the child say? "I don't want the principle of motherhood. I want my mother." I'm grateful that all our principles are embodied in a person, wrapped in warm flesh. My religion is at once personal because it is in contact with a Person.

But the message of the Person and the Kingdom does something else: it makes our faith at once social. If we have a relationship with this Person, we have a relationship with the order embodied in the person - the Kingdom of God. Then you have a relationship with something that is intensely and all inclusively and unavoidably social. Doesn't that make your religion at once personal and at once social? Not now personal and not then social; it is both. I want both because God is not an half God ruling over half realms, saying he's going to save the individual but the social does not matter. I don't want a social gospel that talks about changing the social order but doesn't change the individual. A religion that doesn't begin with the individual doesn't begin. However, if it ends with the individual, then it ends prematurely. It's got to be both.

I am not interested in an individual gospel or a social gospel. I am interested in one Gospel and that Gospel is all inclusive, demanding the total obedience in the total life. And when it (an individual) does so it (the individual) experiences a total redemption. So then our message is not the Order and not the Person – it's both the Order and the Person *together*.

You look down through the Acts of the Apostles and you find that these (two concepts) were put together. Philip went down to Samaria preaching the gospel of the Kingdom *and* of Jesus. Paul as well preached about the Kingdom of God *and* Jesus. The last verse in the book of Acts says that Paul proclaimed the Kingdom of God *and* taught about the Lord Jesus Christ with all boldness and without hindrance. He spoke about the Kingdom of God *and* the name of Jesus.[10] He put those two things together. It is the absolute person and the absolute order coinciding.

Now the early church didn't know what to do with this and it slipped away because it was too immense. By the time the creeds were written, the Kingdom of God had slipped to the edges. The Apostles Creed[11] mentions how many times the Kingdom of God? Not at all. The Athanasian Creed[12] mentions it how many times? I couldn't expect you to answer that very well — it's a long one (creed) — not at all. The Nicene Creed[13]

---

10 Acts 28: 30.

11 Legend has it that the Apostles wrote this creed on the tenth day after Christ's ascension into heaven. That is not the case, though the name stuck. However, each of the doctrines found in the creed can be traced to statements current in the apostolic period. The earliest written version of the creed is perhaps the Interrogatory Creed of Hippolytus (ca. A.D. 215). The current form is first found in the writings of Caesarius of Arles (d 542). <http://www.creeds.net/ancient/apostles.htm>

12 The Athanasian Creed (Quicumque vult) is a statement of Christian Trinitarian doctrine traditionally ascribed to St. Athanasius, Archbishop of Alexandria, who lived in the 4th century. However most of today's historians agree that in all probability it was originally written in Latin, not in Greek, and probably originated in Gaul around 500. Its theology is closely akin to that found in the writing of Western theologians, especially Ss. Ambrose of Milan, Augustine of Hippo, and Vincent of Lérins. < The Columbia Encyclopedia 6th ed., s.v."Athanasian Creed" [database on-line]; available from Questia, http://www.questia.com/PM.qst?a=o&d= 101230399; Internet; accessed 31 March 2007.>

13 The original Nicene Creed was first adopted in 325 at the First Council of Nicaea, which was the first Ecumenical Council. At that time, the text ended after the words "We believe in the Holy Spirit," after which an anathema was added. The second Ecumenical Council in 381 added the section that follows the words "We believe in the Holy Spirit" (without

mentions it marginally and places it beyond the borders of this life — after the resurrection — "thy Kingdom is an everlasting Kingdom," but that was beyond the borders of this life — beyond the resurrection. The three historic creeds of Christendom mentioned once, marginally, what Jesus mentioned a hundred times. Obviously, a note had dropped out; something had been missed and a crippled Christianity went across Europe leaving a crippled result.

The Kingdom of God began to be pushed back into the inner life as personal experience—a mystical, personal experience. Then it began to be pushed out beyond the borders of this life, as a collective experience in heaven. And between this personal, mystical experience within the heart and the collective experience in heaven, what was left out? The social, the economic, and the political, were all left unredeemed. We created a void between the inward mystical/personal and collective experience in heaven. Into that void rushed all the totalitarianisms. They said: "All right, we will give you your mystical experience in the heart now and your collective experience in heaven hereafter. In the meantime we will take over the social, the economic and the political." They took over where we abdicated, and then we began to get harmed. And we began to say, "Is this the result when the churches abdicate?"

Then we went back again to the New Testament and we discovered to our amazement that here was a totalitarianism more total than these people (with their earth bound

---

the words "and the son"); hence the name "Nicene-Constantinopolitan Creed", referring to the Creed as it was after the modification in Constantinople. The third Ecumenical Council reaffirmed the 381 version, and stated that no further changes could be made to it, nor could other creeds be adopted. < The Columbia Encyclopedia 6th ed., s.v."Nicaea, First Council Of" [database on-line]; available from Questia, http://www.questia.com/PM.qst?a=o&d=101261260; Internet; accessed 31 March 2007.>

totalitarianisms) were presenting. It was a total answer to the total life.

Now the church began to feel around for something to match against these earth-bound totalitarianisms. And it has fastened on the ecumenical church as the answer.

I believe in the ecumenical church. Those of you who know me best know that I am trying in a feeble way to get the churches together, to make our church an ecumenical church. Maybe someday I will talk to you about that. I believe that those who belong to Christ automatically belong to all those who belong to Christ. I believe in the ecumenical church. I wrote a letter, rather an article, to *The Christian Century* after the Great Madras Conference held in 1938,[14] where the missionary forces of the world met just before the coming of the war in 1938. I wrote a rather disturbing article, entitled *Where the Madras Conference Missed Its Step."* I said that the Madras Conference stressed with great emphasis the ecumenical church as the answer to Communism, Fascism and Nazism. I replied, there you are putting over against one relativism these totalitarianisms and another relativism, the church. And you can't match against the relativisms of Nazism, Communism and Fascism the relativism of the church. You should have put over against the relativisms of the Nazism, Fascism and Communism — the absolute relativism — the

---

14 The International Missionary Council was established at London in 1921. The IMC linked some 14 interdenominational associations of sending societies - such as the Division of Foreign Missions of the National Council of Church of Christ, USA - with some 16 interdenominational field bodies, such as the National Christian Council of India. The International Missionary Council early on became a focus of the emerging ecumenical movement. Several major international conferences were held where members explored questions on topics such as missionary freedom, general and theological education and many others. The Madras conference in 1938 was held in Tambaram, India where the main topic was the study of the Christian message in a non-Christian world. < http://www.library. yale.edu/div/imcpart2.htm>

Kingdom of God. The church is the best agent of that Kingdom, but not *the* Kingdom.

Suppose I should come to you and say "repent for I am at hand." What would you say? What would you say? You'd tap your head wouldn't you? That's a little cracked. Suppose I should go out and say repent for the Ashram is at hand. Would you laugh again? Yes. Suppose I should go out and say repent for the church is at hand. No. Suppose I should go out and say repent for the Kingdom of God is at hand. Is that all right? You wouldn't laugh, would you? Do you feel like getting on your knees? Why? It's the absolute isn't it? You see — we missed our step when we said that the ecumenical church is the answer. Oh no, the Kingdom of God is the answer. And to the degree that the ecumenical church embodies that Kingdom, to that degree it embodies the answer.

But the church and the Kingdom are not one, are they? Only the Roman Catholic Church makes the church and the Kingdom one. They say anybody who's outside of the church is outside of the Kingdom. Then of course they have to go on and make the church infallible or the representative of the church infallible. And so they built up the infallibility of the Pope. You see you have to have an absolute order with an absolute infallibility in that order. But there's been nothing infallible about the Roman Catholic Church, except it's been infallibly fallible just like the rest of us. And (the church is) most fallible when it talked about its infallibilities.

The church is made up of you and me, isn't it? Are we fallible? Are we absolute? No, we are relative. We are the subject of redemption, aren't we? Christ loved the church and gave himself for it that he might cleanse it by the washing of the water, by the word. The church is the subject for redemption, isn't it? Now you don't build the Kingdom of God, do you? You build the church — "on this rock I shall build my church." You build the church, don't you? Do you build the Kingdom? "This is the Kingdom built from the foundation of the world

— built into the structure of reality. The Kingdom is! If the Kingdom *is* — what then do you do if you don't build it?

Modern people talk about going out and building the Kingdom. You're never told in the New Testament to build the Kingdom. You're told to accept it; to preach it; to suffer for it—but never to build it. It's the absolute order, which you get into by submission, surrender and faith. Now then we're in the process of rediscovering the Kingdom of God and that's one thing that the totalitarianisms are going to do for us. They're becoming a mustard plaster on our backs. They're making us think. And if they make us think and make us rediscover the Kingdom of God then they'll do us a service. God uses some instruments that he can't approve of - just as he used Sirius – "my servant Sirius" who was an outsider. God can stimulate us and push us into doing something that we ought to have done without that prodding or sting. He can use instruments that he doesn't approve of.

Now we are in the process of rediscovering the Kingdom of God, and when we do there is going to be a burst of spiritual power across this world such as we have never seen. Life is going to be organized around the will of God. But somebody says, "Look here. What is the use to talk about the Kingdom of God? It won't come until Jesus comes." As if there will be no Kingdom without the King. And therefore, nothing can be done about it. Well now, let's look at that a moment. In the passage which I read to you were these words: "Jesus said the Kingdom of God is like a grain of a mustard seed, second like unto leaven in the dough; that grain of a mustard seed grew into a great tree; yeast within the dough leavened the whole lump, until the whole loaf was leavened."[15]

These and other passage teach us that the Kingdom of God will come by gradualism, by permeation, by a pervasive growth—first the seed, then the corn, and then the full ear of corn. A number of these passages teach that the Kingdom of

---

15 Luke 13:18-20.

God will come gradually by permeation. Now some people would say that the leaven/yeast is evil, for in Paul's epistles it says: "cleanse out the old leaven," therefore leaven is a symbol of evil. But it would be a clear misinterpretation that would make Jesus say, "The Kingdom of God is like unto evil," wouldn't it? He said: "The Kingdom of God is like unto leaven." If he would say the Kingdom of God is like unto evil, which is like unto leaven, that would be a clear misinterpretation.

There are one or more passages that teach the Kingdom of God will come gradually; there are another set of passages which teach that the Kingdom of God will come suddenly by apocalyptic means with the return of Christ. "He went into far country to receive a Kingdom and returned." This and other passages teach that the Kingdom of God will come suddenly with the return of Christ.

Now which set of passage shall we believe? Some people believe one set; other people support the other set of passages. I can't do that. They are both integral parts of the account and one can't be taken from the other without disrupting the account. Then I must take both and I need both. The gradualism gives me my task — I can be the agent of the coming of this Kingdom now. And when I pray saying, "Our Father ... may thy Kingdom come," I can put myself at the disposal of the Kingdom and say: through me now. *The gradualism then gives me my task. The apocalyptic, or the sudden coming of Christ, gives me my hope.*

My hope is that the last word will be spoken by Christ and that perhaps he will do it suddenly when I least expect it, and that last word will be victory. History hasn't exhausted itself so I can't rule out the coming of Christ. I have no timetable — I have no map for that future. I used to be able to tell you all about it. I knew the whole business. Then I knew I had to learn humility. I didn't know as much as I thought I knew. Because every time people set dates they have to find an anti-Christ to precede the coming of Jesus so we have fastened on this one, that one, or the other, such as Hitler or Stalin. You leave a wake of confusion and disappointment behind you and that is morally unhealthy. I simply don't know and Jesus told me I wouldn't know. He said: "You know neither the day nor the hour." Nobody knows, not even the Son, only the Father. So I put up my question mark against the future and I said there it is. I don't know. But it says he is going to come all right. In the meantime I have my task. So if he comes suddenly, I say: "All right, this is the thing I would like to be found doing when he does come."

There is a third set of passages that teaches us that the Kingdom of God is! It is when we pray the Lord's prayer, we say, "Our Father .... may thy Kingdom come." Then Jesus concludes the prayer by saying, "Thine is the Kingdom" not will be, but *is*. Can we say that the Kingdom *is*? Yes. It's written into the nature of reality. It is. It is written into the laws of our being, the laws of the universe. It is written into the nature of reality; and we don't break these laws; we break ourselves on them. The Kingdom is manifesting itself in our frustrations if we won't live the Kingdom life. Instead, we live the kind of life that we do now, full of frustrations, neuroses, fears, anxieties and guilt, because the Kingdom is working as frustration in us, but it is there. We are not doing away with the Kingdom; we are just doing away with ourselves and getting hurt in the process.

God is reigning, God has never abdicated. We are not breaking his laws; we are breaking ourselves on them. We revolted against God and found to our surprise that we have revolted against ourselves. In God's universe are God's laws — God's Kingdom — and we are getting hurt badly when we break them, (God's laws). Now this is the message which I believe we are in the process of rediscovering. In focusing on the Kingdom of God, we are coming to grips with another way of life. And that other way of life is also totalitarianism — a humanistic totalitarianism.

In one of my books entitled, *Christ's Alternative to Communism*, which I wrote in 1935, after I had been to Russia, I said it something like this: "This generation or at the most the next must decide between materialistic, atheistic, communism and the Kingdom of God on earth. And the decision will be made not according to argument but by the production of a better order." I ended up the book by saying: "The Kingdom of the atheistic man and the Kingdom of God are at the door of this generation." I thought it would take about a generation before that choice would be realized — made. Those words were written in 1935. However, in half a generation, in 15 years, we are now faced with this choice. The world is now facing a momentous decision between a kingdom that is atheistic and humanistic and the Kingdom of God on earth. And this Kingdom is to be on earth mind you. Jesus said when you pray "Our Father may thy Kingdom come and may thy will be done on earth." However, this "Kingdom" is not confined to the earth; rather, it goes out and stretches into eternity.

Do we believe that there is a goal in history? What is it? The Kingdom of God on earth…is that the goal in history? Then does history have meaning, purpose and goal? On the walls of our Ashram at Sat Tal we have this motto "Philosophers have explained the world we must now change it." Where did that come from? The quotation that I gave to you came from Lenin. Is it a good motto? Philosophers have explained the world we must now change it. Is that good? Wherever it came from? If it came from the devil would it be good? Yes, if it is true. Philosophers have explained the world and we must now change it. Do you believe that the world can be changed? Or is this something (the situation of the world) that's so hopeless that we've got to abandon ship and get up to heaven? Jesus said "Thy Kingdom come and thy will be done on earth." We believe that the world can be changed, that there is hopefulness at the center.

When I was in Russia, an actress on the train one day said to me – she could speak English and I was glad to talk to her, "I suppose you are a religious man."

I said: "Yes, I suppose I am."

She said, "You're religious because you're weak. You want somebody to hold your hand." And she took my hand to show me what she meant.

I said, "My sister, you're wrong. I don't want somebody to hold my hand. I want God to strengthen my arm to reach out a helping hand to someone else. I don't want God to wipe my tears, I would like for him to give me a handkerchief to wipe somebody else's tears."

Then she said, "Well, I suppose you are an idealist."

And this time I hesitated and said, "Yes, I suppose I am." "Au Revoir, Good bye. I'm a realist."

I began to think. I said, "Am I an idealist or a realist?" I went back to the New Testament to discover whether I was an idealist or a realist. I came out of that study saying "if I follow what's in the New Testament about the Kingdom of God, I am a realist. My book, *Is the Kingdom of God Realism?*, came out of that experience. Acknowledging that realism is at the heart of the New Testament was what I discovered from the shock that the Russian actress gave me. She stung me into going back to the New Testament to discover if I was dealing with realism or idealism. I said "Oh no, if this is what the New Testament is teaching, it's realism." Jesus was a realist—so far ahead of humanity that we think him an idealist. He was a stark realist. Everything he taught was put into operation within himself. It was Realism.

The Kingdom of God is not idealism; it is realism. Moffat puts it: "the realm of heaven," the realm and the realism of heaven. Communism and Christianity both believe in realism. They both believe in the classless society. In the New Testament it says: "In Jesus Christ there cannot be Greek or Jew." There cannot be any race distinction. There is no barbarian or city, culture distinction; no one in bondage or free, socio-economic, class distinction; no male or female, gender distinction. The New Testament teaches a classless and a raceless society, for it

317

is color blind and class blind; a man is a man – a man for whom Christ died.

When I went into Russia – I was hit pretty hard by Russia. I said here they are trying to make a new order in the name of "Atheism." I went to my New Testament for some word of assurance and a verse rose out of the Scripture and spoke to my condition, as the Quakers would say — became authoritative. This verse: "For we have a Kingdom which cannot be shaken."[16] Let us thank God that we have a Kingdom which cannot be shaken. I lived on that verse that day. I said, "Oh, we've got a Kingdom that cannot be shaken—the Kingdom of God." Then the next morning another verse rose: "Jesus Christ the same yesterday, today and forever."[17] "Oh," I said "we've got an unchanging person."

I came out of Russia with two things in my mind and heart: an *Unshakable Kingdom and the Unchanging Person*. Jesus Christ is not changing. The demand is not to change him but to change ourselves—to be made like him. I came out of Russia with two things on my lips, in my heart: An Unshakable Kingdom and the Unchanging Person. They were two then; now they are one. They coalesce and now I have an Unshakable Kingdom— the Kingdom of God embodied in an Unchanging Person, Christ. I believe that to be the answer, and therefore my heart is inwardly steady. I don't know what the future holds but I know who holds the future. The Kingdom is not going to be shaken. Jesus is not going to change. He is the same yesterday, today and forever.

Shall we pray?

16 Hebrews 12:28.

17 Hebrews 13:8.

PRAYER:

Dear Father, Hold us inwardly steady at this hour and give us an answer, thy answer, rooted in us unbreakably, unshakably. And help us to go out and shout our answer to the world and so that all half answers will break down and it is God's answer that will answer to the Pharaoh and to us. Amen

Jones at Keuka Ashram, 1960

10. THE WAY TO MEET UNMERITED SUFFERING IS TO USE IT

COMMENTARY ON "CHRIST AND HUMAN SUFFERING"

IN the sermon, *"Christ and Human Suffering,"* E. Stanley Jones tackles the Theodicy question from the Christian perspective.[1] He does not pursue the matter of God's justice in the form of a theological argument in an attempt to show that God is righteous or just despite the presence of evil in the world and the suffering of the innocent. Rather, he immediately places the question in the context of the cross. Jones begins with the query, "Are there chimes in the cross? Is there music?"

Jones would write in his autobiography, *A Song of Ascents,* that he has often wondered why God created man and made him free:

> That was a dangerous thing to do. Suppose man would go wrong and abuse that freedom; then God would have to stand alongside that will as love. He could not coerce him, for a coerced goodness is not goodness at all. But to stand alongside sin in the loved one means that God would suffer,

---

1   The common argument that haunts theists is as follows. God is omnipotent and perfectly good which implies that he could prevent evil. However, evil exists in our world. Is God therefore willing to prevent evil, but not able. If so, He is impotent. If He able, but not willing, He is malevolent. Herein emerges the mystery of evil. How does the almighty power of the one God relate to the evil in the world and the experience of human suffering? Why can't God's almightiness overcome evil and prevent the tragedy of undeserved human misery? Or more ominously, is God responsible for evil as well as the good? (Gutierrez 69)

for it is the nature of love to insinuate itself into the sins and sorrows of the loved one and make them its own. If love stays out, it is not love. If it gets in, it bleeds (143).

Jones quickly disposes of the matter of merited suffering when he discusses the "fact" that we live in a moral universe where you get results or consequences. It is the matter of unmerited suffering that is troubling and becomes even more troubling to the reader as Jones reviews the answers of the non-Christian traditions, including Buddhism, Hinduism, and Judaism. Christianity, while clearly the backdrop to his sermon, will not succeed as a path of exemption from suffering. Rather, Jones says, *"How can a faith with a cross at its heart offer you exemption when the gentlest and purest heart that ever beat – Jesus, the Son of God, was not exempt?"* (333). The answer to unmerited suffering, according to Jones, is demonstrated by Jesus on the cross:

Jesus took the worst thing that could ever happen to him – his crucifixion – and turned it into the best thing that could happen to the world...namely, its redemption. Jesus did not bear the cross, he used the cross. The cross was sin and he turned it into the healing of sin. The cross was hate and he turned it into a revelation of love. The cross was man at its worst and through it Jesus showed God at his redemptive best (333).

Jones asks, "Can Christians therefore take what comes – good, bad, or indifferent – and use these life events? Can we turn them into something higher (and better)?" Jones answers in the affirmative. As he develops his argument, he first makes use of an illustration from nature:

I watched an eagle circle over a valley one day in the Himalaya Mountains. I had been interested in that eagle because I had climbed a cliff and watched it feed its young. But this day, I was concerned about what was going to happen to my eagle because there was a dark and terrible storm brewing up in the head of the valley. There were dark clouds and the flashing of lightening and I could hear the rolling of the thunder. What would happen to my eagle when the storm struck down through this narrow valley? Would it fly before the fury of the storm? Would it hide in the cleft of the rocks or be dashed to pieces down upon the pitiless rocks? The storm was now breaking. I watched the eagle breathlessly. The eagle did *none* of the things that I expected it to do. It circled and wheeled and went straight toward the storm and when the storm struck it — it went up, up, and up - way, way up yonder. Far above the storm it flew in majestic circles above the fury of the story. It did not bear the storm, it did not escape the storm, and it was not broken by the storm. It *used* the storm. The set of the wings did it. Had the wings been set this way, the eagle would have fallen to the earth, bleeding, broken, and blighted, but the wings were set this way and when the storm struck it - the eagle went up. What does the Christian faith say for you and me? It gives you a set of the soul, an attitude of mind. It sets your wings. So that when trouble and sorrow and difficulty and frustration strike you — you go up — not down (335).

Moving from the natural world back to the pages of the New Testament, Jones points to the passage, *"Who did sin this man or his parents that he should be born blind?"* Jesus said, *"Neither did this man sin nor his parents that he should be born blind, but that the works of God should be made manifest – in him."* It is the phrase, "made manifest – in him," that is relevant here. Can something come out of this blindness, out of any one's affliction or suffering?

In addition to "using" suffering, Jones suggests that, in our pain and distress, we can experience the company of Christ. God does, in fact, suffer with us, as we have seen in the unmerited suffering of Jesus on the cross.[2] God suffers not

---

2   "A God who is only omnipotent is in himself an incomplete being, for he cannot experience helplessness and powerlessness. Omnipotence can indeed be longed for and worshipped by helpless men, but omnipotence is

because he is forced to suffer, but because he freely wills to reach out in costly love toward all of His Creatures (Johnson, 92).

Does it help to consider that God is sorrowful about the evil in the world? Was God not heart-broken by the cross of Jesus Christ? Is God not weeping for those who suffer injustice, for the innocents who suffer? If God is working to redeem the world by the *cross*, then conceivably sorrow can be redemptive and of value to others. Jones repeatedly states that suffering can be used and is less painful when it is surrendered to God who gives us the promise of transformation. The theologian, Moltmann, also emphases the meaning of the cross as he discusses human suffering:

> In a civilization that glorifies success and happiness and is blind to the suffering of others, people's eyes can be opened to the truth if they remember that at the center of the Christian faith stands an unsuccessful, tormented Christ, dying in forsakenness. The recollection that God raised this crucified Christ and made him the hope of the world must lead the churches to break their alliances with the powerful and enter into solidarity of the humiliated (ix).

It is "Jesus' suffering above all that demonstrates God's full embrace of our human condition" (Johnson, 168). Soulen states that, in "going beyond the reaching out to the lost, Jesus took the place of the lost on the cross, bearing all alienation in order to overcome it" (2/2/2006). We cannot minimize the anguish of Jesus but will see again and again that Jesus used suffering redemptively. Is Jesus an example and a message for how to deal with suffering?

Jones points us to the pages of the New Testament to illustrate how Jesus met suffering; we find that his way is utterly

---

never loved it is only feared. What sort of being, then, would be a God who was only 'almighty'? He would be a being without experience, a being without destiny and a being that is loved by no one." (Moltmann 223) That is not our God!

different from the prevailing way. We must also acknowledge that we so seldom use his way. Jesus accepted the fact of human suffering; he did not explain it away. He embraced it, and thereby transformed it into something that could be borne and even used. We can see in the death of Christ that Jesus lets life do its worst:

> Jesus takes on the injustices of life in solidarity with any of us who have experienced injustice and through it shows the very best that God or man can offer (Mathews 90).

Here is the remarkable thing — that when we are open to it, no human experience, no suffering, and no joy is immune from the presence of Christ who transforms all human experience into possibilities, even suffering and injustice. Jones states that when we experience injustice, it can be the occasion for a testimony. He cites this verse: "And when they shall deliver you up before Kings and Governors for my namesake, they shall turn to you for a testimony."[3] "Oh," Jones says, "Can I turn everything — injustice — everything into a testimony? Can I use everything and can I bear witness to everything?" He affirms that it is possible and then reminds us that Paul's letters were written during his imprisonment. Paul loved to preach, and if he had not been imprisoned, no doubt he would have continued his public speaking and we would not have had his writings: *"While his sermons are gone, his epistles live on. Paul turned that impediment into an instrument, his jail into joy. Paul did something with what happened to him. He used suffering"* (336).

Jones believes that God is in the process of saving all of creation. We know this because of Christ's resurrection — for the end of the story of salvation is given to us in the midst of our lives, inserted into human history. Part of the joy of being

---

3   "But before all this occurs, they will arrest you and persecute you; they will hand you over to synagogues and prisons, and you will be brought before kings and governors because of my name. This will give you an opportunity to testify" (Luke 21:12-13).

a Christian is celebrating the profoundly paradoxical character of God's salvation through Jesus Christ. The incarnation is scandal enough: that the Lord of all universes should enter a single time and space in the form of an infant baby born to impoverished parents. That the incarnate God should not only experience death, but the most shameful form of violent death as an executed criminal: "Here is extreme paradox. And here is the reason why Christian language is so filled with tension and energy, as it strives to express how blessing can come through such incongruous means....if we experience blessing through means so contrary to anything humans could ever conceive, we know we are in the hands of our God" (Johnson 165).

Professor James says, "This positive active way of dealing with sorrow gives a new dimension of life," and Professor Royce adds that "No man is safe unless he can stand anything that can happen to him." (338) Jones will concur, "The Christian is safe because he can not only stand everything that happens to him, he can use everything that happens to him, and that is the victory." Jones concludes with this affirmation:

> "Everything furthers those who follow Christ — if you know how to use it. In Jesus everything is opportunity. Shall I repeat that sentence? In Jesus everything is opportunity because you can make everything into something else" (337).

A religion with a cross at its center doesn't offer mere comfort, a drying of tears – it offers a moral and spiritual master that turns sorrow into song and a Calvary into an Easter Morning" (Jones, *Christ and Human Suffering,* 15).[4]

---

4 Jones' last book, *The Divine Yes,* illustrated in his life his conviction that suffering can be used and suffering can be a testimony.

"THE WAY TO MEET UNMERITED SUFFERING IS TO USE IT" "CHRIST AND HUMAN SUFFERING"

SERMON

IN Holland, in front of a chapel was a huge concrete cross. The center of it was hollowed out and in the center were chimes. Are there chimes in the Cross? Is there music?

One of the problems that is troubling the minds of men is this matter of unmerited suffering. It has been the pressing problem of the East. Merited suffering we can understand. This is a world where we reap what we sow. We live in a world where we get results or we get consequences. If you work with the moral universe you get results, it will back you, sustain, further you, and approve of you. You will have cosmic backing. But if you go against the moral universe you will get consequences you will be up against it and frustrated. Some people go through life getting results – others get consequences. You are free to choose, but you are not free to choose the results of the consequences of your choices. They are in hands not your own.

I understand that. But what about this unmerited suffering, where other people sow and I reap, and you reap and we reap. It is at the place of unmerited suffering that the mind of man reels and rebels and cries out — Why? My son, the world is dark with grief and graves so dark that men cry out against the heavens. What is the Christian answer to unmerited suffering?

First of all let us look at some of the answers that others give. We can see the Christian answer then in the background. There is the message from the ancient Stoic who said, "my head might be bloodied but it will be unbowed under the bludgeons of chance."[5] The Stoic would steel his inner life

5   William E. Henley (1849-1903) was an English poet. This reference is from the poem Invictus and the exact quote is "In the fell clutch of

against outer circumstances. Very noble, but not good enough — in shutting out suffering the Stoic has to shut out love and pity because if you let in love and pity, all the world's trouble and sorry would come behind that love and pity. They would troop in and take over.

Then there was Omar Khayyam the great Persian poet who reacted strongly against this kind of world and said, "Oh love, I would like to take the sorry scheme of things entire and smash it and remake it according to the heart's desire."[6] Lovely poetry but you can't smash the sorry scheme of things entire and remake it according to the heart's desire. You have got to accept things as they are, modified within (inaudible). Margaret Fuller once said, "I accept the universe."[7] Carlyle's response was, "Gad she had better."[8] There is nothing else to be done.

---

circumstance, I have not winced nor cried aloud. Under the bludgeonings of chance, My head is bloody, but unbowed." <Buckley, J.H. William Ernest Henley: a Study in the "Counter-Decadence" of the Nineties (Princeton, NJ: Princeton University Press, 1945, accessed 31 March 2007), iii, available from Questia.com/PM.qst?a=o&d=4919076; Internet.>

6 Omar Khayyam (1048-1131) was a poet, mathematician and astronomer. He is believed to have written over one thousand four line poems. The quote is from the Rubâiyât of Omar Khayyâm as translated by Edward Fitzgerald. "Ah, Love! could thou and I with Fate conspire, To grasp this sorry Scheme of Things entire! Would not we shatter it to bits- and then Re-mould it nearer to the Heart's Desire!" <Fitzgerald, Edward. The Rubaiyat of Omar Khayyam, The Astronomer Poet of Persia /. Philadelphia: J. C. Winston, 1898. Book on-line. Available from Questia, http://www.questia.com/PM.qst?a=o&d=102294138. Internet. Accessed 30 March 2007.

7 Sarah Margaret Fuller (May 23, 1810 - June 19, 1850) was a journalist, critic and women's rights activist. She was also a well known in the Unitarian church. The quote is in reference to her conversion. < Madeleine B. Stern, The Life of Margaret Fuller, 2nd Rev. ed. [book on-line] (New York: Greenwood Press, 1991, accessed 31 March 2007), iii; available from Questia, http://www.questia.com/PM.qst?a=o&d=15714158; Internet.>

8 Thomas Carlyle (1795 – 1881) was a Scottish essayist, satirist, and historian, whose work was hugely influential during the Victorian era. He was also a Calvanist who lost his faith in Christianity while in college.

Then there is the answer of Buddha who sat under the Bodhi tree at Bodh Gaya[9] and pondered long and deep upon the problem of suffering and came to the startling conclusion that existence and suffering are one. The only way to get out suffering is to get out of existence and the only way to get out of existence is to cut the root of desire to become desireless then you go out into that passionless and actionless state of Nirvana — the state literally of the snuffed out candle. I asked a Buddhist monk in Ceylon if there any existence in Nirvana. He said, "how could there be, there is no suffering, thus there is no existence." Buddha would get rid of the problems of life by getting rid of life.

Then there is the answer of the Hindu — he says that what happens (to you) is the result of a previous birth — so that whatever is, is just. If you are suffering now, then you were sinful then — "just as a calf will find its mother among a thousand cows, so your deeds will find you out among a thousand rebirths."[10] Accept it. It is yours. Whatever is, is just.

Interestingly this quote is also attributed to Henry David Thoreau, Ralph Waldo Emerson and Winston Churchill. < http://www.britannica.com/eb/article-9020374/Thomas-Carlyle>

9   Siddhârtha Gautama was a spiritual teacher from ancient India and the historical founder of Buddhism. He is universally recognized by Buddhists as the Supreme Buddha of our age. The time of his birth and death are uncertain; most modern historians date his lifetime from 563 BCE to 483 BCE. < Roger J. Corless, The Vision of Buddhism: The Space under the Tree, 1st ed. [book on-line] (St. Paul, MN: Paragon House, 1989, accessed 31 March 2007), xvii; available from Questia, http://www.questia.com/PM.qst?a=o&d=34672870; Internet.>

10 Karma is a main tenet of Hinduism. It is the belief in "Right Action" and is described as the moral law of cause and effect. Kharma is also closely related to the Hindu philosophy of reincarnation, i.e. that wrong actions committed in one life will follow an individual into the next life (lives) until the action is made right. ommitted in one life will follow an individual into the next life (lives) until the action is made right. < http://en.wikipedia.org/wiki/Karma>

Parenthetically, let me say that a good many Christians are turning to reincarnation as a way to explain the inequalities of life. There is not a line of scripture to back it. Jesus repudiated it when the people asked, "Who did sin, him or his parents when he was born blind?"[11] Jesus said, "neither did this man sin nor his parents."[12] The Christian has another answer for the inequalities of life and they are not hypotheses like reincarnation.

I say that reincarnation is a hypothesis for if you are suffering now why don't you remember what you did? And if you are being rewarded now why don't you remember what you did to get it? Reward and punishment in this system is not connected by memory. What kind of system would that be to reward you but give you no memory of what the reward is all about? You say that some people say that they remember their rebirths. I have my question marks. However, suppose they do. Everyone should remember; everyone should know why it is that I am what I am if it is because of what I have done. However, we don't have the link of memory and so this system (of reincarnation) is a poor system. Besides, we have another way to account for the inequalities and they are scientific and working now.

First, inequalities are passed on through the physical heredity. For example, weak parents on the whole bring forth weak children. Strong parents on the whole bring forth strong children. Inequalities are passed on down through innate heredity. Second, inequalities can occur through social heredity. Society is organized in favor of some and not in favor of others. Many things are passed on through the social heredity and they make for inequalities. And third some inequalities occur through one's own choices. One may take advantage of what he receives by way of innate physical heredity or have certain

---

11 John 9:2.

12 John 9:3.

advantages through social heredity and go up or he may not take advantage (of the advantages of social heredity) and go down. These three things account for supposed inequalities and they are all remediable. We can pass on a better innate heredity and a better social heredity and we can make better choices now.

A Hindu said to me one day that Jesus must have been a terrible sinner in a previous life because He suffered so much in this life. According to the strict law of Karma he was right. But, I would suspect the premise which brought him to that conclusion. Then there is the answer of Islam which says whatever happens is the will of God. Accept it. Islam literally means submission — submission to the will of God. But I question whether everything that happens is the will of God. If so, what kind of God is there? His character is gone. Then there are two answers in the Old Testament. Habakkuk says "Although the fig tree does not blossom, and no fruit is on the vines; though the produce of the olive fails, and the fields yield no food; though the flock is cut off from the fold, and there is no herd in the stalls, yet I will rejoice in the Lord; I will exult in the God of my salvation."[13] Beautiful but the usual answer of the Old Testament is that you will be exempt if you are righteous. "No plague will come nigh your dwelling only with your eyes shall you behold and see the reward of the wicked and it will not come nigh thee."[14] The righteous will be exempt. However, it is difficult to fit that in with the happenings of life. They found that the righteous did suffer — sometimes because they were righteous.

Society demands conformity. If you fall beneath its standards it will punish you and if you rise above its standards it will persecute you. Society seems to demand a grey average conformity. The righteous are a departure upward and their heads are lifted above the multitude and therefore their heads

---

13 Habakkuk 3:17-18.

14 Psalm 91:10.

get whacked. If they don't get whacked then they are not above the multitude. Jesus said, "Woe unto you when all men speak well of you."[15] You are like them. When we now turn to the New Testament some Christians give the Islamic answer, "It is the will of God;" or the Old Testament answer that you will be exempt, "suffering won't come nigh you."

A professor walked across a street in Chicago and was knocked down by a truck and suffered a broken leg. After many weeks in the hospital he came back and stood up in a University chapel service and said, "I no longer believe in a personal God. Had there been a personal God he would have whispered to me to alert me to the danger. But he did not whisper to me and so when my leg was broken, my faith was broken." This professor apparently believed that if you were only righteous, motor trucks would not knock you down. Suppose the righteous were exempt. What kind of universe would we have? We would have a very chaotic one. If a good man were to lean over a tall building and leaned over too far, the law of gravity would be suspended. However, if a bad man leaned over too far, it (the law of gravity) would be in operation. You would not know whether the law of gravity would be suspended or in operation — for you would not know the character of the person concerned. Now when I lean too far over the parapet of a tall building I know that the law of gravity is not going to ask whether I am good, bad or indifferent. It will pull me down. It is a hard school, but I know the rules and it is dependable. Suppose it could be proved that trucks would never knock you down if you were righteous. What would happen to the righteous? They would be the champion jay walkers of the world. They would roam around amid the traffic meditating and vegetating. And that quickness of decision that comes from a world of chance and circumstance would be taken away and that exemption would be their elimination. Now when I cross the street I know that if I don't belong to the quick, I will soon belong to the dead. And so it sharpens my wits and so I watch.

---

15   Luke 6:26.

In China, during the Chinese-Japanese war, there was a church that was not bombed while everything around it was bombed and smashed and that church was exempt (from the bombing) and the people crowded in. "Oh" they said, "This is the true religion and they got so many people to join the church that they had to build a new one. However, on the day that they dedicated it a bomb fell and smashed it and rightly. Because if you had based religion on that false notion you would have said, this is the place to be safe. You would have thought that you would be exempt!

How can a faith with a cross at its heart offer you exemption when the gentlest and purest heart that ever beat — the Son of God was not exempt? The bystanders who stood around His cross said, "Let God take Him down. Then we will believe." But God did not take Him down. Jesus dropped His head on His pulseless bosom and died. And where is the answer (to suffering)? The answer, I believe, is right there on that Cross. Jesus took the worst thing that could ever happen to Him — his crucifixion — and turned it into the best thing that could happen to the world, namely its redemption. Jesus did not bear the cross, He used the cross. The cross was sin and He turned it into the healing of sin. The cross was hate and He turned it into a revelation of love. The cross was man at its worst and through it Jesus showed God at his redemptive best.

Is that the answer? Take what comes, good, bad and indifferent and turn it into something higher? Are we not to merely bear suffering but to use it? Yes, I believe that is the answer. I quoted earlier that passage, "who did sin this man or his parents that he should be born blind?"[16] Jesus said, "Neither did this man sin nor his parents that he should be born blind, but that the works of God should be made manifest in Him."[17] I used to question that verse as it sounded wrong. However, one day I heard this story. A Japanese professor mid-career

---

16 John 9:2.

17 John 9:3.

was suddenly stricken by blindness. His retina was detached. He staggered and reeled and he went to his Buddhist faith and was told that he had sinned in a previous birth. He said, "I can't believe it." Someone suggested that he go to the Christian scriptures where he read that passage about the blind son. He said, "Could the works of God be made manifest through my blindness? Could I make something out of this? Could I use it?" He opened his heart to the love of Christ. He came out of it victorious and became a wonderful evangelist. People crowded his presentations to hear from the man who took the worst (life offered him) and turned it into the best. He went to Scotland and took a doctoral degree in theology and returned to Japan to teach seminarians. He wrote books and was loved, honored and respected. He did not bear that suffering. He used it. Is that what we are to do? Yes.

Where did those matchless parables of the Lost Son, Lost Coin and the Lost Sheep[18] come from? They came out of pain. The Scribes and the Pharisees said that He (Jesus) eats with publicans and sinners because He is like them — in an attempt to take away His good name. Did Jesus bear that? No, he used it. He turned it and used it. You see through those parables the very heart of the seeking God. When others attempted to take away His good name, He turned it into something else – higher.

You remember the story of the man with the withered arm in the synagogue. They watched Jesus to see if he would heal on the Sabbath. He said to the man, "Stand up, stretch forth your arm." And the man stretched it forth and he was well. The Scribes and the Pharisees were beside themselves with rage and they took counsel to see what they would do with him.[19] What they would do with him was to kill him to stop him. Then the account says, "Now during those days he went out to the mountain to pray; and he spent the night in prayer

---

18 The three parables are stories told by Jesus to illustrate loss and redemption. The Lost Sheep is told in Luke 15:3-7; The Lost Coin in Luke 15:8-10; and the Lost Son (The Prodigal Son) in Luke 15:11-32.

19 Mark 3:3-6.

to God. And when day came, he called his disciples and chose twelve of them, whom he also named apostles"[20] Evidently Jesus had seen in the night what was going to happen (to him). He called his apostles together and chose twelve, whom he named apostles. He said all right if they are going to do away with me, I am going to trust my movement to the twelve. That was one of the most constructive things Jesus ever did. He was probably going to do it at some point but this (His experience with the Scribes and Pharisees) hastened it and He acted. And about those twelve, you know what happened? They filled the world with His teaching and His love and His power. Jesus did not bear that attempt to take away His life, rather He used it and turned it into something higher.

I watched an eagle circle over a valley one day in the Himalaya Mountains. I had been interested in that eagle because I had climbed a cliff and watched it feed its young. But this day I was concerned about what was going to happen to my eagle because there was a dark, terrible storm brewing up in the head of the valley. There were dark clouds and the flashing of lightening and I could hear the rolling of the thunder. What would happen to my eagle when the storm struck down through this narrow valley? Would it fly before the fury of the storm? Would it hide in the cleft of the rocks or be dashed to pieces down upon the pitiless rocks? The storm was now breaking. I watched the eagle breathlessly. The eagle did *none* of the things that I expected it to do. It circled and wheeled and went straight toward the storm and when the storm struck it, it went up, up, and up — way, way up yonder. Far above the storm it flew in majestic circles above the fury of the story. It did not bear the storm, it did not escape the storm, and it was not broken by the storm. It *used* the storm. The set of the wings did it. Had the wings been set this way, the eagle would have fallen to the earth, bleeding, broken, and blighted, but the wings were set this way and when the storm struck, the eagle went up. What does the Christian faith do for you and me? It gives

---

20 Luke 6:12-13.

you a set of the soul, an attitude of mind. It sets your wings. So that when trouble and sorrow and difficulty and frustration strike you, you go up, not down.

The same event can strike two people. One writhes in the dust in agony and bitterness stating, "My God why?" The other rises on wings of love into higher heights. It is a question of your attitude and of your mind and heart. The Christian faith then teaches you not to bear suffering but to take what comes and use it. Just like the Lotus flower reaches into the muck and mire and takes up the muck and mire into the purpose of its life and transmutes it into the beauty of the Lotus flower, so you and I are to take what comes — the raw material of human life good, bad, and indifferent. Some of it is pleasurable and some of it painful, some of it complementary and some of it critical. We are to take it up into the purpose of our lives and transmute it into character and into achievement.

I remember when this dawned on me. It was during a time in India when I was puzzled. And then I read this verse, "And when they shall deliver you up before Kings and Governors for my namesake. They shall turn to you for a testimony."[21] "Oh," I said. "Can I turn everything — injustice — everything into a testimony? Can I use everything and can I bear witness to everything? Yes that is possible.

If Paul had been out preaching all of his life, that would have been beautiful and that is what he wanted to do. But he got into trouble through his preaching and was put into jail. It was in jail that Paul he wrote those deathless epistles. Suppose Paul had been out preaching all the time, we would have never received his sermons. There were no tape recorders or stenographers in Paul's time. But when Paul was put in jail, and when he had the leisure to meditate and pray he wrote those deathless epistles. His sermons are gone; his epistles live on. He turned that impediment into an instrument; his jail into

---

21 Luke 21:12-13.

joy. He did something with what happened to him. He used his suffering.

I have just been in Finland. The Finns are a wonderful people. They were unjustly attacked by Russia. The whole peninsula was taken away and five hundred thousand Finns had to be repatriated back into Finland. The Finnish government did it (the repatriation) by simple expediency. There were five million Finnish residents and five hundred thousand had to be absorbed into the country and so the government said, "Everyone has to give ten percent of their land or their money." We will absorb them straight. They did. The country then had to pay a heavy indemnity. They paid it. Then the Russians said that Finland had to give them sixty-four ships but the Finns were not a ship building people so they had to learn how to build ships. After they learned it and gave back the sixty-four ships they said, "Why should we not keep on building ships?" And so they did and now they are a ship building people. In building the ships, they had to construct a great deal of machinery as they were not at that time a mechanized people. They said, "All right, we have learned how to produce machinery now and so let's keep on going." Their unjust attack from Russia was used to the benefit of Finland. In fact it kicked them upward and forward.

Everything furthers those who follow Christ, if you know how to use it. In Jesus everything is opportunity. Shall I repeat that sentence? If you forget everything else (remember) in Jesus everything is opportunity because you can make everything into something else.

Somebody said to me, "In light of all the criticism you get, don't you get stomach ulcers?" I said, "No, I have learned how to deal with criticism. If it is true, I change. So, I have made my critics the unpaid watchmen of my soul. They have furthered me a great deal. I owe them much and I am grateful." But suppose the criticism is unjust? I determined that I would not allow it to change my attitude toward my critics. As far as I know I have no enemies because I have no enmity. It is a very simple way to get rid of your enemies. Have no enmity and they are all gone. But someone said to me, "I don't believe that you know when you are insulted." I said, "Yes, I suppose I don't. Because as Luther said, 'my soul is too glad and too great to be the enemy of any man.'" It is simple. Use your critics. If they are right, change. If they are wrong, don't change. It is that simple.

A woman who thought that her home was intact and beautiful and believed that her husband was faithful and everything was all right, got a cable one day from Mexico saying "divorced in Mexico and remarried here." That news came out of a blue sky. She learned that her husband had married a Japanese woman and that they were now living in Okinawa with two children—two girls and that he now had tuberculosis. She cabled her husband and said, "Please send those girls to me and let me take care of them, so that your wife will have the time to serve and help you." The children came and she took them into her home and treated them like her own daughters. Then she heard that the husband had died and so she sent a telegram to the Japanese wife and said, "Please come and live in our home and take care of your children here and be a part of our family." And when she went to meet the Japanese woman at the airport, she said that my one prayer was this, "Oh God, please help me accept her and love her with as much joy as I would experience if it were Carl — her husband — coming back to me again." And I did with the grace of God and took her into my home. We became a real family of God. She did not bear her suffering and loss, rather she used it.

Professor James says this positive active way of dealing with sorrow gives a new dimension of life.[22] Professor Royce says that "No man is safe unless he can stand anything that can

22 Professor William James, (1842-1910) was a pioneering American psychologist and philosopher. He wrote influential books on the young science of psychology, educational psychology, psychology of religious experience and mysticism, and the philosophy of pragmatism. The quote, from *The Varieties of Religious Experience* (1902), is "A solemn state of mind

happen to him."[23] But the Christian is safe because he can not only stand everything that happens to him, he can use everything that happens to him, and that is the victory that we are going to partake of this morning. It is all in the bread and the wine. Take it, use it and make something out of it. It is the open door.

---

is never crude or simple — it seems to contain a certain measure of its own opposite in solution. A solemn joy preserves a sort of bitter in its sweetness; a solemn sorrow is one to which we intimately consent." < Paul Jerome Croce, *Science and Religion in the Era of William James* [book on-line] (Chapel Hill, NC: University of North Carolina Press, 1995, accessed 31 March 2007), iii; available from Questia, http://www.questia.com/PM.qst?a=o&d=94842669; Internet.

23 Josiah Royce (1855-1916) was an American objective idealist philosopher. The heart of Royce's idealist philosophy was his contention that the apparently external world has real existence only as known by an ideal Knower, and that this Knower must be actual rather than merely hypothetical. <Royce, Josiah, and Josiah Royce. *Royce's Logical Essays: Collected Logical Essays of Josiah Royce.* Edited by Daniel S. Robinson. Dubuque, Iowa: Wm. C. Brown, 1951. Book on-line. Available from Questia, http://www.questia.com/PM.qst?a=o&d=76793736. Internet. Accessed 30 March 2007.>

II. LOVE IS THE STRONGEST FORCE IN THE UNIVERSE AND WILL WIN

COMMENTARY ON THE NEW BIRTH

ON THE PATTERN OF JESUS

The text for this sermon is taken from Hebrews 1:1-3:

> Long ago God spoke to our ancestors in many and various ways by the prophets, but in these last days he has spoken to us by a Son, whom he appointed heir of all things, through whom he also created the world. He is the reflection of God's glory and the exact imprint of God's very being, and he sustains things by his powerful word. When he had made purification for sins, he sat down at the right hand of the Majesty on high, having become as much superior to angels as the name he has inherited is more excellent than theirs.

According to E. Stanley Jones, this text offers the definitive word about the exalted Word — Jesus Christ.

I understand that this particular sermon was addressed to a group of Methodist ministers to whom Jones affirms his hope that the church will be not merely an *organization* but an *organism* of the Holy Spirit. He observes that they had been raising questions — perhaps brought forth by members of their congregations — such as "Why is Jesus necessary? Why can't we go straight to God?" Jones is very clear that understanding the "place" of Jesus is critical to understanding Christianity. He tells of the Gnostics *who believed that they could bypass the historic Jesus and know God without the revelation of God in Christ*

(269). Jones is certain, as is the author of the Gospel of John, that the "Word became Flesh" and so we must not bypass Jesus but come to know him. Jones then reminds these ministers that whatever we preach about in Christianity, such as the Holy Spirit or the new birth, we must connect it experientially, not abstractly, with Jesus. The Holy Spirit and the new birth must be linked to Jesus or they will have no relevance.

Jones then presents his case for the necessity of Jesus "who puts character into God." He is adamant that we cannot know God apart from Jesus, for in Jesus we see the very being of God. Now as to the timing of the arrival of Jesus into human history, Jones notes that *all of the great philosophies of the world and the great moral concepts were completed just before the coming of Jesus* (349). It is as if, according to Jones, that man had gone as far as he could go in his search for God — now God would come to man in the form of a son. Jones repeatedly states that the Gospel is God's search for man and that, in Jesus, God revealed himself.

This sermon reviews in detail the facets of Christ that help us to understand God. Jones will systematically explain how the person of Jesus transforms concepts and moral qualities such as love and purity by making them "real" in the divinity of Christ's life. For example, Jones states that,

> Literature can never rise higher than the life that surrounds the word. The life that surrounds the word puts content and meaning into the word. Suppose God should then give us a book from heaven with all his will written in it. Would that be a perfect revelation of God? Hardly. You and I would see those words and we would read into them our highest experience of those words.
>
> I'd see the word love, and I would read into it my highest experience of love, but my highest experience of love is not love — it's my highest experience of love. It is partial and incomplete. I'd see the word purity, and I'd read into it my highest experience of purity, but my highest

experience of purity is not purity. It would be partial and incomplete (350).

Jones states that we can take *every quality of Jesus and transfer them onto God without loss or degradation to the thought of God* (351). What, then, is the revelation of God? Jones affirms that it is in the person of Jesus, it is in the Word become Flesh, the *divine* Word become flesh. God came to us as the God/Man, not as a teacher, but as a savior. Jones asks, "How are we to understand the concept of this God/Man, the reality that Jesus is both like us and unlike us?"

> Jesus is so like me that I can put my hand upon his shoulder and say "brother man," but when I'm about to do it – I can't. He steps on the side of God with an offer that no man dare to offer another. **"Come unto me. I am the way, the truth, the life."** No man can offer that without blasphemy. He's like me and unlike me. He had to be like us to show us how to live; he had to be unlike us (God) to redeem us (353).

C.S. Lewis, in *Mere Christianity*, reiterates Jones' comments on this incredible offer from Jesus, "Come unto me. I am the way, the truth and the life." Lewis writes:

> A man who was merely a man and said the sort of things Jesus said would not be a great moral teacher. He would either be a lunatic — on the level with man who says he is a poached egg — or he would be the Devil of Hell. You must make your choice. Either this man was, and is, the Christ, the Son of God; or else a madman or something worse. You can shut Him up for a fool! Or you can fall at His feet and call Him Lord and God. But let us not come with any patronizing nonsense about His being a great teacher or prophet. He has not left that open to us (40-41).

Being the God-Man, then, is Jesus a miracle? Jones would answer affirmatively and state that he does not believe in the Jesus because of the miracles, but he believes in the miracles because of Jesus who is the central miracle.

The central miracle is this divine invasion of us in the incarnation. Grant that, and the lesser miracles fall into place. You say, "Of course." Opening blind eyes, that is nothing. Unstopping deaf ears — that is nothing. The big thing is God's redemptive invasion of us *in flesh*. That is the miracle, the miracle of being. Grant that and everything follows (354).

Another emphasis in this sermon is that the *Christian Way* is the "natural" **Way** to live. While the Christian way is primarily thought of as the way of salvation; that is not Jones' primary interpretation. Jones would often say that the Christian Way is the way to think, act, feel and be under every conceivable circumstance and he believed that this was his most exciting theological discovery. He would insist that the Christian **Way** is written into human nature, into our blood, nerves, tissues, and being as the way we are all created to live.

Every cell of my being is made by Him and for Him. The Christian way is the way to do everything, to think, to act, to feel, and to be under every conceivable condition. The Way represents the touch of Christ upon all creation in that everything is made to work in His way, and when it does so, it works harmoniously. We are predestined to be Christian. When we work against His Way, we work toward our own destruction (356).

Jones then links the inherent reality of the **Way** to the fact of God's love for us. Jones often followed psychotherapeutic literature, and in this sermon, speaks about having recently read Menninger's *Love Against Hate*. (Jones' interest in psychotherapy and mental health prompted him to create the Nur Manzil Psychiatric Center in Lucknow, India; a psychiatric hospital providing an emphasis on spiritual as well as psychological and physical treatment and healing.) He uses material from Menninger's book to emphasize humanity's deep need to love and be loved. If God is love and God made us in his image, says Jones, then our nature is love, and when we love we realize our true self. Love is the core component of the nature that God stamped into all of us. The deepest need in man and the highest in God do not conflict – they coincide. (Jones, *Conversion*, 78) Jones echoes Paul's famous verse, "So faith, hope, love abide, these three; the greatest of these is love." (I Cor. 13:1-13).

Jones affirms that:

Jesus is God's answer to the world's need to be redeemed from sin. Jesus has come to cleanse and save the world. Jesus is Lord! This Jesus — is Lord of the past, he saves us from our sins and guilt. Jesus is Lord of the present as he gives us power to face life and Jesus is Lord of the future for Jesus is the resurrection and the life (360ff).

Jones then tells these ministers that all they have to do each day is to walk upon the **Way.** When we surrender our lives to Christ, we walk upon that **Way**. Jones reminds the ministers that, as they preach the importance of the new birth, they hold something special in their hands. They are not preaching barren doctrines, or points of view; rather they are preaching a person – Jesus: *"With these convictions, can we help but go out and preach the new birth, and help people get into this new birth?"* (364).

LOVE IS THE STRONGEST FORCE IN THE UNIVERSE AND WILL WIN

THE NEW BIRTH ON THE PATTERN OF JESUS (1957)

SERMON

SHALL we bow our heads in a moment of silent prayer?
Amen

Let me say before I take my text, that I am grateful for the purpose of this conference and the spirit of it. I go away with a great hope about the Methodist Church. This is the kind of thing (this meeting) that rekindles fires that need to be rekindled and I go away with a great feeling that the Methodist Church is not going to be merely an organization but an organism of the Holy Spirit.

In the first three chapters of Hebrews is a passage upon which I think that I have never heard a sermon preached and I have not preached a sermon on it either for these many years except just recently. Yet perhaps if I were to pick out a passage that sums up the meaning of the Christian faith in its breadth and height and depth... the total sweep... this perhaps would be the crowning verse. "In many and various ways God spoke of old to our fathers by the prophets; but in these last days he has spoken to us by a son, whom he appointed the heir of all things, through whom also he created the world. He reflects the glory of God and bears the very stamp of his nature upholding the universe by his word of power. When he had made purification for sins, he sat down at the right of the Majesty on high."[1]

---

1   Hebrews 1:1-3. RSV

Since I have been here many of you have been raising questions with me. First of all is Jesus necessary? Cannot we go directly to God? Where is the place of Jesus?

Now I am persuaded that this is the crux of the whole matter. I have just spent two years studying First John. The background of First John was the threat of Gnosticism for that is what he was talking about. The Gnostics took Christian nomenclature and thought that they could bypass the historic Jesus and could know God immediately without the revelation of God in Christ. Therefore John begins his first epistle with a head on and sweeping statement about Jesus. "That which is from the beginning, which we have seen and heard and our eyes have looked upon and our hands have handled concerning the word of Life."[2] That was his sweeping answer to Gnosticism...the *word* become *flesh.*

Now I think that we have rightly talked about the New Birth and we have rightly talked about the Holy Spirit and we have rightly talked about doctrines. But if we talk about them abstractly, apart from Jesus, they will soon become hollow shells and without substance. For the new birth, apart from Jesus, becomes a doctrine to be talked about instead of something to be experienced and known. The new birth is never discussed in the New Testament apart from Jesus. "If any man be Christ, he is a new creature." The new birth was tied up to Jesus. The Holy Spirit was tied up to Jesus. The Holy Spirit had a pattern after which he was fashioning men. The pattern was Jesus. The whole of the Gospel comes from Jesus foremost. You cannot say God until you first say Jesus. For Jesus puts character content into God. You don't begin with God, for if you begin with God you begin with your ideas of God which are not God. And we don't begin with man for if you begin with man you begin with the problems of man and if you begin with a problem you will end with a problem and in the process you will probably become a problem. It was said of a modern minister

---

2   1 John 1:1.

"without a problem spake he not unto them."[3] We are a problem-obsessed people and we have become problems dealing with problems.

We don't begin with God and we don't begin with man. We begin with the God-Man and from Him we work out to God and from Him we work down to man. Christianity has its doctrines but it is not a doctrine. It has its rights and ceremonies but is not a rite or ceremony. It has its institutions but is not an institution. It has its creeds but is not a creed. At the center is a person. Christianity is Christ. Christians are people who believe in God and man and life through Christ. There is our starting point to work out to God and to work down to man. In His life we see life. If you begin with God you will probably lose God. A member of the Unitarian faith asked me to speak at one of their conferences. She asked me to help them get God back into their church. We are becoming humanists. I said to myself that is interesting for they who specialize in God were losing him. I, who specialize in Jesus, have found God in the face of Jesus. Wherever Jesus is dimmed there is decay, and wherever He is emphasized there is revival and it works with a mathematical precision.

We believe that we see in Jesus Christ the very being of God. The account says in this passage, "When in former times God spoke to our forefathers, he spoke in fragmentary and varied fashion through the prophets. But in this the final age he has spoken to us in the Son whom he has made heir to the whole universe, and through whom he created all orders of existence..."[4] Through the prophets revelation was progressive coming up and up and up and up and up until it burst forth in final, full and complete revelation in the Person of his Son. It was initially fragmentary and varied but now God has spoken to us not by a Son, which is the phrase used in the Revised Standard Version of the Bible, but in a Son. The New English

---

3   Matthew 13:34.

4   Hebrews 1:1-3. ESV

Bible has the word in (a Son) for we have to see God before we can understand Him. We couldn't have believed Him through words. All religions are man's search for God, therefore there are many religions. The Gospel is God's search for man, therefore there's but one Gospel.

Now it's interesting that all the great philosophies of the world and all the great moral concepts were completed just before the time of the coming of Jesus. In the great philosophical nations — Greece, India, and China — great philosophies were created which were the high water mark of man's search for God. The Hindu philosophies had reached their acme. The Chinese philosophies had reached their climax and the philosophies of Greece had reached their end. The prophets had prophesized moral and spiritual teaching and had reached their end. Humanity was seeking up after God and then when their philosophy and moralisms had taken man as far as he could go, the account says, "… God spoke to us *in a Son.*"

Now, I am grateful for those up reaches after God, grateful for any light that is in any of these. Jesus said, "I have come not to destroy but to fulfill."[5] His word was a generic term locally applied to the law and the prophets but capable of application to any truth found anywhere. He has not come to destroy the long quest of the Hindus or the Chinese or the Greeks or the Hebrews. He came to fulfill it. They spoke truths and He came forth as the Truth embodied.

That is why I said that religions are man's search for God — the up reach of man as far as he could go. But the gospel is God's search for man — the down reach of God. Therefore there are many religions but there is but one Gospel. God had to finally reveal himself through a person. God can and does reveal himself through nature. I look up through nature and I come to the conclusion that God is law. I am grateful that God is law and that He does not work by whim, notion and fancy but by law and order. Grateful but not satisfied. I want to know not

---

5   Matthew 5:17.

that God is law but whether God is love. Nature can't quite frame the words God is Love. Its voice is equivocal.

God can and does speak through prophet and teacher but not perfectly because the medium is imperfect. God can and does reveal Himself through a book but not perfectly because a book is impersonal and God is the infinitely personal. Therefore God could not perfectly reveal Himself through a book. Besides, words take their meaning from the life that surrounds the words. I used the word home today and for some of you it is a place of comfort, and it is heaven. For some of you it is hell, a place of bitter conflict. One word but two diametrically opposite meanings.

Literature can never rise higher than the life that surrounds the word. The life that surrounds the word puts content and meaning into the word. Suppose God should then give us a book from heaven with all His will written in it. Would that be a perfect revelation of God? Hardly. You and I would see those words and would read into them our highest experience of those words.

I'd see the word *love* and I would read into it my highest experience of love, but my highest experience of love is not love; it's my highest experience of love. It is partial and incomplete. I'd see the word *purity* and I'd read into it my highest experience of purity, but my highest experience of purity is not purity. It would be partial and incomplete. I'd see the word *God* and I'd read into it my highest experience of God, but my highest experience of God is not God. I'd pull those words to the level of my life — my highest experience. So would you. The book then would not be so much the revelation of God as a revelation of us.

What then do we need for a perfect revelation? It seems to me this: a life must come among us, a divine life. A life which will take these words, which we drag to the level of our lives, and put the divine content to them — a divine content through a divine illustration — so that we would no longer see those words in the light of what we are but in the light of that divine illustration. We think that's happened.

A life came among us and lived publicly for three years. I no longer see the word *love* in the light of my poor partial love but in the light of a love that prayed for enemies while upon a cross. "Father forgive them."[6] I no longer see the word *purity* in the light of my poor stained purity but in the light of the purity that shared my temptations minus my faults. I no longer see the word *God* in the light of my imagination of God but in the light of Jesus' uncovering of the nature of God in understandable terms — human terms. And my heart almost stops beating and I say to myself, "Is God like that? In character is He a Christ-like God?" If so, He is a good God and trustable. I know nothing higher. I could be content with nothing less.

I can take every quality of character in Jesus and transfer them to God without loss or degradation to the thought of God. Loss or degradation? The highest compliment that you can pay to God or man is to say that he is a Christ-like. The highest adjective to describe character in any language is the adjective Christ-like. If God is not like Christ in character then He is not a good God and He is not trustable. If He is like Jesus, He is a good God and trustable. The revelation had to come through a Person.

We do not believe that the Bible is the revelation of God. It is the inspired record of the revelation. The revelation (of God is what) we see in the face of Jesus Christ. Shall I repeat that sentence? The Bible is not the revelation of God. It does not say the word became printer's ink. It says the word became flesh![7] The Bible is not the revelation of God; it is the inspired record of the revelation. The revelation was seen in the face of Jesus Christ. Therefore I go to these words everyday and I say these words, "Has thou seen him who my soul loveth?"[8] And

---

6   Luke 23:34.
7   John 1:14.
8   Song of Solomon 3:3.

these words take me by the hand and take me beyond themselves to the Word made flesh. And it's there that I find Him—the Word amidst the words. But the revelation is the person in the face of Jesus Christ. "He has in these his last days spoken to us in a Son."

In one place Jesus is called the word. "In the beginning was the word"[9] Why the word? I suppose because the word is the manifestation of the hidden thought. I stand here without a word and you say "I don't know what he's thinking." However, when I put my thought in a word, you say, "I got his thought, projected to me in a word." The thought and the word are one.

Here is the hidden God/spirit. He projects Himself into humanity as the word. Not a verbal word but a vital word— the Word become flesh. I take hold of Him, look at Him and say, "Oh, now I know what the hidden thought behind the word is like." It is like this that I have seen in Jesus. So the thought and the word are one. Jesus said, "I and the father are one."[10] But Jesus also said "the Father is greater than I (am),"[11] which seems to be a contradiction. But the thought is always greater than the word because all expression means limitation. I have to look around to get words into which I can put my thoughts. I say "I can't quite express it." Whenever I put my thought into a word, I limit it. So the thought is greater than the word. The unexpressed thought is greater than the expressed thought—the word. The unexpressed God is greater than the expressed God. He had to limit Himself to get to our (communicate with) mentality. He emptied Himself and yet Jesus could say, "I and the father are one." But the father is greater than I. Of course, because God had to limit Himself to get to our mentality.

---

9   John 1:1.

10 John 10:30.

11 John 14:28.

Weatherhead[12] gives the illustration of a scientist who was an expert in ants. He said that they could find food provided they were "told" once. The ant colony had scout ants out searching for food. And when they would find the food they would come back and tell the ant colony that they had found the food. And then the ant colony would follow the scout ants around the round about way they took to find the food in the first place. They would go all the way this way and all the way back that way. They wouldn't take a shortcut even when my friend put food almost right in front of them. The ants would not deviate from their path. They would not take the short cut and go directly to the food. They'd go all the way around and all the way back. My friend said, "I wish I were an ant so I could show them how to do it. They could save a lot of time." "However," he said, "if I became an ant I'd probably have an ants' mentality and would do exactly what they are doing. The only way for me to help them would be to become an ant and retain a man's mentality. I would have to be an Ant/Man to help them. I could be like them and I would have to be unlike them if I were going to help them."

If God came to us as a teacher, He would become a man, but God would then be like us and could not help us. But suppose He became like us and unlike us. I see two things in Jesus. I see He is like me. He faces life as a man. He calls on no power that is not available to us for His moral battles. He is so like me that I can put my hand upon His shoulder and say "brother man," but when I'm about to do it, I can't. He steps on the side of God with an offer that no man dare to offer

12 Leslie Dixon Weatherhead (1893-1976) was an English Christian theologian in the liberal Protestant tradition. Renowned as one of Britain's finest preachers in his day, Weatherhead achieved notoriety for his preaching ministry at City Temple in London and for his books, including The Will of God and The Christian Agnostic. < D. W. Bebbington, Evangelicalism in Modern Britain: A History from the 1730s to the 1980s [book on-line] (London: Routledge, 1993, accessed 31 March 2007), v; available from Questia, http://www.questia.com/PM.qst?a=o&d =109064142; Internet.>

another. "Come unto me. I am the way, the truth, the life."[13] No man can offer that without blasphemy. He's like me and unlike me. He had to be like us to show us how to live; He had to be unlike us to redeem us. And so God had to be like us to be our example, and He had to be unlike us to be our redeemer. If He'd only been like us, He'd only have been our example. If He were only unlike us, He would only be our redeemer. But I need somebody to show me the way, then somebody to dispose me to walk in that way after I see the way. I need a redeemer. He is like me and unlike me.

That is one reason why I believe in the Virgin Birth. In His virgin birth He was like us — born of a woman — but unlike us — born of God. I see the likeness in His being born of a woman and I see the unlikeness in that He was born of God. I see the same things in His life. The likeness and the unlikeness coincide. I don't believe in Jesus because of the Virgin Birth. I believe in the Virgin Birth because of Jesus. He carries the miracles; the miracles don't carry Him. I don't believe in Jesus because of the miracles. I believe in the miracles because of Jesus. The central miracle is the Person. He rises in sinless grandeur above saint and sinner — a moral miracle, a miracle of being. Then being a miracle, would He perform miracles? The answer is that being a miracle, it would be a miracle if He did not perform miracles. I don't believe in Jesus because of the miracles. I believe in the miracles because of Jesus. He carries them. The central miracle is this divine invasion of us in the incarnation. Grant that and the lesser miracles fall into place. You say, "Of course! Opening blind eyes, that is nothing. Unstopping deaf ears, that is nothing." The big thing is God's redemptive invasion of us *in flesh*. That is the miracle, the miracle of being. Grant that and everything follows.

It says, "Who he (God) appointed the heir of all things." This is a strange thing to say of a man who walked our dusty roads, slept upon our hillsides and was crucified upon one of our trees and was put in our rock tombs. He was to be the

13 John 14:6.

354

"heir of all things." That everything was to come out at His feet. Why? Because I believe that everything is made in its inner structure to come out at His feet. That next verse must be put with the first verse to explain it, "Through whom he created the world." Now that is a strange passage. Did God create the world through Jesus? It says the same thing in the first Chapter of John[14] and in Colossians,[15] again, it says the same thing. But I thought that God created the whole world millions of years ago. And here is Jesus. Why do we say that God created the world through Jesus? What do they mean? They must mean something like this—that everything has the touch of Christ upon it—that the touch of Christ is on all creation. Everything is made in its inner structure to do His will. And when it does His will, it works perfectly, and when it goes against His will, it destroys itself. I believe that when God made you and me and the universe He stamped within us the *Way.*

What does it mean that the Christian way is called the way? Does it mean the way of salvation? Yes, but it means something very much more. A commotion arose over the use of this word, **the Way**—the way with a capital W. We usually make this the way of salvation. It is the Way of salvation but the verse doesn't make that link explicit. It says it's the way, unqualified. Is the Christian way the way unqualified? Is it the way to-do everything, to think, to act, to feel, to be—under every conceivable circumstance for God and man, individual and collective? Is Jesus the way? Are there just two things in life: the Way and not the way? And is the Christian way always the Way? And is the unchristian way always not the way and are there no exceptions? I believe that to be the case and I believe it with all my heart. That is the deepest conviction of my life. I believe there are just two things in life: the Way and not the

---

14 John 1:3 "all things were made through him, and without him was not anything made that was made."

15 Colossians 1:16 "for in him all things were created, in heaven and on earth, visible and invisible…"

way. If you don't believe that, just you try to spend the rest of your life trying to disprove it.

Does it mean that the touch of Christ is on all creation? That everything is made to work in His way? Does it mean that when it works in His way it works well, harmoniously, adjustably and happily? And if it works some other way, it works to its own ruin? If that is true, then the Way is not merely written in the Bible. Am I predestined to be a Christian?

There are just two things: the *Way* and not the way. I believe that I'm predestined to be a Christian by my makeup. I believe that the Way is not just written in the Bible; it is written in my blood, my nerves, my tissues and my being. Every cell of my being is made by Him and for Him. I'm destined and predestined to be a Christian. It says in Romans 8:29, "For those whom he foreknew he also predestined to be conformed to the image of his Son." Am I predestined to be in the image of his Son? And is that destiny written not in mere scripture but in my blood, my nerves, and my tissue? Strange that I who have my roots in Methodism am standing in this pulpit here before a group of Methodist preachers preaching to you *predestination*. I am predestined to be a Christian. I can live according to that destiny if I want to, or I can live against it if I want to. But if I live against it, I will get hurt automatically. An African chief who had recently been converted, got up and said in a meeting, "I'm doomed to be a saint." I think he meant he was destined. Am I destined to be a Christian? Yes, I believe that I am. I am destined to be made in His likeness. When God made you and me and the universe, He stamped in us His image and God is love, agape love.

I read a book some time ago, Karl Menninger's *Love Against Hate*.[16] As I read it I said to myself, "Good gracious, if love so

---

16   Karl A. Menninger (1893-1990) was an American psychiatrist and psychoanalyst. The book Love Against Hate examined the human capacity to overcome self-destructiveness. < Karl Menninger, Theory of Psychoanalytic Technique [book on-line] (New York: Basic Books, 1958, accessed 31 March 2007), null3; available from Questia, http://www.questia.com/PM.qst?a=o&d=100967876; Internet.>

builds us up and hate tears us down, is love not the most basic urge in human nature?" Is the love urge deeper than the self, sex or herd urge which I thought were the basis urges? Is the urge to love and be loved the deepest urge in human nature? I had not seen that and so I talked with Dr. Boss[17], the head of the Psychiatric Association of Europe. I said, "What about this, Dr. Boss? Is the urge to love and be loved the deepest urge in human nature?"

"Yes, this (love) is the root; those (self, sex, herd) are the branches."

"Oh," I said, "that is interesting." I asked Dr. Boss this question, "You are a Christian and a psychiatrist and how did you get them together?

Dr. Boss said, "Well, I had trouble in my early days getting them together. But the demands of human nature drove me to the Christian position."

That was important — that what human nature demanded, the Gospel offered? When we find the gospel, we find ourselves.

I always looked askance at the word "love." Thou should love thy God, thy neighbor. I said to myself, "how can you command love?" I thought that you couldn't put that commandment over man and make him love. How can you command love? You love or you don't. You can't produce it by a command. But when He says thou shall love, what does our

---

17 Medard Boss (1903 - 1990) was a Swiss psychoanalytic psychiatrist who developed a form of psychotherapy known as Daseinsanalysis. Boss believed that modern medicine and psychology, premised on Cartesian philosophy and Newtonian physics, made incorrect assumptions about human beings and what it means to be human. He addressed an existential foundation for medicine and psychology in an eponymous text, Existential Foundations of Medicine and Psychology (1979). < Roger Frie, "Introduction," in Understanding Experience: Psychotherapy and Postmodernism, ed. Roger Fire [book on-line] (New York: Routledge, 2003, accessed 31 March 2007), 10; available from Questia, http://www.questia.com/PM.qst?a=o&d=108487331; Internet.>

nature say? Thou shall love. So what He commands, my nature commands. And so when I love, I fulfill myself. If I don't love, I wither. Then I am made for that commandment as the eye is made for light. And when I fulfill His will, I fulfill my deepest will. I believe that when God made us in His image, He made us in the image of love—agape—and that you and I are made in the inner structure of our being to love God and to love man and when we do, we fulfill ourselves. Ah, but you say, "the baby is not born that way. He is born squalling and crying and grasping." Is he? What happens when the baby is squalling and crying and grasping for itself? It is automatically unhappy. Who decided that? The baby's own nature. When it gives back love, it is happy. When it responds to love, it is happy. Then here is a primary nature which God gave us, and here is what Montesquieu[18] calls a second nature which we build up, which is the nature of sin. This is a second nature, not a primary. The primary nature that God stamped into you and me is to love and be love—to love Him and be loved—that is primary. This secondary nature we have turned into love for self, love for the herd. We have prostituted that love, built up a second nature, what Paul calls the flesh, and original sin. It is a second nature, not primary. Can that second nature be cleansed away? Of course! We produced it, and God can wipe it out. But He will not wipe out the primary nature. The primary nature is there to love Him. Fundamentally, we are designed to love Him, and when we do, we realize our true nature; we become ourselves. "His yoke is easy and his burden is light."[19] For His burden is the same burden that wings are to a bird, that sails

---

18 Charles-Louis de Secondat, Baron de La Brède et de Montesquieu (1689 – 1755), more commonly known as Montesquieu, was a French social commentator and political thinker who lived during the Enlightenment. He is famous for his articulation of the theory of separation of powers, taken for granted in modern discussions of government and implemented in many constitutions throughout the world. The quote philosophy is from his book The Persian Letters. . < http://plato.stanford.edu/entries/montesquieu/>

19 Matthew 11:30.

are to a ship, that love is to the heart, and when I find Him, I find myself. I am never so much my own as when I am most His. I am never so free as when I am bound to Him absolutely. Why? His will is my freedom. It is not hard to be a Christian, it is hard not to be a Christian for we are living against our nature and against the reality of God. When we try to live against this second nature, which we built up, this nature of evil and sin, it is not us; we produced it, and what we produced and made, now God can unmake it. We can return to the original purposes and that is the purpose of redemption—to love Him. We are made for love. I wish I had time to go on.

The text says "he reflects the glory of God."[20] Two little girls, ages 8 and 9, daughters of a theological professor, were talking as they washed the dishes. One said, "This is what I want to know—did Jesus speak as though God were in Him, or did He speak as God?" Pretty deep for eight and nine. The answer is both. He was the God/Man. He reflects the glory of God and bears the very stamp of His nature. He not only reflects God but he is inherently divine. When you see the nature of Jesus, you see the nature of God. Analyze the character of Jesus and you can tell what is in God. Then He goes on and says, "Upholding the universe by the word of his power." He now sustains the universe, for the moment the universe departs from His ways, it falls to pieces. Any life that steps out of Christ, goes to pieces. Then He goes on to say, "When he made purification of sins the center of the revelation of that divinity..."—the cross—He came to save us from sin—this thing that estranges us from God.

He did not come primarily to heal us. Now, I believe in healing but when you make healing the center of the Christian faith, you are off center. The primary business of the Christian faith is to reconcile us with God. Therefore it reconciles us with ourselves and with our bodies and therefore with others. And when I am reconciled with God then I am reconciled with

---

20 2 Corinthians 3:18.

myself, and when I am reconciled with myself, I am reconciled with my body. My body and my spirit are not at cross purposes and therefore health comes into me automatically. He quickens our mortal bodies by the spirit that dwells within us.

Now Jesus did not want to be known primarily as a healer. He said, "keep quiet." I am here to reconcile you with God – redemption. A part of that redemption is the healing of the body, but if I make the healing of the body of the center, then I am the center and God serves me and He keeps me well, therefore He is my servant. He is my cosmic errand boy to keep me well.

Or, if the primary purpose is to make me successful, then I use God. God helps me to be successful; I am the center. But if redemption from estrangement is the center, then God is the center and I am reconciled with God and that makes God the center. If as a by product of that (reconciliation with God) healing comes then it (healing) is wonderful. But, when it is at the center, it is off center and eccentric. I believe that God heals, but the primary purpose is the healing of our relationship with God. If He doesn't save us from sin, He doesn't save us from anything.

I believe that Jesus is God's answer to the world's need to be redeemed from sin. Sins that we have committed and sins that we inherited – the whole business. He has come to cleanse us. It says that when He made purification for sin, He sat down at the right hand of the majesty on high. He went to the final place of authority in the universe. Now this is a wonderful statement that this man who walked our dusty roads is at the final place of authority and will have the last word in human affairs. This Jesus will have the last word. That is the most breath taking conclusion that men ever came to, and note the Hebrews came to that conclusion.

The earliest Christian Creed (and the shortest and the most profound) is Jesus is Lord! It was used as an early confession, the earliest Christian creed. They reduced all of religion to three words: Jesus is Lord. They say that all great discoveries are a reduction from complexity to simplicity. On the wall of the Director's office in an Akron, Ohio rubber works factory is this motto, "The answer when found will be simple." Of all the reductions from complexity to simplicity "Jesus is Lord" is the greatest. Jesus is Lord—not will be, but is! And He will have the final word in human society now. That is breathtaking and that came out of Hebrews—"Jesus is Lord!"

How did they come to that conclusion? Not lightly. They saw that His touch upon life was the touch of God. Jesus was doing things that only God could do, and they came to the startling conclusion that this man who walked our dusty roads was at the right hand of the final authority and had the last word in human affairs. That is wonderful! Why did they come to that conclusion? They found that He was Lord of the past, the present and the future.

They found that He was Lord of the past and that past held guilt. They found that when He touched them, guilt was gone, and only God could lift guilt because it is against God we have sinned. Jesus could lift that guilt out of the past and make us free. We can't just offer our guilt to God. Don't offer your blood to God, rather accept the gift of the blood of the Son of God. He died for you. Take the gift! We need to empty our hands and take the gift. Jesus is Lord of the Past! That is good news.

Jesus is also Lord of the present. Carl Jung says there is a difference between my psychiatry and that of Freud. "Freud says that the basis of neurosis is in childhood. I say that it is in the present."[21] Jung asks, "What is this thing that the person is unwilling to face? Why is he dodging out of responsibility into illusion and illness? What responsibility is this person refusing to accept?" Jung said this is the basis of neurosis. If Jung is right, does Jesus function here? Does He give us power to walk into the present and face everything that comes—good, bad and indifferent? Yes, for Jesus walked up to His cross and took

21 Carl Jung (1875-1961).

the cross—the worst thing that could happen to Him—and turned it into the best thing that could happen to the world, namely its redemption. When you can take the worst thing that can happen to you and turn it into the best thing that can happen to you, then you know how to live—if not on account of, then in spite of. Jesus can make you go into life with all of the escapism gone. Jesus helps you walk straight into life and assume responsibility and use everything that life offers. He helps you turn your Cavalry into Easter morning, your impediments into instruments. Jesus gives you power over the present. Jesus is Lord of the present and gives us the power to face anything.

Jesus is also Lord of the future. Many people are afraid of the future because it holds death. Did Jesus do anything about this matter of death? Yes, He went down to it and came out the other side. He said, "I am the resurrection and the life. He that believeth in me shall never die."[22] If I am in Him, I am deathless. He is Lord of that death, and therefore that fear is gone. The happiest woman that I ever saw in my life was in Wilmore, Kentucky. A dying woman, she lay there clapping her hands as death approached. She said, "They tell me that this is death, but it is life. Oh, Death throw open thy gates." People came to look upon her angelic face as death approached and were converted by her bedside. I knelt alongside her bed and tried to pray for her, but I could not. There was nothing to pray for. She had everything, including death. I knelt there dumb. There was not a thing to pray for. She had everything. While I could not pray for her, she prayed for me. She put her hands on my head and prayed that I might preach this gospel message of joy in spite of death and everything else. I was ordained by a Bishop, and I am grateful, but the mightiest ordination I ever received was from this dying woman. When I preach, I feel her hands upon my head as she says, "Stanley preach it. In the face of death, preach it." I was ordained to it by a dying woman. If we belong to Christ, we don't belong to death, death belongs to us. It is our servant and it will swing open the gates.

Many people are not afraid of death but of this thing called time. The time rolls on and leaves its marks and we get frightened, the graying hair and the wrinkles. Then some look in the looking glass and seeing and get frightened and go off and try to turn back the clock. It is a losing battle, my sister or my brother. You will never be 25 again so accept the age you are. They say that the tree of life bears twelve manner of fruits, each month having its own fruit. If that is true can each month or period of life have its own beauty and joy? Yes, if we know how to use it. I loved being 23; I loved being 33; I loved being 43; I loved being 53; I loved being 63, and now I love being 73 most of all. I would not be 23 for anything. This is too much fun! It is fun to be 73 and a Christian and getting more fun all the time.

All I have to do each day is to walk straight out on this Way. I say to myself, "Stanley Jones if you want to live, this is the way. If you don't want to live, live some other way and you will get hurt." He is Lord of the Future. He is Lord of decay and, in Him, I am deathless.

Three years ago the Lord said to me, "I am going to give you the best ten years of your life – the next ten ahead." When I get to the end of this first ten years, I am going to ask for an extension of ten more. I am giving advanced notice. When I get to the end of that second ten years, I am not so certain (if I will ask for another extension); we will have to see how things are going. It is fun to be His! And it is getting more fun all the time.

The idea of anybody retiring is odd, I went across the line three years ago for retirement and I didn't feel a bump. I have not done a thing differently as far as I know. It is wonderful to feel like this, to have a Savior like this and a Gospel. Jesus is Lord. If that is true, it is tremendously true.

Now you and I can go out and preach new birth. We can preach the Holy Spirit. We can preach all of these basic doctrines, but (they must be) tied up closely to Jesus. He puts the life blood into all of these. We are not preaching barren doctrines; we are preaching something that is vascular. Cut it anywhere and it will bleed with the blood of the Son of God. With those convictions, can we help but go out and preach the new birth and help people get into this new birth?

Shall we pray?

PRAYER:

Dear Jesus, We are at thy feet. We began here and we will close here. Thou art the Alpha and the Omega. You have the keys of life and death. I don't know what the future holds, but I know who holds the future. Glory be! Bless us as we go from here for Jesus sake and put thy nail pierced hand of ordination upon us all again on all of us we go. We cannot but speak the things that we have seen and heard. In Jesus' name - Amen

12. JESUS IS LORD

COMMENTARY ON "THE WORD BECAME FLESH"

The text for Jones' sermon, "The Word Became Flesh," is Hebrews 1:1-3. Jones will share the profound message of God speaking to humanity in a Son — the Word become Flesh!

> When in former times God spoke to our fore fathers, he spoke in fragmentary and varied fashion through the prophets, but in this final age he has spoken to us in a Son whom he has made heir to the whole universe and through whom he created all orders of existence. The Son who is the effulgence of God's splendor and the stamp of God's very being and sustains the universe by his word of power. And when he brought about the purgation of sins he took his seat at the right hand of the majesty on high.

In this talk, Jones communicates his understanding of the progressive revelation of God. God revealed himself first through his creation, then through the Bible, and finally through the perfect revelation of his son, Jesus. Jesus, according to Jones, is the human life of God and the very being of God. Jesus is God revealed as a person. God in a person was the only way for humanity to understand God's message. A word does not convey the complete message, nor do teachers or prophets. The full message of God can according to Jones only be conveyed in the Person of Jesus. Jones says, *"It seems to me this: a life must come among us, a divine life. We think that's what happened. A life came among us and lived publicly for three years."* This life — this Jesus — tells us that God is deeply interested in us. He created us, and he is interested in our re-creation — our conversion. Jesus is the human life of God, God understandable, and God approachable. Jesus is the Way to God.

This sermon has an excellent summary of what Jones experienced as he took his views about the "uniqueness" of Christianity into Asian culture and confronted the Asian religions. His first book, *Christ of the Indian Road*, tells in detail how Jones worked to separate the message of Christianity from India's experience of Western colonialism, which was often negatively associated with Christianity. Jones speaks of his efforts to make Christianity distinct from Hinduism, only initially to find that each apparently "unique" Christian distinction was paralleled in Hinduism. For example, when the New Testament talks about going the second mile and turning the other cheek, Jones was told that the sacred Hindu texts said virtually the same thing: *"The sandalwood tree which when smitten by the axe pours its perfume upon the axe that smites it"* (380). In an effort to further distinguish Christianity, Jones then told his Indian friends about God giving himself in redemption for the world. His Hindu friends countered that the Rig Veda says that the Lord of Creatures gave himself for them. He was their sacrifice (380). Jones was initially "dumbfounded":

> Where is my (Christianity's) uniqueness? And then one day it dawned on me and I saw the difference and it was this. In all that they said, it was the word became word — a philosophy or a moralism. "Be like the sandalwood tree which when smitten by the axe pours its perfume upon the axe that smites it." That is an exhortation not an exhibition. But when Jesus hung on the cross and prayed, "Father forgive them for they know not what they do." That was not an exhortation that was an exhibition. That was the Word become flesh (380).

Jones realized that the Hindu texts were describing the word become word. In Christ, God gave us a Person, not a word. He concluded that Christianity was unique for it was God's search for man and God came to us in a Person. There is no possible way that God could reveal himself except through a person, the Word become Flesh (381). Therein lies Christianity's distinctiveness:

> Suppose this Gospel of ours really is God's invasion of us? Does that make it different? Yes. Once the divine Word became Flesh — that makes all the difference in the world (381).

Jones reflects on the significance of Christ being both like us (flesh) and unlike us, (Divine):

> Christ had to be like us to show us how to live; he had to be unlike us, i.e., God to redeem us. And so God had to be like us to be our example, and he had to be unlike us to be our redeemer. If he'd only been like us, he'd only have been our example; if he were only unlike us, he would only be our redeemer. But I need somebody to show me the way and then somebody to dispose me to walk on that way after I see the way. I need a redeemer (384).

Jones returns frequently to the passage from Hebrews that serves as the theme of this sermon, and he emphasizes this astonishing statement: *"that God created all orders of existence through Christ."* Jones believes that these words mean that the *"touch of Christ is on* all *creation."* Humankind is made by Christ for Christ. Jones states that, when we find Christ, i.e., when we surrender ourselves to Him, we find ourselves and the Way to live — the Way we were "meant" to live. Jones categorically states that the Christian Way is the Way for everything and everybody, everywhere and in every circumstance. In fact, according to Jones there are just two paths to live one's life, the **Way** and not the way. Jones turns to the verse in Romans 8:29, "For those whom he foreknew he also predestined to be conformed to the image of his Son..." He states that we are predestined to be Christian and to be in the image of Jesus. So not only did God create everything through Jesus, but we are

367

predestined to be in the image of Jesus. Jones would bet his life on that reality — the reality of the Way!

As with many of his sermons, Jones punctuates this one with frequent illustrations. For example, as he explains that even in our physical make up, we are created to live in a Christian way, in the Way of Jesus; Jones quotes a great surgeon who said:

"I discovered the Kingdom of God at the end of my scalpel — my operating knife — it's in the tissues."

I said, "Go on."

He said, "the right thing morally — the Christian thing is always the healthy thing physically."

"Oh," I said, "Doctor, say that again.... you said something."

Then he said, "the right thing morally — the Christian thing is always the healthy thing physically."

I then said, "morality is not merely written in the Bible, it's written in our blood, our nerves, and our tissues." He said, "Yes." (386)

Jones continues and elaborates his illustration that the Christian Way is the Way for all of life.

> This time a leading economist came up and said, "I'd like to put it this way...the right thing morally - the Christian thing is always the healthy thing economically." Then I said, "There is a way to get along with material goods and that is God's way." He said, "Yes." Then a leading sociologist came up to me and said, "I'd like to put it this way...the right thing morally the Christian thing is always the healthy thing sociologically." I said, "Then there is a way to get along with people and that's Gods way and God's way is Christ's way." You don't have to love your neighbor — you can just love yourself. But if you don't love your neighbors and only love yourself - you can't get along with your neighbor and you can't get along with

yourself. God's got us hooked. You can't revolt against Christ without revolting against yourself. So he's got us hooked. (386)

Jones insists that Jesus is the author of the whole of creation and that fact means that everything in creation is designed to work together harmoniously. Revelation and science each come out at the feet of Jesus and if we want to know God, we look in the face of Jesus. Jones testifies that when we expose ourselves to Jesus and his converting power, a miracle takes place: *"If I am in Jesus (converted) life holds together and has meaning, purpose, goal, rhythm, and harmony."* The reason — and necessity — for conversion is in order to be reconciled with God, reconciled with ourselves, reconciled with our neighbor, and ultimately reconciled with life. We are ready to meet life when we surrender to Jesus. Jones affirms that "Anything can happen to us when we let Jesus in our lives," and he illustrates this assertion with another story:

> A pastor went past a church. He was broken and beaten, discouraged and about to give up the pastorate when he saw a sign on the church — *Jesus Christ is in this place. Anything can happen here.* He said, "I wonder, I wonder." So he went in and knelt down at the place of prayer. Something did happen when he exposed himself to Jesus; he knelt there and said, "Here I am. I am discouraged and defeated. I'm done for." Jesus spoke the healing word. The pastor rose up and came out of that church a new man. Now he is the center of contagion in his own church. He is on fire and on top of the world (393).

Jones closes his sermon with an invitation for self surrender. He tells his listeners,

> Jesus Christ is in this place…and anything can happen here if we are open to the miracle of change, the miracle of conversion … Expose yourself to Jesus Christ, and the moment you do, miracles will take place (393).

THE WORD BECAME FLESH
"JESUS IS LORD"

SERMON

I am going to re-read a passage, which was read to you this morning. It is so packed that it needs to be re-read again and again. I'm reading from the New English Bible, Hebrews 1:1-3, "When in former times God spoke to our fore fathers, he spoke in fragmentary and varied fashion through the prophets, but in this final age he has spoken to us *in* a Son whom he has made heir to the whole universe and through whom he created all orders of existence. The Son who is the effulgence of God's splendor and the stamp of God's very being and he sustains the universe by his word of power. And when he brought about the purgation of sins he took his seat at the right hand of the majesty on high."[1]

I find myself responding in a peculiar way this morning following the Open Heart.[2] I wish to give you a message that will speak to the various conditions which you revealed this morning. No one could sit here for two hours and hear people opening their hearts and revealing the depths of their

---

1   Heb 1:1-3 (NRSV), "Long ago God spoke to our ancestors in many and various ways by the prophets, but in these last days he has spoken to us by a Son, whom he appointed heir of all things, through whom he also created the world. He is the reflection of God's glory and the exact imprint of God's very being, and he sustains all things by his powerful word. When he had made purification for sins, he sat down at the right hand of the Majesty on high."

2   Each Ashram opens with the experience of the Morning of the Open Heart where the participants respond to a series of questions: "Why have you come? What do you want? What do you really need?" (Jones, *A Song of Ascents*, 224).

experiences and then rise up lightly and say, "Well I hope that God will do something for them." I do not wish to give you a slogan but a Savior, nor a formula instead of a Fact with a capital F! What have we to present to these needs that have been revealed here this morning? Certainly nothing earth-born because our needs are in fact earth-born. Earth born needs cannot be met by earth-born remedies. We have got to hear the answer from heaven for the God that created us must be in some way interested in our re-creation. So you breathe a prayer this morning that I'll not skirt the problems involved, but try to meet them head on. However, I know that my message will be inadequate (to meet your needs) however good. It is only as I interpret something that God did, (that your needs can be met.) Remember that Joseph said to Pharaoh... "it is God's answer which will answer to the Pharaoh." Today it is God's answer which will be the answer to the needs revealed this morning and it will be a total answer!

We've been saying that Christ is the answer but Mary Webster[3] with her amazing insight said, "Christ is not the answer. He is the Way to the answers...to all of them." A schoolteacher who would give the answers to her children would never (help them) develop if she would just say "All right, this is the answer to your problem." Instead, a teacher gives *the way* to find all the answers and shows her students a way to find the answers for themselves.

Jesus is not the answer in the sense that he is a fixed formula. He's the Way. Take his Way and you will find all the answers, but that means self-commitment to His Way, and if you'll take his Way you're on the Way to find all the answers in heaven and on earth. But it is the Way.

---

3   Mary Webster met E. Stanley Jones in 1950 at an Evangelistic meeting and was later trained as a Lay Evangelist and often accompanied Brother Stanley and others serving as a part time secretary and lay evangelist in his meetings. She was a powerful witness for Christ and a delightful and engaging speaker.

Now a great many of you who are facing life are wondering about this question … about what role Jesus plays in the process of finding the Way. At our last Ashram some young people said to our director, "What about this Jesus business — why can't we go straight to God?" Many don't ask the question in such rough language but they do ask it. "Why can't we go straight to God?"

Well you can't go straight to God, because if you went straight to God you would go through your ideas of God which are not God. The mediator would be your ideas, which are earth-born. God has got to reveal himself. But some of you would say, "Wait a minute, don't go too fast. Tell us whether there is a God." Forgive me if I take a moment or two to gather up some of the minds that are halting at this place.

The modern person wants a faith in God, for life without the great companion God is empty, meaningless and goal less for when God goes – goal goes. When goal goes — meaning goes — when meaning goes — value goes – and then life turns dead on your hands. "If there is no God" said Rousseau, the great skeptic, "we would have to invent one to keep people sane, for life would be a mad house." "Life would be a tale of an idiot full of sound and fury signifying nothing."[4] If there is no God how did this universe come into this being? Did atoms floating in space happen by chance upon universal law and order – a law and order, which stretches from the lowest cell to the farthest star and everything between. Did that happen by chance? If so you would have to spell chance with a capital C and call it God. How long do you think it would take for you to stand in a printing office and throw up a font of type and have it come down by chance into a poem — say of Browning? I asked a printer that once and he said, "the type would wear out first," and so would you.

---

4   The Tragedy of Macbeth, V, v, 26-31. < William Shakespeare, The Tragedy of Macbeth, ed. Brooke, Nicholas [book on-line] (Oxford: Oxford University Press, 1998, accessed 30 March 2007), iii; available from Questia, http://www.questia.com/PM.qst?a=o&d=72302821; Internet.>

Sir James Jeans,[5] a great scientist said, "It would take a hundred thousand monkeys seated at a hundred thousand typewriters pecking away at random over the keys for a hundred million years before they happen by chance to create the plays of Shakespeare. Then after they arranged the letters they wouldn't know what they meant." Somebody figured out how many chances to one that the world happened by chance. And the figures go around the world 35 times. "That many chances to one that the world happened by chance — a preposterous figure," said Dr. Madigan.[6] No we can't believe that – that strains our credulity too much.

When I pick up a newspaper, I see that there is intelligence in it and I know in back of that intelligence is an intelligent mind – expressing itself through that intelligence. I look up at the universe and I think to myself — it's an intelligent universe – it can be studied intelligently — it responds to intelligence — apparently intelligence has gone into it for intelligence comes out of it. Then in back of that intelligence must be an intelligent mind, and since the intelligence seems to be universal, the mind behind it must be a universal mind—we call that universal mind – God.

If there is no God then where did you and I come from? You and I who have intelligence—did we come out of a non-intelligent universe? Did the non-intelligent produce the intelligent? If so that is a materialistic miracle. You and I have

---

5   Sir James Hopwood Jeans (1877 – 1946), an English physicist and mathematician, was the first to propose that matter is continuously created throughout the universe. He made other innovations in astronomical theory but is best known as a writer of popular books about astronomy. < The Columbia Encyclopedia 6th ed., s.v."Jeans, Sir James Hopwood" [database on-line]; available from Questia, http://www.questia.com/ PM.qst?a=o&d=101251626; Internet; accessed 30 March 2007.>

6   Colonel Patrick S. Madigan (1877 – 1944), known as "The Father of Army Neuropsychiatry," was assistant to the Surgeon General of the United States Army from 1940 to 1943. < http://www.mamc. amedd.army.mil/pao/COL%20Madigan.htm>

purpose – we can decide between ends. Did we who can decide between ends and who have purpose come, did we come out of a purposeless universe? Did the non-purposeful produce the purposeful? If so, that too is a materialistic miracle. It is simpler to believe that the purposeful came out of the antecedent purposeful...the intelligent out of the antecedent intelligent. For life produces like. We call that antecedent intelligent purpose – God.

But some say, "Couldn't evolution account for the whole thing? Resident forces within nature — couldn't they have produced the universe without the necessity of the hypothesis of God?" But when you say that – you have to quickly park your intelligence because the moment you begin to think it, it falls to pieces. How can resident forces within nature move toward intelligent ends without themselves being intelligent? You see you've smuggled intelligence or God into the process and then say God isn't necessary. But God would be as necessary for evolution as for direct creation. God could create all at once, but suppose he created something, which could create something which could create something? Which takes more intelligence, foresight and skill? To drive a billiard ball at one blow into the pocket or to strike a ball which strikes another and then another and then another and then another until the last one goes into the pocket. Obviously the latter would take more intelligence, foresight and skill. God could create everything all at once, but suppose He chose to create something which could create something which could create something and on and on it moves toward a universe of moral freedom where you and I are no longer pushed from behind by blind and instinctive forces, but beckoned to from before. Wouldn't that process take more intelligence, foresight and skill to produce a world of moral freedom with free beings who can choose? I repeat if there isn't a God — there ought to be one.

But most of you say. "Yes, but what is He like?" There is where the Christian faith steps in and says, "We think we know." What is God like? I look up through nature to God and

I come to the conclusion that God is law, dependable law. I am grateful that God is law...that he doesn't work by whim, notion and fancy but by law and order. The universe is an orderly universe because God's mind is an orderly mind. I am grateful that God is law, but not satisfied. For I am not a subject asking for a law. I am a son asking for a father. I want to know whether God is love. To my view, nature can't quite frame the words God is love, its' (nature's) voice is equivocal.

I'm grateful that God can and does reveal himself through the prophets and teachers. I am grateful but again not satisfied. Because the medium through which this message has come is an imperfect medium and the message coming through that imperfect medium partakes of that imperfection.

I am grateful that God can and does reveal himself through a book. Grateful but again not satisfied. For God couldn't reveal himself perfectly through a book. First of all a book is impersonal and God is the infinitely personal. When I state *"infinitely personal"* I don't mean that he is an enlarged man seated in the heavens.

In personality there are four things: *intelligence, feeling, will and self-consciousness*. So when we say that God is personal we think that He thinks, that He feels, that He wills and that He has self-consciousness. He couldn't be less than that. For personality is the highest category of being that we know of in the universe. But how could the infinitely personal God reveal himself perfectly through an impersonal medium like a book? We know that literature takes it's meaning from the life that surrounds the literature. Literature can never rise higher than life. I used the word *home* here this morning. To some of you it is heaven. But to some of you it's hell. One word — two diametrically opposite meanings because the life that is surrounding the word in one context puts a high and lofty content into it. The life that is surrounding the word in the other context, puts a low content into it. Literature (and the meaning of words) can never rise higher than life.

Suppose God then should give us a book from heaven with all his will written in it. Would that be a perfect revelation of God? Hardly. You and I would see those words and we would read into them our highest experience of those words. I'd see the word *love* and I would read into it my highest experience of love, but my highest experience of love is not love, it's my highest experience of love. I'd see the word *purity* and I'd read into it my highest experience of purity, but my highest experience of purity is not purity.

I'd see the word *God* and I'd read into it my highest experience of God, but my highest experience of God is not God. I'd pull those words to the level of my life — my highest experience. So would you. The book then would not be so much the revelation of God, but a revelation of us.

What then do we need for a perfect revelation? It seems to me this: a life must come among us, a divine life. A life which will take these words, which we drag to the level of our lives and put a new content to them ... a divine content through the divine illustration, so that we would no longer see those words in the light of what we are, but in the light of that divine illustration. We think that's happened.

A life came among us and lived publicly for three years. I no longer see the word *love* in the light of my poor partial love, but in the light of a love that prayed for enemies while in torturous grasp upon a cross. "Father forgive them." Oh I said, say to myself, is that love? I no longer see the word *purity* in the light of my poor stained purity, but in the light of a purity that shared my temptations minus my faults. I no longer see the word *God* in the light of my imagination of God, but in the light of the uncovering of the nature of God in understandable terms — in human terms. One day one of His disciples said, "Lord show us the Father, then that is sufficient." Jesus quietly said, "He who has seen me has seen the Father." And my heart skips a beat and I say to myself, "Is God like that? In character is He a Christ-like God? If so, He is a good God and trustable. I could ask nothing higher. I could be content with nothing less."

Jesus is the human life of God. Jesus is God understandable. Jesus is God approachable. Jesus is God lovable. When I say God, I think Jesus and I cannot think of God in terms higher than to think of Him in terms of Jesus. And if God isn't like Christ, I'm not interested in Him. If He is, He can have my heart without qualification or reservation. If the heart that is back of the universe is like this gentle heart that broke upon the cross for our redemption, He can have my heart without qualification or reservation.

We believe that we see in Jesus Christ the very being of God. The account says in this passage, "When in former times God spoke to our forefathers he spoke in fragmentary and in varied fashion through the prophets..." Through the prophets revelation (of God) was progressive coming up and up and up and up and up until it burst forth in final and full and complete revelation in the Person of his Son. Fragmentary and varied, but now God has spoken to us not by a Son, which is the phrase used in the Revised Standard Version of the Bible, but *in* a Son. *The New English Bible* has the word *in* (a Son — a person) for we have to see God before we can understand him. We couldn't have believed it through words. All religions are man's search for God, therefore there are many religions. The gospel is God's search for man; therefore there's but one Gospel. God, after all of these ideas of Him go as far as they could go, has in these last days spoken to us in a son.

Now it's interesting that all the great philosophies of the world were completed just *before* the time of the coming of Jesus. The great philosophical nations — Greece, India, and China—created great philosophies which were the high water mark of man's search for God. They (*these philosophies*) piled word upon word upon word upon word and syllogism upon syllogism to reach God. I listened to Dr. Hocking,[7] the great

---

7   William Ernest Hocking (1873 - 1966) was an American Idealist philosopher at Harvard University. He considered Christianity a great agent in the making of world civilization. E. Stanley Jones met Dr. Hocking at the International Missionary Council meeting held in Jerusalem in April

Harvard philosopher, speak at the Jerusalem Conference (April 1928), he said, "Man takes himself up as high up as he can go with his own efforts. But he hasn't the resources within himself to complete himself, and then something from without must complete him." I held my breath, "Oh," I said "he's going to say the word, but he didn't." He went on and said something else. At the close I came up to him and said, "Dr. Hocking, why didn't you say the word?" He said, "What word?" I said, "The Word became Flesh. You said that man hadn't resources within himself to complete himself and therefore something from without must complete him. Why didn't you say the Word became Flesh?"

"Oh," he said, "I am a philosopher and I can't say it. You are a religious man and you can say it."

"But," I said, "Dr. Hocking I'm not content for you to see it and not say it."

Philosophy can only pile words on words on words on words and say it must be there,[8] but it can't say it."[9]

1928. <The Columbia Encyclopedia 6th ed., s.v."Hocking, William Ernest" [database on-line]; available from Questia, http://www.questia.com/ PM.qst?a=o&d=101249394; Internet; accessed 30 March 2007.>

8 "Whether through implication or revealing silences, philosophy does say the word. It points to the need of conversion, of being born from above" (Jones, Conversion, 22).

9 In a sermon that Jones preached in the early 1960s he included this addendum to the Hocking story. "I told that story to his son who is also a philosopher at Emory University. He said, 'That is a very interesting story, you might be interested to know that someone asked my father what was the most beautiful and precious verse in the scriptures to him.' And you would have thought that the great philosopher would have said, "You shall know the truth and the truth shall make you free," that would be the word for the philosopher. 'You know what he said? The most precious verse in the scripture is, for me, 'Behold I stand at the door and knock and if any man will hear my voice, I will open the door I will come in and sup with him and he with me.' That personal approach from the unseen, that satisfied the heart of not a philosopher, but a person who was philosophical. Hocking could not be content with principles, he wanted the person."

Shankar, the great Hindu philosopher, piled words on words on words on words. He wrote fifteen volumes to explain *Maya*. Maya is illusion. Then somebody asked him to explain Maya in a sentence. He said, "Well, it's the son of a barren woman." It took him fifteen volumes to say that.

What is the difference between the Christian faith and all others? I found my back up against the wall after I got to India, (as I tried to answer that question). Everything that I brought up (to distinguish Christianity), they'd bring up some parallel. I would talk about going the second mile, turning the other cheek, loving your enemies and they would say, "Yes we have the same thing in our sacred books." Our sacred books say, "That you are to be like the sandalwood tree, which when smitten by the axe pours its' perfume upon the axe that smites it." "Oh," I said, "Yes, that's very beautiful." That is loving your enemies. That is going that second mile. That is turning the other cheek. And when I talked about God giving himself in redemption for us – they'd say yes the *Rig Veda* says the Prajapati,[10] the Lord of Creatures gave himself for them, he was their sacrifice. I said "What? Prajapati, the Lord of creatures gave himself for them he was their sacrifice? Isn't that God sacrificing himself for us?" And then they talked about Shiva redeemed us at a cost to himself. That he drank poison for our sins that we ambrosia of eternal life taste? Yes, Shiva[11] — is

---

10 The Rig Veda tells the story of Prajapati, the first god who created the world. Prajapati means "Lord of Creatures." Prajapati was sacrificed to himself by the younger gods Indra, Agni, and Varuna, and out of his body the whole universe was made. The Rig Veda says that each of Prajapati's other parts turned into a different group of people, so that Indian people thought of themselves as belonging to one of four castes, or groups. This idea of caste seems to be an Aryan idea. < http://www.themystica.com/mythical-folk/articles/prajapati.html>

11 Shiva was a Hindu fertility god, who is thought to make the crops grow. He was not mentioned in the Rig Veda. But around 300 BC, in the Mauryan period, people began worshipping Shiva. This might be another name for the Harappan god Rudra. Shiva (or Rudra) was less like a real man than Vishnu, and scarier. People thought Shiva spent most of his time

called the blue-throated Shiva because he has a blue patch on his throat. He drank poison that we might ambrosia taste and the patch on his throat is the poison lodged in his throat. Isn't that God drinking the poison of our sins?

I was dumbfounded. Where is my *(Christianity's)* uniqueness? And then one day it dawned on me and I saw the difference and it was this. In all that they said it was the word became word — a philosophy, a moralism. "Be like the sandalwood tree which when smitten by the axe pours its perfume upon the axe that smites it." That is an exhortation not an exhibition. But when Jesus hung on the cross and prayed, "Father forgive them for they know not what they do. " That was not an exhortation, that was an exhibition. That was the Word become flesh. And the Rig Veda passage about Prajapati, the Lord of creatures who gave himself for them. He was their sacrifice. That's a stray verse with no historical basis. There is nothing under it. It's the word of divine sacrifice become word, but in Jesus it wasn't the word of divine sacrifice become word. He came. He went to the cross, and He bore our sins in His own body on a tree. That's God giving himself for us. The Word of sacrifice become flesh. And the blue-throated Shiva – Shiva himself was a legend. And therefore his drinking the poison of our sins - "that we might the ambrosia of eternal life taste" — is nothing but legend. It is not in history, but Jesus did drink the poison of our sins. He bore our sins in his own body on a tree – and became sin for us. I said, "I see the difference." All of these were the word become word — man search for God and then I saw that this other was the Word became Flesh. It was God's search for man. It dawned on me the uniqueness–the uniqueness is just there!

---

meditating (sitting and thinking) on top of Mount Kailas in the Himalayas, and it was this meditation that made the spiritual energy that ran the universe. Sometimes people made statues of Shiva, like this one here, but more often they showed him in the form of a lingam, a short stone pillar. <http://www.historyforkids.org/learn/india/religion/shiva.htm>

Now what do we do in our seminaries? We take the idea that Christianity is the word become word — a set of ideas - a theology. And so we study comparative religions. We find that this religion has this idea, this religion has this, this, this, this idea and compare the ideas and come out to the idea that the Christian faith is a little better, a little clearer, a little bit more comprehensive, a little bit more moral, and a bit more consistent. It's a *little bit more!* And you come out at the end of your theological course with a little bit of a Gospel, but with nothing to preach except a very little bit... As a result, we are left with no head-on (*direct*) answer to man's total need. There is no message. But suppose this Gospel of ours is God's invasion of us? Suppose all of these other ideas are man's search for God. Suppose this is God's search for man. Does that make it different? Yes. The difference is this - all other religions are the word become word, a philosophy or a moralism. Once the divine Word became Flesh — that makes all the difference in the world. The only possible way that God could reveal Himself is through a person. The Bible is not the revelation of God, that would be the word became printer's ink, but the Bible is the inspired record of the revelation. The revelation was seen in the face of Jesus Christ — the Word become Flesh!

Last year while I was here I showed you this picture. As you see it is a figure of Jesus done by a Korean artist, beautifully done, but the uniqueness of it is this...that the whole of the New Testament is written from this corner down to that corner beginning with the Gospel of Matthew and ending up with the book of Revelation. It is all written in minute letters by hand in English. There are 185,000 words from this corner down to that corner — about a thousand words on a line.

Note that he hasn't imposed the figure of Jesus on the words but he has inked the words light or dark to bring out the form and figure of Jesus. So that out of the words arises the Word. These words take us by the hand and take us beyond the words to the Word - the Word made Flesh. Out of the Gospels arises the Gospel. Jesus was the Gospel. He didn't come to bring the

Gospel. He was the Gospel. The Gospel lies in His person. He himself is the Good News.

There are twenty-seven little figures (angels) around the edges of the picture. The little angels represent the twenty-seven books of the New Testament all looking at Jesus. The whole of the Christian Gospel then is converging in this Person.

"In these last days he has spoken to us not by a son—that would be the word became word—but **in** a Son, that was the Word became Flesh." This picture represents this unique distinction. The artist who painted this picture was a refugee from Northern Korea and a Presbyterian layman from Seoul. The picture took him two years to create. The words are so minute that most people cannot read them with the naked eye – it dates your birth. At the close you can come up to see if you can read the words or not, but the significant thing about this picture is that the artist saw that the Gospel lies **in** the Person of Jesus. "Having these last days spoken to us **in** a son," not by…that would be the word become exhortation. But if we are spoken to as **in** a Son, that is the word become exhibition. We couldn't see God unless we could see God and see him coming as He is.

A friend of mine was an authority on ants…he said that the ant colony has scout ants out searching for food. And when they would find the food they would come back and tell the ant colony that they had found the food. And then the ant colony would follow the scout ants around the circuitous way they took to find the food in the first place. They would go all the way this way and all the way back that way. They wouldn't take a shortcut even when my friend put food almost right in front of them. The ants would not deviate from their path. They would not take the short cut and go directly to the food. They'd go all the way around and all the way back. My friend said, "I wish I were an ant — so I could show them how to do it." "However," he said, "if I became an ant I'd probably have an ants' mentality and would do exactly what they are doing. The only way for me to help them would be to become an ant but retain a man's mentality. I could be like them and I would have to be unlike them if I were going to help them."

I suppose God's problem was that if he would become a man and only a man then God would have a man's mentality – he'd probably do what we'd done. He had to be like us to show us how to live; he (God) had to be unlike us to redeem us. And so God had to be like us to be our example and he had to be unlike us to be our redeemer. If he'd only been like us he'd only have been our example, if he were only unlike us he would only be our redeemer. But I need somebody to show me the way, then somebody to dispose me to walk on that way after I see the way. I need a redeemer.

Incidentally, the likeness and the unlikeness (to humanity) in the life of Jesus is seen in the likeness and the unlikeness in his birth. In his birth he was like us...born of a woman, but unlike us ... born of God. I see the likeness in that he was born of a woman and I see the unlikeness in that he was born of God. But that is not unique, for I see the same things in his life. He is like me in that he faces God as a man calling on no power that is not at your disposal or mine. He is so like me that I can almost put my hand upon his shoulder and say brother man, but when I'm about to do it — I can't. He steps on the side of God with an offer that no man dare to offer another. "Come unto me, I am the way, the truth, the life." No man can offer that without blasphemy. He's like me therefore unlike me. All the way through the New Testament, we see likeness and unlikeness in a way that does not conflict with his birth, but coincides. It's all a part of a seamless road. This Jesus is God manifested in the flesh.

Now let's go back to our text for a moment, it says *"God who at various times and at diverse manners hath spoken to us in the prophets has in these last days spoken to us in a son, whom he has made heir to the whole universe and through whom he created all orders of existence."* That's an amazing statement. That God created all orders of existence through Jesus. The church has never taken these strange passages seriously.

Passages like this – "through whom he made the worlds..." Without Him — Christ—was not anything created? By whom and through Christ were all things created? Things visible — things invisible. In heaven and on earth. What do these strange passages mean? Did God create the world through Christ? But I thought He created it billions of years ago and Christ appeared just two thousand years ago. What does this mean? Does it mean that the touch of Christ is upon all creation? That everything is made to work in His way? Does it mean that when it works in His way it works well — harmoniously, adjustedly, and happily and if it works some other way, does it works to its own ruin? Are we made by Christ and for Christ? And when we find Him do we find ourselves?

There are a number of passages in the Acts of the Apostles which say that the Christian way is the Way with a capital W. "A commotion arose over the use of this word, **the Way.**"— the way with a capital W. We usually make this the way of salvation. It is the Way of salvation, but the text does not make that explicit link, it says it's the way — unqualified. Is the Christian Way the Way unqualified? Is it the way to-do everything: to think, to act, to feel, to be under every conceivable circumstance for God and man — individual and collective. Are there just two things in life: the Way and not the way? And is the Christian Way always the Way? And is the unchristian way always not the way and are there no exceptions? I believe that to be the case and I believe it with all my heart. I believe there are just two things in life — the Way and not the way. If you don't believe that you just try to spend the rest of your life trying to disprove it.

I am going to spend the rest of my life watching it (*this truth*) unfold. It's proving itself. There are just two things — the *Way* and not the way. I believe that I'm predestined to be a Christian by my makeup. I believe that this way is not just written in the Bible it is written in my blood, my nerves, my tissues and my being. Every cell of my being is made by Him and for Him. I'm predestined to be a Christian. It's says in

385

Romans 8:29, "For those whom he foreknew he also predestined to be conformed to the image of his Son." Am I predestined to be conformed to the image of his Son? And is that destiny written — not in mere scripture but in my blood, my nerves, my tissues? Strange, that I who have my roots in Methodism am standing in this pulpit here and preaching to you *predestination*. It is supposedly a Presbyterian doctrine. But I do preach it. I am predestined to be a Christian. I can live according to that destiny if I want to or I can live against it if I want to. But if I live against it I will get hurt — automatically.

An African chief got up and said in a meeting "I'm doomed to be a saint." I think he meant he was destined. Am I destined to be a Christian? Yes. Is that destiny in me? Yes. Is it therefore inescapable? Yes. Have I a Christian stomach? Yes. Christian nerves? Yes. A Christian brain? Yes. Am I made for Him? Yes.

A great surgeon said to me some time ago, "I discovered the Kingdom of God at the end of my scalpel — my operating knife — it's in the tissues."

I said, "Go on."

He said, "the right thing morally - the Christian thing is always the healthy thing physically."

"Oh," I said "Doctor, say that again…. you said something."

When he said, "the right thing morally — the Christian thing is always the healthy thing physically."

I then said, "morality is not merely written in the Bible, it's written in our blood, our nerves, and our tissues." He said, "yes."

Again I quoted it, this time a leading economist came up and said, "I'd like to put it this way… the right thing morally — the Christian thing is always the healthy thing economically." Then I said, "There is a way to get along with material goods and that is God's way." He said, "Yes." Then a leading sociologist came up to me and said, "I'd like to put it this way...the right thing morally the Christian thing is always the healthy thing sociologically." I said, "Then there is a way to get along with people and that's Gods way and God's way is Christ way." You don't have to love your neighbor – you can just love yourself. But if you don't love your neighbor and only love yourself — you can't get along with your neighbor and you can't get along with yourself. God's got us hooked. You can't revolt against Christ without revolting against yourself. So he's got us hooked.

John Hay, the great statesman, said, "after trying the various ways for nations to get along with one another, I've discovered the only way for nations to get along with one another is to love your neighbor as you love yourself." I say, "But that's Christian." Then clear from the international down to the sociological on into the economic back into the physical and then straight on into the moral and spiritual – all up and down the whole gamut of life — the right thing morally — the Christian thing, is always the healthy thing and the unchristian thing is always the unhealthy thing. You can take it or leave it but it's there.

I was talking to a man in India, a politician, who was challenged by the Oxford Group Movement.[12] But he wasn't prepared to base his life on the four absolutes of the Oxford Group movement — "absolute honesty, absolute purity, absolute unselfishness, and absolute love." He was living with another woman other than his wife and to ward off my appeal

---

12 The Oxford Group was a Christian organization founded by American Christian missionary Dr. Frank Buchman. The group promoted a belief in divine guidance: one should wait for God to give direction in every aspect of life and surrender to that advice. Buchman's program emphasized acknowledgment of offenses against others, making restitution to those sinned against, and promoting the group to the public. The Oxford Group changed its name prior to WWII to Moral Re-Armament and believed that divine guidance would prevent WWII from breaking out. Moral Re-Armament would later change it's name to Initiatives of Change. <http://www.britannica.com/eb/article-9057830/Oxford-movement>

that he cease this behavior, he told me about a British General who had also been challenged by the Oxford Group Movement but he too was not willing to build his life on the four absolutes, so this British General half seriously and half humorously said that he was going to organize another group movement — not the Oxford Group Movement, but the Cambridge Group Movement (the other major university center in England). The Cambridge Group movement was going to have the opposite absolutes, i.e., "absolute dishonesty, absolute impurity, absolute selfishness, and absolute hate." He told me that and waited for me to laugh. I looked him straight in the face and I said, "why not?" I said, "Why don't you organize a movement on absolute dishonesty, absolute impurity, absolute selfishness, and absolute hate — if you believe in evil why didn't you go ahead and make it absolute? Why are you so tentative about evil? Why don't you sin with the stops out?" He looked at me and said... "No I couldn't do that." I said, "why not?" He said, "you see it wouldn't work." "Ahhh" I said, "then you've given away the case. The only way you can keep evil going is to throw enough good around it to keep it alive." For the word **evil** is the word **live** spelled backwards. It's an attempt to live life against itself and it can't be done. Therefore evil is not only bad but it's stupid. It's trying to live life against itself and it can't be done.

Carlyle[13] says... "Sin is, has been, and ever shall be the parent of misery." And you can't make it the parent of happiness — everybody who tries it ends up saying I played the fool. Then what conclusion must I come too? This ... I challenge you to build a society on absolute dishonesty — nobody would trust another, on absolute impurity it would rot, on absolute selfishness — nobody would think in terms of another, on

---

13 Thomas Carlyle (1795 – 1881) was a Scottish essayist, satirist, and historian, whose work was hugely influential during the Victorian era. The quote is from his book The French Revolution: A History, Book 1, Section VII. < http://www.britannica.com/eb/article-9020374/Thomas-Carlyle>

absolute hate — nobody would love another — it would be so centrifugal it would spin off into pieces…then what conclusion should I come to? This …that every dishonest man is a parasite upon the honesty of some honest man whose honesty holds together that situation long enough for him to be dishonest in it.

Shall I repeat that sentence? Every dishonest man is a parasite upon the honesty of some honest man whose honesty holds together that situation long enough for him to be dishonest in it. Every impure man is a parasite upon the purity of some good man whose purity holds together that situation long enough for him to be impure in it. Every selfish man is a parasite upon the unselfishness of some unselfish man whose unselfishness holds together that situation long enough for him to be selfish in it. And finally, every man of hate is a parasite upon the love of some good man whose love holds together that situation long enough for him to be hateful in it.

There's a Way and there is not the way. And the account says… "Jesus is the author of the whole of creation." And therefore everything in its makeup is made to work in His way and when it works in His way it works rhythmically, harmoniously, happily and adjustably. If it works in some other way it works to its own ruin. That is the greatest drama of my life, and I keep alive now just to watch that drama, just to look at it, and watch it. Talk about a cinema - that is nothing — this is the movie of life. I watch it, I watch it, and I watch it. Living life according to the Way is the greatest, greatest news that ever came to our planet.

Now if you go back again to that passage where it says… "Whom he made heir to the whole universe." Are all things in the universe going to come out at Christ's feet? Yes. If you work from Revelation down and from the facts up — the method of Christianity and the method of science — do you come out at the feet of Jesus? Yes. When you work from Revelation down and you unfold the facts of science — and these facts are unfolding day by day — these facts lead you straight to the feet of Christ. If you want to live – you have got to live according to him. Some day the scientists are going to put down on the table these facts and say… this is the way, this is the way, this is the way, this is the way, and this is the way to live and not this way and not this way and not this way and not this way. And we look at it and say: "But brother man the way you say is the Way to live is the Christian way. And the way you say not to live is the unchristian way." "Well" they'd say, "we don't know anything about that, but this is the way life works."

Everything is going to come out at His feet. Jesus is going to be the heir of all things. All the other ways will break down. We'll go through trial and error and bump ourselves and hurt ourselves and then disillusionment will toss us to his breast. He is the heir of all things. And then the Son, it says, "who is the effulgence of God's splendor, and the stamp of God's very being." If you want to know what God is like look into the face of Jesus.

A Sunday school teacher was teaching some slum children and she said to the children, "what do you think of Jesus?" A little grimy hand went up and a little boy said, "Miss, Jesus is the best photograph that God ever had took." "Was it? Yes." He's the express image of God's person. If you want to know what God is like look full into the face of Jesus and you will know what God is like in character. And if that doesn't set your heart singing … I would say that's all right. The universe means well and it means to make me well. Jesus sustains the universe by his words of power. Everything that listens to his word stands together and everything that goes away from his word falls to pieces. You speak of a certain man – and say "that man is going to pieces." And he does — he just disintegrates — you just watch it.

People come to this Ashram and in the hour of the Open Heart reveal themselves and we see that they are full of conflicts. One man heard what was said in the Open Heart and he said, "Good gracious — have you got all the maladjusted people in the country together here?" I said ... "No. You just got a cross section of church life turned honest." We come here to the Ashram and we open our hearts. But I said, "Stay around until the end of the week and if you listen in to what they are saying in the Overflowing Heart[14] – you would look at me and say, "Good gracious have you got all the rhythmical, harmonious, adjusted and integrated people in the country all together?" And I said "No, it is the same people as a week ago but what they have done is that they have exposed themselves to Jesus Christ and surrendered in faith. And a miracle takes place – he's now holding life together. You will go back (home) with life together. You'll say, "This is the way to live. I was broken to pieces and now my pieces have come together like a jigsaw puzzle and it's all making sense, before life added up to nonsense." Now life adds up to sense.

He sustains us with the word of his power. I know what happens to me. If I'm in Jesus — life holds together; it has meaning, purpose, goal, rhythm and harmony. If I step out of him and into myself then life adds up to nonsense. I become cynical. I become bitter. I become out of sorts. If I am not in his word of power then I am in the land of weakness.

And then verse goes on and says, "... when he brought about the purgation of sins he took his seat at the right hand of the majesty on high." This whole thing was for what? For the forgiveness and purgation of our sins? God has one intention, to get out of our lives the thing that is alien, the thing that is creating this whole upset. We have used our freedom to turn away from God. The whole purpose of redemption is to get rid of sin and alienation. It is to make us clean within. To be reconciled with God, means that we will be reconciled with

---

14 The morning of the Overflowing Heart occurred at the end of each Ashram and was the time when the participants told how the internal and external barriers in their lives had been broken and how their relationships to God, to themselves, and to others were forever changed. (Graham 350)

ourselves, we will be reconciled with our neighbor and we will be reconciled with life. It is all going to converge on that. It is not a light remedy or slogan. We don't say, "Now you be a good boy and you be a good girl and don't do it again and then you will be happier and you'll be freer…it is not that." Rather, Jesus says, "I have come to cleanse you from that." We are crying, "Jesus heal us at the heart and let the world come on. Heal us from our sins in our bosom and then let the world of circumstance and difficulty and problems come on." We are ready to meet them. But when we are unhealed at the heart then nothing takes place, except frustration and difficulty. So He has come to purify us from our sins. So we're not going to just say some nice comforting things or give you slogans…no, not at all. Not a bit of it. It's a **purification** of sin and when you get rid of those sins and bury them in the love of God then you walk out of here free.

The whole business of religion is to convert us from perversion. Conversion is conversion from perversion. We've perverted these good things God gave us and turned them into sin and now when he purges us from that (life of sin) we come back to know ourselves – as sons of God.

One more word. The final thing it says is "when he made **purification** of sins he sat down at the right hand of the Majesty on high." In other words he went to the place of final power and he allowed us to say… Jesus is Lord! Not merely the Lord of my sins, but Lord of this thing called time — Lord of death; Lord of everything…He's Lord.

When Gandhi died by an assassins bullet, it was on Friday. On Sunday Mrs. Naidu, the great Indian poet and orator, gave an address over the radio to the Indian people. She's not a Christian, but she had been influenced by Christianity. She's a Hindu and she said this over the radio, "O Bapu (*which means little father*) we're orphaned without you, come back and lead us. This is the third day—rise again from the dead and come back and lead us. Oh Bapu, we are lost without you." I bowed my head in sorrow with the stricken nation, but all the time my heart was singing. I said to myself, "Thank God I do not have to cry that cry — "Oh Jesus we are orphaned without you, come back and lead us. This is the third day; rise again from the dead come back and lead us." No, my grateful heart said he is alive. He's alive and he's alive forever more. If that's true — then what are problems in the face of this Person?[15]

A pastor went past a church. He was broken and beaten, discouraged and about to give up the pastorate when he saw a sign on the church — *Jesus Christ is in this place. Anything can happen here.* He said, "I wonder, I wonder." So he went in and knelt down at the place of prayer. Something did happen when he exposed himself to Jesus; he knelt there and said, "Here I am. I am discouraged and defeated. I'm done for." Jesus spoke the healing word. The pastor rose up and came out of that church a new man. Now he is the center of contagion in his own church. He is on fire and on top of the world.

Jesus Christ is in this place. Roughhewn as this exterior is, and we are rough people, none of us great, none of us mighty – all of us needy, but Jesus Christ is in this place and anything can happen here. We can expect miracles of change, conversion, of the filling of the Spirit, of release of powers. Anything can happen here since Jesus Christ is in this place. Do you believe that? I believe that and I shall see it with my eyes, I know it because you are going to expose yourself to Jesus Christ and the moment you do miracles take place.

Shall we pray?

---

15 In a letter written to his daughter soon after Gandhi's murder, Jones writes, "For some days the radio gave nothing except speeches about Gandhi from national leaders but none of the ideas of Hinduism fitted Gandhi. So they set them aside and quietly adopted Christian ideas. Instead of Karma, the suffering was vicarious. Instead of Gandhi entering Nirvana they wanted him to come back and guide them. Instead of transmigration, they wanted him to come back as Gandhi and have his presence lead them. None of the Hindu ideas fit their need. Only Christian ideas ruled their thinking and the Christian scriptures were quoted a lot" (Graham 418).

PRAYER:

Father God, we thank thee that in the quietness of this morning hour that heart is going to be given to heart and will to will and being to being and life to life. And we are going to rise from this hour not merely experiencing a miracle but becoming a miracle. The word of miracle become flesh in us — may it happen in each one of us and all of us, because thou art alive and forever more. AMEN.

13. JESUS IS THE ONE PERFECT GIFT WE HAVE TO GIVE TO THE WORLD

COMMENTARY ON THE MARKS OF THE CHRISTIAN CHURCH

In this sermon, Jones makes the point that we are Christians today because of the efforts of the early Christians at Antioch. *Antioch, not Jerusalem, was the birthplace of the Church.* Two quite different Christian communities emerged from these two cities: "The roots of Western Christianity are in Antioch, not Jerusalem, for it was out of Antioch that Paul went to spread the gospel to Europe, and hence to us" (Jones, *The Way*, 310). The Christians in Antioch preached the Gospel to the Greeks and then to the world – this "Antiochian" Gospel had universality stamped on it — whereas the Jerusalem church was parochial and custom-bound. "An international mind went into the making of the church. The Jews preached the gospel only to Jews. This bringing of an internal mind to the situation was important, for God guides within the framework of our thinking, and it was from the framework of that thinking that Paul was sent to Europe and to us" (Jones, *The Way*, 310). The Antiochian church was free to move into the world, in part because it was promulgated by *laymen* who were able to imbue their message with the meaning of Christ. "When the church tried to be an apostolic church, centered on the apostles who were in Jerusalem, rather than a Christian church, centered on Christ, it did and will continue to miss its mark for it is built on a weak human foundation" (Jones, *Christ at the Round Table*, 38).

Jones was convinced that the revitalization of the church was going to come through the laity. He points out for example that Jesus was a layman. (Jones, *Christ of the Roundtable,* 43). The early "lay" disseminators of the Christian message were also persons who were *persecuted and had suffered* for following Jesus. Christianity cost them something, and so they valued and protected the gift. "The cross was in it; hence the gift of the Resurrection was in and through it. If our faith costs nothing, it contributes nothing" (Jones, *The Way,* 310). This group of scattered non-Apostolic Christians founded the church at Antioch. It was an error, Jones believes, when in the third century the laity was pushed to the edges of the church, and the clergy became the focus and central decision makers (*Christ at the Round Table,* 46).

> I have the feeling that the disciples made a blunder when they said, "We will give ourselves – to prayer and the ministry of word. And we'll turn over this other work to the lay people, that is, the serving of tables." Now that seemed a very spiritual step. Personally I have come to the conclusion that I think they missed their step. At this point, **they drove a wedge into life between the material and the spiritual.** The spiritual was up here and the material was down here. They would give themselves to the spiritual and another group, a lay group, would give itself to the material. I believe that it drove a disastrous wedge into life between the secular and the sacred, between the spiritual and the material (403).

Jones believed that the church must remedy this past blunder and re-engage the laity:

> If the church is pastor centered then the output will be rhetoric, if it is lay centered, the output will be action. It will be the Word become Flesh, not the word become word (Jones, *Christ at the Round Table,* 109).

The church created in Antioch was also cohesive and strong. It was a *classless society.* It broke down barriers between class and race. Jones reminds us that much of America is Christian because Simeon (called Niger or black) laid his hands on Barnabas and Paul. Then they were sent to preach the gospel in White Europe. (*Christ at the Roundtable*, 86) There is no place, according to Jones, for discrimination or segregation in the church. Jones was well known for his commitment to racial equality in the United States and throughout the world. The church at Antioch is the model then for the Christian church in that regard. There were no divisive characteristics of the church in Antioch. All were welcomed and all were accepted. Jones affirms that, "Our churches must be a house of prayer for all the nations, or else they will be a den of thieves where we steal privileges intended for all, and try to make them exclusively our own. For if they don't belong to all, they belong to none, if they are not shared with all, they disintegrate" (Jones, *Christ at the Roundtable* 91).

> Something new had come into society—that was a man – a man for whom Christ died. He was no longer a man. He was a man for whom Christ died. Classes had been wiped out. Here was a new class—a man for whom Christ died. That placed humanity into an entirely different category of being, and it lifted Christianity to a whole new level (410).

That was the only class that mattered![1]

This Antiochian church, according to Jones, also held together the *radical and conservative* elements of the church,

---

1   Prabhakar illustrates Jones' deep belief that the church breaks down all race barriers with one of Jones' stories: "An African American minister arose in a train in Nazi Germany, gave a German lady his seat and stood for four hours. When the German lady was about to leave, she tried to thank him, but he couldn't understand her German, nor could she understand his English. Finally she wrote out a scripture reference from Isaiah and handed it to him. "The Lord make thee like a watered garden..." Isaiah brought together an African American minister and a German in Nazi Germans. These Christians love each other even before they are acquainted!"

i.e., the prophets and the teachers:

> The prophet is the one who believes that the values of the past should be applied to the present and the future in ever-widening areas of application. The teacher is usually the conservative, conserving the values of the past. The conservative has a real function in human society. The good of the past must be brought into the structure of the present (411).

Jones was adamant that the church must embrace these two elements and not permit a split into either a radical or a conservative faction. Jesus held both facets in his character and the church should maintain them as well. It may be instructive to consider just how this viewpoint could speak to the rifts in the Christian church today. Jones insists that the church needs both elements to be universalized, and to its credit, the church at Antioch embraced strong differences among its members.

The Antiochian church was known as a church that cared for its people and met their needs by taking action. Members did not pass a resolution or extend verbal sympathies in response to needs, but responded directly.[2] They shared in the total life of their society. Jones writes in *The Way*, "A civilization saves or damns its soul by the way it wins its bread" (313).

This church was also redemptive and forgiving. Jones highlights the transformation of Paul's view of John Mark, whom he once judged to be inadequate, i.e., not good enough to work with the Apostle. Paul later forgave him and asked for John Mark to come to his side. The church at Antioch emphasized conversion, recognized the possibilities of change and redemption, and this creative contagion – this *evangelism*

---

2   "At that time prophets came down from Jerusalem to Antioch. One of them named Agabus stood up and predicted by the Spirit that there would be a severe famine over all the world and this took place during the reign of Claudius. The disciples determined that according to their ability, each would send relief to the believers living in Judea; this they did, sending it to the elders by Barnabas and Saul" (Acts 11: 27-30).

impacted the entire world with its message of redemption and reconciliation.

When the church focuses on the person of Jesus Christ, it then has the capacity to create changed character. When it does less than that, it is the man made church – it is off center and focused on the non essential, but when centered on Christ it is centered on Life. The church must offer conversion! (Jones, *Conversion*, 97).

Jones was once asked if the Christian church would be relevant in a future generation.[3]

> Yes, if it stands behind its core values and focuses on the Kingdom of God, the person of Jesus Christ, the possibility of conversion, the power of the Holy Spirit, the fellowship of believers and the promise of service to all. However, if the church of this age marries the spirit of this age, then in the next generation, it will be a widow. For this generation of secularism will be succeeded by another generation of secularism, and secularism has no fixed basis. We must be fixed to something universal and timeless; there are two things that qualify – reality and love (Jones, *Christ of the Roundtable* 19).

While the following conversation with Gandhi is not recorded in this sermon, it is such a prescient observation on Christianity and the Christian church that I am including it as complement to this sermon. Jones reports this conversation with Gandhi regarding the emergence of the Christian church in India. The dialogue includes Gandhi's words along with Jones' internal "responsive commentary."

> 'Mahatma Gandhi I am very anxious to see Christianity naturalized in India so that it shall no longer be a foreign thing identified with a foreign people and a foreign

---

3 The seven last words of a dying church are, "We never did it that way before." Personal communication with E. Stanley Jones.

government, but a part of the national life of India and contributing its power to India's uplift and redemption. What would you suggest we do to make that possible?' He very gravely and thoughtfully replied, 'I would suggest first of all that all of you Christians, missionaries and all begin to live more like Jesus Christ.' He needn't have said any more - that was quite enough. I knew that looking through his eyes were the three hundred millions of India and speaking through his voice the millions of the East saying to me, a representative of the West itself, 'If you will come to us in the spirit of your master we will not be able to resist you.' Never was there a greater challenge to the West than that, and never was it more sincerely given.

'Second,' he said, 'I would suggest that you must practice your religion without adulterating or toning it down.' This comment is just as remarkable as the first. The greatest living non-Christian asks us not to adulterate or tone Christianity down, not to meet them with an emasculated Gospel but to take it in its rugged simplicity and high demand. But what are we doing? As someone has suggested we are inoculating the world with a mild form of Christianity, so that it is now practically immune to the real thing.

'Third, I would suggest that you must put your emphasis upon love, for love is the center and soul of Christianity.' He did not mean love as a sentiment, but love as a working force, the one real power in a moral universe, and he wanted it applied between individuals and groups, and races and nations, the one cement and salvation of the world.

'Fourth I would suggest that you study the non-Christian religions and culture more sympathetically in order to find the good that is in them, so that you might have a more sympathetic approach to the people.'

He was quite right. (Jones, *Christ of the Indian Road*, 101).

Jones would use Gandhi's prescient and constructive comments as he worked to be a servant of the church and a follower of Jesus.

JESUS IS THE ONE PERFECT GIFT WE HAVE TO GIVE TO THE WORLD

THE MARKS OF THE CHRISTIAN CHURCH

SERMON

I thought I would talk to you tonight about the marks of a Christian church. I am going to turn with you to Antioch, where the account says the disciples were first called Christians. I think it was no mere accident that they were called Christians first at Antioch.[4] For Christianity apparently did not come into its own in Jerusalem. Jerusalem was too bound up with racism to become the mold of a world movement. Christianity had to break out of that and move into another setting before it could spread into all the world and so Antioch became that setting.

In those days they gave names to persons according to their perceived character. We give names because we like the sound of a name. But in those times they gave names according to character. For example, when they saw that a person's character changed they changed the name. Barnabas was called Joseph before he surrendered everything to the feet of Christ. The word Joseph literally means "one more." I suppose he belonged to a large family and when they got down to him they ran out of names and so they said we will call him Joseph "one more."

---

4   "Then Barnabas went to Tarsus to look for Saul, and when he had found him, he brought him to Antioch. So it was that for an entire year they met with the church and taught a great many people, and it was in Antioch that the disciples were first called "Christians" (Acts 11:25-26).

But they saw that now he wasn't just "one more." He was then a whole multiplication table so they called him Barnabas – "son of exhortation, the son of consolation."[5]

When the people looked at this Christian community in Antioch, "Oh" they said "they're Christians." The Spirit of Christ had become embodied in this fellowship group and so they were called Christians first at Antioch. Now I want to look with you at Antioch because our roots (as a Christian church) are primarily in Antioch and not in Jerusalem. The missionary movements that swept across Europe and swept across Asia came out of Antioch, which was the base for Paul and Barnabas. So we got our gospel primarily from Antioch. I'm grateful we got it from Antioch because the stamp of universality is upon the type of Christianity found in Antioch. Antioch is our spiritual mother. The gospel first preached at Antioch then spread up into Asia and then on up into Europe and then consequently into America. We are the result.

Let us think about some of the things that went into making of that church at Antioch. First of all it was founded by *laymen.* When the persecution arose in Jerusalem over Stephen many Christians left the city and were scattered.[6] Some went down to Samaria and others to Antioch. It was that lay group of "scattered Christians" that founded the church at Antioch. It said that they were all scattered except the apostles. I used to think the apostles were the braver ones because they stayed behind in Jerusalem. However, I have now come to the conclusion that the Jewish people believed that this lay group was the more dangerous. These laymen were breaking down the barriers. The apostles stayed because they fit into the Jewish molds better than this lay group.

As I study the *Acts of the Apostles* I'm persuaded that when the crisis arose over the feeding of the widows that the apostles missed their step. Although they seemed to be taking a very

5   Acts 4:36.

6   Acts 11:19.

spiritual one. You remember that the race question came up for the first time in the Christian church when the Greeks said: "Why are you neglecting our widows in the daily administration of food." The apostles said: "All right, if you feel we're doing that, we'll tell you what we'll do. We'll appoint seven men to look after this."[7] And they did; they appointed seven men and all of them Greek. In other words, they said: "All right, if you think you're being wronged, we'll turn it (the food distribution) over to you to distribute." On its surface, this all seems very gracious and very wonderful.

However, I have the feeling that the disciples made a blunder when they said, "We will give ourselves – to prayer and the ministry of word. And we'll turn over this other work to the lay people, that is, the serving of tables." Now that seemed a very spiritual step. The apostles would give themselves to prayer and to the ministry of the word and turn over to the seven the management of the material side of things. Personally I have come to the conclusion that I think they missed their step. At this point, they drove a wedge into life between the material and the spiritual. The spiritual was up here and the material was down here. They would give themselves to the spiritual and another group, a lay group, would give itself to the material. I believe that it drove a disastrous wedge into life between the sacred and the secular, between the spiritual and the material.

In Christianity, as seen in the incarnation of Jesus, there is but one, there are no distinctions between the spiritual and the material. There is the Word, the divine word, become flesh.

---

7 "Now during those days, when the disciples were increasing in number, the Hellenists complained against the Hebrews because their widows were being neglected in the daily distribution of food. And the twelve called together the whole community of the disciples and said, "It is not right that we should neglect the word of God in order to wait on tables. Therefore, friends, select from among yourselves seven men of good standing, full of the Spirit and of wisdom, whom we may appoint to this task, while we, for our part, will devote ourselves to prayer and to serving the word" (Acts 6:1-4).

The spiritual and the material were to come together to illustrate the divine revelation. They (the Apostles) separated what God had joined together. They made a distinction between the spiritual and the material. However, in the incarnation the word became flesh. "I know I come to do thy will, a body thou hast prepared me."[8] In other words, the spiritual was to manifest itself in material terms.

I believe that early distinction (in the Church) has impoverished the spiritual because it has made it up here, often high and dry apart from the matters and the relationships of life. This separation has also de-spiritualized the material. The man who does the material things says, "Oh my, mine is a second rate calling, so I don't need to be anything but a second-rate Christian." However, in Christianity everything is sacred. Everything is lifted up from the sordid into the sacred and you do everything for the love of God. Every man has a sense of mission: to put the love of God into everything that he is doing. I believe that we have to get back into the laity a sense of mission: that they are just as divinely called to imbue the material sphere of life with a sense of God's mission as the minister is called to deal with so-called spiritual sphere. I think all life is sacred, if done for the love of God and for the glory of God.

I know a judge in India, who gets up at 4:00 in the morning and has an hour of prayer. While still kneeling he writes the judgments for the day, trying to take his experience of divine justice and make it function in terms of courtroom justice. A lawyer got out of hand one day in his court and the judge said, "I'm very sorry but I've got to fine you for contempt." The lawyer said, "Well, your honor, if you do I'll take it as from the very judgment of God, for when you speak, God speaks." Don't tell me that that secular calling as a Judge was any less sacred than my calling to be a minister and a missionary and an evangelist.

---

8   Hebrews 10:5-7.

Now these apostles said, "It's not fitting that we should serve tables, we'll give ourselves to prayer and ministry of the word." They became more spiritual than their own master. For Jesus taught, preached, healed and lived all as part of the coming of the impact of the Kingdom of the God. They were more spiritual than their own master—saying that we can't feed others, but Jesus fed as a part of the coming of the Kingdom of God. In Him the divine ideas walked; they had flesh and blood so therefore it was realism, not idealism.

An interesting thing happened after they separated the seven and said: "Now you deal with the material." Those seven then become the center of spiritual power. The revival in Christianity breaks out through them. First it was Stephen who precipitated a revival in Jerusalem and paid for it with his own martyrdom. Then Philip, taking up the banner from the fallen Stephen, went down to Samaria and a great revival broke out there. Then the apostle Philip sits down with Peter and John to learn what was happening (the revival) and to regularize what they couldn't produce. Then you remember there was great joy in this city of Samaria when they accepted the word of God and it was through one of the seven — not the twelve. You also remember the story about the Abyssinian, the Ethiopian eunuch, how Philip met him on the way and got up into his chariot and talked to him about Jesus. This Ethiopian eunuch was converted and baptized and went on his way rejoicing.[9] Tradition says that the encounter laid the foundation of the Christian church in Abyssinian and that Ethiopian started

---

9   Then an angel of the Lord said to Philip, "Get up and go toward the south to the road that goes down form Jerusalem to Gaza. So he got up and went. Now there was an Ethiopian eunuch, a court official of Candace, queen of the Ethiopians, in charge of her entire treasury. He had come to Jerusalem to worship and was returning home; seated in his chariot, he was reading the prophet Isaiah. Then the Spirit said the Philip, "Go over to his chariot and join it." So Philip ran up to it and heard him reading the prophet Isaiah. He asked, "Do you understand what you are reading?" He replied, "How can I, unless someone guides me?" And he invited Philip to get in and sit beside him" (Acts 8:26-31).

the Abyssinian (Ethiopian) church which is still going on today. So it was that this lay group that first preached the gospel outside of Jerusalem and into Samaria and through the Ethiopian to the utmost parts of the earth. They were the first ones to fulfill what Jesus said: this (Gospel) ought to be in Jerusalem, in Judea, in Samaria and the utmost parts of the earth. The spiritual initiative (to share the Gospel) seemed to be taken on by this lay group because apparently they were keeping life together as a unit, (i.e., the material and the spiritual) whereas the Disciples were separating it.

These laypersons were scattered by the persecution which arose over Stephen, and went down, the account says, as far as Antioch and there they preached the gospel — the word of God to those from Cyrene and from Cypress. The account says the strong hand of God was among them.

Two things are important to note. In the beginning we see that Christianity was promulgated by the laity. I believe that we have got to get back to the idea that the center of gravity in the Christian church is not the pulpit; it's the pew. We've got to have a lay movement within Christianity. I have just been in Japan and we had 36,000 people sign decision cards to become Christians. That is the most astonishing thing I had seen anywhere in the world. People said, "Well what about it; are they (the pastors) going to follow this up?" Well we turned it over to the pastors but I have to say to the pastors: "Your church is a pastor's church. It is as if you believe that nothing can happen without you — the pastor." In my view, when the whole church revolves around the pastor, the result is the creation of weak laymen without initiative. I don't believe that you will ever be able to save Japan by pastors or missionaries alone. It's got to be a lay group and the Christian movement has to become a lay movement if it is going to become a mighty movement."

The famous historian and theologian Harnack[10] said, "All the early "conquests" (of the Church) were carried out through laymen." A lay group was on fire with the love of God. We have to get that back into our churches, and we are getting that back through visitation and lay evangelism.

Another thing that I noticed in the making of that church at Antioch was that the people who founded it were those who had suffered. Their Christianity cost them something. Therefore it was worth something. The mark of the cross was in the founding of that church. Another important occurrence that contributed to the making of that Antiochian church was the presence of Barnabas. The Christians in Jerusalem made a good choice in sending Barnabas to Antioch. Barnabas was a good man, full of faith and the Holy Spirit and he could rejoice in the work of somebody else. When he saw the grace of God he was glad and he urged them "that with purpose of heart they should cleave unto the Lord."[11] Now when Barnabas went down there and saw this type of Christianity, he did something that was formative for the Christian movement. He said to himself, "this is the place for that young man, Saul, this is real Christianity." So he went off to Tarsus to seek Saul and brought

---

10 Adolf Van Harnack (1851-1930), German theologian and church historian. He was professor of church history successively in the universities of Leipzig, Giessen, Marburg, and Berlin. He was director (1905-21) of the Royal Library, Berlin, and president of the scientific research foundation, Kaiser Wilhelm-Gesellschaft. His great work, Lehrbuch der Dogmengeschichte (4 vol., 1886-90; tr. The History of Dogma, 7 vol., 1895-1900), has exerted an important influence upon modern theological study. Other translated works include Monasticism (1895), What Is Christianity? (1901), The Apostles' Creed (1901), The Expansion of Christianity in the First Three Centuries (2 vol., 1904-5), and Luke the Physician (1907). < The Columbia Encyclopedia 6th ed., s.v."Harnack, Adolf Von" [database on-line]; available from Questia, http:// www.questia.com/PM.qst?a=o&d=101248267; Internet; accessed 31 March 2007.>

11 Acts 11:23.

him to Antioch exposing Saul to this church.[12] The spirit of Antioch came upon Saul. It was at Antioch that Saul's name was changed to Paul. The roots of Paul's spiritual life then were in Antioch and the kind of Christianity that he exported throughout that ancient world came out of Antioch. Saul, or Paul, was a son of Antioch.

Now let's look at some of the marks of the Christian church. These are some of the things that went into the founding of it: first of all, they had a strong corporate[13] sense (of community). They were not just a worshiping body of believers, that is individuals coming together for a day of worship or a period of worship each week, and then going back into their vocations. They had a strong and continuing communal sense. How do I know? Two reasons, I think. The account says that Paul and Barnabas were guests of the church. Now we would have made them a guest of some rich man in the church, but "No," they said, "they are our guests as a total body" and for two years they were guests of that church.

---

12 "Now those who were scattered because of the persecution that took place over Stephen traveled as far as Phoenicia, Cyprus and Antioch, and they spoke the word to no one except Jews. But among them were some men of Cyprus and Cyrene who, on coming to Antioch, spoke to the Hellenists also, proclaiming the Lord Jesus. The hand of the Lord was with them, and a great number became believers and turned to the Lord. News of this came to the ears of the church in Jerusalem, and they sent Barnabas to Antioch. When he came and saw the grace of God, he rejoiced, and he exhorted them all to remain faithful to the Lord with steadfast devotion; for he was a good man, full of the Holy Spirit and of faith. And a great many people were brought to the Lord. Then Barnabas went to Tarsus to look for Saul, and when he had found him, he brought him to Antioch. So it was that for an entire year they met with the church and taught a great many people, and it was in Antioch that the disciples were first called "Christians" (Acts 11: 19-26).

13 Here corporate means to be done by individuals acting together; "a joint identity"; "the collective mind"; "the corporate good." < wordnet.princeton.edu/perl/webwn>

Another thing that makes me feel that they had a strong corporate sense is this: The account says, "While they were worshipping the Lord and fasting, the Holy Spirit said to the whole group, "Set apart for me Barnabas and Saul for the work to which I have called them." Then after fasting and praying they laid their hands on them and sent them off. Barnabas and Saul then went forth on their mighty missionary journeys.

In my view, the old society was breaking down, it had lost its nerve; it didn't know how to love. But here was the emergence of a new society that knew how to love widely and deeply and across all race and class barriers. Into that society pressed people for spiritual nourishment and security. "Ah" they said, "Here are a people (a community) who know how to love and live and have faith. The future belongs to them." And the people joined this new (Christian) society not merely because of the message but because they found there a spiritual security which they could not find elsewhere.

Another aspect that is a mark of this church: is that they became a *classless* society. In the account of the prophets and teachers which were in Antioch they named one man, Manaen, a member of the court of Herod as a teacher. They said that in the church of Antioch there were prophets and teachers. Barnabas and Simeon called Niger and Manaen a foster brother of Herod![14] This foster brother of the king would have been seen as a very prominent person. Some would have made his conversion to Christianity a big deal, to think that the foster brother of the king was converted to Christianity. "Look at that we've got this big man, Manaen, the foster brother of Herod the king!" We would have made him as "exhibit number one," but they put him into that account not at the first place of prominence or the last place of prominence but just about in the middle. In other words they didn't exhibit him as something great. He was just a man, a man for whom Christ died.

---

14 Acts 13:1.

Something new had come into society — that a man was a man for whom Christ died. He was no longer a man. He was a man for whom Christ died. Classes had been wiped out. Here was a new class — a man for whom Christ died. That placed humanity into an entirely different category of being and it lifted Christianity to a whole new level.

Another thing that I note about this church was that it was a group obviously lifted above *race*. The account says among the prophets and teachers was Simeon called Niger and the word *Niger* is literally the word black. Simeon was evidently a black man. Simeon was among the prophets and teachers — not one of the people on the edges, rather, he was at the center. There was clearly a place for a man of color in the early church. This early church was color-blind, class- blind and race-blind – they saw a man as a man – a man for whom Christ died. Note also that Paul and Barnabas were ordained by a black man as they were sent out to preach the gospel to white Europe. So the gospel that we have came out of a group of teachers and prophets, one of whom was a black man. Simeon laid his hands upon Paul and Barnabas and sent them forth to preach the gospel to white Europe. The early church was color-blind. It saw a man, as a man for whom Christ had died.

Now had we been true to that vision, that vision of the oneness of humanity, we would have swept the world. We would have made a brotherhood of the whole world. However, instead of our pushing our principles out into the world, the world has pushed its principles into us. It has taken us over. We have succumbed to standards which are less than Christian and often anti-Christian because we've divided ourselves up and essentially said there is this class and that class and this race and that race. However, in the New Testament there is a new standard. In Jesus Christ there cannot be ethnic, race, cultural, socio-economic or gender distinctions. These distinctions have all been wiped out in Jesus. A person was a person – a person for whom Christ died. However, we have unfortunately allowed the culture around us to prejudice the

Christian faith. We have succumbed to the culture instead of coming to Christ.

It is good news that we now see that these distinction and barriers are falling down. In fact, in many instances they are falling down in places outside the Christian church. The Christian church instead of leading is being led. Regrettably, it is behind the procession instead of leading the world boldly forward in the name of Christ. For many years I have been saying to the American church that I believe that every white church should have at least one member of an ethnic minority as a symbol that we do not believe in class or color lines. And every ethnic minority church should have a least one white member at least as a symbol that they don't believe in color-lines either.

Another mark of the Christian church as seen in that group in Antioch is this – they held together – *the conservative and the radical elements of the church.* The account says that in the church of Antioch (there) were prophets and teachers. Now the teacher is usually the one that conserves the values of the past and passes them on to the next generation. They are typically the "conservatives." Teachers have a great function in society, to conserve values and pass them on to the next generation. The prophets are those who want to apply those values to larger and larger areas of life – they are called the "radicals." Now the church at Antioch had both the conservative and the radical elements and the church held them together and rightly so. The human mind is inclined to choose between the conservative and the radical. We seem to want to be one or the other. The conservative wants to conserve values and the radical wants to apply those values to wider and wider areas of human living. The Church at Antioch knew that the church would need both the conservative and the radical. If the church were one or the other – that is if it were all conservative it would dry up and if it were all radical it would "bust up." However, between the resistance of the conservative and the surrender of the radical the church makes balanced progress. Therefore I

411

want the Christian churches to hold within them people who want to conserve values and others who wish to apply those values to wider and wider areas of human living.

Let me illustrate some of the "conservative" values. Something happened in the incarnation of Jesus. God met us in human flesh; (He) suffered, bled and died upon the cross to redeem us with His own blood. He rose again from physical death and is now spiritually alive for evermore. God comes into our hearts by the Holy Spirit to regenerate us. We can't lose those core (conservative) values; we've got to conserve them. Yet if we only turn back to those values and don't apply them to life as life confronts us, then we only have a half Christianity. We've got to have both: the conservative and the radical. A conservative journal discussed sometime ago: *"Is Stanley Jones a Modernist?"* The came to the conclusion that I had a fundamental soul and a modern mind, which wasn't so bad. That's what I'd like to have.

The church is also built on the foundation of the *fundamentalist* and the *liberal*. I support these two elements coming together and giving each other what they have and sharing their perspectives. However, there is something beyond the fundamentalist and beyond the liberal and that's the Christian. And all of us are just Christians in the making. And I hope that the churches won't split on that (fundamentalism vs. liberalism) but hold these two groups together, each giving the other what they have that is worthwhile.

Another thing I noticed in this early church was this: the Church held together two strong men who *differed widely.* After Barnabas and Paul came back from their missionary journey they were just bubbling over with what had happened. They spent some time recounting what the Lord had done for them and through them. Then after some weeks the "call" came upon them again and Paul said, "Let's go back again. Let's go back and see how they're getting along." Barnabas said, "Good, let's go and let's take John Mark with us." I can see the face of Paul harden: "No, we can't do that. John Mark turned back from

412

Pamphylia on that last journey did not accompany us in our work. We can't take a man who turns back that way."[15] But Barnabas said, "But Paul, we don't break a man because he makes one mistake, do we? I thought our movement was redemptive; now let's not break John Mark. He got weak and turned back. I know he did but he's got something in him. Let's take him back again." And Paul's face hardens and says, "No, we can't take him. I won't have a man like that. We've got to have a pure Christian movement." But Barnabas said, "This Christian movement has got to be redemptive." The account says that the contention was so sharp between them that they parted, according to Moffatt's translation, — *in irritation.* Barnabas took John Mark and Paul took Silas.[16]

Then the account says that they were both commended by the church to the grace of God. Now I think that you can read it and looking at it fairly, that it seemed as though the church committed both of those men to the grace of God, as much as to say: brothers, you both need it (grace). But the church says, "when you come back, you come back home." This is home to you. When Barnabas and Paul came back again they both came back to Antioch. In other words, Antioch's wisdom was big enough and ample enough to embrace strong men who differed widely. Don't let a church be split over honest and true men who differ on things and differ widely, but who love Christ perhaps equally well, but who may differ in regard to certain policies. The church is big enough and great enough to do that.

---

15 Acts 15:37-39.

16 "After some days Paul said to Barnabas, "Come let us return and visit the believers in every city where we proclaimed the word of the Lord and see how they are doing." Barnabas wanted to take with them John called Mark. But Paul decided not to take with them one who had deserted them in Pamphylia and had not accompanied them in the work. The disagreement became so sharp that they parted company; Barnabas took Mark with him and sailed away to Cyprus. But Paul chose Silas and set out, the believers commending him to the grace of the Lord. He went through Syria and Cilicia, strengthening the churches" (Acts 15:36-40).

Then I want you to notice that this church was *redemptive.* Years later, I can see (this redemption illustrated) the aged Paul is dictating a letter to an amanuensis – when he comes down to that last epistle to Timothy he dictates this sentence: "Bring John Mark with you for he is profitable to me for the ministry."[17] And I can see the amanuensis look up and gaze at Paul with a quizzical smile and Paul settles back into his chair and says, "Yes, I know what you're thinking – you're thinking about that time when Barnabas and I quarreled over John Mark. Barnabas was a better Christian than I was. He was always taking people nobody else would take. He took me when nobody else would take me. And he took John Mark when I wouldn't take him and he has made a man of him. A wonderful Christian that man Barnabas is — a better Christian than I was. I want you to write exactly what I said: 'bring John Mark with you.'" John Mark had come back to the bosom of the church at Antioch and Antioch had made him over again. Aren't you glad? Aren't you glad that they didn't break him? Barnabas had taken him and remade him and made him into the man who wrote the gospel that blesses our spirits.[18]

---

17 "Do your best to come to me soon, for Demas, in love with this present world, has deserted me and gone to Thessalonica; Crescens has gone to Galatia, Titus to Dalmatia. Only Luke is with me. Get John Mark and bring him with you, for he is useful in my ministry" (2 Tim 4:9-11).

18 This story is included in Jones' book, *The Reconstruction of the Church, After What Pattern?* This book was published in 1970. This footnote illustrates how Jones developed themes in his sermons that would often be later included in a book on the same topic, almost verbatim. Here is the text from Jones' book. "We saw that Barnabas and Paul parted "in irritation" over the question of John Mark and his going with them on a second evangelistic tour. Did this leave permanent sores which refused to heal, or was redemptive grace at work completely healing those sins? Redemptive grace was at work. The years come and go and Paul, now the aged, is dictating his last letter, Second Timothy. He dictates to his amanuensis this sentence: 'Bring John Mark with you for he is profitable to me for the ministry.' (2 Tim 4:11) I can see the writer lay down his quill, look up at Paul, and smile. Paul, reading its meaning, must have replied: 'Yes, I know what you are thinking about – that quarrel that Barnabas and

I shall always be grateful to a little group in the church where I was converted — in Baltimore. I was gloriously converted. I've no pride. It is just a fact. For a year I was on fire, radiant, I know. But then I tripped and sprawled. I didn't actually fall but tripped and sprawled. And then I said to myself, "What is the use of going to the Bible study tonight; I have nothing to say." We went to a weekly meeting where we told each week what had been happening to us. I had nothing to say, my music had died but I resisted that temptation and went anyway. The rest of them were telling what Christ had done for them and I sat there with tears streaming down my cheeks. I was broken-hearted and for the first time in a year there was a cloud over my spirit. After everybody had spoken the class leader, the layman, John Zincs said, "Stanley, tell us what is the matter." I said, "I can't, but pray for me." They got on their knees as one man and took me into their arms and took me back to the bosom of God. When we got up from our knees I knew that I was reconciled with God, with myself and with the group. I shall always be grateful to that little group. They could have broken me for I was a very bruised reed. They could have said, "Yes I told you so. It is too good to be true." They could have snapped me. They could have put out the spark, but they never uttered a word of criticism, only words of love. They were a place of redemption and that is what the Christian church must be. These Christians in the making must know that when they fall, they've got a place where they can go back and find people who love them in spite of everything that they have done.

I had over John Mark. Barnabas was a better Christian than I was.' (A tear must have trickled down the furrowed cheek of the ancient warrior), 'I was hard and unbending and unforgiving, But Barnabas took John Mark, nursed him back to spiritual health, and made a wonderful man out of him. They tell me that John Mark has written a Gospel God forgive me. Yes, I want him. So write exactly what I say. I really want him and need him.' The wound was healed and no scars were left. The mainstream of the Christian movement (Paul) was redemptive again, made so by Paul's saying, I was wrong, I'm sorry and by restoring John Mark to his fellowship" (100).

In Korea there was a woman who knocked on a door of a Christian church and said, "Is this the place where they mend broken hearts?" Yes, the Christian church ought to be a place where they mend broken hearts and broken hopes and broken lives and broken homes—broken everything—and make them over again. And everybody must feel that if they stumble and fall, well, they can go right back straight to the church again and get love and sympathy and redemption. The church redeemed John Mark and I am grateful.

The last thing that I see in that church at Antioch is this, that church was creative! Out of it came a movement that went to the ends of the earth and we are the result of that little group of people hearing the voice of God saying, "Separate me Barnabas and Saul for the work to which I have called them." Now when a group listens to God instead of listening to contemporary society, it becomes creative. Movements begin to break out from it – redemptive movements, touching situations at home and abroad. God is still saying, "Separate me this man, that man, this woman, this boy, this girl, I want them." And then these persons become the agents of a great creative movement – the whole western civilization would ultimately "listen" to God. It all started in the small group in Antioch.

Now these are some of the marks of the Christian church and I think that you would agree with me about the people who looked at them and said, "Why, they are Christians!" Yes, they were. The spirit of Christ was becoming incarnate and we've got to re-baptize ourselves in that original spirit and catch the same mind that was there at Antioch. And I hope that will happen in your lives. My time is exactly up so I have to stop.

Shall we pray?

PRAYER:

Dear Jesus: Put thy hand upon this group and may the churches represented here, all these different denominations, become incarnations of the spirit of Christ in human society. We ask this for Jesus sake. Amen.

V

CONCLUSION

JONES wrote and spoke for the general public. There is little doubt that his words brought hope and refreshment to multitudes all over the world (Mathews 15). We have discovered in these Fifteen sermons that Jones was a man of contagious and transparent faith. When he preached about Jesus, it was as if he knew Jesus personally and could reach out and touch him. Jones described himself as an evangelist....the bearer of the Good News of Jesus Christ. Jones would not keep this "good news" to himself, but wanted to put his arms around the world and share Christ with everyone. He emphasized self surrender and conversion in his sermons, in his books, and in his life. Jones would repeatedly tell his audience that the Christian **Way** is **The Way** to live. This **Way** is written into the nature of reality, into human nature – into all of life. Jones easily moved from the personal message of self surrender and conversion to the implications of a life in Christ and a life lived upon the **Way**.

As noted earlier, Jones' preaching did not require people to leave their intellect at the door; his presentation of Jesus engaged both the intellect and touched humanity's desire to experience the living Christ in their lives. The countless illustrations found in his sermons speak to a cross section of humanity and demonstrate, in a multitude of ways, the transformative impact of Jesus Christ on human existence. Few listeners could miss identifying with one story or another — virtually all listeners would find stories that touched their lives. All were offered hope that they too could experience the transformation available through self surrender and conversion.

E. Stanley Jones presented Jesus as the redeemer of all of life and used his wide ranging study of the non Christian religions, medicine, psychology, philosophy, science, history, and literature to make the case that the touch of Christ is upon all creation — that the totality of life was created by Christ and for Christ. We were all created to live upon the Way.

In these sermons, we have found that Jones moves from the individual to the social, the economic and the cultural implications of living a life following Jesus. Many have said that the social realm was Jones' *garden* for the application of the message that the Christian Way is the way to live in all spheres of being. Jones uses the redemptive principles of the Kingdom of God, which is built into the nature of reality, and applies them in support of redemptive possibilities for all of life. E. Stanley Jones has been called a spiritual genius whose work on the Kingdom of God, the Holy Spirit, and the application of those areas to social and political thought was timely and much needed. (Graham 396). The Ashram movement was one such application of the Kingdom of God.

The sermons that were the focus of this book illustrate that E. Stanley Jones' core convictions ring as true today as they did nearly fifty years ago. His sermons affirm the fact that Jesus is Lord – Lord of us and Lord of the Universe. His twelve convictions now have the last word!

♦ The moral universe that God created is dependable. We experience results or consequences in this universe that God created. Jones *and* our experience tell us that the message of

Revelation and the facts of science both end up at the feet of Christ.[1]

♦ The creator of this universe is a God who is love and who seeks all of humanity as the object of his love. The New Testament tells us that God revealed himself in His most perfect and loving form in the person of his son, Jesus Christ.[2]

♦ Jesus is God become man. The divine word became flesh in Jesus Christ. Jesus shows us how to live in that He is our example and disposes us to live in that He is our redeemer.[3]

♦ The cross represents the reality of God's full identification and experience with our suffering. "What fell on Jesus fell on God, what he bore, God bore; his cross was God's cross.[4]

♦ Self surrender enables us to take the gift of God which transforms us and lets us live upon the Way! We travel that Way by grace and receptivity.[5]

♦ The **Way** is written into the nature of reality and into our natures. We are most free when we rest in Him. Christian living has cosmic backing for it is the natural way to live.[6]

♦ The Holy Spirit makes Christ our contemporary for the Holy Spirit is Christ in us now![7]

♦ The Kingdom of God is to be taken seriously as a present reality. Jesus believed in life and in its redemption. The Kingdom of God is the collective redemption of all mankind.[8]

♦ Unmerited suffering and injustice can be used. Jesus took the cross, the symbol of death, and turned it into the symbol

---

1   Two Approaches to Life: Faith and Science.
2   God's Search for Man.
3   Who Do You Say That I Am?
4   Self Surrender.
5   How are we to be changed & transformed?
6   Christian Faith and the Body.
7   Sermons on the Holy Spirit.
8   The Kingdom of God.

of redemption. All injustice and evil can be the occasion of a testimony to the glory of God.[9]

♦ Love is the strongest force in the world and will ultimately win.[10]

♦ Jesus is Lord, and if we have any doubt, we can simply recall the resurrection on the third day. "Put out the candles, the sun is up." Jesus is alive and Jesus is Lord.[11]

♦ Jesus is a gift to be shared with the world: "In the person of Jesus Christ the Christian church holds within itself a motive and a power that produces changed character"[12]

Jones would repeatedly affirm that it does not take much of a man to be a Christian, but it takes all there is of him. It doesn't matter how much you've got; it matters much how much He's got of you. I concur thoroughly with Graham who observed that "God certainly had all of E. Stanley Jones, and that was enough to change the world" (391).

---

9   Christ and Human Suffering.
10 The New Birth on the Pattern of Jesus.
11 The Word Became Flesh.
12 The Marks of a Christian Church.

APPENDICES

‌▬ ▬

Appendix 1

THE TEN PILLARS OF THE UNITED CHRISTIAN ASHRAM

BY E. STANLEY JONES (1971)

In the first part of my work, Theophilus, I wrote of all
that Jesus did and taught from the beginning until the
day when, after giving instructions through the Holy
Spirit to the apostles whom he had chosen, he was taken
up to heaven. He showed himself to these men after his
death, and gave ample proof that he was alive; over a
period of forty days he appeared to them and taught
them about the kingdom of God. While he was in their
company he told them not to leave Jerusalem. 'You must
wait,' he said, 'for the promise made by the Father, about
which you have heard me speak, John, as you know,
baptized with water, but you will be baptized with the
Holy Spirit, and within the next few days.'"

- Acts 1:1-5 (New English Bible)

1. THE WORD BECAME FLESH

The Gospel begins with Jesus. We begin with Jesus. That is
where Luke began. Jesus is the self-revelation of God. Jesus is
God breaking through in understandable terms. Jesus is the
human life of God. I cannot think of God in terms higher than

425

Jesus. He is the unfolding of the nature of God. Everything apart from Jesus is off-center. We think of God in terms of Jesus. We think of Christ in terms of Jesus. We think of the Holy Spirit in terms of Jesus. If I were to put my finger upon the most important verse of the scripture, I would put my finger on: "The Word became flesh." Jesus did not bring a message from God: He was the message from God. He is not a mediator between us and God, but He is a mediator in the sense that He mediates God to us.

2. THE WORD BECAME DEED

Jesus was the word become flesh, and Jesus did: "All that Jesus *did* and taught." When we see Jesus, we see what God is like and what man can be like in a revelation of both God and man. He did *to do* as well as *to be*. So, the revelation of God was not only in what He was, but what he did. He was an act breaking through. Therefore, we don't teach a philosophy; we teach a fact! The fact of Jesus! "All that Jesus did" – you've got to preach this deed, not this philosophy, but this fact of doing and everything that Jesus taught, He did. You can't tell where His words end and His deeds begin. They came together with what He was. We have got to be deed — something has to happen to us, in us, through us before we can teach. Christianity is not a teaching of a code of words, but it is a presentation of a person, it is the incarnate God who incarnated His principles and His attitudes and His love.

3. THE WORD BECAME TEACHING

"All that Jesus did and taught." Teaching is third and not first. Jesus never came to teach a religion. He came to present Himself as God's answer to man's total need. His teaching was a fact. The word must become flesh in us, then we can teach. The teaching will be a self-revelation of what has happened to us. It is experience. It is autobiography!

426

4. THE WORD BECAME ATONEMENT

Love came in contact with hate and evil. Where there is sin in the loved one, love has the task of bleeding on it. It becomes atonement. Because it is the nature of love to involve itself in the sin and sorrow of the loved one, love had to live alongside of sin in the loved one, and that turned it into a cross. The moment man sinned, the lamb was slain. The lamb was slain not merely two thousand years ago, but from the foundation of the world. It is the unseen cross upon the heart of God. The outer cross was lifted in order that we might see the unseen cross in the heart of God. The cross was inevitable. It was bound to happen – it is a fact of the redemptive movement. Therefore, we believe in the cross. The cross lifts-up the nature of God as redemptive love. We believe that the heart of the power of the universe is self-giving love. Jesus had to die that we might live and that means that at the heart of our relationship, we must choose to lose ourselves in order to find ourselves again.

5. THE WORD BECAME VICTORIOUS

We raise all the questions against the love of God and in the resurrection. He answers them, not by a verbal answer but by a vital answer – the resurrected Jesus. He was the answer to all the questions raised from the cross. So, we believe that the word became victorious. The last word is not the cross; the last word is victory — resurrection. That is good news! Jesus is alive forevermore. We are not orphans. He has come back in triumph. He is here! So, we believe in the resurrection and the resurrected Christ. *This* Jesus is alive right now. He is available for everything you need.

6. JESUS HAS BECOME INCARNATE IN A GROUP

As a little flock to whom God was to give the kingdom met together, they were the koinonia. They became the seed of a new order. I believe in the church. With all its faults, it is the greatest servant institution upon earth. It has many critics, but no rivals in the work of human redemption. There isn't a spot on earth, from the frozen north to the tropical islands of the sea, where we haven't gone with schools and hospitals, orphan asylums, leper asylums, churches, gospel, everything to lift the soul, the mind, the body, and the race. I am a part of the church. Its sins are my sins. I belong to the church but the church also belongs to me. I belong to something beyond the church. I believe in the kingdom. Now, the church is a relativism. Christ loved the church and gave Himself for it that He might redeem it. Therefore, the church can't give redemption. It is the subject of the redemption.

7. THE WORD BECAME AUTHORITY

He talked with them for forty days about the kingdom of God. In other words, His first word was the kingdom of God. His inner word was the kingdom of God, and His last word was the kingdom of God. He went out preaching the gospel of the kingdom of God. The coming of the kingdom of God would be the doing of the will of God on earth which is done in heaven. The will of God is done in the individual will, as well as in the corporate will. It is a completely total order demanding a total obedience in the total life. We are to preach the kingdom *now* which ventures into something that demands it in the total life. The kingdom is the unshakable order, the unshakable kingdom, which cannot be shaken. We are to preach the kingdom in the individual level and in the social level. The total life is to come in the total allegiance, individual and collective. So, an individual gospel without a social gospel is a soul without a body, but a social gospel without an individual gospel is a body without a soul. I want one gospel that lays its hand upon the individual will and says, "Repent, be converted." It is the total answer to man's total need. We emphasize the kingdom at every Ashram because it makes us relevant on every front. The power behind the gospel of the kingdom is the power of the Holy Spirit.

8. THE WORD BECAME ADEQUATE RESOURCES – BAPTIZED WITH THE HOLY SPIRIT

We are to preach the kingdom and back our message with the power of the Holy Spirit. We need adequacy and power to bring in God's order upon earth. The power behind the gospel of the kingdom is the power of the Holy Spirit. If the Holy Spirit emphasis is taken away from Jesus, it ends up in confusion. The three things necessary before this Gift of Gifts could be given had now been accomplished; Life has been shown in His Life; Life had suffered so that the three things that cripple life — sin, suffering, death - might be cleared away; Life had utterly overcome in the resurrection, and now Life was ready to be given. He lived, He died, He rose again, He gives Himself in experience — these four facts stand together and constitute our gospel. To take the first three but to stop short of the fourth is the supreme tragedy of present-day Christian living. We emphasize His life, His death, His resurrection, but we also need to emphasize the experience of the Holy Spirit.

9. THE WORD BECAME PERSONAL

We belong to Christ. We belong to Him through self-surrender. The last thing we ever give up is ourselves. Jesus asks us to lay down that last thing. Self-surrender is the door to abundant life and there is no other door. Self-surrender is the basis of all real love. The Divine Self-surrender to us has been complete. The cross is its sign. God can go no further; He has gone to the utmost limit. The only thing lacking is our self-surrender. When that comes, love turns into being. It is spontaneous, inevitable. Spiritual power is a by-product of something deeper. It comes out of an inward fellowship with God and abandonment of His purposes. Surrender to Christ as Lord gives you the absolute security of belonging to Him who has the ultimate and final authority; therefore, it can and does give absolute security. Let the stimulus of "Jesus is Lord" play upon your life continuously and the sickness – producing stimuli of fear, resentments, and anxiety are counteracted and cancelled by this glorious positive – Jesus is Lord!

10. THE WORD BECAME UNIVERSAL MOVEMENT AND MESSAGE

We are to be witnesses to the ends of the earth. The evangelism of Jesus was an evangelism to the total man. He did not love people's souls alone — He loved people and would lift everything: that cramped body, soul, and mind.

Christianity is at the parting of the ways. It is now at the point of decision where it must decide in the larger way to be definitely Christian or vaguely religious. The whole pressure is toward a synchronism. In East and West, the demand is that we draw a line through the word "Christian" and put in "Religious." This is in the supposed interests of universality. In reality, it leads to a "mist of amiability." You cannot be more universal by being less Christian. Whenever you strike a truly Christian note, you strike a universal note. If we want universality, then back to Pentecost! For there the universal Christ becomes universal in experience, and this experience breaks into universal forms.

Christianity did not come into its own in Jerusalem for two reasons: it was too racial and too authoritarian. The Christian gospel was free to express its very nature and purpose at Antioch. The matrix of Jerusalem was too narrow (Jewish racialism) and too high (too authoritarian) to be universalized. The Christian movement had to be put into a new matrix, Antioch, to come to its own.

As for the "Great Commission" being an interpolation, we reply that it has not yet been proved; but even if it were, we would still be comitted to this whole enterprise of sharing Him with the world, for it is not based upon a command, but upon the very nature of the gospel itself, upon Him. Last command or no last command, we must share Him, for the necessities of human life command us to give a savior such as Jesus. But of the deep necessity comes the imperious voice, "Go into the world and preach the gospel."

Here we have a ten-fold program and I believe it is all around Christ Jesus. It is the gospel of the kingdom and the gospel of the Holy Spirit, and its gospel sends us to the ends of the earth because this is the only thing that people need anywhere and everywhere. It is the Word. It is THE WORD! It has become incarnate, it is being lived out and it is adequate. And I believe that if we can become incarnate with these ten things, we are going to be a spearhead of the kingdom of God. We won't be the perfect answer. We are an imperfect people with the perfect message, a perfect goal, and a perfect incarnation of the goal. And so we don't go out apologizing. We shout it from the housetops, for if we keep quiet the stones will cry out. The hard, bare facts of life will cry out for Jesus. So we believe in cosmic backing, we therefore need not be afraid. Jesus is Lord!

Note: The Ten Pillars is a Theological Position Paper based on an Address given by Dr. E. Stanley Jones (Brother Stanley) at the Oklahoma Christian Ashram, Oklahoma City, on December 7, 1971. This was one of the last official Ashram addresses by Jones which was secured for us by the Reverend Ray Owens, Director of the Oklahoma Ashram. Summarized and Edited by: Roberto Escamilla.

Appendix 2

WHAT IS CONVERSION?

By E. Stanley Jones

"Except you be converted, and become as little children, you shall not enter in the kingdom of heaven" (Matthew 18:3 KJV). Rabindranath Tagore, the great Indian poet and philosopher, said this passage was the most beautiful passage in the Bible.

But what is conversion? Converted comes from "con", with and "vetare", to turn — "to turn with." The big question in life is, is my face or my back toward Christ? The first step in the new life is to turn your back on the old life and face toward Christ. You do not do that alone—there is the "with." The moment you throw your will in His direction, He is there *with* you. He helps you to do what you can't do — to break with the old life. However, that decision to turn around is your decision. There you stand alone and as a free moral being you make the decision alone, severely alone. The moment you make it, however, He is "with" you.

Second – we must "become as little children" — we must acquire a new spirit. You are given a new spirit — the spirit of a little child — You have a fresh beginning with a clean slate. That emancipation from the old guilt, from the consequent sense of inferiority, of estrangement from God, man, yourself, and the universe, is the most important and radical emancipation imaginable. "If the Son makes you free, you will be free indeed." This is an "indeed" freedom — nothing, absolutely nothing is like it. You're not only emancipated from the past but you become receptive. A child is receptive. The new spirit is the spirit of receptivity. You can now take life by the handfuls and heartfuls and beingfuls. You are no longer struggling with life — you take it open-armed. You are alive to life to your fingertips.

*Third... we must "enter the kingdom of God"*We gain a new sphere of living. Your circumstances will be the same, but you will now live in two world at once, the world of physical relationships and the world of the Kingdom of God. This inner world makes new the whole outer world. You will do things now from a new motive, a new spirit and a new outlook. As one of the most alive Christians I know, says "The one thing that has changed is your reason for living."In this new sphere of living you supply the willingness and He supplies the power. Life is no longer alone, struggling, tense, anxious and uncertain. It is relaxed, released, reassured, and receptive. You are no longer living on the unit principle, but on the cooperative plan.

To sum up: The first step, "the new direction," is yours; the second step, "the new spirit," is His; the third step, "the new sphere of living," is yours and His. This is Conversion.

Conversion may be described in a most striking way " If any man...be in Christ, he is a new creature: old things are passed away; behold they (the old things) have become new."(II Cor. 5:17, ASV). The American Standard version makes everything clear. You are a new creature — "old thing have passed away; those "old things" have become new."

A psychiatrist came to where I was writing in the Himalayas for the express purpose of surrendering himself to God. His 'conversion' happened on the way when he was still twenty miles from where I was staying. He describes it, "I was dead tired from a sleepless night - tired and upset. When suddenly as I made my surrender to God, my tiredness and frustration dropped away. I was a new man. I came to Sat Tal striding across the mountains as though I had on seven league boots. And I have never seen Sat Tal so beautiful before. It was alive with beauty." He was happy with a divine gaiety. Reconciled with God, he was reconciled with himself, with his body, with his brothers, with nature, with life and with his psychiatry. Psychiatry was no longer for him, dominant, proud, self-sufficient in its own techniques. Now it has a point from which to work out to life — Christ. It was servant, no longer a master. All life fell into its place, and all life began to add up to sense and meaning, a powerful example of a life transformed of conversion.

In other words, *"Conversion is a reaction in which Christ is central."* When you make Christ central you are converted. When self-surrender takes place God moves in from the margin and takes possession of the center. He is no longer "marginal and vague;" he is now "focal and dynamic." As someone said, "I expose myself to His everything." Jesus is Lord!

SOURCES CITED

Anderson, James D. "Black Rural Communities and the Struggle for Education During the Age of Booker T. Washington, 1877-1915." *PJE. Peabody Journal of Education* 67, no. 4 (1990)

"Athanasian Creed." In *The Columbia Encyclopedia* 6th ed., edited by Lagass, Paul. New York: Columbia University Press, 2004.

Bebbington, D. W. *Evangelicalism in Modern Britain: A History from the 1730s to the 1980s*. London: Routledge, 1993.

Buckley, Jerome Hamilton, *William Ernest Henley; A Study in the "Counter-Decadence" of the Nineties*, Princeton, New Jersey, Princeton University Press, 1945.

Bundy, David, *The Theology of the Kingdom of God in E. Stanley Jones*, Wesleyan Theological Journal 23:58-80, 1988.

Carlyle, Thomas, *The French Revolution, A History*. Book 1, Section VII, , London, Chapman Hall, 1898.

Chesterton, Gilbert Keith, *The Everlasting Man*. New York, Houghton & Stoughton, 1927.

Coffin, William Sloane, *Some Christian Convictions*. New Haven, Connecticut, Yale University Press, 1915.

Corless, Roger J. *The Vision of Buddhism: The Space under the Tree*. 1st ed. St. Paul,MN: Paragon House, 1989.

Croce, Paul Jerome. *Science and Religion in the Era of William James*. Chapel Hill,NC: University of North Carolina Press, 1995.

Eldridge, Paul. "Hope," In *Infidels and Heretics: An Agnostic's Anthology*. 58-60. Boston: Stratford, 1929.

"Emerson, Ralph Waldo." In *The Columbia Encyclopedia* 6th ed., edited by Lagass, Paul. New York: Columbia University Press, 2004.

Epps, John L., (Ed.) *Bending History: Talks of Joseph Wesley Mathews*. Resurgence Publishing, 2005.

"Feng YÜ-Hsiang." In *The Columbia Encyclopedia* 6th ed., edited by Lagass, Paul. New York: Columbia University Press, 2004.

Fitzgerald, Edward. *The Rubaiyat of Omar Khayyam, The Astronomer Poet of Persia*. Philadelphia: J. C. Winston, 1898.

"Francis, Saint." In *The Columbia Encyclopedia* 6th ed., edited by Lagass, Paul. New York: Columbia University Press, 2004.

Frie, Roger. "Introduction," In *Understanding Experience: Psychotherapy and Postmodernism*. Edited by Fire, Roger, 1-26. New York: Routledge, 2003. Book on-line. Available from Questia, http://www.questia.com/PM.qst?a=o&d=108487331. Internet. Accessed 31 March 2007.

Graham, Stephen A., *The Totalitarian Kingdom of God: The Political Philosophy of E. Stanley Jones*. Lanham, Maryland, University Press of America, 1998.

— — — — —, *Ordinary Man: Extraordinary Mission: The Life and Work of E. Stanley Jones*. Nashville, Tennessee, Abingdon Press, 2005.

Grant, Frederick C. *The Earliest Gospel: Studies of the Evangelic Tradition at Its Point of Crystallization in Writing*. New York: Abingdon-Cokesbury Press, 1943.

"Harnack, Adolf Von." In *The Columbia Encyclopedia* 6th ed., edited by Lagass, Paul. New York: Columbia University Press, 2004.

"Hocking, William Ernest." In *The Columbia Encyclopedia* 6th ed., edited by Lagass, Paul. New York: Columbia University Press, 2004.

James, William, *The Varieties of Religious Experience*. London, Collier Press, 1961.

Jensen, Lionel M. *Manufacturing Confucianism: Chinese Traditions & Universal Civilization*. Durham, NC: Duke University Press, 1997.

Johnson, Luke, Timothy, *The Creed: What Christians Believe and Why It Matters*. New York, Doubleday Press, 2005.

Johnson, Martin Ross, *The Christian Vision of E. Stanley Jones: Missionary Evangelist, Prophet, and Statesman*. Ph.D. Dissertation, Florida State University, 1978.

Jones, E. Stanley, *Christ of the Indian Road*. New York, Grosset & Dunlap, 1925.

— — — —, *Christ at the Round Table*. New York & Cincinnati, Abingdon, 1928.

— — — —, *The Christ of Every Road: A Study in Pentecost*. New York, Cincinnati & Chicago, Abingdon, 1930.

— — — —, *The Christ of the Mount: A Working Philosophy of Life*. New York & Nashville, Abingdon-Cokesbury, 1931.

— — — —, *Christ and Human Suffering*. New York, Cincinnati & Chicago, Abingdon, 1933.

— — — —, *Christ's Alternative to Communism*. New York, Cincinnati & Chicago, Abingdon, 1935.

— — — —, *Victorious Living*. New York & Nashville, Abingdon-Cokesbury, 1936.

— — — —, *The Choice Before Us*. New York, Cincinnati & Chicago, Abingdon, 1937.

— — — —, *Along the Indian Road*. New York, Cincinnati & Chicago, Abingdon, 1939.

— — — —, *Is the Kingdom of God Realism?* New York & Nashville, Abingdon-Cokesbury, 1940.

— — — —, *Abundant Living*. New York & Nashville, Abingdon-Cokesbury, 1942.

— — — —, *The Christ of the American Road*. New York & Nashville, Abingdon-Cokesbury, 1944.

— — — — —, *The Way*. New York & Nashville, Abingdon-Cokesbury, 1946.

— — — — —, *Mahatma Gandhi: An Interpretation*. New York & Nashville, Abingdon-Cokesbury, 1948.

— — — — —, *The Way to Power and Poise*. 1949, New York & Nashville, Abingdon-Cokesbury, 1949.

— — — — —, *How To Be A Transformed Person*. New York, & Nashville, Abingdon-Cokesbury, 1951.

—————, *Growing Spiritually.* 1953, New York & Nashville, Abingdon, 1953.

—————, *Mastery: The Art of Mastering Life.* New York & Nashville, Abingdon, 1955.

—————, *Christian Maturity.* New York & Nashville, Abingdon, 1957.

————, *Conversion.* New York & Nashville, Abingdon, 1959.

————, *In Christ.* New York & Nashville, Abingdon, 1961.

————, *The Word Become Flesh.* New York & Nashville, Abingdon, 1963.

————, *Victory Through Surrender.* New York & Nashville, Abingdon, 1966.

————, *A Song of Ascents: A Spiritual Autobiography.* New York, & Nashville, Abingdon, 1968.

————, *The Unshakable Kingdom and the Unchanging Person.* New York & Nashville, Abingdon, 1972.

————, *The Divine Yes.* New York, Cincinnati & Chicago, Abingdon, 1975.

Lewis, C.S., *Mere Christianity.* New York, MacMillan & Company, 1960.

Logan, James, C., Ed. *Theology and Evangelism in the Wesleyan Heritage.* Nashville, Tennessee, Kingswood Books, 1994.

MacNicol, Nicol. *Indian Theism: From the Vedic to the Muhammadan Period.* London: Oxford University Press, 1915.

Mathews, James K. & Mathews, Eunice J., *Selections from E. Stanley Jones, Christ and Human Need,* Nashville, Tennessee, Abingdon Press, 1971.

Menninger, Karl. *Theory of Psychoanalytic Technique*. New York: Basic Books,1958.

Newbigin, Lesslie, *The Open Secret, An Introduction to the Theology of Mission.* Grand Rapids, Michigan, Eerdmans Publishing Company, 1995.

Outler, Albert C., *The Works of John Wesley, Volume 1, Sermons I 1-33.* Nashville, Tennessee, Abingdon Press, 1984.

"Nicaea, First Council Of." In *The Columbia Encyclopedia* 6th ed., edited by Lagass,Paul. New York: Columbia University Press, 2004.

Parker, William & St. Johns, Elaine, *Prayer Can Change Your Life: Experiments in Prayer Therapy.* New Jersey, Simon and Schuster, 1972.

Placher, William C., *Jesus The Savior, The Meaning of Jesus Christ for Christian Faith.* Louisville, Kentucky, Westminster John Knox Press, 2001.

Prabhakar, John, A., *A Homiletic Analysis of E. Stanley Jones' Devotions and Meditations.* 2003, Delhi, India, Cambridge Press, 2003.

Reeves, Jeremiah Bascom. *The Hymn in History and Literature.* New York: Century, 1924.

Royce, Josiah, and Josiah Royce. *Royce's Logical Essays: Collected Logical Essays of Josiah Royce.* Edited by Daniel S. Robinson. Dubuque, Iowa: Wm. C. Brown, 1951.

Ryce-Menuhin, Joel, ed. *Jung and the Monotheisms: Judaism, Christianity, and Islam.* New York: Routledge, 1994.

Schott, Ben, *Schott's Original Miscellany.* New York, Bloomsbury Press, 2002.

Shakespeare, William. *The Tragedy of Macbeth.* Edited by Nicholas Brooke. Oxford: Oxford University Press, 1998.

Sheehy, Noel. *Fifty Key Thinkers in Psychology.* New York: Routledge, 2003.

Soulen, R. Kendall, *Lectures in ST 305, Systematic Theology I & II.* Fall 2005, Spring, 2006, Wesley Theological Seminary, Washington, D.C.

Stark, W. *Montesquieu: Pioneer of the Sociology of Knowledge.* London: Routledge & Kegan Paul, 1960.

Stedman, Edmund Clarence, ed. *A Victorian Anthology, 1837-1895: Selections Illustrating the Editor's Critical Review of British Poetry in the Reign of Victoria.* Boston: Houghton Mifflin, 1895.

Stern, Madeleine B. *The Life of Margaret Fuller.* 2nd Rev. ed. New York: Greenwood Press, 1991.

Stoodley, Bartlett H. *The Concepts of Sigmund Freud.* Glencoe, IL: Free Press, 1959.

"Tagore, Sir Rabindranath." In *The Columbia Encyclopedia* 6th ed., edited by Lagass, Paul. New York: Columbia University Press, 2004.

Tennyson, Alfred Lord, *Selected Poems, Flower in the Crannied Wall*, London, Penguin Classics, 1992.

"Thomas, Gospel Of." In *The Columbia Encyclopedia* 6th ed., edited by Lagass, Paul. New York: Columbia University Press, 2004.

Thompson, Francis. *Poems of Francis Thompson.* Edited by Terence L. Connolly. New York: D. Appleton-Century, 1934.

Tillich, Paul, *The New Being,* New York, Scriber & Sons, 1955.

"Tocqueville, Alexis De." In *The Columbia Encyclopedia* 6th ed., edited by Lagass, Paul. New York: Columbia University Press, 2004.

United Methodist Church, Book of Hymns, Nashville, Tennessee, The United Methodist Publishing House, 1964.

United Methodist Church Book of Discipline, Nashville, Tennessee, The United Methodist Publishing House, 2000.

Van Dusen, Henry P., *Spirit, Son and Father,* New York, A. & C. Black, 1958.

Wells, H.G., *The Outline of History,* New Jersey, Garden City Books, 1962.

Whithall-Smith, Hannah, *The Christian's Secret to a Happy Life,* Christian Witness Company, 1875.

ABOUT
THE AUTHOR

DR. ANNE MATHEWS-YOUNES is a psychologist who currently works for the U.S. Federal Government. In 1980, she completed her doctorate in Counseling and Consulting Psychology from Harvard University and has worked in State and Federal mental health agencies for the past 40 years in programs designed to prevent school violence and suicide, promote mental health and prevent mental and behavioral disorders, treat child trauma, and support disaster, terrorism and bioterrorism preparedness and response.

Dr. Mathews-Younes has also completed a Master's Degree in Theological Studies at Wesley Theological Seminary in Washington, D.C., as well as a Doctoral Degree in Ministry from that same seminary. Both of her theology degree theses focused on the life, mission and theology of her late grandfather, E. Stanley Jones, with whom she traveled extensively throughout India and Africa.

Dr. Mathews-Younes is the President of the E. Stanley Jones Foundation (www.estanleyjonesfoundation.com), which is dedicated to preserving and extending the legacy of the late E.

Stanley Jones, who blessed millions of people around the world with his preaching, teaching and prolific spiritual writings. She has also served as the Vice-President of the United Christian Ashrams Board, a spiritual retreat organization founded by E. Stanley Jones. Her book, *Living Upon the Way: Selected Sermons of E. Stanley Jones on Surrender,* was initially published in 2008 and this 2018 edition is a reprint.

Anne can be reached at:
Email: anne@estanleyjonesfoundation.com

Anne with Jones in India, 1968

ABOUT THE E. STANLEY JONES FOUNDATION

The E. Stanley Jones Foundation is dedicated to bold and fruitful evangelism which shares the life-changing message of Jesus Christ to persons of all ages, backgrounds, life situations and locations. The Foundation is also dedicated to preserving and extending the legacy of the late E. Stanley Jones who blessed millions of people around the world with his preaching, teaching and prolific written words proclaiming Jesus is Lord! Our vision is to reach every generation with the message of Jesus Christ; enlighten spiritual growth through education and inspiration; prepare both Christian leaders and laity to be followers of Jesus Christ, and make known the Kingdom of God today.

For more information and our current programs, kindly visit us at:

www.estanleyjonesfoundation.com

Thank you!

OTHER PUBLICATIONS
FROM THE E. STANLEY JONES FOUNDATION

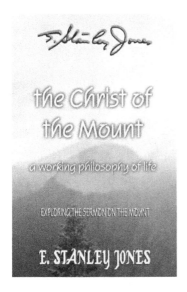

The Christ of the Mount:
A Working Philosophy of Life
Authored by E. Stanley Jones
List Price: $15.99
6" x 9" (15.24 x 22.86 cm)
Black & White on Cream paper
312 pages
ISBN-13: 978-1542896030
(CreateSpace-Assigned)
ISBN-10: 1542896037
BISAC: Religion / Biblical Meditations /
New Testament

The Life and Ministry of Mary
Webster: A Witness in the Evangelistic
Ministry of E. Stanley Jones *Authored*
by Anne Mathews-Younes
List Price: $14.99
6" x 9" (15.24 x 22.86 cm)
286 pages
ISBN-13: 978-
1544191799 (CreateSpace-Assigned)
ISBN-10: 1544191790
BISAC: Religion / Christian Life /
Spiritual Growth

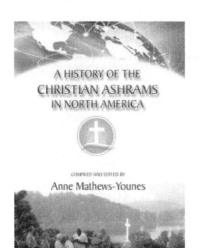

A History of the Christian Ashrams in North America
Compiled and Edited by Anne Mathews-Younes
List Price: $34.99
6" x 9" (15.24 x 22.86 cm)
Black & White on White paper
528 pages
ISBN-13: 978-547229017
(CreateSpace-Assigned)
ISBN-10: 1547229012
BISAC: Religion / Christianity / History / General

Is The Kingdom of God Realism?
Authored by E. Stanley Jones, Foreword by Leonard Sweet, Afterword by Howard Snyder
List Price: $19.99
6" x 9" (15.24 x 22.86 cm)
Black & White on Cream paper
428 pages
ISBN-13: 978-1976151514 (CreateSpace-Assigned)
ISBN-10: 1976151511
BISAC: Religion / Christianity / General

IS THE KINGDOM
OF GOD
REALISM?

E. STANLEY JONES

Foreword by Leonard Sweet | Afterword by Howard Snyder

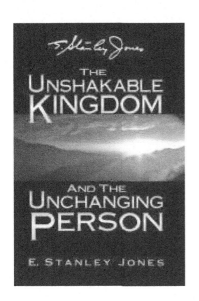

The Unshakable Kingdom and the Unchanging Person
Authored by E. Stanley Jones
List Price: $18.99
6" x 9" (15.24 x 22.86 cm)
Black & White on Cream paper
408 pages
ISBN-13: 978-1974132935
(CreateSpace-Assigned)
ISBN-10: 1974132935
BISAC: Religion / Spirituality / General

Victory Through Surrender
Authored by E. Stanley Jones,
Preface by Anne Mathews-Younes
List Price: $12.99
6" x 9" (15.24 x 22.86 cm)
Black & White on Cream paper
166 pages
ISBN-13: 978-1717548474
(CreateSpace-Assigned)
ISBN-10: 1717548474
BISAC: Religion / Christian Life / Professional Growth

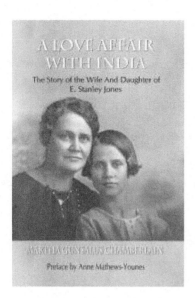

A Love Affair With India: The Story of the Wife and Daughter of E. Stanley Jones
Authored by Martha Gunsalus Chamberlain, Preface by Anne Mathews-Younes
List Price: $14.99
6" x 9" (15.24 x 22.86 cm)
250 pages
ISBN-13: 978-1984960276 (CreateSpace-Assigned)
ISBN-10: 198496027X
BISAC: Biography & Autobiography

A History of the Sat Tal Christian Ashram (USA Edition)
Authored by Anne Mathews-Younes
List Price: $15.99
6" x 9" (15.24 x 22.86 cm)
238 pages
ISBN-13: 978-1722847524 (CreateSpace-Assigned)
ISBN-10: 1722847522
BISAC: Religion / Christianity / History /General

ALL PUBLICATIONS OF
The E. Stanley Jones Foundation
are available for purchase from:

www.estanleyjonesfoundation.com

www.createspace.com

and

www.amazon.com

Order your copies today!